The Barrel of a Gun

SOUTHERN QUESTIONS

Decolonisation was the major historical process of the twentieth century. Its unfinished projects continue to shape our present. The defeat, withdrawal, and reconfiguration of Western colonial power in the postwar decades have affected almost everyone alive today, with stunning unevenness. The Southern Questions series features first-hand accounts – memoirs, novels, pamphlets – written by participants in the drama of decolonisation and its aftermath. Alongside these titles, Southern Questions presents new histories, reportage, and literary criticism devoted to nations, regions, and zones in the South.

Adom Getachew
Thomas Meaney
Series Editors

Titles in this series from Verso Books:

Everybody Loves a Good Drought by Palagummi Sainath

The Cameroon War by Thomas Deltombe, Manuel Domergue and Jacob Tatsitsa

Literature at the End of History by Pankaj Mishra

My Country, Africa by Andrée Blouin

This Fiction Called Nigeria by Adéwálé Májà-Pearce

The Barrel of a Gun

Political Power in Africa and the Coup d'État

RUTH FIRST

With a foreword by Christopher J. Lee

VERSO
London • New York

This edition first published by Verso 2026
First published by Allen Lane 1970

The manufacturer's authorized representative in the EU for product safety (GPSR) is LOGOS EUROPE, 9 rue Nicolas Poussin, 17000, La Rochelle, France
contact@logoseurope.eu

1 3 5 7 9 10 8 6 4 2

Verso
UK: 6 Meard Street, London W1F 0EG
US: 207 East 32nd Street, New York, NY 10016
versobooks.com

Verso is the imprint of New Left Books

ISBN-13: 978-1-80429-944-9
ISBN-13: 978-1-80429-945-6 (UK EBK)
ISBN-13: 978-1-80429-946-3 (US EBK)

British Library Cataloguing in Publication Data
A catalogue record for this book is available from the British Library

Library of Congress Cataloging-in-Publication Data
A catalog record for this book is available from the Library of Congress

Printed and bound by CPI Group (UK) Ltd, Croydon CR0 4YY

CONTENTS

FOREWORD
THE WAY OF THE GUN

Every Communist should grasp the truth that political power flows out of the barrel of a gun.

– Mao Zedong (1927)

If Frantz Fanon had not died of cancer in 1961 at the age of thirty-six, what kind of sequel might he have written to *The Wretched of the Earth*? What political issues of the post-colony might have he confronted? And what developing theories of post-colonial state power might Fanon have conceptualized and proposed? Ruth First's *The Barrel of a Gun* – her study of post-colonial elites and military power – provides one possible answer to these speculative questions. *The Barrel of a Gun* is several things at once: a razor-sharp analysis of post-colonial power dynamics in Africa; a political history of Africa during the 1960s; and a document of First's life and political views at a time when the promise of revolution in Africa was coming up short. A communist committed to liberation struggles across the continent, but particularly in her native South Africa, First was profoundly influenced by Fanon's work. Her archived personal papers indicate plans to write a biography of him, and his name appears early on in *The Barrel of a Gun*. Picking up where Fanon left off, this book outlines the dangers and political cul-de-sacs of decolonization and post-colonial politics. Yet it is neither a derivative work nor a pure act of homage. As a member of the South African Communist Party (SACP), First sought to situate themes of political violence, armed struggle, and revolution, which had preoccupied South African activists during the preceding decade, in a wider context.

Published in 1970, *The Barrel of a Gun* came together after First left apartheid South Africa for exile in London in 1964. The previous fifteen years had been defined by her involvement in her country's liberation struggle as a leading figure of the underground SACP and its close ally, the African National Congress (ANC). First's commitment culminated with her arrest by the Special Branch – the white minority government's secret police – and her incarceration without trial under the apartheid regime's ninety-day detention law. Before being forced into exile, First had been engaged in debates within the ANC and SACP about whether to pursue armed struggle – a strategy which the two organizations ultimately adopted. By the time she was developing *The Barrel of a Gun*, she and other activists questioned the potential of the military as a revolutionary force. First was particularly preoccupied with how such militarism could reinforce elite power, even when the soldiers and officers involved came from the popular masses and claimed to represent them. First sought to examine and understand how power over the means of violence could turn against political ideals, bringing uncertainty and even self-destruction to the post-colony. For this reason, her ideas and conclusions still apply to struggles around the world.

Ruth First may appear as an unlikely inheritor of Frantz Fanon's legacy. White, Jewish, middle-class, and, not least, a woman, First contrasts Fanon and his best-known acolytes, like Steve Biko and Huey P. Newton, in numerous ways. But they both committed their lives to liberation struggles and sought to advance those efforts through rigorous political analysis. *The Wretched of the Earth* is a treatise on the structural legacies of colonialism, a diagnostic account of the effects of violence on the colonized and the colonizer alike, and, above all, an argument for the decolonization of the Third World. Decolonization, for Fanon, was not exclusively a political act. Indeed, in his chapter 'On Violence', he expresses anxiety that the approach of diplomatic resolution leading to political independence would amount to little fundamental change for the colonized with a colonial class structure transferring unrevised to the post-colony. *The Wretched of the Earth* elaborates this economic prognosis with chapters on the limits of nationalism through discussions of national consciousness and national culture and a penultimate chapter consisting of individual medical cases that collectively illustrate the psychological impact of total war on civilians and combatants alike. Fanon famously concludes his book with a call for a new humanism, thus underlining his belief that decolonization was not simply political but cultural, psychological, and ultimately humanist, in the most profound sense of the term.

The Barrel of a Gun extends Fanon's perspectives and arguments by addressing the world that came after independence – not only the unmaking of colonial power but also how post-colonial societies faced their own undoing through emergent elements of elitism and militarism abetted by familiar foreign forces of the past. First's ideas and commitment, like Fanon's, were born through political activism and the displacement of exile, which introduced elements of freedom and insecurity into their lives and writing. Like *The Wretched of the Earth*, *The Barrel of a Gun* reflects its time, blending analysis and argument as a means of thinking through the failures and ongoing ambiguities of the present. First embraced a pan-African perspective with implications that extended across the Third World. *The Barrel of a Gun* reveals the unique set of circumstances that informed First's life and politics, as well as those of the South African liberation struggle more generally.

Born in Johannesburg on 4 May 1925 – coincidentally, the same year as Fanon – Heloise Ruth First grew up in a Jewish, middle-class household that presumed her path to university education, becoming a wife, and eventually having three daughters. Each of these qualities informed her activism in distinctive ways, positioning her at different moments as a political outsider, a party confidant, a fiercely engaged intellectual, and a mother both protective and absent, influenced by the shifting circumstances of exile. Her husband, Joe Slovo, was a prominent figure in the SACP and a founder of uMkhonto we Sizwe (MK), the military wing that the ANC and SACP established in 1961. He later became general secretary of the SACP and minister of housing within South Africa's post-apartheid government during Nelson Mandela's presidency. First's life reflected this personal and political partnership, with her actions and outlook shaped by their marriage, if not always determined by it.

First's parents were equally political. Her father, Julius, and mother, Tilly, had emigrated to Johannesburg from Latvia and Lithuania, respectively, as part of a broader influx of Jewish immigrants to South Africa during the first decades of the twentieth century. Both became involved with the Communist Party of South Africa (CPSA), as the party was named after it was founded in 1921. First consequently grew up in a political household that shaped her socialist outlook and activist future, especially after she arrived at the University of the Witwatersrand.

At Wits, as it is known in shorthand, First met Slovo, who was a returning veteran of the Second World War. She also met Mandela and other student activists like Harold Wolpe, who later became a Marxist economist known for theorizing the concept of racial capitalism. Her budding political engagement soon extended beyond campus with the 1946 mine workers' strike, involving approximately 74,000 Black workers and resulting in the deaths of at least 9 and more than 1,000 injured. She discovered journalism as a vocation, working for the *Guardian* in Johannesburg, where she covered Black politics. First and Slovo became romantically involved in 1948, the year the conservative National Party came to power with its extremist platform of racial segregation known as apartheid. They married the following year in 1949.

The 1950s were a heady period of activism, and even optimism, until the Sharpeville Massacre of 1960, which struck a devastating blow to the struggle. The Suppression of Communism Act passed by the apartheid government in 1950 forced the CPSA to dissolve publicly and reform underground as the SACP. This shift also converged with a growing alliance between the SACP and ANC, a partnership that had origins going back to the 1920s, when James (Jimmy) La Guma of the CPSA and Josiah Tshangana (J.T.) Gumede of the ANC attended the 1927 League Against Imperialism conference in Brussels and went on to Moscow where they met with Nikolai Bukharin, then general secretary of the Communist International (Comintern). This meeting resulted in the Native Republic Thesis, a two-part political strategy for South Africa that argued for Black national liberation in advance of socialist revolution.

Though the thesis was dropped as a platform by the Second World War, it informed the ANC–SACP alliance in the decades ahead, as well as intellectual debates over the national question and the idea that South Africa reflected a 'colonialism of a special type'. Under the leadership of Chief Albert Luthuli, the ANC spearheaded the multiracial Congress Alliance during the 1950s, with such mass actions as the 1952 Defiance Campaign – a national initiative that included strikes, boycotts, and civil disobedience against pass laws, which restricted movement by requiring Black South Africans to carry documentation at all times. This resistance culminated with the Congress of the People in 1955, held in Soweto, at which the member organizations of the Congress Alliance adopted the Freedom Charter, which, among many aspirations, demanded a multiracial democracy for all South Africans. The apartheid government responded swiftly to this event, arresting 156 activists for their involvement and accusing them of attempting to overthrow the state. First was among those detained. The Treason Trial that subsequently ensued from 1956 to 1961 stymied the political momentum that had been mounting over the previous years. However, it also provided a spectacle and stage for activists to promote their agenda to a global audience and ultimately unified different factions across organizational, racial, and gender lines. Among the accused were Nelson Mandela, Oliver Tambo, Walter Sisulu, Moses Kotane, Helen Joseph, Ahmed Kathrada, and Alex La Guma. Mandela would later quip in *Long Walk to Freedom* (1994) that the trial was 'the largest and longest unbanned meeting of the Congress Alliance in years'.

Though all accused were eventually acquitted, the Treason Trial created an opening for other parties to emerge, most notably the Pan Africanist Congress (PAC). Founded by Robert Sobukwe, a former ANC member, the PAC emphasized Black African nationalism in contrast to the multiracial front of the Congress Alliance. Sobukwe, therefore, served as a forerunner to Steve Biko and the Black Consciousness movement of the late 1960s and 1970s. On 21 March 1960, the PAC organized a pass law protest in Sharpeville involving an estimated 5,000 to 7,000 people. Police opened fire, killing at least 91 and injuring hundreds more. Just over a week later, on 30 March 1960, a second protest took place in Cape Town, again organized by the PAC, but this time the number of participants had swelled, with an estimated 30,000 to 50,000 people marching from the township of Langa to the central police station in Caledon Square. The police responded with unrestrained violence once more. The white minority government declared a national state of emergency the same day and, a week later, banned both the PAC and the ANC. Thousands of activists were arrested and detained as a result.

The Sharpeville Massacre marked a turning point in the anti-apartheid struggle – one that spurred the emigration and exile of thousands of protestors. The PAC based its early exile headquarters in Maseru, Lesotho. Over the preceding decade, the ANC had already launched an international strategy, known as the 'external mission', establishing connections abroad that would serve as the foundation for its diplomatic exile after the ban went into effect. First herself had travelled to the Soviet Union and China in 1954, only a few months after her youngest daughter, Robyn, was born. However, more significant, Sharpeville also initiated ANC and SACP members' formal turn to armed struggle in 1961. Mandela and Slovo were key architects of this new strategy, marking a generational shift away from the civil disobedience approach of the older Luthuli. The next several decades would be defined by the maneuvers of MK, aligning the ANC and the SACP with other liberation organizations in Africa as well as similar movements in Southeast Asia, Latin America, and Palestine.

First was not peripheral to these discussions. Alongside Slovo, she was centrally involved in planning and recruiting MK members. The question of armed struggle and the role of militaries and war as an alternative method of politics therefore informed her thinking leading to *The Barrel of a Gun*. The apartheid state's ban on the ANC and the escalation of police surveillance that followed Sharpeville had forced First to uproot her life more generally. She travelled to Swaziland (present-day Eswatini) with her daughters shortly after the state of emergency was declared and her husband was detained. First eventually returned to her work as a journalist, under increasingly oppressive conditions. The situation began to unravel in 1962 once Mandela and other activists were arrested for their militant activities, leading to the Rivonia Trial and the sentencing of eight, including Mandela, to life imprisonment in 1964. First and Slovo had been involved in the purchase of Liliesleaf, the MK safehouse and headquarters where Mandela and others were apprehended.

First herself was arrested in August 1963 after police raided her home and found 'illicit political material'. Slovo had already left South Africa in June for what was planned to be a temporary mission for MK. Incarcerated under the 90-day detention law, First spent 117 days in prison. Her subsequent memoir, *117 Days* (1965), described in visceral detail the psychological torture she endured while in solitary confinement. 'Left in that cell long enough, I feared to become one of those colourless insects that slither under a world of flat, grey stones, away from the sky and the sunlight, the grass and people,' she recalled. The book brought international attention to the reality that the apartheid system's brutality affected not only Black South Africans but every South African, even white, middle-class women like herself. Her memoir also laid the foundation for the major themes that would continue to animate First's written work, particularly the role and function of the state, the forms and uses of violence, and the agency of individual people within systems of inequality and oppression, whether apartheid, colonial, or post-colonial in nature. *The Barrel of a Gun* elaborated these interrelated concerns on a much broader canvas, demonstrating the freedom of thought that exile had granted her.

Released from prison in November 1963, First left South Africa in March 1964, never to return. She was greeted as a celebrity when she arrived in London with her daughters Robyn and Gillian. As with many others, exile proved to be a complex experience, at once personally liberating but at a cost of losing touch with one's homeland. Political work competed with domestic responsibilities. The external mission of the ANC and SACP involved diplomatic trips and speeches at numerous venues, whether Trafalgar Square or the United Nations.

During the same month as Sharpeville and Langa, ANC Deputy President Oliver Tambo left for London, where his assignment was to establish an overseas diplomatic front for the ANC. Tambo understood all too clearly the vital responsibilities at hand. Just before the Rivonia arrests and trial, in May 1963, he had represented the ANC at the founding of the Organisation of African Unity, followed by additional diplomatic visits to the USSR and the People's Republic of China. Perhaps most significantly, Tambo delivered a speech at the United Nations, which motivated the passage of UN Resolution 1881 (XVIII) on 11 October 1963, demanding the release of all South African political prisoners. Following the Rivonia verdict, the ANC established offices in Algiers, Cairo, Lusaka, and Dar es Salaam by 1965, reflecting the speed and early success it had in launching an international presence under Tambo's guidance. Dar es Salaam served as the ANC's initial headquarters. Indeed, what remained of the Congress Alliance was informally reflected by location and where the leadership was stationed: many Black activists emigrated to African countries, whereas white, Indian, and Coloured activists largely relocated to London. This provisional plan accorded with the 'African image' approach that positioned Black activists as a political vanguard. It also generated unresolved intra-organizational tensions. Exile had encouraged a moment of ideological and tactical reflection. While it had been agreed that Black nationalism should take precedence, this course of action left non-Black Congress Alliance members unclear as to their organizational role and standing.

London was initially disorienting for First – politically and culturally, as well as with the new sense of freedom and agency she had. Though her ongoing activism grounded her, it was First's intellectual life and work that blossomed. She assisted in the editing and completion of SACP and MK leader Govan Mbeki's *The Peasants' Revolt* (1964) and Mandela's *No Easy Walk to Freedom* (1965), which was an early version of his autobiography *Long Walk to Freedom*. (As co-defendants at Rivonia, both Mbeki and Mandela were imprisoned on Robben Island at the time. Mbeki's son Thabo would become post-apartheid South

Africa's second president after Mandela.) First also attended classes at the London School of Economics and at the Institute of Commonwealth Studies starting in 1966. She met and became friends with fellow writers and academic members of the New Left such as Tariq Ali and Ralph Miliband, associations that demonstrated her intellectual and political independence considering the SACP's pro-Soviet stance. Indeed, ideological frictions surfaced between First and Slovo following the Soviet invasion of Czechoslovakia in August 1968, with First critical of the blatant abuse of military power to suppress popular dissent. She also helped produce a television documentary involving Fanon and other figures, entitled *Power from Beyond*. Overall, exile inspired First, with her experience as a journalist encouraging her to think about longer works of scholarship and political theory after the publication of *117 Days*. It was a period of intellectual exploration and personal reinvention.

In May 1965, First wrote a letter to Peter Worsley, a staff member in the Department of Social Anthropology and Sociology at the University of Manchester, a former member of the Communist Party of Great Britain, and a founder of *New Left Review*. He was also among the first scholars to mainstream the idea of the Third World with his 1964 book *The Third World*, which examined colonialism, nationalism, and revolution across the new states of Asia, Africa, and Latin America. Its scope provided a model for First. In her letter, she described how she had 'been feeling more unsettled than ever' despite having been in Britain for twelve months, reflecting 'a false settling-in year with a little bundle of work commissions that kept my nose to the grindstone'. The 'size of London and the anonymity' provided some enjoyment, and though her children said 'they'd never go back to South Africa', First insisted, 'I would, but it seems we're in for a very long stay here.'

This letter is included with her archival materials concerning *The Barrel of a Gun*. It is clear that writing and intellectual engagement motivated First, but the origins and gestation of her book were initially opaque and somewhat chaotic. In her letter to Worsley, she elaborated her project on 'Africa's new bureaucrats' by discussing a range of issues she wanted to address:

the professionals who run the government, the civil service, the party, the co-ops, the trade unions, the lot. Who are they? What infleunces [*sic*] played on them? (The colleges they went to, specially abroad; the influence of the mission stations and schools, political influences abroad). Not a who's who but an examination of the important men at the top. Then the influences behind the planning in the take-over of government period [*sic*]; how Africanisation works; government and party (is party an instrument of government, or government an instrument of party).

She also proposed six countries as case studies – Algeria, Kenya, Tanganyika, Ghana, Mali, and Zambia – though she also feared this program would be too ambitious, since she hoped to spend time in each country. 'Just very tentative thoughts,' First concluded, 'but what do you think?'

By August 1965, First had reached a decision to focus on coups. By the end of September, her project 'Coups in Africa' had received interest from British and American publishers. In February 1966, First was exploring travel options to Abidjan, Bamako, Brazzaville, Leopoldville, Duala, Nairobi, Dar es Salaam, Benghazi, Tripoli, and Algiers – all initially imagined as part of a single journey. She ultimately focused on Sudan, Nigeria, and Ghana. However, as indicated in the somewhat facetiously titled 'Scoreboard' that appears at the beginning of *The Barrel of a Gun*, her concern was always continental, even Pan-African. Despite her case study approach, First never lost sight of the broader post-war trend that had unfolded across Africa, starting with the Free Officers Movement in Egypt that placed Lieutenant Colonel Gamal Abdel Nasser into power in July 1952 and a similar officers' coup in Mali that toppled the Modibo Keita government in November 1968. During the intervening sixteen years, military coups, successful and unsuccessful, had taken place in over a dozen other countries, including Sudan, Ethiopia, Togo, Congo-Kinshasa (present-day Democratic Republic of the Congo), Algeria, Central African Republic, Burundi, Nigeria, Ghana, and Sierra Leone, with some countries experiencing multiple instances. Independence in many African countries proved fragile. The initial optimism of self-determination turned out to be short-lived in many places, replaced by wild swings of power backed by militarism. The guns of liberation pointed in new directions.

The Barrel of a Gun consists of six parts and spanned approximately 500 pages in its first edition. The book offers historical background, accounts of three case studies, and an analysis of the connections between militaries, economies, and political leaders. As First explains in her introduction, the book is concerned with positioning 'a general theory of power for newly independent states', focused especially on why they were 'so vulnerable to army interventions in politics'. Primary attention was paid on politics and state power rather than the role of militaries per se in the post-colony. First recognized that a single coup could be too exceptional and anecdotal to illuminate the larger elements of this theme, hence her decision to address four recent coups in particular, including two in Sudan, one in Nigeria, and one in Ghana. Additional coups in Algeria and Egypt are also included. Still, *The Barrel of a Gun* is not a survey. First emphasizes her interest in the perceptions of ordinary people, 'the sense of pulsating life in the streets of West Africa' and the way that 'rumbustious spirit' reflects 'something of the way people see, and say things about, their condition'.

As a result, *The Barrel of a Gun* is wide-ranging in scope but also intimate. For First, it was not an academic exercise but an attempt to understand a political problem that was obstructing a revolutionary project to which she was deeply committed. The tone is critical, even cynical at moments, and the narrative is often fast-moving. The text reflects First's skills as a journalist as well as her analytical acuity. In Part I, 'Silent Clamour for Change', she wastes little time in mentioning her first-hand encounters with soldiers and a coup in Freetown, Sierra Leone. 'Army men have by now unmade and remade governments in one out of every four of the continent's independent states,' she remarks, jesting bleakly, 'Sandhurst and St Cyr, the journalists were saying, had succeeded the London School of Economics and École Normale William Ponty in Dakar as the training-ground of Africa's leaders.' She goes on to compare the trend of coups in post-colonial Africa as rendering the politics of the continent similar to those in Latin America, a sense of Third Worldism at play. Coups in Africa were becoming 'infectious' because they were 'so effortless': 'Get the keys of the armoury; turn out the barracks; take the radio station, the post office and the airport; arrest the person of the president, and you arrest the state.' Through this ease, coups were becoming a form of conventional wisdom and a type of political common sense. 'Power lies in the hands of those who control the means of violence,' First observes. 'It lies in the barrel of a gun, fired or silent.'

This logic of violence, First argues, was underpinned by an economic logic. 'African development has been held to ransom by the emergence of a new, privileged, African class,' she writes in the book's first chapter. 'Few of them read Frantz Fanon, yet they are living out his description of them: "Spoilt children of yesterday's colonialism and of today's governments, they organize the loot of whatever national resources exist."' *The Barrel of a Gun* expands on these ideas, critically analyzing the systemic problems of the post-colony of which Fanon could only garner a glimpse before his untimely death. Going further, if Walter Rodney's *How Europe Underdeveloped Africa* (1972) attributed Africa's economic stagnation after independence to the centuries-long history of Western resource extraction, *The Barrel of a Gun* can be grasped as a political analog: how Europe *politically* underdeveloped Africa. 'Many of Africa's new states entered independence, though nominally nation states, more divided than united,' First writes at the start of Part IV. 'Conquest had resulted in the establishment of colonies within artificial boundaries, and diverse societies had been administered piecemeal without any national integrating political system. The test of independence politics was to rest largely on the attempt of the parties and the politicians to devise a unifying political purpose for their countries and peoples.'

Colonialism, in sum, left African states with weak and anti-democratic systems of governance. Though the initial sections of her book replicate many of Fanon's ideas and his criticism of the unreconstructed nature of post-colonial elites from their colonial predecessors – indeed, many of them were not simply beneficiaries but the same people – First goes further, describing the inability and failures of revolutionary leaders to implement structural transformation. In the case of Kwame Nkrumah, Ghana's charismatic and anti-imperial first president, she writes that 'his limitations as a theoretician and a leader' rested in his belief that change was 'to be promoted by edict, from the pinnacle of government, by himself, a strongman and charismatic leader'. Nkrumah ultimately failed due to this stance, which left colonial hierarchies and protocols unreformed, rendering him 'solitary in government'. His presidency 'alienated those who hoped to improve their personal and political fortunes by independence; but it did not disarm them, or displace their influence'. Indeed, in a section some readers may find controversial, First asks whether the CIA was essential to the toppling of Nkrumah. 'The basic structures of African society in new states, Ghana and Mali included, hold the seeds of a coup d'état within themselves,' she argues provocatively. 'It is precisely because foreign powers and bodies like the CIA understand this well, that their interventions, even very indirect ones, are so effective.'

In this case and others, *The Barrel of a Gun* highlights the importance of coups as events and militaries as political litmus tests, revealing the workings of power and institutions in the postcolony. In her words, perhaps reflecting her own perspective on MK, 'there is no such thing as a non-political army'. Rather, through their personnel, constituents, training, and other features, 'Africa's armies are reflections of society and encompass all its interests and conflicts'. Militaries are not always aligned to ruling elites. Soldiers identify with numerous factors, whether regional affiliation, generation, ethnicity, or ideological inclination. 'Armies are agglomerations,' First contends. 'They thus play shifting roles, and they adjust to the shifting state of African politics.' Taken together, African militaries must not only be approached as forces of liberation, as perceived at the time within South Africa's anti-apartheid struggle, but also as ambiguous elements within post-colonial orders, at times reinforcing the gatekeeper state, as historian Frederick Cooper has called it, and at other times short-circuiting it. Her book's title, drawn from Mao Zedong and displaying once more her unorthodox thinking beyond the doctrinaire SACP, captured this tense uncertainty.

⋆

On 30 October 1970, the *Guardian* ran a feature article on First titled 'The Loneliness of the Long Distance Revolutionary', a paraphrase of Alan Sillitoe's classic story of working-class anger and dissent, 'The Loneliness of the Long-Distance Runner' (1959). 'I call myself a revolutionary. I am absolutely committed, committed to the struggle for change,' First is quoted as saying. The occasion for this feature profile was the publication of *The Barrel of a Gun*. In First's words, the book 'is a documentary polemic against a going establishment in independent Africa, an attempt to prod people who are disabused with the proceedings of the professional politicians and the bureaucrats, the political corruption, the conformism to Western standards'. Against polite paternalism, she further called 'to stop the sentimental attempts to protect Africans, not to hurt feelings, to save them from their own worst deeds, for that too is a form of patronage'. First reaffirmed her commitment to 'Fanon's disinherited, the wretched of the earth'.

Certainly, a dispiriting mood had descended on South African activists by 1970, given the failure of MK after the decisive setback of the 1967 Wankie Campaign, which had attempted an invasion of South Africa via Rhodesia. The Durban Moment of 1973 and the Soweto Uprising of 1976 were still to come, unimaginable at the time. Pessimism reigned. Under these conditions, First described the challenges of writing *The Barrel of a Gun* as a wife, mother, and activist all at once. 'There always seems to be the laundry to take in or something,' she remarked. 'I have a husband who believes in women's liberation,' she said, and, of her children, 'I think they respect our commitment – even if they don't fully understand it.' She further commented, 'I don't feel I am an exile, I feel I live in transit.' As the reporter pointed out, however, she did consider herself African in *The Barrel of a Gun* – 'I count myself an African' – though a sense of distance levied a cost. 'I miss the real commitment,' First explained. 'I had developed up to a point where I was capable of a certain involvement, a point where your whole existence is tied up to political struggle, violence if necessary. I feel rather academic in Britain.' In her words, the overriding political question ultimately had to be: 'Which revolution, when, how, in what way?'

The answer for First proved to be Mozambique, which won independence from Portugal in 1975 under the leadership of the Marxist-Leninist Frente de Libertação de Moçambique (FRELIMO). Excited by its revolutionary possibilities, First moved there in 1978 to head the Centre of African Studies (Centro de Estudos Africanos) at Universidade Eduardo Mondlane in Maputo. Revolutionary Mozambique presented a new political horizon for southern Africa and Africa generally when other countries had failed. It was also proximate to her native South Africa. First was able to return to a region that was close to home, if not home specifically.

Despite her optimism, First's relocation was a risk that ended in tragedy. On 17 August 1982, she was brutally assassinated by a parcel bomb sent to her office at Eduardo Mondlane by the apartheid government's Special Branch, the same police unit that had interrogated her decades earlier. She was fifty-seven years old. Like Walter Rodney, who was also assassinated by a bomb in June 1980, and Frantz Fanon, First died far too young. Like them, she became a political martyr, remembered in South Africa to this day for her activism, commitment, and intellectual independence.

The Barrel of a Gun is emblematic of these qualities. Women remain largely absent in the canon of post-colonial revolutionary thought. This book is an important corrective. It returns to perennial questions in her work, going back to *117 Days*, about violence, the rule of law, and the role and fortunes of the state. It reveals the expansiveness of her mind as well as her grounded-ness in terms of research and her ability to face unflinchingly the varied political realities of Africa's post-colonial condition. These virtues are also found in her later book, *Libya: The Elusive Revolution* (1974), which forms a sequel to *The Barrel of a Gun* through its critical analysis of the coup that brought Colonel Muammar Gaddafi to power. Ralph Miliband would recall her as 'the least utopian of revolutionaries'. Military coups continue to be a significant issue. Since 2010, there have been over forty coups and attempted coups in sub-Saharan Africa. Coups are not a political feature of the past but an ongoing phenomenon of the present that demands attention.

Still, *The Barrel of a Gun* reveals an unwavering belief in future possibility. It is a testament to the political imagination of those who went into exile. Ruth First never witnessed the birth of a new, fully democratic South Africa. Nonetheless, she played a crucial role in preparing for it, laying the groundwork for its intellectual and political prosperity, which to this day awaits complete fulfilment.

Christopher J. Lee

After God, it is above all to our armed forces that I must express the gratitude of the nation.

President Senghor of Senegal, after an abortive coup against his government.

It wasn't a coup. We only relieved two quarrelling Presidents of their duties.

Colonel Alphonse Alley of Dahomey

INTRODUCTION

This book is about army interventions in politics, but more about politics than armies. This is in the hope that, from an examination of the crisis in politics, coup and counter-coup, there will grow, tentatively at least, a general theory of power for newly independent states which explains why they are so vulnerable to army interventions in politics. It is not, accordingly, a book about the mechanics of armies and coups d'état, their logistics and command structures, but about the way army interventions in politics reveal the nature of political power and its areas of failure in Africa. The army coup d'état is plainly a short-circuit of power conflicts in a situation where arms do the deciding. What is the kind of conflict? And what does the decision entail?

Tracing the development of a single African army coup d'état does, I believe, tell more about soldiers and politicians, and their clashes and compromises, than a mere factual inventory of all the coups on the continent. On the other hand, while the coups d'état in Africa may spring from like causes, they are not identical. And so, more than examination of a particular coup d'état is needed. I have looked especially closely at Nigeria and Ghana; and at the Sudan (with its two very different coups in a decade). Algeria and Egypt figure, too; for the coup d'état is a feature of political crisis in all parts of the Third World, and the inclusion of these countries, with their bodies in Africa but their heads in the Middle East, is an opportunity to consider Africa from Third World perspectives. Most of the other coups make incidental appearances.

An account devoted exclusively to fact could present an Africa that is desiccated and dull. It must lose, for instance, the sense of pulsating life in the streets of West Africa, where the rumbustious spirit seems so incompatible with the earnest political futility in high places. I have tried to convey something of the way people see, and say things about, their condition, in the scattered, sometimes unattributed, quotations throughout the book. One word about titles: they are often omitted not out of casualness or disrespect but because, especially in these new and heaving states and armies, they change so often. I have drawn heavily on much of the writing about Africa and about armies in the new states, and am indebted to it, though in the course of this investigation I changed most of my – and many of the accepted – notions about independent Africa. There has been the risk, in the range of countries I have selected, of advancing propositions based on selective example. I have tried to avoid this by including sufficient detail, consonant with the purpose of each example, and sufficient generalization to make the exercise relevant to more than those immediately affected.

The account of the coups is based on what 'official' accounts there are – the Ghanaian army men have been prolific in print – and on what press coverage, African and European, exists; but mostly on interviews with as many participants and close witnesses as I could meet in visits to Africa between 1964 and 1968. The rather numerous footnotes and references are there that others may test the evidence; for much about these contemporary events is still controversy rather than record. There were numberless interviews. Some of those interviewed are quoted anonymously, for they preferred it so.

In particular I would like to thank the following: Patrick Lefevre and Chris de Broglio helped with the French material, and Dr Farouk Mohammed Ibrahim, Omar al Zein, Tigani al-Taib and very many others in the Sudan with the Sudanese. Countless people in West Africa generously gave both information and hospitality. Tom Wengraf helped me with material on Algeria, and Dan Schechter of the Africa Research Group and *Ramparts* magazine helped with American sources. Discussion with and a paper on the military by Desmond Morton during a London School of Economics seminar conducted by Dr Ralph Miliband helped sharpen the topic for me. Ken Post read the first draft and talked over and helped tackle some of the problems the book raised; his own work is frequently acknowledged in the chapters of this book. Professor Thomas Hodgkin criticized searchingly, though with never-failing courtesy; he is in no way responsible for any good advice not followed. Albie Sachs read and suggested textual improvements to the first draft. Ruth Vaughan helped with typing and early research.

I am grateful for a grant from the Leon Fellowship of the University of London. Ronald Segal thought of the subject and steered the book through its life. Above all, my husband Joe Slovo bore with it, and with me, as this book was written; he inspired much of it, and made its writing possible. Its faults are all mine, of course.

Harsh judgements are made in this book of Africa's independence leaderships. Yet this book is primarily directed not to the criticism, but to the liberation of Africa, for I count myself an African, and there is no cause I hold dearer.

London
November 1969

SCOREBOARD

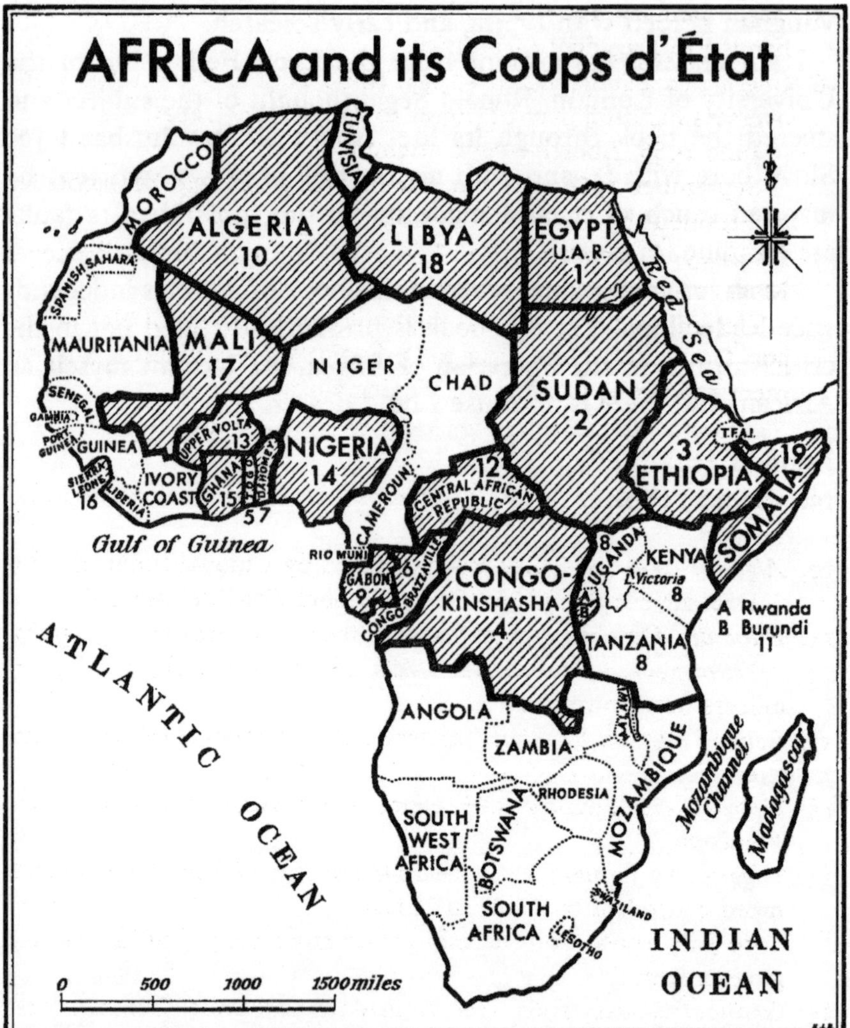

1. *United Arab Republic* (Egypt). July 1952. Monarchy overthrown by Free Officers' Movement.
2. *Sudan*. November 1958. General Abboud seizes power, military junta rules till 1964.

   May 1969. Free Officers' Movement seizes power for popular front government.

3. *Ethiopia*. December 1960. Abortive coup d'état against the Emperor by the Imperial Guard.
4. *Congo-Kinshasa*. General Mobutu seizes power temporarily in 1960, and again in November 1965.
5. *Togo*. January 1963. President Olympio killed in coup, power handed to President Grunitzky.
6. *Congo-Brazzaville*. August 1963. Abbé Youlou overthrown, army oversees handing over of power to Massemba-Debat.

   June 1966. Abortive coup attempt.

   September 1968. Captain Raoul takes power, to be succeeded as President by Colonel Ngouabi.
7. *Dahomey*. December 1963. Colonel Soglo overthrows President Maga, re-arranges the government.

   December 1965. General Soglo intervenes again in November, and December. December 1967. Soglo is deposed and a government headed by Colonel Alley is installed.
8. *Tanzania, Kenya, Uganda*. January 1964. Army mutinies, put down with the help of British forces.
9. *Gabon*. February 1964. Coup d'état reversed by French intervention.
10. *Algeria*. June 1965. Ben Bella deposed by Colonel Boumedienne.

    December 1967. Coup led by Colonel Zbiri defeated.
11. *Burundi*. October 1965. Army officers overthrow monarchy.

    November 1966. Captain Micombero and a group of army officers take power.
12. *Central African Republic*. January 1966. Colonel Bokassa deposes President David Dacko.
13. *Upper Volta*. January 1966. Colonel Lamizana deposes President Yameogo.
14. *Nigeria*. 15 January 1966. Coup d'état initiated by young officers taken control of by General Ironsi.

    29 July 1966. Coup wrests power from Ironsi, installs Gowon government.
15. *Ghana*. February 1966. General Ankrah and Police Commissioner Harlley form a government after the deposition of Nkrumah.

    April 1967. Abortive coup led by Lieutenant Arthur.
16. *Sierra Leone*. March 1967. Lieutenant Colonel Juxon-Smith heads a government which takes power from Sir Albert Margai.

    April 1968. A coup from the ranks results in the return to civilian rule, under Siaka Stevens.
17. *Mali*. November 1968. Young officers' coup headed by Lieutenant Moussa Traoré removes the Modibo Keita government.

18. *Libya*. September 1969. A Revolutionary Command Council which includes two army officers deposes the monarchy.
19. *Somalia*. October 1969. A group of lieutenant-colonels and colonels installs a Revolutionary Council in place of the Somali Youth League government.

And, in the years between and after, numbers of other coups d'état, like abortive attempts in Niger (December 1963), in Senegal in 1962, in the Ivory Coast in 1963; the attempted overthrow of Colonel Ojukwu's government in Biafra, several attempts to unseat the government that rules Mali; and a reported coup attempt in Congo-Brazzaville in November 1969.

Part I

Silent Clamour for Change

During the years I was in the State Department, I was awakened once or twice a month by a telephone call in the middle of the night announcing a coup d'état in some distant capital with a name like a typographical error.

George W. Ball, *The Discipline of Power*

Gentlemen and Officers

'Army coups in Africa?' friends said caustically. 'You had best suggest to the publisher a loose-leaf book, or a wad of blank pages at the back.' Army men have by now unmade and remade governments in one out of every four of the continent's independent states. Since I started planning this book, nine states have been taken over by their armies. As I prepared to visit Nigeria, a West Indian friend, who had gone to teach in West Africa as a devotee of African power on the newly free continent, was leaving. He had found himself in the thick of two military take-overs, at intervals of six months from one another, and had narrowly escaped being taken for an Ibo during the massacres in the North. He wanted still to stay in Africa, to teach and to write, but in a quiet spot this time. 'No more coups, I think it'll have to be Sierra Leone.' Nine weeks after he arrived in Freetown, there was an army coup. A year later, on my way back from Nigeria and Ghana, I dropped in to see him in Freetown. The very night I arrived we were stopped by armed soldiers at a road-block. A coup to end the regime installed by the coup of a year earlier was in full swing. From his house veranda, we watched soldiers searching the neighbourhood. They were rounding up the officer corps.

Sandhurst and St Cyr, the journalists were saying, had succeeded the London School of Economics and École Normale William Ponty in Dakar as the training-ground of Africa's leaders. (The Sandhurst and St Cyr curricula were probably over-due for change.) Africa was becoming another Latin America, where political instability has long been chronic. There, modern political history is a chaotic account of coups and counter-coups, of precipitate but meaningless changes of president, minister, cabinet, government and army chief. One professional soldier replaced another at the head of government. Sometimes the military unmade the very power formation they had themselves installed. A coup every eight months, or twelve, in some states; elsewhere, a breathing space, before another spurt of *golpe cuartelazo* (barracks-room revolt), or *golpe de estado* (coup d'état), or some combination of the two. The very language of coups has attained a peculiar finesse in Latin America. Violence has nearly always been present; fundamental change, virtually always absent.

By the time the coup d'état reached Africa, men of more blasé societies – whose own nation states had evolved through revolution and civil war, but in an earlier era – were already adapted. The Sierra Leone coup, said a United States Embassy official in Freetown, was just 'a Mickey Mouse show'. African countries, said the sceptics, were like television stars: in the news with a coup today, forgotten tomorrow, or confused with each other in a succeeding coup.

It has proved infectious, this seizure of government by armed men, and so effortless. Get the keys of the armoury; turn out the barracks; take the radio station, the post office and the airport; arrest the person of the president, and you arrest the state. In the Congo, where the new state disintegrated so disastrously so soon after independence, Colonel Mobutu, army chief-of-staff, 'clarified' the situation by taking the capital with 200 men. At the time it was a larger force than any other single person controlled in Leopoldville. In Dahomey, General Soglo, who had come to power by a coup d'état, was overthrown by sixty paratroopers in December 1967. In Ghana 500 troops, from an army of 10,000, toppled supposedly one of the most formidable systems of political mobilization on the continent. In the Sudan two bridges over the Nile command Khartoum; and the unit that gets its guns into position first, commands the capital. In Dahomey a Minister of Foreign Affairs was heard to boast about one of that country's three coups d'état, that not a shot had been fired, not even a blank; not a tear-gas grenade had been thrown; and not a single arrest had been made. Dahomey's army men staged three coups in five years and thus far hold the record for Africa.

It seems to be done with little more than a few jerks of the trigger-finger; and there are, often, no casualties; Nigeria and Ghana were exceptions. Sierra Leone had fewer than half a hundred officers in her army by 1968. The coup that toppled the military government, itself brought to office by a coup d'état a year earlier, was organized by privates and by non-commissioned officers. The army consisted of one battalion. A barracks on a lovely flowered hillside in the capital was the single power centre. The billiards room in the officers' mess was the scene of a brief tussle for control. The following morning, the debris was slight; some broken Coca-Cola bottles and cues lying awry on the green baize, and, in a ditch not far from the barracks, a car belonging to an officer who had tried to escape. After this coup, the entire army was in the control of two officers recalled from abroad – the rest were confined to the Pademba Road police station – and the police force was in the hands of two officers brought back from retirement. In Ghana Colonel Afrifa, or, as he came to be called after promotion, 'The Young Brigadier', was criticized for the detail he included in his chronicle of the Ghana coup. All that a conspirator had to do was read the relevant chapter, it was said. Lieutenant Arthur did, in fact, stage an abortive counter-coup a year later, following much the same pattern as Afrifa had outlined. There had not yet been an instance of a lieutenant staging a successful coup in Africa, said Arthur. He aimed to be the first to do so. For the formation of the new military junta, he had counted out all colonels and above.

The facility of coup logistics and the audacity and arrogance of the coup-makers are equalled by the inanity of their aims, at least as many choose to state them. At its face value, the army ethos embodies a general allergy to politicians; a search for unity and uprightness; and service to the nation. Nigeria's First Republic collapsed, said General Gowon, because it lacked high moral standards. Nzeogwu, the young major who made that particular coup, talked in more fevered but comparable terms of a strong, united and prosperous Nigeria, free from corruption and internal strife. In the Central African Republic Colonel Jean Bedel Bokassa's Revolutionary Council announced a campaign to clean up morals, that would forbid drum-playing and lying about in the sun except on Saturdays and holidays. Colonel Lamizana of Upper Volta said, 'The people asked us to assume responsibility. The army accepts.' It is the simple soldier's view of politics, a search for a puritan ethic and a restoration of democracy unsullied by corrupt politicians. It is as though, in the army books and regulations by which the soldiers were drilled, there is an entry: *Coups, justification for*; and beside it, the felicitous phrases that the coup-makers repeat by rote.

The coup is becoming conventional wisdom not only among Africa's army men, but among her young intellectuals. In the exile cafés of Paris and the bed-sitters of London, and on the university campuses of the United States, young aspirants for power, or social change, consider the making or unmaking of African governments in terms of their contacts within the army. Power changes hands so easily at the top, and the political infrastructure is so rapidly rendered tractable. Government shifts in a single night from State House to barracks. There are fresh names, ranks and titles to be learned. The photographers ready their cameras for the new official pictures: uniforms instead of double-breasted suits; the open army look instead of the politician's knowing glance. In place of laws lengthily disputed in debating chambers, come swift decrees in civil service jargon. There is more punctuality, less pomp, total pragmatism. 'Efficiency' becomes the outstanding political principle. Political argument, once exuberantly fatuous in the mouths of career politicians, is stilled. In the political vacuum where the soldiers rule, the role and purpose of armed men go unquestioned. At the outset, it is enough for them to announce that they rule for the nation. Power lies in the hands of those who control the means of violence. It lies in the barrel of a gun, fired or silent.

What is this Africa that soldiers are taking over? The Third World consists of three vast continents, and Africa is one of them. She is united with Latin America less by any close resemblance between, say, Brazil, Venezuela or Peru, and Algeria, Uganda or Ghana, than by their mutual relationship to forces outside the three continents, which aggravate their poverty, their dependence and their dilemmas. Latin America has had its spate of military coups; Africa seems to be in hot pursuit. Neither continent has found countervailing forces against the firepower of the clique in uniform. In Latin America, though, there is Cuba, capital of social revolution for the continent, where a popular guerrilla army and popular rising displaced the putsch and achieved a seizure of power different in character. Africa, for her part, has Guiné Bissau, where Amilcar Cabral and his party propose to lead a social revolution through armed struggle by an army of political volunteers. Both continents grapple with the threat and the reality of outside intervention, with the visible and concealed roots of dependence, with mounting national indebtedness and the prospect of stability in massive want and conspicuous corruption.

Not that the continents of the Third World are the same, or their political crises and uniformed presidents interchangeable. In Latin America the military emerged in alliance with the traditional power of land-owners; and later, when new social and economic forces developed, intervened in contests between the forces of the countryside and those of the city, between indigenous vested interests in industry and organized labour.[1] In some countries there is a long history of student protest with an explosive revolutionary content. There has been a long-standing United States defence and security policy of keeping the continent 'stable' by coddling dictators, especially those in uniform.* In Africa the economy is less developed by far; social forces are still largely inchoate; and the continent, except for some key areas like the Congo, and Ethiopia on the Red Sea and near the Middle East, is lower on the foreign-policy lists of the big powers. What Latin America endured yesterday, Africa may encounter, with due variation, today. Yet the identity of plight and purpose between the continents of the Third World is obscure or irrelevant to the vast majority of the men who rule over most of Africa. I rarely heard them talk about Vietnam, or China, or Cuba, or even Guiné-Bissau. The revolutionary turmoils of the Third World in our century are passing them by. Africa is one, of course, but it is a skin-deep connexion. About the vast and vital areas of the unliberated south there is concern, but only

* A confidence in the military that may wane now that the army leaders in Peru have begun expropriating US oil interests.

ricocheting knowledge. Ghanaians, supporters of both Nkrumah and Ankrah regimes, have said to me that the Southern African liberation movement should 'struggle' for independence as Ghana did. 'We had twenty-nine shot dead before we gained our independence,' they admonish. There seems so little awareness of the structure of White power in the south; no insight into the strategies of struggle there, of how far back it goes and how many hundreds have lost their lives. What independent Africa has not herself experienced, she does not easily recognize. She can be only too careless in her ignorance, and smug in her superiority. Men who still struggle for independence are considered unrealistic, for all the advice that they should struggle onwards. They should know better than to espouse hopeless causes or to fight for goals beyond the reach of the manipulating politician or the coup-making officer. I cannot forget the remark of a young Nigerian politician, who not long before had enjoyed a reputation for radicalism and even been imprisoned for his politics. He and a friend were discussing the then recently reported death of Che Guevara at the hands of the Bolivian army and the CIA. 'What could he expect if he went messing about in other peoples' countries?' he exclaimed. In Britain, the United States and Cuba, Black Power advocates declare: 'We will hook up with the Third World. We will go for the eye of the octopus, while our brothers sever its tentacles.' Many in Africa have not yet recognized eye or tentacle.

Africa is the last continent of the Third World come to political independence. She is the deepest sunk in economic backwardness. She has the most appalling problems. And she revels in the most effusive optimism. In the offices of the world organizations, the international diagnosticians, planners, technocrats – experts all, if not partisans – retreat steadily from hope. Their figures and graphs show that the continent is more likely to slide backwards than to stride forwards. The assets of three United States corporations, General Motors, Du Pont and the Bank of America, exceed the gross domestic product of all Africa, South Africa included. What Africa produces, with a few exceptions like copper and oil in fortunate places, is less and less wanted by the international market. Prices are dropping;

Africa's share in the total of world trade is declining. Schemes for commodity price stabilization, if they can be agreed, may help for a while. But even as the parties bargain, the chemical laboratories are making synthetically what Africa strains to grow.

Africa is a continent of mass poverty, but the obsession of the ruling groups is with luxuries. The same could be said in indictment of countless societies. But those who came to power mouthing the rhetoric of change faced the critical poverty of their countries with frivolity and fecklessness. Their successors, the soldiers, have an ingenuous faith in 'efficiency' and the simple army ethos of honesty. They detect the problems no more acutely than did the men they overthrew, probably, indeed, not as much. They discuss the problems less often, for such are 'politics'.

There has been eloquent, inexhaustible talk in Africa about politics, side by side with the gaping poverty of political thought. Down there on the ground in Africa, you can smother in the small talk of politics. Mostly it is about politicking, rarely about policies. Politicians are men who compete with one another for power, not men who use power to confront their country's problems. The military formations, the uniforms, the starch, the saluting aides-de-camp, the parade-ground precision might look, at last, like the decisiveness of purpose that Africa needs in its leadership. They camouflage a regimented sterility of ideas and social policy.

Africa is not everywhere the same, of course. Ethiopia is ruled like Machiavelli's polity: with Prince, aristocracy, palace intrigue, Church and army; and an American military base and Israeli-trained security service thrown in for good measure to reinforce an ancient dynastic power base built on an utterly wretched peasantry. Liberia, with an economy dominated by an international rubber company, is ruled by a Black settler élite, crowned by twelve families and a top-hatted President, disdaining the rights of 'indigenous' Africans as American whites once disdained those of the freed slaves, who were the founding fathers of this American-style plantation colony. In some states monarchs these days behave like presidents, and presidents aspire to be monarchs. In others, party programmes conjure splendid visions of African-style democracy, even socialism; yet the problem is to generate not only enthusiasm, but, more difficult, capital accumulation for development. In Kenya, and in the Ivory Coast, much of the surplus is absorbed by a combine of foreign corporations, with their resident representatives, and the related small circle of Africans on the make. West Africa is a whirlpool of candidates for quick profits, contracts and commissions, rake-off. Tanzania's under-development bred a sense of egalitarianism, albeit in poverty, which has now been augmented by attempts to proscribe the growth of a privileged group. Here and there are political systems committed to austerity and development, not spectacular consumption. Across the continent from West Africa, along the Nile, there is a greater austerity of living, but the same massive poverty and lack of policy. In Egypt a generation of army officers and students, pampered to lead their country and uplift the peasantry, dream of the night-clubs and neon-lit shop windows of Europe.

Everywhere, under the mobilization systems inaugurated by Nkrumah, Modibo Keita and Sékou Touré, Julius Nyerere and Kenneth Kaunda, as well as under the free enterprise of the Margais, Okotie-Ebohs and Mobutus, African development has been held to ransom by the emergence of a new, privileged, African class. It grows through politics, under party systems, under military governments, from the ranks of business, and from the corporate élites that run the state, the army and the civil service. In some countries, its growth is virtually free, in the sense that, though resources themselves may be fast exhausted, there is no social or economic policy to limit the size or dominance of this class. In other countries, policy is opposed to its very existence, but it persists all the same. National styles, territorial distinctions, and even divergent policy commitments blur into the continent-wide style of the newly rich. They are obsessed with property and personal performance in countries where all but a tiny fringe own hardly more than a hoe, a plastic bucket, an ironware cooking pot or two, and perhaps a bicycle. On the plane from Rome to Lagos there was a young man who had spent a year in Milan training to operate a computer. On his little airline trolley he carried as much haul as a peasant family in Africa or even Italy might work a decade to earn. Milan, he said, had been all right, but the Italians, though they worked so hard, 'don't seem to be getting anywhere'. Africa's élite is working hard at getting somewhere. Few of them read Frantz Fanon, yet they are living out his description of them: 'Spoilt children of yesterday's colonialism and of today's governments, they organize the loot of whatever national resources exist.'

There are, of course, those who have always been convinced that Africans are unfit to rule themselves, that Empire opted out of Africa too quickly, and that the continent was bound to go into decline after the premature granting of independence. But the crises of Africa have nothing to do with any such supposed incapacity of Africans to govern themselves. Independence delayed longer would have made the continent less, not better, able to meet the political and economic challenges of independence. Those who seek comfort in the tumult because they can ascribe it to black inferiority close their eyes to the depredations of the slave trade; the colonial role in Africa; and the political horrors perpetrated in Europe and elsewhere, by Whites and European political systems on a far more shuddering scale. It is the old paternalism of seeing London, Washington or Paris as the norm, which the rest of the world must follow, at peril of Western censure. It is time to judge Africa by what Africans need and want, and not by what the West finds congenial.

On the other hand, Africa needs a pitiless look at herself. It must be a long look, without the sentimentality which is the other side of colonial patronage. It is no answer to an indictment of the way Africans have handled their independence to ask, 'Could others have done better?' If they had not managed, they should have been subject to the same sharp criticism. Yet it is, after all, less than ten years since Africa became independent. That is no time at all to advance a continent as ravaged as any other, and that started with fewer advantages than most. Africa rightly rejects a time-scale that measures her need by the time taken by others to assuage theirs. 'We took a hundred years, after all; have patience', is chilling comfort. There is no patience. Too much time has been lost or squandered.

Much that needs to be said on the continent is not said, or not so that others can hear. James Ngugi, the Kenya novelist, has warned of the 'silent clamour for change that is now rocking' Africa. Yet, sounding close to despair, Wole Soyinka has anticipated that the African writer will before long envy the South African the bleak immensity of his problems. 'For the South African still has the right to hope; and this prospect of a future yet uncompromised by failure on his own part, in his own right, is something which has lately ceased to exist for other African writers.' Soyinka was considering the failure of writers; but of others, too, more directly culpable. The velvet-cushion commandos, he once called them in his own country, the men who rode to office and prosperity on the wave of independence, while the great majority saw no change from colonialism to independence.

Is there a group compromised by failure? Perhaps for some the anti-élite invective in this book will be too strong. Criticism made of persons or their roles is only incidental to a criticism, substantially, of systems and of policies. The targets are not individuals, but their place in an interest group. Civil servants come under fire not because Africa cannot produce some of the best, but because the very virtues avowedly possessed by a bureaucracy are inimical to the growth of self-government. Politicians condemn themselves out of their own mouths by their professed purposes and their subsequent performance. The army, whatever its declarations of noble intent, generally acts for army reasons. Where it does not, it has, in the nature of army structures and ethos, the greatest difficulty in initiating more than a temporary holding action. Above all, traditional armies believe that it is possible to create a policy without politics. This opens not new avenues but new culs-de-sac.

For many, the indictment should not be of Africans, whatever their record, but of the outside forces responsible, ultimately, for the plight of the continent. That indictment stands. It cannot be framed too often. But that approach, too, on its own, is a form of patronage; for it makes the African ever victim, never perpetrator. If independent Africa is far from the political promise of independence, let alone from social change, this is not because she does not need it. She needs change no less, at least, than Latin America; but the Americas seem closer to change and their needs therefore nearer assuagement. She is far from change because there are formidable world forces against it, and because her colonial experience hangs a dread weight upon her; but also because she has produced few leaderships, these independent years, that want it. The old generation of independence politicians is largely played out, exhausted. There are too few exceptions – until new forces stir – to stop the débâcle in all but a few enclaves. The generation, whether politician, administrator or soldier, that comes forward to replace *les anciens* from the euphoric days of independence, is greedy for its prizes; and, for the most part, even less concerned with the polity, let alone the people. A different force is stirring, among the secondary-school students, the urban unemployed, the surplus graduates of the indulged coastlines, the neglected and impoverished of the northern interiors. As yet the pockets of discontent are scattered, hesitant and unassertive, or easily obliterated. The disaffected are bewildered by the confusions and lost causes in the litter of the generation that wrested independence, and are fumbling for a coherent resolve. They are not rebels without a cause, but, stirring to rebellion, are still unsure of their cause, and the means to advance it. Will the search for change be pre-empted or pursued by the entry of the army into government?

Think-Tank Theories

Coups have become a growth industry for academics as well as for military men, and the models and theories, up-dated and re-shaped, are coming thick and fast. An early classification encompassing the whole world was that of Finer.[2] His man on horseback, the military, intervened in politics according to levels of political culture, which were determined by the strength or weakness of attachment to civilian institutions. The higher the level of political culture, the fewer would be the opportunities for the military, and the less support the military would receive.

The lower the level of political culture, the more numerous the opportunities, and the greater the likelihood of public support. (The coup is taken as the index of civil–military relations; but military organizations can exert a strong influence on government policy without recourse to a coup.) This framework, Ralph Miliband has said,[3] is not necessarily harmful, but it is not very illuminating either. The theory does not answer the question why coups occur in some states of 'minimal political culture', and not in others, and why they take one form in some states and another somewhere else. It is a universal classification that leaves much unaccounted for and unexplained.

The search for an overall classification system has been punctuated by quantitative studies probing for the role of the isolated common factor: stage of economic development; types of political organization; length of independence period; size of army. The computer as a substitute for social analysis has produced arid or trivial conclusions – such as that the chances of military involvement increase year by year after independence. (Self-evident, one would think, seeing that only after independence did Africans get control of armies and politics, and any assault on a colonial administration would fall into the category not of coup, but of rebellion.) Janowitz has explored the relationship between economic development and limitations on the political role of the military in a sample of fifty-one developing nations. Empirical results, he found, were mainly negative or unreliable. The argument that the more economically developed a nation, the less likely a military intervention, was not borne out.[4] The size of the army and its firepower have not been decisive; nor has the proportion of the state's military expenditure as a percentage of gross domestic product. Others[5] have traced the correlation between coups and one-party, two-party, multiparty, no-effective-party states; but coups have occurred with a fine disregard for these earnestly constructed systems. (Some tried to explain the coup as the logical outcome of the one-party system, where the army played the role of opposition; but Dahomey and the Congo, Sierra Leone and Nigeria were scarcely one-party states.) As Van Doorn said, summarizing the work of the experts, 'almost every tendency shows its counterpart'.[6]

Scrutiny directed to the political party or the political system next turned to the social structure and motivation of the army. Records of military training schools have been combed for the social background of officers, and their attitudes, with the army's promotion structure studied for sources of tension between professionals competing to advance their careers, for motives of intervention in politics. Throughout Africa, with the exception of Algeria, Finer argued, armies had a low flashpoint, or small propensity to intervene. Yet they intervened. Disposition to intervene, as Finer showed, proved to be a skein of motives, mood and opportunity. But descriptions of military organization and the social origins of soldiers are not likely to be helpful outside the context of the social and political system. In many instances, the origins of a coup are obscure, and the intentions of those staging them are mixed. The army acts for army reasons, but for others as well. A military coup needs the participation of a professional army or core of officers, but it need not be precipitated, or even planned, by the military alone,[7] for military reasons.

Some general theories have emerged. There is the theory that the army in under-developed countries is the modernizer; that soldiers are endowed with all sorts of virtues as dynamic, self-sacrificing reformers.[8] For from where else are new social policies and institutional reform to come?

A volume planned as *The Politics of Change in Latin America* became, in the course of writing, *The Politics of Conformity in Latin America.*[9] Social groups committed, it was thought, to producing structural change, have attained power, but not to implement reforms; rather, they have worked to integrate themselves into the existing social structure. An apparently new middle group has turned out to be an extension of the traditional upper class, in economic position and in basic values. Reforms considered essential for the continent have not taken place. Groups which seemed likely to promote economic development 'have not even managed to achieve recognition, much less the capacity to dictate policy'.[10] Guerrilla struggle in Latin America is posed precisely to break up the politics of conformity, as Robin Blackburn has pointed out.[11]

The false model for Latin America has been Europe's early bourgeoisie (with, behind it, a distinctive method of primary capital accumulation) and the Western parliamentary system. It has been the wrong model. In Latin America, intelligent and facile answers have been given to the wrong questions. The model for Africa cannot be Latin America, for conditions, once again, are too disparate; and, besides, the model has plainly not worked in Latin America. What are the right questions for Africa?

Armies, it was said, would not move into politics in Africa because they were so small.[12] The strength of the army has turned out to be the weakness of other forces in the society. This can be illuminated only by looking at both army and politics, and their mutual inter-action. Many questions have to be asked. Who rules Africa under independence? What are the main elements in the chronic instability of these states? How is political power concentrated or dispersed, and why can the action of a small armed group so effortlessly capture it? Why, thus, when there has been a blow at the top of the power structure, does it seem so irrelevant to the polity as a whole? What of the institutions of state, and in particular the management of the economy? What of the people, down below? Who is dispossessed by a coup; who raised to power? Was the conflict over who exercised power, or how it was exercised? Why does the army, and not some other group, play the pivotal role in new states? Who are the military men under their uniforms; whose sons and brothers? Do they represent distinctive social forces? The dispossessed? Themselves alone? Do captains of the army hope to become captains of industry, or of commerce? What triggers the coup? Does the army act for inner army reasons, or for reasons that flow from the wider polity? Or both? Coups, clearly, decide who will rule for the moment; but do they, could they, change the character of the society or its political system? Do they promote change, or conformity? Where coups have failed, what have been the sources of their defeat? Are all army coups equivalent, all military governments comparable? What can the barracks produce that the politicians, or the economic planners, have not? Does the army file back to barracks on its own?

These questions apart, there is the issue of foreign intervention. A theory of conspiracy sees all the ills of the Third World as visited on her by outside forces. Very many of them are. No doubt, in time, more information will come to light about exact connexions between foreign states, military attachés and coup-making army officers. Until the evidence does become available – and that, in the nature of things, will take time – this account of coups d'état calculates on intervention playing an insidious and sophisticated role, but not the only role, and often not even a decisive one. For there are two sets of causes for a coup. The one is deep-seated, in the profound dependence of Africa on external forces. The economic levers that move or brake Africa are not within her boundaries, but beyond them. Nkrumah was brought down as much by the plummeting price of cocoa in the world market as by his army and police officers. Whether governments are working well or badly – and his was working badly – the state of particular commodity markets or a drying up of loans could be their undoing. Apart from the tripwire of France's military presence in Africa (of which more in a subsequent chapter), any economic breeze in Paris blows gales through African economies; and M. Foccart, France's Secretary for African and Malagasy Affairs, is generally better able to decide their role than the African presidents themselves. The second set of reasons lies in the tensions and fragility of the African state. This book focuses mainly on this set of reasons. Foreign powers and counter-insurgency agencies reckon acutely on them as I try to show in Part 6. Agents, counter-insurgency teams, mercenaries like 5 and 6 Commando in the Congo, undoubtedly exist; but there are also patient, knowledgeable and deliberate probes of the weak points in a state which it is policy to assail. The shadow-play of neo-colonial politics is often improvised locally, Roger Murray has said.[13] In a search for the genesis of the coup, Africa must address herself not only to the airports where agents arrive, but to her own inner condition. The Bay of Pigs assault on Cuba did not bring that government down. The column of soldiers that marched on Flagstaff House from the garrison at Tamale did. The reasons are important. It is the groundswell of African politics which makes army coups possible, and while giving armies internal reasons for striking, gives other forces little or no defence.

Not all army, or armed, interventions in politics are equivalent, nor do they all take the shape of coups d'état. Zanzibar is usually included in lists of army interventions: but in January 1964, when the Sultan and a minority government entrenched under a colonial constitution were overthrown, it was by popular, armed insurrection. In Congo-Brazzaville, also usually included in the list, the Youlou regime was brought down in 1963 by strikes, demonstrations and conferences of youth activists and trade-unionists; and the army – though its refusal to fire on the crowds massed outside the presidential palace made it the decisive force in overturning the government – played a self-effacing role. Only during a subsequent political crisis, in 1966, did the army strike its own blow against the state and enter government. Uganda is generally not included in lists of African coups d'état, except as one of the three East African states which experienced a brief and easily suppressed army pay mutiny in 1964. Uganda has not experienced an army take-over, and has no army men in her government. But in May 1966, a long-festering conflict there between the central government and the kingdom of Buganda came to a head, and the army was used to subdue the Kabaka and his palace guard. The action was directed by President Obote's civilian regime. But the Uganda army was crucial in that confrontation, and has been the nexus of power in Uganda ever since.[14] Army interventions on behalf of government, such as that in Uganda, can be taken for granted as an extension of their role as guardians of the state; they can also be by virtual self-invitation, as in Gabon, where President Bongo made room in his cabinet for several of the senior army command, in what looked like a bold attempt to pre-empt the army's taking the seats for itself.*

The army coup d'état, though, is not equivalent to *any* political use of the army by government. Nor is it equivalent to

*March 1969.

any use of violence to effect change; or even to any sudden, forceful substitution of one ruling element for another. These could be rebellion or revolution, where groups, small and conspiratorial, or representing great masses of people, act to seize the state: either to press for changes within the accepted framework, or to substitute new forms of government and political system. The coup can only be undertaken 'by a group that is already a participant in the existing political system and that possesses institutional bases of power within the system. In particular the instigating group needs the support of some elements of the armed forces.'[15]

The coup d'état can pre-empt revolution, or lead to it. It can install a military, or an alternative civilian, government. It can maintain, or change social policy. In its essence, the coup is a lightning action at the top, in which violence is the ultimate determinant, even if it is not used. The conspiratorial strike is the secret of its success, not the mobilization of popular masses or their mandate. Any armed group can, theoretically, effect a coup; but it would have to immobilize or confront the army, police and other security apparatus of the state. Army coups d'état involve the army as principal protagonist and conspirator, even if it withdraws to the barracks once the action is over.

The army does not always move monolithically. A successful coup may be staged by the army command itself, by a section of the officer corps, by non-commissioned officers, or even by privates, if each such group can take the necessary steps to immobilize counter-action from the levels of command above it. Senior military commanders have tended to identify with the government in power and to have substantial stakes in preserving the *status quo*. Younger officers have tended to identify with their generation in politics or the civil service; if that generation is critical of the political order, its representatives in uniform may employ arms to re-arrange the order itself. The critical coup-making rank was generally considered to be the colonels and other middle-grade officers, who have command of men and also access to army communications and arsenals. But most ranks have been protagonists in one or other African coup d'état.

Whatever the political background to a coup d'état, when the army acts it generally acts for army reasons, in addition to any other it may espouse. Corporate army interests may be predominant, or they may be secondary to other more generalized political grievances; but army reasons are invariably present. The army may long brood over its discontent, biding its time until its contemplated action coincides with a general state of anti-government feeling, as in Ghana; or it may seem oblivious to popular opinion and strike precipitately when it feels it is being affronted or brought under attack, as in Togo.

The striking feature of army interventions in politics is that to almost every coup there is a counter-coup. (Congo-Kinshasa has so far proved a notable exception.) The coup spawns other coups. Some are successful, some fail. And in a single coup cycle, each successive coup tends to be set afoot by a rank lower in the army hierarchy than the one that initiated the sequence. Causes, sequels, and the purpose to which the coup is put, alter; but once the army breaks the first commandment of its training – that armies do not act against their own governments – the initial coup sets off a process. The virginity of the army is like that of a woman, army men are fond of saying: once assailed, it is never again intact.

The Contagion of the Coup

In the sequence of coups on the continent, Egypt was first with its 1952 army-led revolution; but this was an event to which Africa – the Sudan excepted – gave hardly more than a sidelong glance. Nasser came into his own in Black Africa as a soldier-revolutionary only when young majors, like Nzeogwu of Nigeria, diagnosed their political systems as rotten, and sought texts and models for making and justifying a coup to a soldier generation taught that it had no place in politics. The momentous precedent for the coups that have swept across Africa was the overthrow of Lumumba's government, with the murder of Lumumba himself, and the part played by General Mobutu and his army in carving the shape of politics in the Congo. This was the first time that the legitimacy of the colonial inheritance was defied and denied. And it was done with the connivance – where not the collaboration – of the West and even of the United Nations. The Lumumba government had achieved power by electoral primacy, by constitutional means, by parliamentary choice. But the constitution was one thing, as was the election; the army proved to be quite another. The Congo had a traumatic effect on Africa (especially on Nigerian and Ghanaian army officers who served there, and watched the soldiers arbitrate between or coerce the politicians). Power and control depended on who commanded, and used, the army, and for what purpose. In a political crisis, the army was the only decisive instrument. (One other was more decisive, and this was the role of foreign intervention; for when it was brought into play, it could overrule the decision of the army.)

The politicians were slower than the soldiers to realize the power of the army. It was only after the initial coup d'état that political leaders planned for the eventuality of another (in Ethiopia, in the Sudan and in Tanzania, where methods were, variously, to split the army command so that one section could be used to prevail against another, or to try and enrol the army in the purposes of government). Even the soldiers were slow to use their striking power for general political ends; and in the beginning, when they moved it was to assert corporate army interests, rather than to make any special political point. Independence was still young, and crisis was not yet mature. Thus the first army coups were pay strikes, to secure better conditions for the army. Each coup grew to larger political purpose; and the later wave of coups had wide political objectives and initiated thorough military take-overs of government. After staging a coup in the early phase, the military were content to return to barracks, having installed a new civilian government, or extracted something from an old one. In the later phase, the military abandoned their inhibitions about seizing and running government itself. The Congo, Togo and Dahomey went through early and late phases, both; Ghana and Nigeria established military juntas from the beginning.

Internal characteristics account for the difference, between coups d'état and their sequels. One could erect a Heath Robinson coup mechanism, to show how in a particular coup, and in one compared with another, coup-making levers are jerked into play: political and army grievances often correspond; external pressures can be decisive; political levers are jerked by stresses between parties, regions and personalities. The range of minor differences is wide. More significant is what exists in common among Africa's military interventions in politics: the resort to colonial-type, bureaucratic control; the dominance of the administrative class, the civil servants, in the military–bureaucratic governing partnership; the re-arrangement of the personnel operating the political system, without significantly affecting the social and economic structures. The coup as a method of change that changes little has become endemic to Africa's politics.

It has certain contagion. What the military of one state do today, their confrères next door may do tomorrow. Since independence, states have become part of inter-acting sub-systems for regional economic, political and other purposes. They co-operate, and they intervene, directly and indirectly, in one another's affairs. Tensions with Niger aggravated Dahomey's internal crisis.[16] Congo-Kinshasa is vitally concerned, and involved, in developments across the river in Congo-Brazzaville. Soglo has explained his take-over in Dahomey as prompted by fear that the scheduled elections might produce disorder similar to that which followed the Western Nigerian elections (many Dahomeyans are Yoruba, and they follow closely Western Nigerian developments).[17]

The strongest source of contagion, however, lies in the old-boy network of the African armies, and related inter-army inspiration. The military leaders of the former French colonies trained together, fought the same wars together, and several of them (Soglo, Lamizana and Bokasso) are intimates. The young Alley of Dahomey and Eyadema of Togo grew up in the post-Second World War French military tradition. (And if they were seeking an outstanding military prototype, why not General de Gaulle, who came to power on the strength of the army, by subsequently concealed but none the less evident coup d'état?)

The senior officers of the British-trained West African armies have almost interchangeable careers. Nzeogwu and Afrifa, the young coup-makers of Nigeria and Ghana, were two course-terms apart in their Sandhurst training. Ghanaian coup-makers recount how they were spurred into action by taunts that the Nigerian soldiers who made the coup were Men, after all. What was wrong with Ghana's soldiers? This may be a rationalization; but if anything made the Ghanaian coup inevitable, it was the staging of the Nigerian coup a month before. The continent-wide cycle is far from complete.

Part II

The Colonial Sediment

The crisis of Africa's independence governments, which one after the other have fallen victim to army coups d'état, cannot be discussed without a close look at the colonial period.

Independence is seen as a watershed in the development of the contemporary African condition. And so it was. In 1960 there occurred changes scarcely credible ten years before. But despite the great wave from colonial to independent government, there remained a continuity between the old dependence and the new. Many of the means and ends that made up colonial administration were inherited virtually intact by the independence governments. For the sediment of colonialism lies deep in African society. The armies are colonial products; the political system is largely a transplant, and a bad one at that; while the political rulers were trained or constrained by the colonial system. Africa was a continent of bureaucratic rule, with armies behind the administrators ready to prove whenever necessary that government existed by conquest.

Have we not had enough of the colonial period by now? It may be charged that such excursions only encourage the tendency to find excuses for failure on the African continent in the heritage of colonialism, or the machinations of outside forces; and that it is time we stopped blaming everything on the colonial past. For Africans have taken over now. But independence in many countries is not yet ten years old; and while it is said that, in such independence, there was an African revolution, we must ask – how complete a revolution? If Africans have taken over now, what have they inherited or discarded? Which of the faults in their politics are intrinsic to the condition in which colonialism left the continent? And which, given clearer purpose, properly pursued, might Africa have surmounted? To answer these questions, it is necessary to examine the state structures built up during the colonial period and taken over at the time of independence; and how, in the phase of decolonization, power was transferred, through virtually unchanged institutions of government, to largely hand-picked heirs. These heirs are the new ruling groups of Africa. Their aspirations, their fears and their conflicts, in a system still subjugated within the world economy, and developing too slowly to make room for all claimants – among them, the military men – to membership of the ruling and privileged groups, are the political crises of Africa, punctuated so frequently by the coup d'état.

The Grid of Administration

The numerical weakness of the colonial general's troops impelled them to discover in the country to be conquered the resources necessary for completing the conquest: manpower by recruiting natives, intellectual power by studying the populations and getting used to them. Action undertaken in this way is patient and solid. It raises up native allies.... Conquest became organisation on the march.

R. Delavignette, *Freedom and Authority in French West Africa*

Conquest, diplomatically and officially speaking, became a sustained venture of the European powers after the Berlin conference of 1884–5, although the slaver, the trader, the fortune-hunter and the missionary had all come before the imperial army, each in his turn or all together softening up the continent for conquest. The division of Africa was an extension of the struggle among the European powers of the nineteenth century, and Africa under colonialism was ruled as a promontory of European interests. Colonialism was trade, investment and enterprise for the benefit of an alien society. Power lay outside the country. African trade, African free enterprise, far from being encouraged, were ousted, or permitted to operate only as very junior partners.

In the conquest of the continent, a show of force was not always necessary; artful negotiation and deft displays of potential were often sufficient. Occupying powers met resistance and made enemies; but they also induced allies among groups which thought that self-interest would be served by joining the invader rather than by opposing him. There were regions of brave and costly resistance. But whatever the pattern of the conquest, whether by war or seduction, conquest it was, and the colonial power insisted upon unassailable authority. That it did not always immediately install this authority, outside of garrisons and the raising of local forces, lest needless trouble break out, did not obscure the fact that the colonial powers owed their presence and their claim to legitimacy to force.

From formal conquest until, more or less, the First World War, colonialism was characterized by pacification, trade and only the most rudimentary forms of administration. Traders, concession-holders and, in some regions, white settlers, were left to install themselves where they were inclined and to exact what premiums they could. French Equatorial Africa, for instance, was divided among forty concession companies at the beginning of the century.[1] Commanding only meagre forces in the field,[2] colonial rule had to be riveted like 'a great steel grid' over the continent.[3] The grid had to be tight and durable, but it had also to be cheap. Lugard's improvised grid, the indirect rule system, was 'the offspring of expediency and parsimony'.[4] It was economical not only of the colonial power's cash resources, on which a large bureaucratic machine would have made heavy demands, but also of its military capacity. Emirs were offered a settlement of conquest without dishonour.[5] Government would be channelled through the chiefs, 'to maintain, strengthen and educate the Fulani and Kanembu ruling races', so that 'the regeneration of Nigeria might be through its own governing class'.[6]

The patents for the administrative grids fashioned in London or Paris, in Brussels or in Lisbon, varied in style and design, since variations had to allow for the aberrations of French,

British, Belgium and Portuguese history, as well as their respective philosophies and styles of administration. The French, once installed, set out to break the powerful Moslem dynasties that had fought them on the battlefield. Lugard himself, searching for a malleable and hierarchical system of authority, found one in the northern emirates of Nigeria. Indeed, this system was one that, in the rigid control of commoners by overlords, recalled, in thrifty combination, the iron discipline of his beloved army and Britain's own rigid class distinctions. To the British, the emirs of Nigeria, with court and protocol, not to speak of purdah, evoked the Indian Raj. Here in Africa were princely states that kept their subjects at a respectful distance, unlike the pushful southern society of the British colonies, whose imitation of British ways made the master writhe with discomfort at the familiarity of it all.

The French tied their territories close to France, seeking, with their penchant for philosophy and system, some coherence in a scheme said to embrace Frenchmen and adopted Frenchmen – the *evolués* – alike. The British were empirical, mostly, or opportunist; they felt easier administering from hand to mouth, stretching such theory as they managed to devise, like Lugard's indirect rule, to inapplicable proportions in regions totally unlike those in which Lugard made the emirs the pinnacle of authority – under him. And the proselytizing that the French undertook with French culture, the British tried with the Christian religion and the mission society. They permitted a bewildering array of mission societies; but through them all, the White man's God laid down the White man's superior morality, to those striving for acceptance through conversion. When it came to government, British administrators focused not on Westminster, the mother of Parliaments, but on her minor children: local government, local councils, local problems. Parochialism recalled a more static age, when the country squire and the justice of the peace kept order in the domain. The pinnacle of achievement was the life and manners of the English gentleman, the English public school, English phlegm.

The French found themselves more comfortable in the company of the *evolué* – and the *evolué* was suitably responsive to the compliment.[7] The British preferred not the jumped-up, educated black Englishman, but the 'unspoiled' villager or peasant tribesman, patiently trying out his model of local government, and knowing his place in the hierarchy of authority, under the chief, who was in turn, of course, under the administrator.

The French, said one of their former colonial governors superciliously, did not have 'a superstitious regard for monarchy'.[8] The chief was not considered a potentate; rather, a useful administrative auxiliary. Cantonal chiefs were appointed only to transmit orders and to collect taxes. The French administrator 'is the commandant, the king of the bush, whose very presence creates a new political unit'.[9] And, to be sure, whether the chiefs were supported under the British or degraded under the French, the colonial official himself was the king of the bush; and of the province, and of the capital, and of the colony. Students and Africanists have dwelt in earnest detail on the main colonial systems, the French, the British and the Belgian. But, scrutinized after the independence experience, the differences fall into academic obscurity. There was the national inclination of each towards its own 'system'; but lines between the French, British, Belgian and other systems are blurred in many places, with policy frequently pragmatic and in conflict with declared principle.

Colonialism in its different variations was more like than unlike in the form of rule it imposed. This was, whether conscious or not, military in conception and organization. More than anything else, colonial administrations resembled armies. The chain of authority from the top downwards was untouched by any principle of representation or consultation. For long periods in some territories, indeed, the colonial administrations not only resembled armies, in their para-military formation and ethos; they were, as in the Sudan, the instruments of military men.

The pacification of the Sudan was brought about by a series of military excursions; but these apart, the army shaped, during the pacification period, the Sudanese administration itself. The Condominium Agreement of 1899, under which the Sudan was governed (actually by Britain, but supposedly by the two Condominium partners, Britain and Egypt), declared a state of martial law in the Sudan so as to give the governor-general full powers in the process of re-occupation, and this martial law remained in force until 1926.* The governor-general, who until 1925 was also commander-in-chief of the Egyptian army, was absolute ruler. Not until the Second World War was anything done to dilute the pure autocracy of government in the Sudan or to find some way of consulting the Sudanese themselves; and when steps were taken, they were too few and too late. The day-to-day exercise of the governor-general's authority devolved on government secretaries, governors of provinces and department heads; but ultimate authority remained unimpaired in the hands of the governor-general, with all officials responsible to him alone. The civil apparatus below him followed a distinct military pattern, with the civil, finance and legal secretaries, the heads of departments, and the governors of provinces, his staff and commanders in the field.[10] All governors, inspectors, senior administrative officers, and even magistrates in the early years, were British officers seconded from the Egyptian army. Under them, in charge of routine work, were Egyptian army officers. The highest posts open to Egyptians were those of *mamur* (subordinate to an assistant-district commissioner) and *sub-mamur*. The Egyptian officials in turn had Sudanese of even lesser rank from the armed forces as their assistants.

The search for civilian administrators was cautious and tentative, though somewhat speeded up by the Anglo-Boer War at the turn of the century, which drew from Sudan some of its military administrators, including Kitchener himself. Each year, through careful selection by a board sitting in London, a few young British civilians were recruited from the universities to meet Cromer's requirements of 'active young men, endowed with good health, high character and fair abilities'.[11] Six were taken out to the Sudan in 1901; by 1905 there were fifteen; and by 1933, forty, making up what was by then the Sudan Political Service, probably the most select and best-paid body of administrators in the colonial world. As late as 1912, no more than

*Article 9 of the Condominium Agreement reads: 'Until, and save as it shall be otherwise determined by Proclamation, the Sudan shall be and remain under martial law.'

two of the twelve provincial governors were civilians. Only very gradually was the administration transformed from a military to a civilian machine, though 'it continued to have a military flavour which survives to this day in the khaki uniform and coloured stripes of the civilian administrators of the independent Sudan'.[12] Between them, Cromer, Wingate and Kitchener, all products of the Royal Military Academy of Woolwich (Cromer and Wingate passed out as gunners; Kitchener, as a sapper)[13] formulated policy for the Sudan – and Egypt – across thirty-six years. Wingate had been Director of Intelligence to Kitchener during the advance on Khartoum, and the man he chose to succeed him when he was transferred to Cairo as High Commissioner for Egypt, Sir Lee Stack, had at one time been his own Director of Intelligence.[14]

No specific Whitehall department in London, no parliamentary supervision (the occasional question in the House apart) controlled policy in the Sudan; and the Foreign Office, which was the only department concerned, could always find evasion and defence behind the fact that, by the clauses of the Condominium Agreement, the governor-general was in supreme control. Around this command, there grew, according to a doubtful tribute by a former senior member of the Sudan Political Service, 'a closely integrated corporation of willing servants of the State, undogged by the tyranny of the pen, concerned with little but their work, their hobbies and their families, and owing a ready allegiance to the embodiment of leadership and power in the person of the Head of the State'.[15] If governors of provinces or members of the secretariat at headquarters had received no previous administrative training, they made up for this or any other inadequacy with the confidence that, as military officers, they had unchallengeable superiority in 'handling men'. Alien as this notion might be to the principle of representative government, and destructive of its future practice, it was the only system operable by a traditional military hierarchy. Men in command, by the nature of their office, knew how to command other men. Any other influences were obstructive.

In the French empire, a military-type administration

developed as naturally as in the Sudan. Military conquest was followed by military administration. 'When the military were replaced by civilian administrators,' a historian of the period has written,[16] 'the latter were inheritors of an administrative infrastructure that was essentially military in conception. Sole authority was vested in the Commandant de Cercle, who, like the colonel of a battalion, had jurisdiction over, if he did not carry out, all fields of administration, including the technical services.'[17] The civilian administrator continued to require that the 'natives' salute him; and to enforce his authority, he had a para-military force at his disposal in the form of the *gardes de cercle*. 'These guards obtained great power in the community because of their police function and because they were frequently used as intermediaries between the administrator and the chiefs.'[18] Just as the French army was organized so that there should be no duality of command but a logical chain of authority from the highest to the lowest, so 'the administrative structures introduced (by the military) in Africa were, even more than those created by Napoleon in the mother country, based on the hierarchical pyramid of the army'.[19] The chiefs of the cantons and circles of the administration were grouped into a hierarchy: *chefs supérieurs de province*; *chefs de cantons*; *chefs de village*. The chiefs were selected for their loyalty to France, on evidence that often involved service in the army or police. And only in 1936 were they granted official civil service terms of appointment.

Lugard's system, likewise, has been described as a classic example of militarism in government. It

> stemmed from his military training and mind, and the system of one man rule which he set up faithfully reflects military rather than civil considerations. Instead of a commercial capital as the seat of government he chose a series of operational headquarters divorced from the economic life of the country. Instead of experienced colonial civil servants, he deliberately sought 'officers' and 'gentlemen' (without previous experience) as his administrators. Instead of embryo civil departments to provide commercial and social services, he created an autocratic command system, running from his headquarters to provincial outposts, and through them to the now-subordinate Fulani Emirates, themselves military in origin.[20]

Whether Sudanese, French-military or Lugardist in form, a hierarchy of officialdom followed each colonial conquest in turn, creating an authoritarian system, in which power flowed from the top downwards and, ultimately, from outside. Here in small measure, there in larger, a handful of approved locals – chiefs or the new educated – might be recruited into the lower and middle ranges of the administrative system. But the system was answerable not to these favoured participants or to the communities from which they were drawn, but to the external, forcibly imposed authority of the imperial government in the metropolis. In the eyes of colonial power, effective self-government, social management from below, was totally incompatible with good government. The problem, after all, was one of administration, not of participation and politics; and who could be better administrators than those trained to administer? Until the late 1950s, colonial officials serving in Africa were still known, technically, as 'administrative officers'. The colonial system functioned in the conviction that the administrator was sovereign; that his subjects neither understood nor wanted self-government or independence; that the only article of faith on which administrators could confidently depend was that all problems of 'good government' were administrative, and that disaster would follow from attempts to conceive of them as political. Even in later years, when administrators were consciously trying to adjust their attitudes to changing situations, the structures were not fundamentally changed, and would not permit any official behaviour other than the administrative–autocratic.

This colonial pattern, wrote Rupert Emerson,[21]

> rests on two assumptions familiar to aristocracies everywhere, that the backward masses, incapable of administering themselves and misgoverned by their own regimes, will receive a far better deal at the hands of their advanced overlords, and that they are primarily interested only in living their lives in peace and quiet, with rising standards of welfare to be provided for them from above. The proper focus of administration is the 'real' people, the simple peasant mass which gratefully accepts benevolent paternalism and which should be protected from the arousing of discontents since it has neither the desire

nor competence to play an active role in its own and world affairs. The occasional outbursts of political agitation reflect not the demands of the 'real' people, but only the self-interested machinations of an untrustworthy few, who, caught in transition between two worlds, represent neither east nor west and seek to make capital out of the academic yet dangerous theories of liberty and equality. It is not to these new pretenders to power that the guileless masses should look for sympathetic understanding, but to the disinterested imperial administrators.

Britain's army of colonial administrators, inbred and insular, was commanded by a senior corps, recruited in its later years from Britain's public schools by a man who has been called 'an unreconstructed Victorian gentleman'. This was Sir Roger Furse, who controlled appointments to civil service posts for thirty-eight years, from 1910 to 1948. Parliamentarians and Ministers of State rose and fell, but his highly personal and intuitive methods of selecting colonial officials screwed that administrative grid into place over the British colonies. Furse himself went to Eton and Balliol, but he confessed that he owed his success more to his training as a cavalry officer. In the years immediately after 1918, new recruits to the colonial service were young ex-officers from the war, selected by interview in London.[22] When the supply of ex-officers dried up, recruits were drawn from the public schools and from Oxford or Cambridge.

Furse was searching for men with special qualities of leadership. Such men, he was convinced, came invariably from certain families and educational institutions. 'The District Officer,' Lugard had said, 'comes from a class which has made and maintained the British Empire.'[23] So Furse visited his friends in public schools, at Oxford or Cambridge, in country houses or in London clubs, looking for men capable of dealing with other men (though black, brown or yellow) and picking candidates by the thrust of their jaw, their firmness of handshake, their athletic prowess, their membership of worthy families and their gentlemanly bearing. His deafness, it has been suggested,[24] meant that he could not easily hear what the candidate up for the interview was saying, but his quick eyes took in personal mannerisms. Following an interview in 1911, he wrote that the candidate was

> tall, light haired, slim but well built . . . a good open face with a good deal of grit in it . . . a very good athlete . . . brains I expect fair . . . a fourth class honours degree . . . but had influenza just before. He has a slightly affected way of shaking hands . . . but made a good impression and is I think really up to East African standard.[25]

Members of the recruiting staff were told to watch out for 'colouring, build, movement, poise', and 'such superficialities as style of dress and hair, health of skin and fingers'.

> But your scrutiny will be directed chiefly to eyes and mouth, for they, whether in repose or in action, combined with speech and gesture, may tell you much. You will have in mind the truism that weakness of various kinds may lurk in a flabby lip or in averted eyes, just as single-mindedness and purpose are commonly reflected in a steady gaze, and firm set of mouth and jaw.[26]

An official inquiry, scrutinizing the colonial recruiting system, in 1929, clearly agreed with the views of a Secretary of State, the Duke of Devonshire, when he said: 'The code which must guide the administrator in the tropics is to be found in no book of regulations. It demands that in every circumstance and under all conditions he shall act in accordance with the traditions of an English gentleman.'[27]

Sir Roger Furse was right: the show could not have been run without the public schools. To Furse and his class and generation, the public school was the 'spiritual child of the tradition of chivalry'. Its product was characteristically set off from the rest of English society, and so could be expected to observe suitable aloofness from the people it would rule in bush or savannah. The men sent out to control the colonies lived by a code of paternalism that had already been eroded in the generation before their own. Some were born to rule; others became rulers through their role in the colonies, which they ran like eighteenth-century shires and parishes. The ethos of a ruling class, that in Britain was fast losing its exclusive claim, became the ethos of the colonial service. And very naturally, one 'aristocracy' gravitated to another: it was not surprising that officials in Northern

Nigeria 'instinctively buttressed the hierarchy they found in existence there, as did their colleagues in Uganda, Malaya and the Aden Protectorates'.[28]

Only after Furse's retirement in 1948 was his service's code of recruitment substantially altered. Indeed, as the Second World War drew to a close, even Furse perceived that the time was past when the main function of the Colonial Office was to deal with traditional chiefs. The 'educated native' had arrived on the scene and challenged, by implication at least, the traditional authorities on which administration had relied. Whereas in earlier times Margery Perham had received inquiries from administrators in the field on how to deal with traditional chiefs, she was now getting requests for advice on how to deal with new and unfamiliar urban authorities.[29] Yet some officials changed not at all, and spent the best years of their lives trying to preserve societies which imperial incursion into the continent had irreparably shattered. These men viewed the urban African, created by their own economic order, as a threat to the stability of that order. 'What these people need,' remarked a District Officer, discussing the urban African, 'is not education, but the stick.'[30]

Some of the men who administered France's colonial empire expressed themselves less like head prefects and more like romantic visionaries, at least in Parisian print. Metropolitan France smelt stale and felt cramped, wrote a one-time Minister of France's Overseas Territories. The fault lay with an impersonal, irresponsible, routine-ridden administration. There was no Command. In Africa, on the contrary, 'we are preserving that function of authority in which resides the vital spirit of the new world'. The Commandant was much more than an official at some district outpost. Not only did he send to the French in Europe the luxuries to which they had become accustomed, but he also 'transmits a sort of energy. . . . The colonial administrator is the unknown electrician in the power house of a new order of life, just as much for Africa as for France.'[31] Europe, in opening Africa up to the world, was acting as a universal civilization rather than as any particular imperialism. In savannah and forest, these carriers of civilization were conducting a race towards civilization, not a conflict between civilizations. The

European powers competed against each other, not like the 'pontiffs of hostile sects', but like runners, to see who would win through first to river or town; who would mark the greatest number of points on the map. In Europe the powers were bristling with conscript soldiers, ruining themselves with armaments. Africa, on the contrary, endowed the powers with an astonishing unity.

And the representative of the commercial house was as much part of the civilizing mission as his colonial office counterpart.* 'The wife of an agent of a chartered company radiates authority as though she were the daughter of the stateliest house in England,' wrote Delavignette. But the French high-born or well-off of the capital was not interested in service outside France except in the army. Most colonial posts were filled from families already in government service, or by those ambitious to achieve a respectable social standing. In French West Africa in 1943, nearly a quarter of the officials, including four governors, were Corsicans;[32] others were from the West Indies and Brittany. Selection for the French overseas service was by examination, not interview. But if the successful candidates often came from social areas below those which provided British administrators, the École Coloniale made sure that if a sense of vocation was not inherited it was none the less imbibed.

The colonial official, French, British, Belgian, or any other, was not the servant of government; he *was* government. His administration was a series of untidy, crowded pigeon holes, buff files and inter-office memoranda. No one who had not read the documents could guard continuity and precedent, and thus take part in the process of government. There was a single column of power in the system, rigidly hierarchical, insulated from outside pressures. Where authority was delegated, it was played out tightly to chiefs-cum-administrators, who were themselves made part of the closed administrative system by being put on the payroll, and made subject to arbitrary dismissal. There

*Colonial society is divided between Administration and Commerce, wrote Delavignette. He gave figures showing that French Colonial administrators were recruited from families already serving the State and Commerce (*Freedom and Authority in French West Africa*, p. 24).

was no place for representatives, only for intermediaries of the system. When a council system was devised on a partly elective basis, it was used not as a forum but as a façade; its members were not to represent the people in government, but to represent the administration to the people. The colonial bureaucracy ruled; as Louis XIV had proclaimed of himself, it *was* the state: though with this difference, that the administrator-kings of the colonial services were not even of the country; and for all their insistence that they were motivated not by political but by administrative needs, it was the needs and the politics of the metropolis which almost exclusively determined the fate of the colonial subject.

At the hands of a colonial bureaucracy, local initiative or popular political organization – the ingredients of self-government – were, if not crushed, at least controlled, or wasted. In the subsequent period the colonizer based his rule and his hopes for a successful decolonization on the bureaucracy and the army. It has been said of the Congo[33] that these were the elements which emerged strongest from political crisis. This is true not only of the Congo, but of all Africa that has fallen victim to an army intervention in politics.

If there was any training and adaptation before independence, it was a schooling in the bureaucratic toils of colonial government, a preparation not for independence, but against it. It could not be otherwise. Colonialism was based on authoritarian command; as such, it was incompatible with any preparation for self-government. Africa was the continent of bureaucratic rule. In that sense, every success of administration was a failure of government. Government was run not only without, but despite the people.

Ways and Means of Decolonization

. . . if, in both colonisation and decolonisation, force has always been the ultimate sanction, it has not always been used. A few decisive military-political actions have established new balances of power for whole regions. The repercussions of the most decisive revolutions, too, established more than a local or even a regional change; they altered the whole field of forces on the world level. In the post-war world, such crucial events were the independence struggle of Indonesia, the Chinese revolution when, in Mao's graphic phrase, China 'stood up'; or Cuba where social revolution, long incubating in Latin America, was placed firmly on the order paper of the century.

Peter Worsley, *The Third World*

The Second World War broke shatteringly into the staid pace of colonial rule. The Dutch tried holding on to Indonesia, by massive force, as the French tried in Indo-China, and subsequently in Algeria, at disastrous cost. The sporadic troubles of the British empire, previously put down by punitive expeditions, were tending to grow into prolonged guerrilla war. Battalions were needed to put down the 'terrorists' in Malaya, and the 'Mau Mau' in Kenya. Cyprus took to arms; the Middle East was seething. The Royal Indian navy mutinied in 1946. The longer the empire lasted, the higher the expenditure on retaining it seemed to grow. Trials of force cost money, and Britain, struggling to maintain the value of the pound and achieve the transition from a war- to a peace-time economy, was in no position to pay for a decisive series of such trials. So, India was allowed to go first in 1948, followed closely by Ceylon and Burma. The withdrawal from Africa started a decade later, by when France, for similar reasons in the altered post-war balance of power, was likewise forced to adjust her imperial rule. In the 1950s and the 1960s, constitutional formulae, constitutional conferences and bargaining dominated African politics. It began with cautious changes, like allowing Africans to enjoy unofficial majorities in legislative councils, and it ended with the cascade of independence constitutions in the 1960s. There was, of course, an agitated fluttering of the old Africa hands. They protested at this ignominious scuttle of empire before Africans and Asians had proved themselves 'fit' for self-government. All the same, argued a former colonial governor and head of the African division of the Colonial Office, Sir Andrew Cohen, Britain needed a changing policy for Africa. She should recognize that 'successful co-operation with nationalism' was the 'greatest bulwark against Communism'.[1] The transfer of power to colonial people need not be a defeat, but a strengthening of the Commonwealth and the Free World.

Decolonization came to Africa in two phases. The first, in the first decade after the end of the war, occurred in those regions which European armies had used as actual theatres of war: Ethiopia, Libya, Egypt, the Sudan, Morocco and Tunisia. The defeat of the Italian army restored to Ethiopia an independence dating from the eleventh century and interrupted only by the Italian invasion of 1935. Libya, another former Italian colony, found herself independent in 1951 by vote of the United Nations, because the big powers could not decide what to do with her. (During the final negotiations, a UN delegate is supposed to have remarked to a colleague, 'At three o'clock this afternoon we free Libya.' His colleague replied, 'Impossible. We freed Libya yesterday.'[2])

Uniquely in Africa, and for reasons closer to Middle East than African developments, Egypt in 1952 achieved more than formal independence in a seizure of power by an army coup d'état that set afoot a social revolution. Egypt's conspiracy of army officers against an ancient and corrupt order of privilege may be matched by several score Latin American and Middle East coups d'état in which generals have displaced politicians. But there, the more that the shadow of power has changed, the more its substance has remained the same. The distinction held by Egypt's Free Officers is that, in a pragmatic stumble towards policy, as in the aftermath of the Suez gamble, they identified with the movement for social change and became, almost despite themselves, its main instrument. Egypt's social order, like China's, had been ripe for toppling; but whereas in China, a political movement with a finely articulated policy for social revolution adopted mass armed struggle to seize power, in Egypt army officers seized the state in one sharp blow at the apex, and then looked about for a political force and a policy to express the change. From his first conventional disavowal of the political interest and role of soldiers, Nasser graduated by 1962 to the thesis that the role of the army was to clear the path of the revolution.[3] Egypt did not want politicians in the army, but the army as a whole would constitute a force in the political process. The ensuing years were to show – not only in Egypt, but also in the Sudan and Algeria – how far an army could 'clear the path of the revolution'; or for reasons intrinsic to the control and style of armies, and such interests as were represented in Egypt's officer corps, it might proceed instead to undermine it.

One of the first fruits of Egypt's own newly seized independence was the independence of the Sudan, her one-time colony. After the reconquest, the Sudan found herself under the control of both Britain and Egypt, though the latter was represented more in the name of the Condominium Agreement than in actuality. Egypt's young officer coup d'état placed Egypt in the position where she could unilaterally make an independence proposal to the Sudan and, having negotiated its terms, present these to Britain as a virtual *fait accompli*. For the first time in her history, the Sudan reaped benefit from having been a bargaining counter between the two states; and the young officer coup in Egypt accordingly resulted in changes not in one African state but in two.

In the French African empire, it was the independence struggle in the Maghreb that was principally responsible for France's accommodation to new policies. In both Morocco and Tunisia – though not in Algeria – France astutely timed independence offers to forestall guerrilla actions and install moderate leaderships: in Morocco, urban underground action and rural struggle were already under way; and in Tunisia, a section of the Neo-Destour Party was advocating the continuance of armed struggle, begun in 1954, when in 1956 France granted independence.

Ghana and Guinea attained independence in the tail years of this first decade. Then came the avalanche of West and Central African independence in 1960, when seventeen colonies of the British and French empires in Africa became independent, and even Belgium, seemingly the most intransigent of the colonial powers, suddenly shortened her timetable for the independence of the Congo from thirty years to seven months. Another five countries became independent during the next two years; then Kenya in 1963, a full ten years after the armed rebellion that disturbed the pace of negotiated independence; then in East and Central Africa, the states of Tanganyika, Malawi, Zambia and Zanzibar, the latter one month before an armed uprising in 1964. The ensuing years saw the conclusion of the process, as small states like Gambia, Botswana, Lesotho, Swaziland and Mauritius joined the independence round.

It looked deceptively easy, this evacuation of empire. True, members of the West African élites, first inspired by Edmund Blyden's messages, had been meeting spasmodically in Pan-Africanist conferences: in 1900, after the First World War, and, more intensively, after the Second World War. They had launched students' federations in London and Paris; nationalist newspapers; and finally, fully fledged political independence movements which, for long patient, mild and pliant, received a stiffening of ex-servicemen, trade-union and radical agitation after the war. Quoting the promises of the Atlantic Charter for a bright new world, these movements began to insist that if Whites, and then Asians, were fit to govern, why not Africans? In Ghana Nkrumah catapulted a positive action campaign into the orderly pace of constitution-making; there were demonstrations by ex-soldiers, with riots and boycotts, in the late 1940s, at a cost of twenty-nine killed and 237 injured. It was events in Ghana, and the British preparations for the transfer of power there, as well as the turbulence of the independence struggle in the Maghreb, that stimulated France's own cautious experiments with the *loi cadre* and other circumspect constitutional reforms.

But inside Africa, apart from Algeria and the other countries of the Maghreb, Kenya, the Cameroun and Madagascar, it was hard to find turbulence enough to explain why, having earlier seemed so resolved to keep the continent, the colonial powers – with the exception of Portugal and the settler-dominated communities – now, after the war, seemed so preoccupied with how to get out of it.

Macmillan's wind of change, which blew independence even into settler-dominated countries, was not a dramatic Cabinet decision, wrote a former Minister of State for the Colonies,[4] but a comment on a decision the tempo of which had been accelerated as a result of a score of different decisions. In East Africa, the tempo was accelerated by the 'Mau Mau' rising; in French Africa, by Algeria's war for independence. It was the struggles in these two countries, though different in scale and duration, that provided the exceptions to Africa's licensed advance to constitutional independence. Both countries, significantly, were dominated by White settler power that had ruthlessly dispossessed the colonial peasantry, and enjoyed a voluble say in metropolitan decisions.

In Kenya, a dominant local white community and the colonial regime between them met African grievances with repression and precipitated the very revolt that these measures had been designed to deny. African political organization had stirred in the early 1920s and been suppressed, had revived, and been beaten back again the following decade. But it continued to sprout in a variety of shapes and forms, an amalgam of 'the secular and the religious, the tribal and the African national, the old and the new, increasingly interwoven in the complex ideological fabric of the Kikuyu peasant masses'.[5] The state of emergency unleashed in 1952 against the underground movement that was preparing for armed resistance was intended to savage the leadership and terrorize discontent into submission. It did the opposite. A plan for revolt, only partly prepared, was triggered into action by lower levels of the leadership, who escaped the police net by moving into the forests and turning them into bases of operation for a guerrilla war. But the struggle began 'without a master-plan for revolution, without cadres trained in the art of guerrilla warfare, without an adequate supply of arms and ammunition, or arrangements for their supply from outside the colony, without the necessary support of tribes other than the Kikuyu, the Embu and the Meru, who had not entered the movement in significant numbers, and without any contact with the outside world'.[6] The fighting groups that remained in the forest after 1956 were small isolated bands, constantly pursued by government troops and offering little co-ordinated resistance.

The revolt lasted for more than three years and was defeated by a combination of overkill and terror against the Land and Freedom army, and the civilian population at large. Though the fighting was virtually over by the beginning of 1956, the state of emergency was lifted only in 1960. The intervening years were almost as important as the years of armed conflict in breaking the back of African resistance and grooming a tame and emasculated generation of politicians for the independence era. For by the time that independence constitution-making for Kenya was begun, less than a decade later, the peasant revolt was defeated, and its aims were all but obliterated.

In the space of a few devious years, Kenyatta, once execrated as a black nationalist leader to darkness and death, had become the grand old man of the settlers. He headed a government of politicians preoccupied with constitutional niceties. White settlers had not only joined but were helping to lead African political parties. The fighters of the forests and the camps, broken in health, landless and unemployed, belonged to a past which the dominant political class of independent Kenya was only too anxious to forget.[7]

Despite the armed rebellion, therefore, independence for Kenya came only after the colonial power had prepared the timing and the manner of the take-over. It came not with victory, at the climax of the military rising, but only five years later, when settler intransigence had turned to 'realism', and the policy of confrontation with African demands had become one of bargaining and negotiation. The generation of militant fighters was dead, imprisoned or black-listed. In its place was a generation that, for the most part, was ready to accept independence as a gentleman's agreement, with the political process as the prerogative of a privileged élite. The 'Mau Mau' had fought a war, but lost it, and the landless poor which that struggle had represented were given no place in the independence settlement.

Algeria's war, by contrast, lasted twice as long and ended in the victory of independence. Far from her conflict being blockaded in the forests, it spread to France, brought down the Fourth Republic and threatened the survival of the Fifth, in a decisive display of the dangers in the settler slogan '*L'Algérie, c'est la France*' (or *Algérie Française*).

The war, begun in November 1954, was fought with unabated ferocity on both sides. And by mid-1958 French military operations were apparently beginning to bear fruit. ALN guerrilla units were scattered, with their command interrupted. But France had herself experienced three crises of government in the space of a year. Power in parliament was an incoherent mixture of Paris and Algiers,[8] racked between the left that was pressing for peace negotiations, and the right wing in France, the lobby of the colons and the army, which had made its influence felt since Indo-China, but never as vehemently as during the Algerian war. The danger rapidly mounted that the army, far from being in the service of the French government, would supplant the government altogether, bringing army and neo-fascist rule not only to Algeria but to France. The generals' putsch in Corsica and the shouts in Algiers of '*les paras à Paris*' were signals for the advance on France. The attempted putsch of 13 May 1958 brought de Gaulle to power at the head of the army. But an army victorious in Algeria would be impossible to subdue in France; driving the conflict to a bitter end in Algiers would transplant it to Paris. The terrorism of the OAS, the combat force of the colons, was proving that. De Gaulle cracked down heavily on the army, especially after the 1961 generals' revolt, led by Salan and Challe. Then, armed with exceptional powers, he felt his way gingerly towards a formula for negotiation, peace and independence. On the Algerian side, the politicians of the government-in-exile, the GPRA, proved amenable to bargaining; and in the latent conflict which had existed in the Algerian leadership, between the fighters of the interior and the old-type politicians like Ferhat Abbas who had joined forces with the FLN, the moderates now had their chance. The Evian Conference decided that Algeria would become an independent state, within limits.

Alone in Africa, Algeria fought a national liberation war for independence which struck at the very basis of French settler-colonialism. But the seizure of power through armed struggle was not followed by a period of concentrated mass mobilization, without which a revolutionary transition to independence cannot be secured. In part this was because Algeria emerged from the war economically exhausted, bonded to her former colonial power and unprepared, in the shape of economic blueprints, for victory. In addition, de Gaulle's initiative for a peace settlement at the Evian talks created a psychological as well as an economic dependence on France. But, above all, Algeria's revolution was stunted because her leadership was locked in conflict. There were the competing claims of the military and political wings of the independence movement, of the army of the exterior, which had waited in reserve during the war, and the peasant guerrilla force of the *wilayas* that had borne the brunt of the combat; and of the divergent strains in the political leadership that could not agree on the post-liberation restructuring of Algerian society.

Despite her own setback, it was Algeria's war for independence that achieved more for the other French colonies than anything that they dreamt of doing for themselves. And yet, in the main, the tempo for change in Africa was accelerated more outside the continent than within it, in Asia rather than in Africa; France's colonies gained their independence as a direct consequence of crisis in other parts of the French empire. In 1944, at the Brazzaville conference, reforms had been suggested for the African territories on the understanding that there was to be no independence other than the independence of France. As for colonial peoples, said the Free French Commissioner for the Colonies, M. René Pleven, 'In the great colonial France there are neither peoples to liberate nor racial discrimination to abolish.'[9] Suddenly, six years later, decolonization flooded first over one colony, then another. What had happened? The French had been defeated at Dien Bien Phu, and this altered the French course not only in Indo-China, in Asia, but also in Africa. Faced with a Dien Bien Phu, Frantz Fanon has written, a veritable panic overtakes colonial government.

> Their purpose is to capture the vanguard, to turn the movement of liberation towards the right, and to disarm the people: quick, quick, let's decolonise. Decolonise the Congo before it turns into another Algeria. Vote the constitutional framework for all Africa, create the

French Community, renovate that same Community, but for God's sake let's decolonise quick.... And they decolonise at such a rate that they impose independence on Houphouet-Boigny.[10]

Independence was breaking out all over the French empire, and the British; and over the Dutch and the Belgian, as well. There were international reasons why. Already by 1945 the war had fundamentally altered the pre-war structure of power. United States policy was to supplant European imperialisms with paternalist and profitable economic ties; in place of old-style colonies, would be put the new containment, in United States free enterprise. There was, thus, a perceptible shift in the priorities of Western powers, which had to take their cue from the most powerful among them. The United States was interested, for its own reasons, in confining traditional European power and its financial freedom to pursue an independent course. For the United States, a historian of the politics and diplomacy of the Second World War has written,[11] support or opposition to European colonialism would depend on the extent to which the interested European nation respected American global goals elsewhere; and also, most significantly for Africa and Asia and Latin America, on the nature of the local political opposition within the colony. If left-wing forces led the independence movement, then the Americans would sustain collaborationists if possible, or a colonial power if necessary.[12] Decolonization was a move to shore up 'stabilizing' forces in restless regions, rather than a recognition of the right of peoples to the independence and the freedom that the phrases of the United Nations so eloquently embodied.

Africa's rapid transition to independence, if it made the early 1960s heady with optimism, left behind a damaging legacy of myth and illusion. Independence came by too many to be seen as a single, sharp act, like running the national flag up the flag-pole. The constitutional agreement once signed, an African state was independent. Indeed, independence was seen by the political careerists not as the beginning, but as the end in a process of change. To them independence was reduced to a constitutional formula in which contesting élites, serviced by lawyers and public relations men, bargained on terms and fixed indemnities for the departing power, which for their part were intent on handing over political power as long as this did not affect their economic stakes.

This is not the version of history that the independence generation of politicians cares to recall. And it is not, to be sure, invariably the whole story in each individual country. But, on the whole, the experience of decolonization in Africa is not one of grass-root struggle, except for brief, unsustained periods. For each individual state, the details and the differences are important. Here, a generation of political leaders that would have fought for sterner guarantees, better terms and a policy of social change, was suppressed, sometimes by the colonial government, sometimes by the authorities acting in collusion with a more conservative branch of the independence movement. Here, the colonial power manipulated the competing wings of a movement across the conference table; played off one delegation against another from the same country. There, withdrawal took place only after the studied creation of constitutional and political structures that were bound to buckle, even break, under independence needs.

In much of Africa, the leaders of the independence movement accepted without undue perturbation the form of independence ordained by the departing colonial authority. 'Gabon is independent,' President M'ba is reputed to have said, 'but between Gabon and France nothing has changed; everything goes on as before.' The only change in fact, commented Fanon, 'is that Monsieur M'ba is President of the Gabonese Republic and that he is received by the President of the French Republic.'[13]

Many of this generation of independence leaders clung with pathetic endeavour to the forms of government transferred to them, or those practised at home by the colonial power. British or French or Belgian constitutional traditions seemed the only permissible, even possible, form. Regular electoral competition within a European-type constitution became the 'pubertal rite'[14] on the independence scene; though, so shortly before independence, the colonial system had been busy locking up its opponents and had never dreamt of paying them salaries to oppose. Nkrumah remarked on the tenacity with which Colonial

Secretaries argued the case for adopting certain types of constitutional arrangement at conferences held to negotiate the independence of African states.

When colonial power, on the other hand, for reasons of its own occasionally suggested a variation of its own governmental forms, African politicians protested that they wanted the model intact. So, London or Paris or Brussels models were prepared for export; and universities, law courts, local government and the civil service were cut according to the master pattern. The élites of the British territories hankered after the so-called Westminster model. The French political leaders copied the autocratic presidential powers that de Gaulle had assumed. These made it difficult for an Assembly to overturn a government; gave the executive comprehensive powers, enabling it to appeal over the heads of the Assembly to the people, by submitting measures to referendum; and eliminated, in large measure, ministerial responsibility to the legislature. There was one de Gaulle in Europe, and a dozen or more little de Gaulles in Africa; though they didn't all prove as secure in office as Senghor and Houphouet-Boigny, or even, for so long, de Gaulle himself.

Transferring the so-called Westminster model was an exercise of dubious value.[15] The British constitution, unwritten just because it is rooted in age-old precedent and tradition uniquely British, serves a society which could scarcely be less like those for which its export model was prepared. The Parliament at Westminster owes its present character to a civil war and several centuries of bitter struggle.[16] The legislature is anything but the sole seat of power; beyond it function the great institutions of the economy from the banks to the stock exchange; the civil service; the education system; the great families; the newspaper chains; the Institute of Directors and the Trade Union Congress; all forms of power diffused through the society. In new African states, patterns of power – or lack of it – are quite different; and, most often, unsettled and unresolved. What sort of a system, political and economic, is it? The issue opens out only with the onset of independence, and sometimes not even then. Who rules? Does power not lie without, rather than within the country? In largely peasant societies, where local élites derive power and authority from a village, district or regional society, does a national parliament automatically displace or unify these power systems? Are there, nationally and locally, competing forces advocating competing policies? Or, under the imported constitutional system, were parties not artificially pressed into the game of parliamentary shuttle-cock between government and opposition, even when these were artificial divisions? In the shadow of Westminster, the constitutions made place for oppositions even where these did not exist, as in Tanganyika, where TANU won every seat but one in the 1961 elections.

In reality, though, the constitution-drafters did not stick precisely to the Westminster 'model', but wrote clauses into its export variety which were in sharp conflict with the British system. The essence of the British system is that there is absolutely no limit on the sovereignty of Parliament. The export models incorporated all sorts of checks and balances for parliamentary power. They made laws subject to judicial review. Bills of Rights were prepared, ostensibly to protect minorities but in fact to hand them extra-parliamentary levers. The notion of transplanting a standard form of government to countries as widely divergent as India, Malaya, Trinidad, Malta and Ghana, did not seem to appal the Colonial Office drafters. The fact that few of the models lasted more than a few years in Africa reflected on the value of the original exercise. From the end of 1960 to the beginning of 1962, thirteen states revised their constitutions or produced altogether new ones.

The assumptions of the imported systems proved untenable in the new states. With the onset of independence, African parliaments seemed notoriously to debate the least important issues of the day. This was because the parliamentary convention of government and opposition politely exchanging the seats of office assumes that the crucial ideological questions have been settled; but, neither settled nor even debated in Africa, they tended to drop into oblivion. Land and economic policy were not scrutinized; social policies and administration were inherited from colonial days, and, for the most part, kept intact. Caught in the parliamentary round, the politicians devoted themselves to electioneering and party manoeuvring, rather than to national mobilization for national needs. A pursuit of expediency and political profiteering began, rather than a search for national policies to defeat poverty and backwardness. It did not take long before the constitutional models showed in practice their manifest irrelevance. One country after another sank into political crisis. The political parties seemed to be dying on their feet, till army juntas swept them away altogether. The causes lay deeper, by far, than a failure of the parliamentary model. Yet, so firm was the faith in the transfer of 'superior' and tested Western systems of government, that many continued to seek explanations in the inability of Africans to govern themselves.

Its very widespread transfer implied that the metropolitan model was the acme of achievement in self-government. The colonial power had itself judged the colony ripe and ready for independence, and the natural prize was a Westminster Parliament, or some other metropolitan equivalent. This in turn implied that the colonial presence had existed to train; and that the training period had been successfully completed. The apologia of colonialism, that it was a preparation for independence, is, in fact, largely fantasy. Studies of particular colonial records, wrote Schaffer, 'show that it is very difficult to trace any continual preparatory process at work, or any signs of a prepared policy until after the war'. Even then the post-war years were too late for preparation, save as a purely political, almost desperate effort to provide an ideology of delay (in the granting of independence). The notion of preparation was to justify the colonial record, as a tactic of delay in the sense that 'you would not seem to be delaying, only training and educating'.[17] The theory of preparation 'emerged after the event', Lord Hailey agreed. A decade after the end of the war, he wrote that there was no trained machinery of administration ready to hand.[18] Little or nothing had been done in the years gone past to prepare Africans for assuming new powers.

If there was a course of 'preparation', it was not only grudging and late, but notoriously badly planned and timed, with precipitate spurts towards the end to make up for decades of earlier stagnation. In any event, if independence was to provide Africa with Western European-styled political systems, the 'preparation' period should have encouraged direct elections, free political campaigning, full opportunities for all political parties to solicit the support of the electorate with their programmes. In the Belgian Congo, there was virtually no devolution of legislative authority in half a century, and a Legislative Council was set up only after the troubles of 1958 and 1959, less than twelve months before independence. In Tanganyika, the first election in which Africans were allowed to stand as candidates was held in 1958, only three years before independence. In Kenya, the first African was nominated, not elected, to the Legislative Council in 1944; and by 1958, five years before independence, only one in four members was African. In Uganda, the Legislative Council in 1950 had thirty-two members, of whom only eight were unofficial African ones. Nigeria had an unofficial majority in the Legislative Council for the first time in 1947; but the constitution provided for three separate regional Houses of Assembly, and a House of Chiefs for the Northern region, so that the constitution contributed to the fragmentation rather than to the integration of a so-called national system. Colonial administrators fought delaying actions against direct elections, precisely because they wanted checks on the so-called 'professional politician'. Full-time political campaigners were bad enough; radical politicians were anathema. In colonial Gabon, Chad, Central Africa Republic and Congo-Brazzaville,[19] the administration had the power to deny recognition to any association, or even to dissolve it. The French administration was markedly skilful in suppressing or defeating the radical wing of the independence movement, to make for a 'safe' transfer of power. A battery of techniques was devised to block the rising Jacobins among African political leaders.

Colonial administrations manipulated local, regional and ethnic differences to emphasize divisive rather than unifying national interests.[20] And such divisions were deposited in independence constitutions, to assail the cohesion and survival of the new states from their inception. The Nigerian constitution, most notoriously of all, not only ensured that politics would be regional, but that the Federation itself would be perpetually on the brink of crisis. In Kenya, the constitution introduced a system of regional government calculated to give the minority settler-backed party, KADU, a built-in advantage over KANU, the majority party that had refused to work any constitution until Kenyatta was released from detention. KANU's first years in office, which the party captured in spite of the obstacles provided by the constitution, had to be spent dismantling a regionalism which undermined the working of the country's independence government. In Kenya, too, the independence settlement bequeathed the dispute with Somalia over her far north-west territory inhabited by Somali, which has flared into persistent warfare. The Somali demand had been voiced long before Kenya's internal self-government period; but by the time Britain called a joint Kenya–Somalia conference in August 1963, Kenya independence was only four months away, and it was too late to act on any of the conference proposals. The Somali issue was left unresolved, to create for the newly independent government of Kenya a major problem of internal security, in the tackling of which they would have to rely heavily on British logistic support.[21]

In Uganda, Britain entrenched a special status for the Buganda Kingdom in the 1963 constitution. (The only way to rule the country was through the Kabaka, Lugard had said.) The country thus had two competing systems of power, two heads of state, two prime ministers, two cabinets, even two armies. This conflict culminated in an abortive plot against Obote that he suppressed only by calling in his army, with whose support he has ruled uneasily ever since. In the Sudan, the independence government was inaugurated to the sound of gunfire in the south. There, the people had been led to expect a future independent of the Arab north; and a section of the army staged a mutiny to hold Britain to her commitment. But by then, Britain had already ceded authority to Khartoum. With that authority went an endemic state of rebellion in the south, the suppression of which has demanded a huge army and military budget that have undermined the Sudan state ever since.

Independence arrived already crippled by the colonial past. And most serious, that heritage was assumed virtually intact by many of the new rulers. Judging by the structures which they took over and left almost unchanged, the new governments of Africa were planning not to break with the pre-independence past, but to maintain close continuity with it, unaware – or, if they were aware, unable to do much about it – that the 'experience' gained under the colonial administration was not only irrelevant, but dangerous, to the new needs of African states.

In much of Africa, and especially in West Africa, where the course of independence was auspiciously placid by comparison with the regions of White settlement, there was markedly little sustained policy for the radical transformation of society; and little prolonged mass or militant struggle for independence. Movements with mass memberships were built to reinforce élite claims for control of government, but they functioned in a largely vacuous electoral fashion. Mass mobilization was limited to brief periods and limited purposes. Government was in the great majority of cases transferred to a virtually hand-picked group that had made its compact with the departing colonial authority.

Though African independence in general follows this pattern of negotiation and circumscribed change, the leaderships of the national movements were not uniformly compromised by their independence agreements with the colonial powers. Ghana, Guinea and Mali in the west, and Tanganyika (Tanzania) in the east, were the furthest committed to social change, even if it had to be initiated from the top by the party leadership. But these states, too, experienced not a revolutionary transition to independence, but a negotiated transfer. 'The characteristics of the resulting state structure will vary appropriately,' writes Peter Worsley. 'Yet in all these cases there is one major common feature: politico-bureaucratic machines are in the saddle from the beginning, and there is no "heroic" period of Cuban-type mass participation in government. Radical social change, if initiated at all, is initiated from the top.'[22]

In the phenomenon of decolonization, the idea of compromise is central, Fanon wrote. Compromise is needed from both sides. Martin Kilson[23] has traced for Sierra Leone that intricate pattern of compromise. Colonialism ruled through the chiefs and reinforced their powers, but at the same time set up new tensions in rural society. In the 1930s there was widespread peasant revolt against traditional rulers and authority. It became particularly strong in the immediate post-war years, and has sometimes flared since then. A commission of inquiry referred to a 'mass disobedience of authority'. These were tax riots. Similar peasant troubles occurred in other African territories: in Nigeria, in Chad, in Uganda, in Kenya. These were Max Gluckman's peasant rebellions, distinct from revolution, for they aimed not at destroying the system of traditional authority, but at ameliorating aspects of its use.[24] Peasant violence was aimed at the property, the person and the authority of the chiefs, because the chiefs were the main rural agencies of the colonial power. Unwittingly, thus, this form of colonial administration had stimulated a mass reaction in the countryside. The behaviour of the rural population was anomic; it lacked sustained, articulate action and demands; but it did create conditions of political instability in colonial society.

It was this 'rural radicalism', Kilson argues from the Sierra Leone experience, that élite leaderships exploited during the pre-independence years, in their drive to 'Africanize' colonial society. As rural protest spread, it was the new middle-class élite that presented itself to the colonial authority as the force to contain this.

> The new elite and the colonial oligarchy had common interests in facilitating constitutional change: the elite required such change to advance their own socio-economic standing; the colonial masters obtained greater efficiency through the advancement of the new elite. The colonial oligarchy also expected greater stability in local society as the new elite, abetted by constitutional change (including ultimately the mass franchise), spread their political influence and leadership into rural society.

It was ultimately this curious identity of interest between the new élite and the colonial oligarchy that facilitated the peaceful transfer of power to African regimes in most of colonial Africa.[25]

Once it had become apparent that the trade and economic policies of the colonial power could be conducted without the apparatus of direct political control, decolonization as a bargaining process with cooperative African élites did not end with the onset of independence, but continued beyond. The former colonial government guarded its options and interests; the careerist heirs to independence preoccupied themselves with an 'Africanization' of the administration which, more than even the transfer of political power, gave them openings previously filled by white men. Africanization, like the transfer of power, occurred within the largely unaltered framework of the colonial system. Power was transferred from a colonial bureaucracy to African auxiliaries in politics and administration. This is Fanon's 'false decolonization'.

In some newly independent African states, African leaders and parties harboured a more radical purpose. They saw decolonization as only the first step. Mass parties were built in Ghana, Guinea, Mali and Tanzania as explicitly anti-colonial instruments. They aimed not to inherit but to transform the system. Their political aims and strategy were to be tested not against the ring of their radical intent, but against the whole substance of colonial dependence – economic, cultural, military and political – that persisted, even tightened, in the independence era.

In states of more conservative cast, outstanding radicals like Ruben Um Nyobe of the Cameroun, and Morocco's Mehdi Ben Barka, who not only led principled opposition struggles but were also formulating a theory of African revolution, were killed in their political prime. Other militants were persecuted into the wilderness for the challenge they offered to élitist politics. Africa has had her political martyrs as well as her political careerists.

But taking the continent as a whole, the independence 'revolution' in Africa was brief, makeshift and leaky. It came precipitated as much if not more by thrusts from beyond the continent as by sustained and articulated social revolution from within. This does not mean that independence was unwanted in Africa, or that her peoples were any less ready for it than any other peoples in the Third World. It means that, in the circumstances of its coming, it could accomplish and change only so much, and no more.

Part III

The Successor State

White Power, Black Parody

The *evolues* are well dressed and wear fashionable clothes. They meet in front of bookshops and look for new books. They read Georges Duhamel, Henri Bordeaux, Roland Dorgèles, all the modern writers. They discuss, rightly or wrongly, current affairs. You meet them in the cafes exchanging ideas on current problems with a rare exuberance.

La Voix du Congolais, writing in 1945

When government was transferred to Africans in the era of independence, there existed, in each independent state, a select circle of heirs. Except in circumstances like those in Northern Nigeria, where the new men of politics were linked with traditional sources of power, political control passed to a Western-educated élite which headed independence movements of relatively recent, effectively post-Second World War origin. These political representatives had not always been the obvious inheritors of government. Older, more traditional heads, the chiefs and the elders, had at first been used as the instruments of the colonial administration; and, after them, an earlier educated élite had expected to inherit. But these groups had either come to terms with the newer aspirants, or been beaten at the post by them. Were these conflicts between contesting social groups and heirs to power decisive and lasting? Were the different streams in the élite always separate from one another, or did they converge? How did the newest displace the older-established? What was the power base of the inheritors? Did they, indeed, possess such a base? Or were they impotent? What were their goals? Mostly, they had acquisitive aspirations, if not resources, and envious eyes fixed on the white man and his estate, together with a marked inability to conceptualize the promise of independence other than in terms of their own immediate interest.

Here and there a section of the élite had a firmer commitment to national rather than to narrow goals, but over time it encountered obstacles either under-estimated or blithely ignored. Were the failings inherent in the independence contract; or were they the consequence of an inept political leadership? Did Africa possess power that she squandered or mis-used; or did she fail because, however she might propose, other forces disposed?

AFRICA FOR THE AFRICANIZED

Under colonialism, power lay with the 'imported oligarchy':[1] the alien administration (in the last resort, its army); the representatives on the spot of government in Europe; and the powerful foreign firms that controlled the economy. Capital came from abroad, and profits were remitted there. External needs and imposed controls began to change the face of African society. The administration needed intermediaries – interpreters, clerks, policemen, junior administrators and teachers – to form a network of communication between the imported oligarchy and its subjects. Colonialism began to fashion an élite.

In West Africa, the first to fashion themselves in the image of the white man were the old coastal élites, which rose in the towns along the shore line where the trading posts were built. Up and down the coast, across the map lines drawn between French and British possessions, these old coastal families produced not only traders, but lawyers, judges, doctors, academics and other pillars of the liberal professions.

By the end of the nineteenth century, however, the coastal élites were no longer regarded as the ideal agents of colonialism. They had begun to show signs of trying to take controlling positions into their own hands. In any event, the colonial phase was passing from relatively simple trading operations to the more intense exploitation of land and people. Once subsistence economies had to be prompted into producing cash crops for the market, and men had to be induced to work on plantation, mine and public works, different kinds of intermediaries were needed. 'If dangerous revolts are to be obviated,' Sir George Taubman Goldie advised,[2] 'the general policy of ruling on African principles through native rulers must be followed for the present.'

What more natural, and economical, than to confirm the traditional authority of chiefs, once this authority had been bent to the purposes of the colonial administration? The old coastal élite receded in importance. Whereas, by the second half of the nineteenth century, the Gold Coast, for instance, was well on the way to developing its own African civil service, with African administrators appointed to high authority, by 1890 the tempo and orientation of British colonization had changed.[3] Members of the educated African élite were being edged not into, but out of, command; and their influence in politics, trade and religion was being curtailed. As late as the 1930s, the British in West Africa were still reducing the percentage of Africans in senior civil service posts, and were up-grading formerly African-held junior posts so that more expatriates might be employed at the centres of administration. Only in Liberia, never a colony in the same sense as the others, did the old creole élite keep its dominance up to the present day; there, its influence on government coincided with the foundation of the state itself. Elsewhere, the political ascendancy of the old élite declined – to revive briefly once again, in alliance with the traditional chiefs, in a contest with the newer generation of educated élite, over which element, in the late 1950s, was to inherit power. Yet if the political vigour of the old élite faded, its tradition of exclusiveness from the people of the interior, the uneducated, the poor and contemptible, did not die. It persists in present-day educated African prejudices and unconcern for the plight of the undistinguished mass.

For the greater period of colonial rule, the chiefs and traditional heads were the most malleable instruments of the alien government. Running the administration through the chiefs was 'colonialism-on-the-cheap'.[4] And, of course, it also gave the chiefs new sources of authority, influence and wealth. Martin Kilson has shown, in his study of Sierra Leone, how initially the colonial administration granted chiefs a variety of financial incentives to administer their subjects. These included stipend payments, rebates on the collection of taxes, court fines, and entertainment allowances; and by 1930, such represented 10 per cent of the expenditure on administration. The cost undermined the capacity of the administration to pay for the social services so needed by the local populace; and meanwhile it augmented the wealth of the traditional rulers at the expense of their subjects, enabling them to enter, and stake important claims in, the modern sector of the economy. Often the man of traditional authority and the man of wealth was one and the same person; and as traditional forms of authority and wealth began to be superseded by new sources of influence, the chiefs and their kin involved themselves to profit from the process. In this way, the new élite that grew was not entirely new, but developed in part from the old.

In the French colonies the administration encouraged the formation of *administratif* parties, based on the appointed chiefs, and particularly after 1951 when the extension of the franchise in the rural areas enabled the chiefs to swing election results, the administration supported chief-based parties to offset the influence of the *Rassemblement Democratique Africain.*[5] In the Gold Coast, as late as 1946, chiefs played an important part. Two years later the Watson Report declared: 'The star of rule through the chiefs is on the wane.' (Though in 1949, the Coussey Committee reverted: 'We believe there is still a place for the Chief in a new constitutional set-up.') The colonial powers had been in some dilemma: was it safer to leave authority with the chiefs or entrust it to the new élite? By the time that power came to be transferred, however, the colonial governments had abandoned the chiefs as the main medium of political authority and had decided to use instead a new élite, more directly sprung from the needs of the colonial system. What were the origins of this new élite; from where had it sprung; and what were its inclinations?

'*Instruire la masse et dégager l'élite,*' the French ordained in their colonies. It was Western education that disengaged an élite and drove the cleavage in colonial society between the chosen minority and the ranks of the commoners. This education at first helped traditional élites to entrench themselves in the new society; for, in the early schools, the sons of chiefs were favoured for entry above others. But the colonial classrooms soon began raising new candidates for élite status. They became the great equalizers. Education was the ladder to a post in the administration or the rank above labourer in the money economy; and because education was free, the sons of humble parents could climb the rungs. The early élites maintained their footholds; but new entrants fast outnumbered them, and the members of the present élites in the African states are drawn predominantly from humble homes.[6] Most rapid expansion occurred in the late 1940s, when the colonial administrators began responding to pressures within the colonies, and in the late 1950s, as independence approached.[7] The French were careful to train only those numbers for which they were willing to find a place in their administrative structure as subordinates to European superiors.[8] In a quarter of a century, the École Normale William Ponty at Dakar, the nerve centre of the African élite in the French colonies, graduated fewer than 2,000 qualified Africans, of whom a third were trained as medical assistants. Only in the late 1950s did a significant number of African graduates – apart from the privileged 'citizens' of Senegal – return from universities in France or the post-war University of Dakar.[9]

Among these and their British-trained equivalents, were the first prime ministers and cabinet ministers of the independent states: the first permanent secretaries, ambassadors and representatives at the United Nations; those at the top of academies, the professions and the civil service. Western education was the curriculum of the new élite; independence, and with it Africanization, constituted graduation. As members of the imported oligarchy left, Africans stepped in to fill their jobs, play their roles, inherit their rates of pay and their privileges, and assume their attitudes, in particular the conviction that the educated in power have a divine right to rule and to prosper.[10]

Between teachers and pupils alike in the colonial schools, there had been a conspiracy to groom Africans in the image of their masters. Edmund Blyden's warning at the end of the nineteenth century – that the subjection of Africans to 'unmodified European training' would produce a 'slavery far more subversive of the real welfare of the race than the ancient physical fetters'[11] –

had fallen on unhearing ears. The élite wanted an unmodified European training. The early élites had to convince themselves as much as others that they could reach the standards set by the 'superior' White race; and so they insisted on competing by white man's standards for the most prestigious posts in the white man's world. What the early élite generations needed for their self-respect, later generations refused to change. White man's values were pursued not so much to prove equality, as because they were regarded as virtuous in themselves.

The educational system was geared not to Africa but to Europe. School textbooks were written and published in metropolitan capitals; students wrote the examinations of metropolitan universities. In British colonies, African children recited the tables of English kings and the dates of English wars. In the French colonies, the children chanted from a history book, 'Our ancestors were the Gauls, and they had red hair.' The language of the élite was the language of the colonial power. Education and a white collar were the gateway to the White world; and what that world practised, the pupils imitated. Before independence, these standards were regulated by the colonial order. After independence, they were retained virtually intact by an élite that needed to entrench itself behind them. In the African universities, it was African academics who resisted changes in the curricula. They showed, wrote an educational critic, a pedantic acquiescence in a pattern which was already abandoned by the new universities in Britain.[12] Indeed, the African universities clung not only to the curricula, but to the archaic traditions of their models: High table; Latin graces; those Michaelmas, Lent and Trinity terms; the separation of the sexes in bars and common rooms. With their large cement buildings in grounds splendidly landscaped, the campuses sited themselves as far as possible, in distance and attitude, from the nearest rumbustious African town, and there did their best to emulate the organized reticence of Oxford and Cambridge. Gown had to be not only superior to town, but well insulated from it.

> Many African academics [wrote a critic, himself an academic], rather than ask themselves how best they can adapt their foreign intellectual baggage to the needs of their country, manifest a concern for 'keeping

the standards' of their alma mater. Their status as scholars seems to depend almost solely on their ability to demonstrate that they can write as pedantically as their European colleagues in esoteric journals, and that they can train students who are as successful as Europeans at taking highly ritualised examinations that bear little practical relationship to European conditions, much less African ones. . . . They suffocate in their gowns, say grace in Latin, quote Shakespeare and Racine (or indeed Nkrumah and Castro) while the masses remain illiterate. . . .[13]

Élite status consisted in this distance from the mob or the 'bush'. ('He's really bush', the wife of the academic, or the academic himself, will say, like the colonial did in his day, of a new countryman arrived in the town.) It lay, too, in the stifling social respectabilities and affectations of a colonial order and a colonial ruling class. Narcissus-like, the élite adored this image of itself in the shape of its colonial predecessor, and worked avidly to enhance it. The imitation was a parody not of twentieth-century society but of the nineteenth, the age of colonialism, not of the average British or French home, but of the middle- or upper-class background or affectation of colonial officials. The deference was to manners as antiquated and as unsuited to Africa as were those steamy tropical coastal town houses of the older coastal élite, stuffed with chandeliers, four-poster beds, parlour mantelpiece knick-knacks and Victorian head-of-the-family portraits. The élite was opinionated and snobbish. It was extravagant and flamboyant. Consumption had to be conspicuous, even spectacular. Partly this was because the new acquisition of wealth and the traditional role of a wealthy, important man converged; for, much as the élitist tried to emulate the insularity of exclusive (white) society, the hullabaloo of the gregarious neighbourhood and the claims of his kinsmen invaded it. Partly, too, the conspicuous consumption was to make up for time lost when it was the white man who was busily inheriting the earth. Now that the black heirs were coming into their own the long ingrained habit of emulation found fresh spurs.

Some of the new men preened themselves in the perfection of the white man's life. Others were torn by ambivalences, admiration and resentment, aggression and subservience, need and rejection. The poets of *négritude* passionately rejected the ways of the white world and the pulls of assimilation. 'I feel ridiculous,' wrote Leon Damas

> *in their shoes, in their dinner jackets*
> *in their stiff shirts, their paper collars,*
> *with their monocles and bowler hats*
> *I feel ridiculous*
> *with my toes that were not made*
> *to sweat from morning to evening*
> *in their swaddling clothes that weaken my limbs*
> *and deprive my body of its beauty.*

Yet despite the poet's rejection, élite status in Africa is instantly recognizable in its habit of over-dress, as though the tropics were the Georges Cinq in Paris or the Dorchester in London; more camel-hair jackets and gold-rimmed spectacles for the one, and sober double-breasted suits for the other, of course, as befits such sartorial distinctions.

In pre-independence days, the cries of the intellectuals were vibrant and their needs passionate after what the continent had suffered. Influenced by the poets and philosophers of négritude, and by the painful awareness of how colonialism was racking African society, African students, especially those who studied abroad, talked, and even planned revolution in Paris and London, as Europe's 1848 generation had done in the same cosmopolitan meeting-grounds. In their heyday, FEANF in Paris, uniting all African students from the French colonies, and WASU and CAO for the British, were the radical leaven of the independence movements. Then came independence. Students who had been volubly dissident went home to be absorbed in the élite. Some of the most politically skilful renounced their opposition to the regimes in power and were rewarded with appropriate posts.[14] Some found it too difficult to leave at all and remained in the metropolis. Sometimes victimization awaited them at home if they persisted in their radicalism. Others, when they were back home, like Mbella Sonne Diphoko's character on the Mungo River of the Cameroun, sitting beside the hurricane lamp and waiting for the first rains, remembered with longing 'the often frivolous conversations with women, the talking and re-talking of what had been talked and re-talked . . . the morning mail and the letters of the afternoon, all those books, breasts, embraces and the caresses under the indulgent look of time'.[15] Before they returned home, many of the students insisted on guarantees from their governments of a high wage, housing, a car. Some returned, and left again, disappointed. The younger generation wanted everything at once – jobs, security, reforms, power and adulation from the masses and their own elders.[16] It was once again Awolowo's first glimpse of white-man superior: a British official, carried in a hammock, an open book on his chest, escorted by carriers, messengers and police constables.[17] Pomp and circumstance, comfort, education and authority, all together: these were the rewards of the élite. When students went on strike in 1968 at Nigeria's Ife University, it was because they objected to having to return their own plates to the service counter of the student dining room. At one of the colleges in the university of East Africa, they rose in protest when asked to double up in their dormitories so as to make room for more students. The conditioning was not only to set an élite apart from and above the common people, but against them.

Yet, like an emergent bourgeoisie everywhere, the African élite identified the general interest with its own. 'I cherish politics and journalism as a career,' wrote the young Awolowo, 'and I desire advocacy as a means of livelihood.' He was writing a request to a prospering compatriot for a twelve-year interest-free loan. 'By helping me to achieve my ambition you are indirectly and even directly helping Nigeria, or even Africa.'[18] Personal initiative was the key to individual success; and individual achievement, a credit to the society as a whole. Were the interests of its shining sons not paramount in any community? Within the élite, the preoccupation with personal initiative was a short step to policies that talked of African socialism but really meant private ownership – by Africans. The members of the African élite were spiritually company directors or property-owners long before they became them in reality.

African socialism and négritude served to equate élite goals with those of the people at large; but once independence had been achieved, the élite addressed itself single-mindedly to its interests. They had become heirs to a successor state that they had, with few exceptions, little inclination to change. They had criticized not so much the system as its incumbents. With independence, they were the incumbents.

WHITE EMINENCE

Always brooding over African society is the presence of the Whites. After independence, when they vacated political and administrative seats, metropolitan economic interests stayed behind, and so, too, did a deeply enduring subservience to colonial standards and attitudes. In many African states, the influence of White disapproval has been as inhibiting as the earlier physical omnipotence. White power could subdue by force, and corrupt with patronage, but also control with contempt. The press was and still is overwhelmingly expatriate-owned and thus influenced. 'Public opinion' is interpreted by editors trained in Western standards and served by Western news agencies. Administrators model themselves on systems devised for European conditions; and military men think of what Alexander, or Napoleon, a Sandhurst or St Cyr instructor might do in their place. Direct or snide criticism from London, Paris or Brussels, wounds deeply. Approval from Europe compensates for estrangement from the poor and illiterate at home. Ghanaians had ample domestic reason to question Nkrumah's policies in the waning years of the CPP; but if anything goaded their military and civil élite into active opposition, it was the withering effect on their self-esteem of the disapproval from the White, Western world. It is never all that remote. White influences continue to renew themselves in the years since independence. The recent arrivals are international businessmen, technicians and expert advisers, rather than the administrators of earlier days. Their sojourn will be as temporary as that of those who once served out their contracts and then went 'home'. But for as long as they stay, they endorse White standards, and dispense White approval and White patronage to an élite desperately eager for approbation.

Whites also make their influence felt more permanently and

more directly. In colonial days, below the tiny but powerful group of administrators and senior officials, there were the settlers or 'expatriates' in the British colonies, the colons or the *petits blanc* in the French, who constituted significant minorities of small-scale businessmen and artisans. In the decade after the Second World War, the White population of French West Africa trebled. The rate of exchange[19] gave each franc made or saved in Africa double its worth at home. Whites and their wives dominated the urban labour market and the middle posts of the administration in the colonies. In 1958, in the Ivory Coast, for instance, there were fewer than a score of top-level African administrative and technical officers. In Senegal, likewise, there were twice as many Whites as Africans in middle-level posts.

Whites living and working in the colonies made their political influence felt. Politicians were offered, or sought, the advice of White lobbies and White political groups. If the advice was followed, protection and sponsorship were not far behind. In the Congo, Whites were behind the formation of African political parties. In Gabon, rival African parties aligned themselves with rival European economic groups.[20] Direct White intrusion into African political activity was especially marked in the former French Equatorial colonies. Administrative officials manipulated employment and patronage as well as election procedures to prevent the spread of parties which they opposed, John Ballard wrote. 'After several years of frustration in fighting the administration, each of these (leaders) had learned to temper his ideas in favour of a partially effective compromise with official views.'[21]

When Africans succeeded to political authority as heads of government, the policies they formulated had to reckon with the presence of potential opposition of Whites – influentially placed not only in the economy but also in the administration. Some African states quite soon found themselves struggling to absorb a surplus of qualified élite members. Others were sorely understaffed and, especially in the former French colonies, drew heavily on France and the French administration. The commitment of almost all the former French colonies to close involvement with France in their economic development brought with it the 'corollary of *political* commitment by the leaderships of these countries to the employment of French expatriates, even when indigenous university graduates were available. Furthermore the French government pays the salaries of its civil servants who are seconded to work with African governments, thus providing an important subsidy to African budgets that would be lost to Africanization.'[22] Only in the Ivory Coast, where expatriate income has grown faster than the gross domestic product, and where the share of gross profits enjoyed by the large corporations has doubled since 1950, has the White population gone as far as trebling itself from 1950 to 1965. But an *eminence blanche* is everywhere present; sometimes out in the front of Ministry offices, sometimes in the rooms behind.

President Banda of Malawi, incurably sycophantic, believes in having his European advisers in the front room. He outraged young administrators and politicians when on one occasion he left the country on official business and appointed his private secretary, a Briton to act in his place. He is given to instructing his Cabinet by holding consultations with the permanent secretaries, all Whites, and then sending messages requiring Ministers to get their briefings from their officials. In Malawi until recently, the highest administrative post held by an African was district officer; in the police force, warrant officer; and in the army, second lieutenant. In many African states, if permanent secretaryships were fairly rapidly Africanized, the command of army, police and security remained the last in White hands. Major decisions hinged frequently not on the purposiveness of the independence government but on the equivocations of White officials. Above all, especially in the French territories, the ultimate arbiters in political crisis were the French military forces. This was so before independence, and afterwards. 'French military forces and the French commandants of national armies (after 1961, when separate national armies were formed . . .) were for several years looked upon as the ultimate source of power behind each regime's authority, and friendship with the French military commanders was often of greater importance to a president than good relations with the French High Commissioner.'[23]

Narcissus in Uniform

Yes, I am a Francophile, the whole of Dahomey is Francophile. We like your country because we have never been asked to do this or that.

General Soglo, *Le Monde*, 30 June 1966

The Nigerian Army distinguished itself in the Ashanti Wars and other punitive expeditions which resulted in the pacification of Nigeria.

Nigerian Ministry of Information, *100 Facts About Nigeria*, Lagos, 1966

More than any institution left behind by colonialism, the armies of Africa were set in the colonial pattern. More than this, the armies of the new states were the identical armies that the colonial powers had built to keep their empires quiescent. After independence they retained, with few exceptions, their colonial pattern of army organization; their dependence on the West for officer training, specialist advice and equipment; and their affinity with the foreign and defence policies of the metropolitan countries. Even when Africanized and run by commanders-in-chief who were nationals of their own countries, Africa's armies were an extension of the West. Where they had gone into battle in the pre-independence period, it had been for, not against the colonial power. And, except for Algeria and to some extent Morocco, they played no part in the independence struggle.

The French and the British empires used their African armies in different ways. Britain had the Indian army as her main reserve of imperial military might, with Africa as a minor recruiting station. The West Africa Frontier Force, which was founded in 1897 as a counter to the French during the critical period of Anglo-French rivalry on the Niger, was to be Lugard's crack corps in opening and guarding the new territories; and he pressed the War Office for the 'best' officers, preferably with Indian or Egyptian experience. At the outset, two WAFF battalions were responsible for the control of something like 300,000 square miles. Then, when conquest was succeeded by administration, the British colonial armies became local constabularies on internal security duty. Except for recruiting spurts during the two world wars, the armies were small. Between the two wars, the British-run units in Britain's African empire comprised some 19,000 Africans altogether.[1] Only in 1939, on the eve of war, did the control of the WAFF pass from the Colonial Office (in fact, the Colonial Governors, who used them as domestic trouble-shooters) to the War Office. Only after the war and the loss of India was it decided in West Africa, as in the Sudan, not to cut the force back to its pre-war size.

France, on the other hand, having no Indian army, used her colonial possessions in Africa as the main colonial reservoir of her military manpower. African armies were used to fight France's wars in Europe and to conquer her colonies around the world. Throughout the nineteenth century, Senegalese troops were used: in the Napoleonic wars, in the Crimean war, in the assault on Madagascar in 1838, and against Mexico. It was African troops under French officers who provided the bulk of the fighting force that brought French Equatorial Africa to heel. The cost of acquiring Congo-Brazzaville, the Central African Republic, Chad and Gabon, was estimated at not more than 700 soldiers killed and 1,200–1,500 wounded, of whom four-fifths were Africans.[2] African troops were thrown into the Moroccan war of 1912 and against the Rif rising of 1925. And African armies not only helped to conquer the empire; they also took part in unsuccessful attempts to defend it. 15,000 African troops fought in France's war in Indo-China, up to and including the last stand at Dien Bien Phu.[3] Over 30,000 were used in the war against Algeria. African forces took part in the French–British–Israeli assault on Suez in 1956.

Until 1910, recruitment into the army in French-controlled Africa was on a voluntary basis. After 1912, obligatory military service was introduced for men between the ages of twenty and twenty-eight. It was hoped to recruit a million men from French West Africa alone.[4] But torn between the demands of the Minister of War for more men under arms, and the demands of the Minister of Production for more provisions from African village economies to sustain an embattled France, the Governor was unable to meet the recruiting targets, and he warned that the colonies were in grave danger of revolt against the unrelenting manhunt. At this point M. Blaise Diagne, Deputy of Senegal who was later to become Under-Secretary of State for the Colonies, came to the rescue of the empire. Appointed High Commissioner for the Recruitment of Troops in French West and Equatorial Africa, with powers equal to those of the Governor-General (who promptly resigned in protest), M. Diagne succeeded in recruiting more than the quota – or 63,378 instead of the 40,000 men required of the West African territories – in his year of office. By the end of the First World War, the French had recruited into the army some 200,000 men from a population of eleven million, compared with only 30,000 West Africans in the British forces (some 2,000 of whom were sent to fight in East Africa and were repatriated just in time to put down the Egba revolt against indirect rule).[5] In the Second World War, however, Britain drew heavily on Africa. Over 372,000 men, including carriers and porters, were enlisted, of whom 166,000 served outside their home territories, with more than half of these in Burma.[6] West African troops fought within Africa in the Abyssinian campaign and in Italian Somaliland.

The Second World War saw a burst of sympathetic enthusiasm for the cause of the Allies from the educated élite of British West Africa, some of whose speeches about the defence of the empire would have graced any London club.* In the French territories, the French forces were, as usual, carried along in the drift of French fortunes. French Equatorial Africa went over to the Free French cause: but in West Africa, the navy, the army and the administration opted for Vichy; and with them, the Legion Française des Combattants de l'Afrique Noire, which in 1941 held a mass parade of 6,000 – including African – legionnaires in Vichy's support. When Free French forces took their place on allied war fronts, African soldiers made up half their total strength.[7]

At home, the ex-servicemen in the French colonies were

*Though, on the whole, support also demanded the application of the Atlantic Charter to the colonies.

among the most loyal and cohesive supporters of the administration. Blaise Diagne, as chief recruiter of French African troops, had stipulated a *quid pro quo* of citizenship rights for help in the First World War. The vote was given to service veterans, men on active service and the widows of veterans who had died in the service of France. In Dahomey by 1948, some 58 per cent of an electorate totalling 54,000 consisted of ex-servicemen or serving soldiers.[8] In 1954, one in five of the job openings in the administration of the French colonies was reserved for veterans. A decision to pay equal rates to metropolitan and overseas troops was well-timed to bring a rush of recruits for the war in Indo-China; and in Chad, for instance, there were said to be so many volunteers that a large number had to be turned away.[9] France's armies in Africa fought the battles for empire, but they were also an opening for the unemployed. Which other branch of the economy offered steady jobs and such good pay?

COLOURING THE TROOPS

Like the Persia of Darius and Xerxes, or the Rome of the Caesars, modern empire looked about for the 'barbarians' of remote areas to do their fighting for them. In British West Africa, the model was India. Few British officers in Africa during the early days had not served with the Indian army, and for a while there were even some Indians in the WAFF.[10] Lugard had gained his military experience in India, and it has been said that the layout of Kaduna was based on a typical Indian cantonment in the last days of the British Raj.[11] The precedent for officer and other recruitment policies was laid in India. There, it was directed, officers should be 'confined to the small class of nobility or gentry . . . it would rest upon aristocracy of birth . . . to gratify legitimate ambitions . . . and to attach the higher ranks of Indian society, and more especially the old aristocratic families to the British Government by closer and more cordial ties. . . .'[12] Seeking to apply the Indian model to Africa, a Governor of Sierra Leone expressed his perplexity. There was, he said, 'no gentleman class in Sierra Leone from which men of a high sense of honour and duty could be found'.[13] The WAFF, accordingly, had no African officers.

In India, the British army had improvised the theory of the 'martial races', and recruitment had been confined to peoples of supposedly unique fighting qualities, such as the Sikhs. Men with an urban background were distrusted and kept out of the officer corps, for they were likely to be infected with nationalist sentiment. 'The clever young men of the Universities were quite unfitted for military work . . . the army officers had long realized that the Indian intelligentsia would never make officers.'[14] This reliance on so-called martial races became conventional army wisdom, as did the principle that officers should, on the whole, be drawn from one tribe or group of tribes, and ground troops from others. In West Africa, recruitment was pressed among tribes with 'warlike traditions' and 'the useful attributes of cheerfulness and loyalty'.[15] These qualities were not necessarily found together. British army officers had a certain reluctant admiration for the military prowess of the Ashanti, who had mounted successive wars against them, with the last as late as 1900; but the recruitment of Ashanti into the Gold Coast regiment of the WAFF was bitterly opposed on political grounds. Armies, after all, were needed as reliable instruments against internal discontent. Between wars they were super police forces, organized for rapid deployment to put down tax revolts, labour disputes or nationalist demonstrations. Thus, it was sound policy for colonial regimes to recruit from groups with manageable aspirations. And these were generally in the economically less developed areas, where army employment offered one of the few openings to young men. The armies were built on recruits from remote tribal groups; and a careful ethnic balance, or imbalance, was developed. In Nigeria and Ghana, recruiting concentrated on the Northern areas, with the result that by the mid-1960s, about 70 per cent of the service troops in the Nigerian army were drawn from the North: not the 'true' North, but provinces like Adamawa and Benue; from the Tiv, the Idoma and the Igbirra; and from Bornu. In Ghana, northern peoples supplied 80 per cent of the non-commissioned officers until 1961. In Uganda, recruiting concentrated on the Acholi; in Kenya, it was chiefly among the Kamba and the Kalenjin, and deliberately not among the politically aggressive Kikuyu.

Even in Tanganyika, where a great number of small tribes and the absence of any dominant majority group promoted national unity, army recruits were drawn chiefly from the Hehe and the Kuria.[16]

MEN OF WAR

Nowhere was the army used more ruthlessly as the tool of colonial coercion than in the Belgian Congo. The Belgians, unlike the French, the British and the Portuguese, sent no metropolitan troops for the colonial contingent. 'The Congo had to be quickly organized so that it would conquer itself.'[17] The Force Publique was founded in 1888; by 1897 it numbered 14,000 men, of whom 12,000 were Congolese. Throughout most of its existence, its strength was about 20,000. By 1953 there were only 788 Europeans with the army, forming a very small corps of expatriate officers. Again, unlike its other partners in colonialism, the Belgians did not draw for recruits almost exclusively on special tribes – though they, too, sought out those 'martial races' – but followed a deliberate policy of having all ethnic groups represented in the army. There were explicit instructions that platoons had to be scrambled to contain representatives of at least four tribes.[18] This was to reduce the chances of mutiny. And certainly the Force Publique attained a high degree of cohesive proficiency in 'disciplining' trouble-makers, from tax defaulters to religious zealots, acquiring in the process a reputation for strong-arm methods that verged on gangsterism. 'Who was sent into the Force Publique?' asked its Belgian commander, General Emile Jannsens: 'The least promising individuals, the pupils who had been expelled from school, the refuse of the nation.'[19] It was General Jannsens' implacable refusal to permit any acceleration of the army's Africanization programme that provoked the post-independence army mutiny, and so placed the Congo at the mercy of foreign intervention. At independence, the Force Publique had three Congolese sergeant-majors. What plans there were for Africanization would have taken generations to fulfil. Overnight the expatriate officer corps disappeared and discipline disintegrated. General Jannsens wrote on a blackboard in front of a few hundred incensed Congolese non-commissioned officers: 'After Independence = Before Independence'.[20] Later that same afternoon, the first instances of outright disobedience to remaining Belgian officers began. That evening, when a column of reinforcements summoned from the near-by garrison at Thysville refused to march and arrested its officers instead, the mutiny was on; and, with it, the breakdown of the Congo's newly independent state.

It was an ex-servicemen's demonstration, demanding Africanization in the army and the granting of regular commissions to African officers, that triggered off the riots of February 1948 in Ghana and the positive action phase which changed the face of Ghanaian politics. 'The large number of African soldiers returning from service with the Forces where they had lived under different and better conditions made for a general communicable state of unrest,' wrote the Watson Commission.[21] The ex-servicemen's march to Christianborg Castle presented a petition to the Governor. 'Your Excellency's loyal and dutiful ex-servicemen who saw active service in World Wars I and II found that 18s or 30s a month disability pension can hardly keep together the life and soul of a disabled ex-soldier, especially when he has a wife and children to look after.' The week before the riot, Danquah and Nkrumah had expressed public support for the claims of the ex-servicemen, who formed a significant slice of the population, especially as they tended not to return to their villages but to settle round the towns, and in particular the capital. A Commission had been set up to handle the Demobilization and Resettlement of Gold Coast Africans in the Armed Forces,[22] but plans for re-settling ex-servicemen were thin on the ground. 'When you get home,' said the instruction formulated by the Commission, 'obey your Native Authority, give honour to age, and be willing to teach others all that you have learned without shouting about what you have done.' Ghana, with a population one-seventh of Nigeria's, had contributed half as many enlisted men.[23] Two-thirds of the soldiers from the Gold Coast had served abroad. About a third had learned army trades; but large numbers of these, among others, found themselves jobless and the war promises made to them unkept. After the firing by police on the demonstrators, the administration declared that an increase in disability pensions had, in fact, been approved and was about to be announced when the trouble broke. But by then the police action had given an enormous fillip to the demands of the nationalist movement and its militant phase of struggle for independence.

In Nigeria, returned soldiers were resentful of inadequate pensions and gratuities (an ex-serviceman with 100 per cent disability drew only £3 a month) and at discrimination in army pay scales and general treatment. Both before and after the war, indeed, the army was a stronghold of discrimination.[24] From the formation of the WAFF until the outbreak of the Second World War, Nigerian soldiers had not been allowed footwear on parade or ordinary duties, only on long marches. African feet were supposedly hardened enough not to need shoes. Their uniform was deliberately made baggy: for free movement, the army decreed; but 'to make us look native', as a Nigerian soldier who rose to the rank of brigadier remarked.[25] The knee-length shorts (known as a longshort) were not provided with pockets, and whether this was official thinking or not, Nigerians suspected it was because the average 'native' soldier was supposed to be a thief, and the provision of pockets would encourage stealing. In the pre-war Nigerian army, the highest post a Nigerian could reach was battalion sergeant-major. A Nigerian soldier of whatever rank had to stand to attention even to a British sergeant, and he had to salute White civilians. Then there was the glaring discrimination in pay scales. 'Those who enlist expect a good salary just as their White brothers earn. To the people death knows no colour and, as such, rates of pay should be adjusted in that spirit,' wrote the *West African Pilot* during the war.[26]

But in Nigeria, unlike Ghana, the grievances and frustration of ex-servicemen were dissipated in the multiplicity of their different organizations, each highly localized. There were, for instance, the Supreme Council of Ex-Servicemen; an organization for Lagos ex-servicemen; a National Federation of Ex-Servicemen's Associations for Nigeria and the Cameroons. Northern ex-servicemen were not even represented in the

Supreme Council, though they constituted the majority of ex-servicemen in the country at large. The returned soldiers were caught up in the regional politics that dominated Nigeria. But the region too, was sometimes not parochial enough. An attempt to organize all ex-servicemen in the Western region failed because Warri and Ilesha did not like the idea of being led by those in Ibadan, which had been projected as the headquarters. 'The brave new world they had fought for has very easily faded into the rotten world of unemployment and frustration,' wrote M. Okoye.[27] There was very little opportunity and sense of direction for the individual man, and Nigerian politicians were too busy with their mutual recriminations, too confused over means and ends, to consider how to use such excellent material in the national cause. The reabsorption of Nigeria's ex-servicemen was punctuated by only one outburst, which was the disturbance at Umuahia in 1951, when the town was held by ex-servicemen for a few days in protest against the requirement that they pay tax even though they were jobless. The protest was suppressed and the ringleaders were jailed; the ex-servicemen dispersed to their homes or the job queues in the towns. For them 'this is the way the world ends, not with a bang but a whimper'.[28]

After the war and the loss to the Empire of India, Pakistan and Ceylon, Britain's African armies became more important in imperial defence strategies. They needed to be bigger, better equipped and better trained. Up to the war they had been mainly infantry battalions with conventional and often anachronistic equipment, and, apart from some African warrant officers, officered by expatriates with no great level of professionalism. If progress towards independence in the 1950s was slow, Africanization in the armies was even slower. In 1953 it was decided that the WAFF, which embraced all four British colonies in West Africa, would be broken down into constituent national forces.[29] This was done in 1956. It was agreed that the four governments would invite the Army Council of Great Britain to appoint a General Officer Commanding-in-Chief. And it was also agreed that Sandhurst should hold twenty places a year for West African cadets. But these places were not fully taken up, so rigorous and reluctant were the selection procedures. The first Gold Coast cadets were sent to Britain for training only in 1953. (In East Africa, the first Ugandans went in 1959, and the first Tanganyikans in 1961.) In the period of so-called 'preparation', but also in the period after independence, the training of African officers was undertaken with the greatest reluctance. Invariably the last functions transferred to African control with decolonization were those connected with internal security or defence. When Ghana achieved her independence in 1957, no more than 10 per cent of her army officers were Ghanaian.[30] In the Nigerian army, by 1958, there were only forty-five African commissioned officers – about half of whom had passed through Sandhurst – or one in seven of Nigeria's officer corps. In the Federal Parliament, Nigeria's Minister of Defence, Alhaji Mohammed Ribadu, was pressed for speedier Africanization. 'Our army in the Congo is being looked after by an officer who is not Nigerian,' said Mr C. O. D. Eneh. The Minister replied: 'The government is doing its best to Nigerianize as much as possible the armed forces, but Sir, as I have said in my speech, experience is very, very important because we do not want to have another Mobutu. . . .'[31]

While the Nigerian army was fully Africanized only by 1965, the officer corps in the Sudan was composed entirely of nationals by the attainment of independence in 1956. Part of the officer training had been done at Khartoum's Military Academy; the rest through crash training programmes in Britain. The Sudan possessed the only army in colonized Africa to be completely Africanized by independence. This and its fairly modern military establishment resulted from its pivotal position between Britain's strategic interests in the Middle East and in East Africa.

From 1925 onwards when it was constituted as the Sudan Defence Force, the army of Sudan was carefully nurtured for its strategic role, with Egyptian officers, units and influence purged from what had started as a section of the Egyptian army. After the 1924 mutiny, the selection of officers and ranks was closely supervised. Recruits for the army were traditionally drawn not from the dangerous ranks of the educated but from respected families propping up indirect rule, and they were trained in that 'typically imperial institution, Gordon College, Khartoum'.[32]

In the Second World War, the Sudanese army saw intensive combat service on vital fronts in Eritrea and Ethiopia during the North African campaign of 1942, when it had to regain the Sudan's eastern provinces. It did not then join in any European arena of the war, but returned to the Sudan for service as a strategic reserve against Egyptian unrest.

> That this was regarded as a continuing function was apparent in the fact that there was only limited demobilisation of the Sudanese army at the end of the war. The loss of the Indian army – historically a key force in Britain's imperial defence system – provided an additional reason for the maintenance of the Sudanese army as an effective military unit following World War II. This was reinforced by the fact that the post-war British Labour government was not prepared, for both political and economic reasons, to offset the loss of the Indian army by an equivalent commitment of military manpower recruited and kept under arms in the United Kingdom.[33]

By 1958 the Sudanese army was about 12,000 strong.[34] Most of the officers commissioned into it when it had been part of the Egyptian army had gone into retirement, though General Abboud (commissioned in 1918) continued to represent his generation as Officer-Commanding, and Abdallah Khalil (commissioned in the Sudanese battalions of the Egyptian army in 1910) kept a proprietary eye on the army as Minister of Defence. From 1924 to 1935, the army was run by British officers and a small number of Sudanese promoted from the ranks. Some sixty officers commissioned after 1937 or promoted during combat in the Second World War had, in the course of active service under British officers, inherited the traditions and outlook of the latter.

In 1953 the Sudan embarked on a crash programme of Sudanization. This included officer training for the army; and between three and four hundred junior officers were drawn from the secondary schools and commissioned in large batches.[35] The recruitment of this generation was to be the equivalent in the Sudan of the entry into the Egyptian army of Nasser and his Free Officers, when in 1936 Egypt's military academy, formerly accessible only to members of the old Turkish families, was thrown open to Egyptians of all classes. Sudanization of the army and the civil service were part of popular political mobilization for ridding the country of British influences. The junior officers, trained in the crash programmes to Sudanize the officer corps, were part of the country's independence generation. They identified themselves vigorously with nationalist aspirations. They also scorned the generation of senior officers, as being inferior to them in education, ability and patriotic ardour. 'It is difficult for Abdallah Khalil (the prime minister) to depend on the Sudanese army because the spirit of national extremism is strong within it,' wrote the *New York Times*.[36] It was public knowledge that the army command was uneasy about the shadow of Nasser's Free Officer Movement, which hung so inevitably over young nationalist army officers. Grumbles about corruption and inefficiency in the Sudanese army led to talk among officers about the formation of patriotic groups within the forces; but the moves seemed tentative and unfulfilled.

Who joined Africa's armies? In countries as far afield as Nigeria and the Sudan, army service was considered a disreputable career for the sons of the educated and respectable. No worthy Lagotian father, no successful lawyer or flourishing trader, would have dreamt of making his son a soldier. In West Africa, particularly, the sons of the middle class or up-and-coming ranks of urban society set their sights on the elevated professions like law and medicine, or on government service. Those who joined the army, to rise through the ranks or, in the later period, to graduate from the military academies, tended to be the sons of minor officials, small farmers and petty traders. They were from families in the rural areas and small towns rather than large city centres, and were the sons of parents who could not afford to educate them further than they had already gone in the mission school. Military education, after all, was free.

The first generation of African army officers, the Abboud–Ankrah–Ironsi–Ogundipe generation, sweated their way slowly up through the ranks; and only with independence and Africanization were they commissioned and promoted to fill the posts of the withdrawing expatriate command. This first generation of officers was generally drawn from the army education and pay services. Nigeria's General Ironsi served as a storeman in the Ordnance Department after he enlisted, and is said never to have sloped a rifle. Nzeogwu, the young major who led the January coup, referred to him contemptuously as a tally-clerk. Ghana's General Ankrah had been a mission teacher who enlisted at the outbreak of the Second World War and spent the war on supply duties, finishing as a warrant officer and getting his commission in 1947. The Sudan's Generals Abboud and Abdallah Khalil worked their way up the ranks through service in two world wars; but the Sudanese officers saw more combat than most others in British Africa. Without their service under the UN in the Congo most British African armies and officers – except for the veterans of the Second World War, who had generally been sent to Burma – would never have fired a shot in anger.

YOUNG VETERANS

The same could not be said of France's armies in Africa, which had fought so many of France's own wars. Until independence, these armies were organized to meet French military needs, with a total disregard for territorial divisions between the colonies. They were centralized at Dakar for French West Africa, and at Brazzaville for the Equatorial colonies. 'The concept of developing embryonic national armies was non-existent; the only legitimate nation was France, with its overseas departments and territories, *une et indivisible*.'[37] The African officer corps, no less than the army, was altogether orientated to France.

Then, with the onset of independence, national armies began to be constituted for the first time. African officers who had served in the French army were appointed chief-of-staff, military adviser to the head of state, or commander-in-chief. They were African army heads, but they differed from their professional counterparts in the French army proper only in the colour of their skin. Their commitment had been to France's army and wars, and their attitudes and experience had been suitably conditioned.

Let us look at the first generation of military men. Dahomey's

General Soglo volunteered for the French army in 1931, at the age of twenty-one. He was a sergeant-major when the Second World War came, was mentioned in dispatches during the French campaigns of 1940, and thereafter served in Morocco's Colonial Infantry Regiment under the Vichy regime, and then moved to the 6th Régiment des Tirailleurs Sénégalais to help liberate French soil. He took part in the Free French landings on Corsica and Elba, and by the end of the war was Colonial Troops Staff Officer. Then, made a military adviser to the French government in 1947, he was promoted to captain in 1950 and sent to Indo-China, where he fought for five years in both the north and the south, and was awarded the Croix de Guerre. When Dahomey became independent, he became adviser on military affairs to the head of state; and, subsequently, his country's first chief-of-staff.

Colonel Jean-Bedel Bokassa, cousin to President Dacko of the Central African Republic, whom he toppled from power in the coup d'état of 1964, served for twenty-three years with the French army. A communications expert, he received twelve decorations in Indo-China, and is passionately pro-French. Lieutenant-Colonel Lamizana of Upper Volta joined the army at the age of twenty, fought for two years in Indo-China and another two in North Africa. Chad's chief-of-staff, Colonel Jacques Doumro, joined the French army when he was nineteen, fought in the Second World War, and for three years in Indo-China with the French 6th Colonial Infantry. He was transferred to the Chad forces in 1961. The Ivory Coast chief-of-staff had a similar history in the French army. It was this first generation of officers, '*anciens d'Indo-Chine*', who, one after another, were seconded to their country's national armies when these were constituted at independence. Their rise in the ranks had been almost as slow as that of their British equivalents, but they had had considerably more combat experience and had achieved a commitment, under fire, to French colonial aims.

More than anything else, it was the Algerian war that groomed the next generation of officers. Junior officers or under-officers were trained at the Centre de Perfectionnement des Sous-Officiers Coloniaux (Centre for Advanced Instruction of Colonial

NCOs) at Frejus and became eligible for promotion to second lieutenant after the course. Among the 15,000 troops who served in Indo-China until 1954, there were twenty officers and 900 non-commissioned officers; but by 1956 there were still only sixty-five African officers in the French army. Afterwards, training was accelerated. In 1958 the first parachutists were graduated from Dakar; and in that year, French West Africa had 500 students at military schools. The second generation of officers were thus younger and more highly educated men, trained as more specialist and technically qualified cadres. Dahomey's Major Alphonse Alley is an example. He went through army secondary school in Dakar, joined the Senegalese Tirailleurs as an officer, and was trained as a paratrooper; he was decorated in the war in Indo-China and also fought in Algeria. Alley played a leading role in the Soglo take-over of Dahomey's government in 1964–5, and became his general's chief-of-staff; then in the junior officers' coup of December 1967, he displaced General Soglo as head of state. His contemporary, Colonel Étienne Eyadema of Togo, joined the French army at the age of sixteen and fought in both Indo-China and Algeria. Now Togo's head of state, he was one of the principal organizers of the 1963 coup against the government of President Sylvanus Olympio. 'A soldier who has been taught to kill, who has an Algerian or a Vietnamese on his conscience, makes no bones about killing one or two Togolese as well,' one of the Togo coup-makers told journalists.[38]

The 1963 coup in Togo was a direct result of French army developments in Africa. As the 1960s opened, France's defence policy was re-orientated towards nuclear strategy, and French military installations on the continent were accordingly reduced. Strategic bases were left in Algeria, at Mers-el-Kebir; in Dakar; in the Malagasy Republic; in Chad, at Fort Lamy; in Congo-Brazzaville, at Pointe-Noire; at Douala in the Cameroun; and in Mauritania, at Port Étienne: but there was a substantial cut-back of manpower stationed in Africa. French policy was to withdraw from Africa but to build, within France, a force capable of intervening at short notice abroad. African service-men were given the option of remaining on service with the

French army, or of taking up service with the newly constituted national armies. About 283,000 men left Africa, including Algeria, between January 1962 and January 1963 and a further decrease of 82,000 was envisaged by the end of 1963. About 20,000 men returned to their home countries, or neighbouring ones, to take up service with African armies. Changed French defence policy thus had dramatic effects in Africa. It deposited large contingents of returned ex-servicemen on small and struggling economies, and on new, tiny armies. Upper Volta, for instance, whose army in 1966 was only 1,500 strong (though at a cost that swallowed one-seventh of the country's total budget) found herself with 150,000 French army veterans, or one adult male in six.[39] About a third of a million French West Africans conscripted for the Second World War had been accorded privileges like the vote and parity of pensions with French metropolitan rates, and some of these ex-servicemen, particularly the non-commissioned officers, lived well in their villages. But soldiers transferred from the French army to African armies in the 1960s had to accept cuts in pay and reduced standards. Both Senegal and the Ivory Coast stepped up expenditure on the army, though they were embarked on general austerity campaigns.

Guinea had to deal with large numbers of repatriated military personnel in the first few months of her defiant vote for independence and her break with France.

> Today [said Sékou Touré], they [the veterans] find an independent country. Instead of coming with courage and confidence, with energy and pride to work for their country, certain of them will say: 'If we are not given work we will do this, we will do that.' In saying this, to whom do they think they are speaking? They are speaking to the people of Guinea, to those same people who obtained the independence of their country. Do they think that the people will let them do such things?[40]

Some 500 of about 50,000 returned veterans were found government employment; and for the rest, Guinea set about trying to build a national army well integrated with the party, so that it could not easily be used against party purposes. Guinea is said to have put one particular contingent of discharged Algerian veterans back on the plane for Paris.

In Lomé, capital of Togo, Sergeant Emmanuel Bodjollé was the spokesman of returned soldiers, and he pleaded for the enlargement of the army to incorporate them. Togo's French military adviser also favoured a larger army and military budget; Olympio resisted, however. He was unwilling to tax Togo's limited resources with a military establishment out of all proportion to the country's needs and finances. He was eventually persuaded by the French officer to add 100 men to the army, but even then he planned to by-pass the French army contingent. He told the Bodjollé delegation, 'I shall use unemployed school-leavers, or people who fought for independence, and not you mercenaries who were killing our Algerian friends when we were fighting for independence.'[41] Togo was the first but by no means the last occasion when French policy had cataclysmic consequences in an African state, this time through a seizure of power by discharged soldiers. But there is another important point to be made about the Togo coup. The returned ex-servicemen who faced unemployment were from the Cabre people, of a relatively poor and undeveloped region in Togo. Independence was young, and already the political class and the élites of the towns seemed to be taking the best for themselves. Well, soldiers could do something about that.

At independence, of all those belonging to the Western-groomed élite, the military looked the least likely avenue to political influence; indeed, the army was not considered part of the equation of power in African states until other sections of the élite found themselves in crisis. Then it made up for lost time.

A SPECIAL CASE: ALGERIA

At independence, Africa's armies consisted of little more than foreign-officered infantry. They were small armies: only three military establishments in sub-Saharan Africa exceeded 10,000 men (the Sudan, Ethiopia and the Congo), and fourteen were below 2,000. Of all the institutions bequeathed from the colonial period, the armies retained their colonial flavour, their foreign advisers and their affinity with the former colonial power longest.

Alone of Africa's armies, Algeria's was different. This was no colonial inheritance; it was an army created to wage a war of national liberation. Yet in post-independent Algeria, the army has acted as a competitor for power; the pattern of government is military–bureaucratic in type; and the political movement of the FLN has visibly degenerated. Somewhere during the course of Algeria's revolutionary war, the process of achieving popular mobilization and devising forms of popular authority for social change under an independent government withered. How did this happen?

There were two distinct phases in Algeria's war for independence, and Algeria's liberation army was affected by them both. The first was from the outbreak of rebellion at the start of November 1954 to the Battle of Algiers of 1956–7; the second was from de Gaulle's seizure of power in France to the Evian agreement between Algeria and France which was signed in March 1962. During the first phase, the ALN (Algerian Army of National Liberation) went on the offensive in fairly classic guerrilla warfare style. The *wilayas*, or guerrilla command groups, won over extensive areas in the interior and advanced to the coastal strip. This assault culminated in the Battle for Algiers, when the capital itself became a field of fighting for the best part of a year. It was after this stage of the war that France summoned new material and tactical resources. She threw a vast army and security force into the task of 'pacifying' or occupying the countryside and the towns. France thus established her military superiority, but she ensured an irreversible shift of loyalty to the nationalists and she thus lost the battle for the political support of the Algerian people. The *wilaya* were forced to withdraw to strongholds and to mountain redoubts, and the French army built the Meurice Line: a formidable system of electrified barriers along the borders, cutting Algeria off from Morocco and Tunisia. These fortifications shut off the *wilayas* from supplies and reinforcements, and divided the ALN into the forces of the interior (the *wilayas*) and the forces outside the country. It was this division which was to have far-reaching political consequences. The Meurice Line was completed in September 1957, and from this time onwards the French forced a rollback of the ALN; the liberation army could not translate its political support into outright military victory, while the French, for their part, had to be content with military superiority and pacification but no outright victory either.

In August 1956, before the French achieved this rollback of the Algerian forces, the critical Soummam Conference had taken place in Algeria under the very nose of the French army. It set out to bring together the *wilaya* commanders of the interior and representatives of Algeria's external delegations; though, in the event, the latter did not manage to attend, and not all the *wilayas* were represented either. This conference decreed the precedence of the political leadership over the military, and the precedence of the forces in the interior over those of the exterior. Military decisions were to be subordinated to political aims, and a collective or collegial system of leadership was to be accepted at all levels. A five-man Executive and Co-ordinating Committee (the CCE), dominated by the internal military commanders, was set up; and plans were made for a national council of the revolution, composed of delegates from all over Algeria, to act as a kind of sovereign assembly over the leadership. This Soummam conference, inspired by young *wilaya* commanders like Ramdane Abbane of Wilaya 1, in the Kabilya, envisaged the growth of a dynamic revolution, in which all national forces would be enlisted in the fight for national liberation, and the army of liberation itself would grow from a guerrilla force into the masses armed and politicized. But Algeria did not develop like China or Vietnam: France increased her military effort, managing to scatter the guerrilla force in the interior, and to disrupt the chain of command so carefully built through the CCE. The CCE itself was forced to seek refuge in Tunis, where it became the precursor to a full-blown government-in-exile, the GPRA (Gouvernement Provisoire de la République Algérienne). This provisional government manned a vast external network of political and diplomatic machinery that functioned from impressive ministry buildings in Tunis, and from other capitals, but was cut off from direct contact with the forces struggling inside Algeria.

There developed, indeed, not only a division between the armed forces of the interior and the exterior, and between the political leadership and the *wilayas*, but also a break-down, inside Algeria, of communication and cohesion among the six *wilaya* regions harassed by the French forces. Each *wilaya* was thrown back on its own military and political resources, and became virtually autonomous in its own field of operation. (Most serious of the divisions created by the isolation of the *wilayas* was the estrangement of that in Kabyle. After a purge in 1959 of young urban intellectuals and radicals in the Kabyle leadership – fomented, it has been suspected, by French intelligence – this degenerated from a stronghold of the guerrilla war, into an isolated and politically alienated camp, resentful at any signs of Arab military or political domination of the Berbers.)

Inside the country, the number of Algerians under arms was dropping under the pressure of the enemy; but across the borders, the ALN mustered some 40,000 men and a highly organized army administration. It was a democratic and political army in which officers and men drew the same pay; each unit had a political commissar ranking with the officer in charge; army journals discussed the politics of the struggle; and the army education programme taught the politics of national liberation laced with some measure of socialism. It was, thus, an army exercised in politics as well as trained – perhaps over-trained – for combat; but it was an army-in-waiting, an army in enforced inactivity. With the exception of rare infiltrations through the Meurice Line, it was cut off from the struggle in the country, and, in the years of intensive preparation but non-involvement, increasingly prone to inner intrigues and struggles for power. To the beleaguered forces of the interior, starved of supplies and reinforcements during the hardest days of the war, it seemed that the army of the exterior was not a reserve force for combat, but, inevitably perhaps, preserving its force for another day.

On the political front, the original inner circle of those who had planned the rebellion (the Club of Nine) had grown to encompass a great range of forces, combining to prosecute the war of liberation. Among them were the representatives of the militants in the towns, workers and students, and also old-style politicians, like Ferhat Abbas, the generation of leaders who had earlier tried to extract concessions from the French and had failed, and who came to the revolution late and despite themselves, there to play the role of diplomats and negotiators abroad. With the formation of the Algerian government-in-exile, the FLN as policy-maker tended to be effaced. And when independence came, after seven years of protracted war, it was negotiated by the politicians who made up the provisional government-in-exile. They concluded the Evian agreement, with all its constraints on full Algerian independence. This limited success promptly opened all the fissures between the forces of the interior and the exterior, the army and the politicians, the divided *wilayas*, and the range of ideologies and interests which had been covered over by the all-purpose structure of the FLN and by a general failure to enunciate the goals of the struggle beyond independence.

In the acute and involved pre-independence crisis, the army under Boumedienne and the government-in-exile were at loggerheads, to the point that at one stage Boumedienne was dismissed from his command. (The order was never operative.) The army had forced a small shift leftwards in the government-in-exile, with the displacement of Ferhat Abbas (who had risen to the top after the French kidnapping of Ben Bella) by Ben Khedda. But the attempt to avoid a neo-colonial settlement through the Evian agreement failed. At this stage the army decided to settle for formal independence as the shortest road to real Algerian power.

When, on the eve of independence, with the opening of the borders, the army and the provisional government entered Algeria, they accordingly came not as a united force, but as contestants for power. They were rivals for internal political support, with the *wilayas* divided between them and from them. Nor was the provisional government itself united. At one point there were even two rival governments in Algeria: Ben Khedda's, which was recognized by thirty-three foreign states, and Ben Bella's, with headquarters first at Tlemcen, then at Oran. Civil war was averted only at the last moment by frantic popular pressure, especially in the capital through demonstrations organized by the trade unions, and by a decision of Boumedienne that the army would support Ben Bella for as long as he did not deviate from what the army considered were the correct revolutionary paths. Ben Bella and Boumedienne thus came to power in tandem. But the real force in Algeria was the army: professional, closely-knit, and, as the army of the exterior, non-combatant in the liberation war.

The advance of the ALN on Algiers was measured, as it began asserting its authority over the *wilayas*. It dissolved them and, where they resisted, crushed them. A few decisive pitched battles even ensued. The army of the exterior was highly organized and intact. By contrast, the *wilayas* had managed with difficulty to maintain a command and an organization at all; and where they had succeeded, these had functioned erratically, clandestinely, and out of contact for years with the army and the political leaders beyond the borders. And on the eve of the transfer of power, the French tried one last manoeuvre. This was the recruitment – by moderate Algerian politicians – of a force for 'law and order', which was composed largely of 'harkis', or native auxiliaries used as counter-insurgency troops during the war. This force sent troops into the *wilayas*; the membership of which was in some instances swollen by hundreds or thousands of men, previously uncommitted to the struggle but hostile to it, and ready for any political adventure.

To the army of the exterior, there was no option but to assert its total, national command over what looked like roaming armed bands. The men of the *wilayas* were ordered to lay down their arms and abandon their wartime structure; where they resisted, they were arrested for illegal possession of weapons. The fighters of the *wilayas* were not absorbed into the army. But half a year later, the army did absorb Algerians who had been officers and non-commissioned officers in the French army; and it was said that much of the general staff in the ALN, which became the ANP (Armée Nationale Populaire) at independence, was largely created from these officers. New regions of military administration, which cut across the old *wilaya* divisions, also played their part in bringing the control of the *wilayas* to an end.

Thus, at the very moment of Algeria's independence victory, after seven years of gruelling war, the very forces which supplied the dynamics of Algeria's revolution were displaced. The forces of the interior, liberated by a guerrilla war which might have led to a genuine popular mobilization for a new political system, were overtaken, even suppressed, by a highly centralized, authoritarian and bureaucratic armed structure. From this time onwards, Algerian independence politics were not peasant-based, as the rural revolt which sustained the war had been; nor were they fired primarily by the worker, student and intellectual militants of the cities, who in great street demonstrations and in the Battle for Algiers itself had thrown their weight behind the FLN in the face of security force terrorism. They became the contests of élite groups, among them the professional officer corps of the career army, manipulating for political and economic vantage points.

In the prosecution of the war, the FLN had combined men of disparate origins and political persuasions – prosperous middle-class merchants, members of prominent land-owning families, workers, trade-union militants, students, intellectuals, poor peasants and religious leaders. When it entered independence, it had little to offer in the way of a programme. 'We will start thinking about Algeria's economy when we are back on Algerian soil,' one FLN spokesman had said. So it was a broad but amorphous and eclectic movement, with anything but a coherent strategy for the post-independence period. When the Tripoli Programme and the Charter of Algiers proclaimed the leading role of the FLN in defining policy and controlling government, this was enshrining a myth. The FLN had been a great wartime resistance front, but it was to atrophy rapidly with independence. The real power in Algeria after independence was not the party, but the highly organized and professional army. It had grown in struggle, unlike Africa's other armies; but after independence, it was more like them than distinct from them. And Algerian politics, fired in a revolutionary struggle for independence, had produced the ashes of élite preoccupations.

Politicians in Business

. . . And I say to this Central African élite which is daily growing before our eyes: don't be ashamed to be bourgeois, don't be ashamed to become wealthy.

President David Dacko, addressing the National Assembly of the Central African Republic, 16 October 1961

'Élite' has been used as a catch-all term to describe those in Africa who were employed originally as intermediaries by the colonial power, and who later came to see themselves as its heirs and beneficiaries. Some members of the élite were born to special status and influence; others acquired it through education or economic opportunity afforded by the changing social system. Within the élite group there were several layers. Apart from the 'traditional' élite, reinforced in their authority by the colonial administration, and the coastal élites that enjoyed an early monopoly of Western education and trading opportunities, a later-educated layer took to the professions or the civil service and became a large and influential administrative élite. Others, especially from rural areas, went into the army. Some achieved membership of the élite through their role as middlemen in trade, or as employees of the import–export houses and other foreign enterprises. A vociferous generation espoused politics in the immediate pre-independence decade, earned the prestige of having negotiated the independence settlement, and, once in power, used politics to try transforming itself from élite group to ruling class. In the first phase of independence, Africa's power élite was dominated by the politicians and their party machines, but it was not confined to them; for around the feet of the politicians in power clambered not only those who exercised economic and political influence by virtue of office, leadership or business, but many more who laid claim to such.

The élite that aspired to the place of the colonialists, and the power élite that in fact came to inherit command, was not a distinct social class, for neither grouping was anchored in economic ownership and control. Neither the governing parties nor the opposition were, in general, class-based. Majhemout Diop, the Senegalese marxist, writing on his own country, had pointed out that nearly all the leaders of the different parties were of much the same social origin, the petit-bourgeoisie or lower middle class; most, he added, had imbibed their ideology from much the same sources, a blend of African nationalism and some marxism.[1]

Class formation is still rudimentary; and class characterization alone, an incomplete guide to the nature of power in the new African state. Society is stratified in complex ways, and class alignments are criss-crossed by kinship, age-group, ethnic and regional affiliations, and patron and client relationships. Though there are those, especially since they obtained control of the state as part of the power élite, who have increasingly constituted both an upper social and a ruling class, and who have found growing opportunity for entrenchment, it remains difficult to equate any one social class with the ruling class. There has been no necessary congruence between wealth and economic power, or between economic and political power, Ken Post has written.[2] But within the élite – and outside it too, of course – a process of class formation is in progress. 'Class formation,' Richard Sklar has written, 'would appear to be more significant than class conflict as a form of class action in contemporary Africa.'[3] It is the scuffling for control of groups within the power élite that constitutes the crisis of the first phase of African independence, and that helps explain the invasion of government by the soldiers.

No bourgeoisie, in the style of Europe's early nation states, has found the power to govern alone; for indigenous ownership and controlling groups had been able to grow only in the shadow of colonial power. Since independence, as before, the large concentrations of capital have been in the hands of foreign companies. Africans have risen to be planters, traders, cocoa-brokers, timber-merchants, transport contractors, and small manufacturers. But Africa's bourgeoisie has been incapable of accumulating capital and creating economic growth independent of the giant international firms. No indigenous capital has existed to challenge the expatriate monopoly of banking, insurance, building societies, shipping lines or large timber concessions. European banks exercise a virtual monopoly in Africa; and banks have ever been loath to lend money for African-run enterprises without 'security'. At the end of the Second World War, three large firms controlled from half to four-fifths of the main exports of Nigeria and Ghana; while three great trading companies dominated the French colonies.[4]

In the years between the wars, a number of small middle-men managed to wedge themselves between the expatriate companies that monopolized the import–export trade, and the small-scale farmer-producers. In Nigeria there were about 100,000 such middle-men.[5] But their profit margins were small. Then, after the war, the marketing boards, through which exports were handled, had power to license buying agents. The large foreign firms began to withdraw from the wholesale buying trade, and this created opportunities for Africans in at least these interstices of the economy. Now African agents, brokers, contractors and traders – among them the market 'mammies' – stepped into their own. By 1964 in Nigeria, for instance, the number of African agents had trebled. Yet, by independence, very few members of the élite had entered it as private businessmen or entrepreneurs. Where they functioned in the commercial world, it was mostly as agents and go-betweens, or as employees of the expatriate firms. Many were living conspicuously in the professions, as lawyers, doctors and academics. Many had graduated into politics. Most were manning the lower levels of the civil service and filling the white-collar jobs in the towns.

Not that glaring inequalities in wealth and ownership did not exist. Indeed wealth was increasingly being concentrated in a few hands. In the Ivory Coast, a planter class of perhaps 10,000, including President Houphouet-Boigny himself – scion of a hereditary chief, political leader and head of government – owns large tracts of land, employs wage labour and has accumulated capital to branch into commerce and transport. In Ghana, by 1959–60, at Kumasi and Accra, the two largest towns, there were traders, with a turnover of £5,000 to £20,000 a year each, who handled direct importing from abroad.[6] Nigeria was said in 1965 to boast half a dozen millionaires, men with incomes of perhaps £100,000 a year.[7] In Nigeria's Western Region, the top 5 per cent enjoyed 26 per cent of the national income, though in Ibadan, the capital, the advertised wage rate for unskilled labour was 5*s*. a day. The same concentration of wealth is at work in most African states. Changes in the law to allow the transfer of land to private ownership has produced strong land-owning differentials in some parts of the countryside. In Togo, by the mid-1950s, less than 5 per cent of the farmers possessed about one-fifth of the planted cocoa land. The crystallization of a bourgeoisie took place mainly in the countryside, or in trade, commerce and property. Indigenous industry was virtually non-existent. There were tiny workshops, employing a handful of men each, but no industrial enterprises worth talking of.*

According to a report on the Development of African Private Enterprise, made in 1964 for the U.S. National Planning Association by T. Geiger and W. Armstrong, the Nigerian Ministry of Commerce and Industries has estimated that 'there are roughly 200,000 Nigerian entrepreneurs, the great majority of whom are partially or wholly engaged in small retailing activities'. Their incomes are mostly low: 'a 1959 report of the Nigerian Government indicated that about 85 per cent of the African traders in Lagos earned less than 420 dollars a year – and this is probably higher than in most other parts of the country.' The same report quotes a 1963 census in Ghana which revealed 'over 100,000 enterprises of all sizes, of which 1,200 employ more than 10 people'; and it adds that most of these, as in Nigeria, are small retailers with low incomes.[8]

An African bourgeoisie was struggling fitfully to emerge, but it was having a hard time of it. Giovanni Arrighi argues[9] that, thanks to the grip of the international corporations on African economies, Tropical Africa may not produce more than a satellite, subordinate, lumpen bourgeoisie, less and less able to stimulate economic growth independently of these corporations. 'The

*In fourteen towns surveyed in Nigeria's Eastern region, 10,728 firms employed 28,721 workers, an average of 2·7 per enterprise, including the manager–owner and apprentices. (*Development of Small Industries in Eastern Nigeria*, prepared for the United States Agency for International Development.)

integration of Tropical Africa with the international capitalist system can be assumed to exclude the possibility of a nationalist capitalist pattern of development.' Decolonization, he claims, was the result of a conflict between two kinds of preserves in the colonies: the big companies, on the one hand, and small planters, small trading houses and marginal enterprises, on the other. With independence, the latter lost. The upshot has been the emergence of a new pattern in foreign investment. The typical expatriate firm operating in Tropical Africa is more and more what has been called the multi-national corporation, 'an organized ensemble of means of production subject to a single, policy-making centre which controls establishments situated in several different national territories'. And, to be sure, foreign investment is increasingly a device for transferring a surplus generated in Africa to the investors. Investment in mining and, of late, petroleum, absorb the preponderance of private funds. Industrial investment is concentrated either in the processing of primary products for the export market, or in import substitution. Heavy industry remains either absent altogether or, 'being export-orientated, totally unrelated to the structure of African economies'. The system of oligopolies provides no basis for the production of capital goods to promote the industrialization of Africa.

Before independence the élite found its political power, ownership and economic advance restricted by the colonial system. It demanded the protection of African business from unfair competition by foreign firms; but only the removal of colonial rule, it was thought, would open the way to African development, African control, African ownership. Political control would come first, and African economic advance would follow, it was supposed. At independence, however, the transfer of authority produced a divided system of power. The oligarchy evacuated government and administration, in staggered stages depending on the speed of the Africanization programmes. Yet economic power remained entrenched in the hands of the oligopolies. 'The problem of independence seemed to have been solved in many of the ex-French territories in a practical spirit remarkably free of doctrine,' wrote Unilever's official historian.[10]

'By the mid-sixties it was evident that a new future had been won for Unilever in the new Africa.' Unilever had come to terms with the new system of bifurcated power; so had its counterparts in the former French colonies, SCOA and CFAO, and its own UAC subsidiary, *Cie du Niger Française*. Beside the multi-national corporation, the African bourgeoisie was feebler than ever. Real power in the shape of economic ownership continued to lie outside the country.

Two power groups accordingly controlled the newly independent states. They worked at different levels, from different bases, with the one distinctly feebler than the other and deeply subservient to it. The successor state of the independence era looked different on a superficial level, sounded different, even craved to be more different still. But while the African élite had inherited political power, the price was a continued dependence on forces beyond its political reach; and the consequence was a lop-sided development of social and economic forces within African society.

By independence, therefore, an indigenous dominant class with power grounded in economic control had not emerged. But if the parties inheriting government did not possess an infrastructure of economic power, they promptly set about trying to build themselves one. The first phase of independence was characterized by the efforts of the power élite to use the state not only as an instrument of political domination but also as a source of economic power, in the interstices of the economy unfilled by external control.[11] Possession of government and the resources of the state proved the decisive means. For the state in Africa is the main source of domestic capital and its accumulation. The state plays the major role in economic activity and development. The state is the principal employer of labour, the chief dispenser of jobs, benefits, patronage, contracts, foreign exchange and license to trade. Manipulation of the offices and resources of the state by the power élite proved the shortest cut to wealth. It was political power that made possible the creation of economic power, not the other way about.

Sometimes the manipulation was a party-managed affair, as in Nigeria, where each of the major Southern parties had its bank, business and financial structures, to make money for the politician–businessman and provide funds for the parties themselves. Sometimes individual politicians improvised their own grafts. In one country after another, African politicians came to be known as Mr Ten Per Cent. Politicians extracted such a commission for services rendered in the exercise of their office. Large expatriate firms and local contractors budgeted for the extra 10 per cent that had to be paid to politician or party in securing a contract. (The 10-per-cent rake-off has become such conventional practice in African states that when the Togo government helped the Nigerian federal government during the war with Biafra, by intercepting £7 million-worth of banknotes smuggled abroad by the Biafrans, it was agreed at a joint meeting between the two heads of state, Major-General Gowon and President Étienne Eyadema, that the Togo government receive an 'indemnity' of £700,000 – or 10 per cent of the total value.)

Nigeria's First Republic became an orgy of power being turned to profit. Political party, public and private financial interests fed greedily upon one another. The men who controlled the parties used them to commandeer business, and the business, in turn, to buy party support. The politicians come to power saw it as their right to rule, and in ruling to profit.* Government resources were freely used to acquire economic interests, and these, in turn, to command more political support. The Coker Commission Report showed how £16·3 million (24 per cent of the Western Region Marketing Board total revenues up to 1962, and one and a half times the regional government's revenue for a year) were misappropriated by the ruling party, which filled

*The former Western Minister of Finance, Oba Cladius Dosah Akran, was sentenced to seven years' imprisonment for stealing half a million pounds belonging to the Nigersol Construction Company some time in 1965. So was Prince Adeleke Ademiluyi, one-time chairman of the West Nigeria Development Corporation. It was alleged before the Somulu tribunal that Oba Akran, while Minister of Finance, had improperly acquired the sum of £2,060,347 10*s.* 2*d.*, this in two years between 1963 and 1965. The ex-minister's wife operated four bank accounts under four different names, the tribunal was told. At the time of the hearing, the tribunal was told, Akran was a retired civil servant of the Posts and Telegraphs Department, on a monthly pension of £19 3*s.*, (*Daily Sketch*, 19 August 1967).

private or party purses behind the cover of loans, bank deposits, investments and inflated prices.[12] The business politicians did not have quite the same freedom of manoeuvre everywhere. In Sierra Leone, neither power élite nor assets were as expansive; but the bank balances of politicians were nevertheless swollen with the 'sweets of office', as a commission into corruption showed when it ordered the former premier to repay the state the sum of £771,037.* When the successor government of Siaka Stevens came to office, it announced ruefully: 'There is not much we can celebrate today, the kitty is empty.'[13] Already by 1967, the reserves of Sierra Leone's Produce Marketing Board had been so vigorously deployed for political patronage that it was unable to pay farmers for crops.[14] In Upper Volta, President Maurice Yameogo went on trial, charged with embezzling £1,212,000 during his spell of office. In Ghana, patronage was more rigorously controlled, for there was a national policy for the development of state enterprise and for the curbing of the private business sector; but the group intent on accumulating property while praising the constraints imposed by the state, often managed to elude them.

'Dash', like traditional gift-giving and jobbery, had long been a feature of West African life. The bigger the man, the bigger the 'dash' for the favour or service received. Thus there developed the Big Man syndrome, of the patron fostering his flock by his fame and fortune. The bigger the politician, the bigger the political or business manipulation. 'Corruption' in the political process was crude and flamboyant. There was the élite's old confusion between the individual and general interest, as when Nigeria's Finance Minister opened a shoe factory, but not before he had legislated tax relief for local industry and a tax on imported shoes. A puritan ethic might have inspired a firmer moral integrity, it is often suggested; but this was more than a rampant moral fecklessness. It was the manipulation of the whole system by a political group in power, which found that only by drawing on the resources of the state could capital be raised rapidly and with relative ease. Beside the financial

*A three-man commission headed by Mr Justice Foster probed the Margai government of Sierra Leone.

manipulations of the advanced world, so quick to admonish the poor for its lack of business morality, Africa's fixers were small stuff, to be sure. This was primary accumulation of capital, slow and insignificant by the acquisitive methods of earlier capitalist classes, but it was incurably damaging to Africa's pitiful resources. It was Africa's open season for primitive accumulation, in a period when the more vigorous the plunder, the sooner came the crisis of political control. Resources were too scanty in these backward and fragile economies for their dispersal not soon to be felt or noticed; and Africa, unlike the European powers in the high noon of capital accumulation, found piracy on the high seas and colonization closed to her.

The group that derived its ownership and control not from its hold on the main levers of the economy, but from the manipulation of the political system, has been called the 'political class'.[15] Its members were not simply people who exploited their tenure of political office to their own pecuniary advantage. Many of them were dependent for their success as businessmen, or for their tenure of traditional office, or even civil service appointments, upon the favours of the party in power. 'It is the requirement of the role of businessmen, rather than simply the opportunities available to politicians, which forces people to become part of the political class,' one observer has written.[16] The political class thus 'includes incumbents of political office but also all whose office, employment and income depend on gaining the favour of the government in power'. Its core was made up of Cabinet Ministers, members of parliament, prominent businessmen who often held directorships of public corporations, and important party officials: all those whose control of government enabled them to disburse government revenues and to use government patronage, so as to consolidate their political dominance. More peripheral groups included traditional heads, smaller businessmen, civil servants, academics and party functionaries at local levels: those not so much in control of, as dependent on, government resources, and the party in power. The party in power was able to make a bourgeoisie, newly emerged or aspirant, dependent on government; and this group, in turn, was able to make the state the instrument of its purpose.

It was the political connexions of businessmen that safeguarded and extended their economic power; and the politicians' use of state resources that built them an economic base. No wonder the political parties clung so tightly to power; they had so much to lose.

The State of Bureaucrats

If independence installed the politician–businessmen as the dominant wing of the power élite, Africanization was responsible for the prodigious growth of an administrative sub-élite and the rapid rise within the power élite of this influential bureaucratic layer. Party leaders and bureaucrats had inherited their kingdoms more or less simultaneously – depending on the pace of Africanization in one country or another – and for a while the bureaucratic élite serviced the political layer and augmented it. Initially, indeed, their roles and interests appeared indistinguishable. The power élite has even been called 'the bureaucratic bourgeoisie': Majhemout Diop used this term for the group of over 1,000 career politicians, lawyers, civil servants, sons of land-owners, traders and richer farmers that controls political power in Senegal and uses government and state positions to acquire wealth and economic footholds.[1] But while the leading civil servants – and army commanders – owed their positions at first to the favour of politicians, they have, in the peculiar nature of the African state, acquired special corporate interests in it; and they also, significantly, represent lower and later levels of the élite. It is the combination of these two factors that has made the group of bureaucrats ever-increasingly a rival power formation to the political class, and in ever sharper conflict with it. In the crisis caused largely by the 'corruption' orgy of the politician–businessmen, the alliance within the power élite rapidly broke down and the bureaucrats found their own road to power most dramatically through the coup d'état. (This is not, of course, to say that their influence and special role are by any means limited to those states which have experienced a military seizure of power.)

Not only is the state in Africa the main source of domestic capital and its accumulation, and the principal employer of labour; but government service is the ladder to promotion and thus to economic status for by far the largest number of the top and lower levels of the élite. Half the wage-earners of West Africa are employed in the public service, which includes the civil service and the public corporations. Of Nigeria's total labour force, 75 per cent are employed in agriculture: but of the rest, 62 per cent, or 300,000, are employed by government, with 122,000 of these in federal or regional ministries; 80,000 working for local government; and the rest in the public corporations, the army, the police and the railways. In five years of independence, Nigeria's civil service increased by one-half again, and some ministries quadrupled in size.[2] In Ghana, by 1960, there were 60,000 trained professionals: one in six was self-employed; and of the remainder, two-thirds were employed in the public sector, leaving only 8,000 in the private.[3]

Alongside this phenomenally swift growth of the government-employed élite, went an equally rapid rise in élite status and living standards. When expatriates left the civil service Africans stepped into their posts to inherit their rates of pay. Discrimination in the scales of reward had been one of the principal grievances of the emerging élite. Now the civil servants of the independence government clung tenaciously to expatriate rates of pay. In Nigeria, where the average national *per capita* income is £29 per annum, university graduates commence their careers with salaries of over £700, which rise to £3,900 for superscale posts, while a ministry permanent secretary receives at least £2,500 in basic salary. And the civil servants demanded not only expatriate pay, but colonial privileges, like the system of subsidized rentals, car allowances and a free passage to England each leave! In Western Nigeria, 2·4 per cent of the government's recurrent expenditure has gone on basic car allowances to its civil servants.[4]* In Ghana, government expenditure rose fourfold between the mid-1950s and the mid-1960s. In part this was due to the expansion of social services; but it was also because African civil servants insisted on equality with expatriates, who had been paid according to the salary scales of the metropolitan countries. Africanization thus multiplied many times the openings for African members of a 'red tape' middle class, and produced unprecedentedly rapid career opportunities for the top men: in ten years an exceptional civil servant could rise to the highest rung of the bureaucratic ladder. In Nigeria, the average age of permanent secretaries is thirty-nine; their rise has been meteoric, and their influence has soared with their status and income. Down in the ranks of the administrators, too, salaries and privilege have been vastly inflated. If the lower levels of the administrative élite are not equal partners of the power élite, they are at least among the prime beneficiaries of state policies which unquestioningly adopted the salary structure left behind by colonialism, and so perpetuated, even promoted, the yawning gap between the living standards of the élite and sub-élite and those of the great popular mass.

Independence thus brought immediate gains to a new and relatively privileged class of administrators which, as it grew, began to consume a greater and greater share of the national product, and to precipitate an uncontrolled expansion of public spending on non-productive activity. Perhaps this process is most dramatically revealed in Algeria,[5] where at the end of the war for liberation, 800,000 colons quit the country within eight months, and Algerians had immediately to replace the departed administering and trading class. Of 450,000 jobs outside agriculture in the mid-1960s, 180,000 were filled by skilled and manual workers, white-collar workers, small entrepreneurs and executives in the urban economy; the rest went to the civil

*Nothing seemed too much for this group. In March 1968, during the war, the Association of Civil Servants called on the Nigerian Federal military government to shoulder direct responsibility for their motor-car advances instead of arranging them through private finance houses. This, as an irate correspondent pointed out to the *Sunday Post* (3 March 1968), when the government's estimates, drafted by these same civil servants, showed a period of national austerity.

service and the army. Apart from the 120,000 military – Algeria has one of the largest armies in the Third World with twelve soldiers to every 1,000 inhabitants – the administration recruited 150,000 new civil servants. In the Maghreb as a whole – however different the pronounced state policies of Algeria, Tunisia and Morocco – in the decade between 1955 and 1965, the number of manual and white-collar workers and artisans rose by only 30 per cent, whereas the number of executives and civil servants earning relatively high salaries multiplied six times. Side by side with this extraordinary inflation of administrators, important and petty alike, and all with privileged living standards, agricultural production in Algeria was dropping, urban unemployment rising and the number of productive jobs growing only imperceptibly. Samir Amin writes[6] that the most striking characteristic of the years in Algeria from 1963 onwards was the sharp rise in public expenditure despite the sudden drop in the level of the country's economic activity. Indeed, the fall of Ben Bella from power coincided with the most acute financial crisis.

In one independent state of Africa after another, there developed this vast and proliferating élite of administrators. Its appearance gave countries very different in their professed political purpose and commitment a common cast, for it was not the size of these administrative cohorts that was alone significant; it was that they battened on the state, and vigorously defended their right to do so, at a time when the resources of these states were needed for the more productive side of their economies, and the productive springs themselves, as Samir Amin calls them, were stagnating.

A few years after independence the state seems to be swallowing its own tail. Each year African governments spend more of their revenues on their own employees. The neutral phrases of the ECA reports[7] describe the steady growth of the 'public sector'; how central government revenues and expenditure each year account for a greater share of the gross domestic product. (The figures generally available relate to central government expenditure only, and not to regional or provincial governments as well, and so the picture is under-stated into the bargain.) Two items have come increasingly to dominate expenditures:

public debt repayments (which in the Congo, for instance, grew from 1·7 per cent in 1963 to 30·4 per cent in a handful of years) and recurrent administration. A close look at government budgets produces a hair-raising picture. Gérard Chaliand[8] has taken just such a close look. Senegal's budget for 1964–5 showed that just under half (47·2 per cent) of the total was absorbed by administrative salaries. A finance commission duly castigated itself, and called for a restructuring of the budget. Running costs, it pointed out, were greater than income; and, as a result, 'we have not been able to devote one franc for investment and we have had to resort to loans to finance the national plan'. But Senegal was no exception. In the Cameroun, administration swallowed 18,550 million CFA francs, and capital expenditure only 1,409 million. The official report on the budget assured the country that the expenditures were 'strictly necessary' for the 'normal' functioning of services.

In the Central African Republic, 81 per cent of the budget went on the civil service; and of that, 58 per cent on civil service salaries alone. In Congo-Brazzaville, the expenditure on government personnel rose 88·8 per cent in four years, to constitute 62 per cent of the budget. The population is 826,000; and on 1 January 1964, there were 10,931 state employees. One detailed set of figures may be cited, for the Ivory Coast. There, the civil service in 1964 comprised 28,314 persons, including army personnel.

Army	7,100
Education	7,405
Public health	3,510
Interior	3,082
Agriculture	2,500
Finance, economic affairs and planning	1,808
Public works	1,559
Justice	754
Ministry of Armed Forces	291
Foreign affairs	147
Presidency	66
Supreme Court	62
Ministry of State	30
	28,314

Omit the 6,000 servicemen and some 6,000 teachers not on the top salary scales, as well as certain other employees not usually classified as civil servants, and there remained 15,000 civil servants, or less than 0·5 per cent of the total population of 3,750,000 in the Ivory Coast. Yet between them, this 0·5 per cent absorbed 58 per cent of the budget. In Dahomey civil service salaries absorb 64·9 per cent of the budget. That country holds the record. As for Ghana, Guinea and Mali, those countries showed the same bureaucratic extravagance. In Guinea, administrative expenditure rose by 80 per cent between 1959 and 1962; in Mali, by 60 per cent; and there, salary structures inherited from the colonial era had hardly been altered.[9]

Chaliand's close look at budgets and trade balances produces yet another alarming set of figures characterizing these states as dominated by a small government-employed élite which lives in the style to which its French colonial predecessors were accustomed. In 1964, in the fourteen former French colonies, six times as much was spent in importing alcoholic drinks as in importing fertilizer. Half as much was spent on perfume and cosmetic imports as on machine tools. Almost as much went on importing petrol for privately owned cars as on the purchase of tractors; and five times as much on importing private cars as on agricultural equipment. The resources of the new states were being devoured by a tiny group whose demands distorted the budgets and the economies of the states they governed. It was René Dumont who commented that the cost of African presidential and ministerial establishments was probably higher, in relation to national income, than the cost to France of the Court of Louis XVI in 1788.[10]

In the Central African Republic, the budget report reflected smugly, if rather too soon, that

> the policy of *austerity* [my emphasis] is general in French-Africa, but while numerous countries have arrived at this state of affairs by the unfortunate road of revolution or coup d'état, it is very agreeable to see that in the CAR the national solidarity and political maturity of the population allows the government to reorientate in this way.

In that country, as in Dahomey and Upper Volta, it was the imposition of so-called 'austerity' measures that precipitated the strikes which brought those governments down and the army to power. The cry of 'austerity' was implausible, even insulting, from notoriously profligate politicians. Yet, significantly, the unions that led the strikes were composed largely of civil servants and other government employees, for these comprise the largest and best organized of those in wage employment, and while, beside the squandering of resources by the politician–businessmen, their wage and bonus demands could have been nothing but just, in the tug-of-war between politician–businessmen and the privileged administrative élite, the greatest proportion of the national income continued to be appropriated by parasitic and unproductive groups, oblivious to the needs of the common people and ranged against any real development policy.

BUREAUCRATS AGAINST POLITICIANS

The tug-of-war between different levels of the élite grew stronger as the experience of independence lengthened, and the politicians rapidly lost their grip. The speciousness and brevity of the independence struggle itself had endowed the political class that came to power with little moral authority. And as it squandered this along with the coffers, it opened itself to challenge and displacement by other competing groups within the élite. Such conflicts have not been fundamental, however, in the sense that different branches of the élite have had divergent policies for their country. The quarrel has been between 'ins' and 'outs' for the same prize, the control of power and patronage.

Élite competition has not always been the trigger, nor the single or central motive, for every army intervention; but in several it has played an important role in precipitating the collapse of a government and, after the military has acted, installing another. If competing élites have not always directly made a coup – because it takes a complex of factors to do so – they have generally taken advantage of it. For the 'outs' in the élite groups, coups become a swift way 'in' to power.

And, to be sure, the first generation of politicians had seen to it that there was virtually no other way to displace them. Among the élite groupings not accommodated by the political class in power were opposition politicians belonging to the generation of agitational independence politics. In addition, the large second-generation élite which consisted mainly of administrators often better educated and qualified than the men in office, saw the first-generation leaders as part of a closed corporation. *Les anciens* occupied the positions of real power. In Senegal, young civil servants talked of politics as 'a basket of crabs'.[11] They knew that dissent from the party leadership would mean the loss of their jobs. So they avoided politics, but returned, degrees in hand, expecting the best jobs and the fullest opportunities through the administration. In Upper Volta, there was the same criticism about *les anciens* in power. And when the coup came in January 1966, it seemed to have brought a significant number of the second generation élite to office. In Dahomey, the coup that forced Maga out of office and placed General Soglo in power was almost certainly engineered by a group of young second-generation élite in the government, trade unions and educational establishment. For three months, until Soglo withdrew from political power in January 1964, the government was dominated by a dozen or so second-generation technocrats. When Soglo re-emerged at the head of the Dahomeyan government in December 1965, there was a wholesale house-cleaning that again brought a group of young technocrats to the fore. The new Soglo government included two doctors, an engineer, the director of a public corporation, a former teacher, and administrators or technicians for the rest.[12]

With independence, the strategic command posts of the society had fallen to politics, and there, to the ruling party. The rewards of the successful politicians had been disproportionate to all others, including those of the technicians and the administrators. When the politicians fell, or were removed, the pivot swung from politics to administration as the principal point of entry to the power élite. The bureaucracy, civil service and army became the new road to power, and the administrators, in uniform or in tailored suits, the new power-bureaucrats.

Post argues[13] that the parties and politicians running the state are always threatened potentially, at times actually, by two corporate groups whose existence is determined only partially by social class. These are the bureaucrats and the army officers.

> In more developed class systems their class affiliations are clear; these are usually with the bourgeoisie, though in the case of army officers they may be with a landowner class. In West Africa classes are just forming. During the colonial period many sons of peasant farmers managed to get the education essential for entry into the bureaucracy or army. . . . The present senior bureaucrats are recruited not through the class system but by the state, through a relatively classless educational system. Their careers are based on their symbiotic relationship with the state. They share its power with the politicians, but the relationship is frequently an uneasy one. The bureaucrats and army officers are corporate groups in that they have their own sense of community, their own consciousness, their own values. . . . The power of the politicians lies with the party; that of the bureaucrats in their technical expertise in managing the state. . . .

The politician–businessmen in office were intent on rapid acquisition and the manipulation of political control for their patently personal economic ends; the soldiers and the administrators – and their counterparts in the managements of expatriate firms – persuaded themselves that they were the agents of rational 'development' and 'efficiency' in management. Civil servants have always nursed a deep resentment of the politicians. The politicians were the upstarts. The civil servants had a function to perform before the politicians entered the scene. They have expertise; the politicians generally do not. The politicians arrive in office talking about making a clean sweep (though they usually sweep anything but clean); civil servants were trained in attitudes that make adaptation and change unsettling. Ideology is rejected. Civil servants, drilled in the notion that political contest should be free and open, with the administration itself disinterested, were quick to accuse the politicians of defiling the neutrality of the service and its incumbents by using government for their own narrow ends. Like its imperial mentor before it, the African civil service develops a contempt for political movements. Its inherited mystique is that efficiency solves all problems; politics is a dirty game, and government would be better off without it.

The civil service does not act directly to seize state power. But once the military does that, it is the civil service that cossets the new regime in its shaky first hours and makes sure it survives. Dahomey and Upper Volta are the outstanding examples of coups triggered by the corporate interests of bureaucrats; and Togo, of a coup by soldiers acting directly in their own interest. But even where coups have not been immediately instigated by either of these corporate group interests, the two have merged very soon after the seizure of power. For while the invasion of government by the soldiers need not be precipitated directly by competition within the élite – any crisis can cause the coup d'état – in the actual rearrangement of the power structure caused by the coup, there is a shift in dominance, temporarily as in Ghana or more permanently as in the Congo, from the politician–businessmen of the power élite to the power bureaucrats.

It was, in fact, in the Congo that the conflict between these two mainstreams of the élite bureaucrats, the army included, rose earliest and swung the pendulum of power furthest into the hands of the power bureaucrats.

The pre-independence handing-over period was exceedingly brief, and the political parties had not time to build popular bases. The only Congolese party with a serious claim to national leadership, the MNC led by Lumumba, was overthrown by a conjunction of external and domestic forces before it could assert its hold on the state machinery. Perhaps the major internal cause of the Lumumba government's fall, indeed, was the challenge to the politicians, to the whole nascent political class, from lower ranks of the élite, the army and the Congolese clerks of the civil service.[14] When the Force Publique mutinied under strong Belgian-officer provocation, this was because it saw no immediate prospect of a share in the fruits of independence.[15]*

*According to Crawford Young, *Politics in the Congo* (Princeton, 1965), p. 315, a soldiers' petition said: 'There will be two branches of Congolese independence. First there will be . . . the class of the great Congolese leaders and their white counselors. These will benefit from all the advantages of the new independent state. . . . A second dishonoured wing, which will include the inferiors, the criers of "Vive Independence" will be and remain the servants of the first branch.'

It was the mutiny and the breakdown of the administration that gave the Belgians the pretext for their intervention and that undermined the authority of Lumumba and his government; had Lumumba been able to rally the army, and so possibly deal with the Katanga secession, there might have been no necessity to call in the United Nations. Without an effective army, the central government was impotent. A few months later, during the United Nations operation, and with the complicity of UN officials, the first military coup led by Mobutu swept the Lumumba government from power. In the subsequent period, the army did not rule directly, but it backed a government of commissioners drawn from the small university-educated elite. Government was conducted by *cabinet de coulisses*,[16] manoeuvring in aisles and back rooms. Apart from the foreign governments and companies, the major power-brokers in the Congo were the men who controlled the army, the police, the security services and 'other channels of communication with friendly foreign powers'.[17] The Binza group included Mobutu as head of the army, security police chief Nendaka, head of internal security Kandolo, Foreign Minister Justin Bomboko, and president of the National Bank, Albert Ndele. The group owed its effectiveness to a political situation where power derived from control of the key political resources in the central government structure at the capital. This, says Crawford Young, was an anonymous coalition, whose existence did not even become widely known until mid-1962, a year after it had started functioning.[18] After the 1964 crisis caused by the Eastern Province and Kwilu peasant rebellions, Tshombe was brought to power; but in the following year, Mobutu staged his second take-over, this time with carefully laid plans to build a political base for the army-run regime.

The swing from politics to bureaucracy-and-army as the centre of power is graphically illustrated in the careers sought by young educated Congolese. On the eve of independence, only three Congolese had reached the top level of the administrative hierarchy (there were 4,642 Belgians in those grades), and so there was a massive exodus of junior Congolese civil servants into politics. There were no outlets in the administration, and politics seemed the answer. Of 137 deputies in the 1960 assembly, sixty-six had been public employees; as had thirty-one of the eighty-four senators.[19] After 1960, the trend was sharply reversed. The university graduates, the best trained members of the younger generation, went not into politics, but into the bureaucracy. It was through the administration and not through the polls that the Congo's new political class was emerging. A certain fusion of interests had occurred between pre-independence politicians and the men running the administration; but the characteristic of post-1960 Congo politics is the rapid recruitment into the new power élite of petty officialdom. Its first instinct was to proliferate the administrative machinery. The number of provinces was increased from six to twenty-one: each with a government; its own administrative personnel; its administrative and political clients; and an assembly of around 700 members. In the urban centres there grew a commercial class born of speculation, inflation, administrative corruption and trafficking in licences for commodities. The new ruling class in the Congo contained, at the political level, some 1,500 important and profitable posts; some 11,000 high-ranking administrative posts, and nearly 100,000 middle ones; and, in the army, some 23,000 men, of whom less than 11,000 were privates or corporals.[20] The administration had been the guiding force in colonial days; once again the single most important source of power lay in the civil service, with the army behind it. Mobutu's second regime turned to reinforcing government at the centre and building a political base for the army through the Mouvement Populaire de la Revolution, organized along the lines of the mass independence parties.

THE DECLINE OF THE PARTIES

When the soldiers struck, what became of the parties?

Some of the independence parties achieved an impressive measure of popular support from the men of property and trade in the towns, from the articulate in the professions, from the lower ranks of the élite among the civil servants, including the teachers, from those newly arrived in the towns, whose voluntary associations maintained close links with their rural communities, and from local communities where the new politicians acted as intermediaries, rather like the political bosses among new immigrants to the United States in the nineteenth and early twentieth centuries.[21] The traders, especially, were formidable financial and political backers of the new parties, from the CPP, where the mammies of the market-places first helped install, and then topple Nkrumah, to the Ivory Coast where to this day the party headquarters are situated in the middle of the market, the heart of trading power.

The parties were not all alike. There were the élite parties that relied on an existing social élite, with chiefs and headmen prominent pillars of support. There were the mass parties which recruited on the basis of political commitment rather than of social status and which aimed to carry out not only a political transfer of power but a social revolution as well.[22] In Ghana there was a distinct shift of political dominance away from the older, more highly educated and better entrenched élite, to the 'veranda' boys of the CPP, the products of the primary rather than the secondary schools. There, as in Guinea and Mali, where the trader and rural bourgeosie was feeble, a younger outgrowth of the élite came to power. In Nigeria, on the other hand, and in the Sudan, traditional heads and traditional support formed an influential amalgam within the power élite. In Mali and Guinea, the trade unions were active in the independence parties; methods of mass campaigning and mass organization were developed; the parties acquired a more radical ideology; and union leaderships were well integrated into the party structures at independence. In Nigeria, by contrast, the parties of the new southern élites had lost their radical momentum even before they came to power. Shrewdly timed constitutional reforms focused political energies on competition by election, and diverted the popular mobilization that the unions were just beginning to achieve. Within the independence movement, the Zikist radical wing and trade-union militants were alike defeated in attempts to influence the shape of the political system that emerged through constitutional negotiation.[23]* There was a shift of political gravity from mass organization to regional assemblies built on communal constituencies, at the same time that the unions began to fragment and so recede in political influence. Of 425 MPs elected to the regional assemblies in 1951, only eight were trade-unionists. Eight years later, in the Federal Parliament of 312 MPs, there were only six. In the French colonies, skilful direction by the French government and their man in French West Africa, Félix Houphouet-Boigny, broke the back of the radical wing of the independence movement, except where it survived to comprise the governments in Guinea and Mali, and to some degree in Niger and the Cameroun. In the Ivory Coast, Houphouet-Boigny showed himself a master at embracing his radical opposition to suffocate it in the bosom of his party. Critics were invited into the Assembly or into government, and student unions that proved too difficult to buy were adeptly out-manoeuvred and displaced by government-approved bodies.[24]

In the transfer-of-power formula, the balance of old and new élites, the type of independence party – mass or élite – and the base of party support, differed from one state to another; but these distinctions faded into insignificance in the face of the military challenge, for the parties of all types had begun to atrophy with independence. There were several reasons.

The anti-colonial independence parties were built on the assumption that there was an interest and goal common to all colonial subjects, the élite and the common men alike. And so there was, up to a point. But few if any political leaders, of élites or commoners, identified the point at which, or the direction in which, interests diverged after independence.

The mass party had been built in the pre-independence period as the party of the potential nation: the nation would be realized through the unity and functioning of the party. The

* Mukwugo Okoye, the secretary-general of the Zikist movement, wrote of the 1949 Convention of the NCNC where Dr Azikiwe led the party's condemnation of the Zikists and ridiculed those who were political prisoners at the time: 'After preaching revolution for a decade he [Dr Azikiwe], a successful businessman and a man of pleasure, was terrified when he saw one.'

mass party and, after independence, the one-party state were created to strengthen the power of the newly liberated 'nation' or people. There had to be one united party; for party proliferation or opposition within the 'nation' was a source of weakness.[25] Thus the parties reconciled divergent standpoints in the common interest and goal of independence. Auxiliary organizations were built, of women, youth and of trade unions, but they had little autonomy to mobilize support in their own right.[26]* If the party declined in vigour and representativeness, its supporting bodies inevitably did so as well. Rooted in the notion that the party equalled the state, and the state the party, and that both expressed the will of the undifferentiated people, the mass party, and its successor the one-party state, presumed a high degree of clarity of political purpose, and a high level of consciousness and mobilization on the part of the 'people'. What ideology there was did not wear well, however, with the experience of independence. Membership of the party was elusive. It was a matter more of loyalty than of organization, a question of feeling an association rather than of holding a party card. Within the party, divergent social and economic interests developed; and it was hard to convince the rural poor and the urban unemployed that politicians and administrators in well-paid posts shared, or understood, their needs. It was not only that politicians waxed manifestly prosperous in office, but that they distorted the party to turn themselves into a new economic class.

The absence or incoherence of an independence ideology and development programme was the first major reason for the decline of the independence parties. The second was the shift of gravity from party organization to state, from the ways of popular mobilization to the methods of the administrator. When the party came to power, its leading cadres deserted it for government and other state jobs. The state asserted itself over the party, not the other way about. Once again, as in colonial days, bureaucratic methods dominated over the political. The

* In Mali, for instance, when the leader of the youth was dismissed from the party's leading committee after a disagreement within the party, the maximum age limit within the youth section was lowered, and the youth branches were brought under the direct political control of the party.

leader of the party became head of state. The committee of the party became the cabinet. Local party leaders were given key posts in local administration. The local party branch blurred indistinguishably with the local administration. Even when the intention was to avoid abandoning methods of popular mobilization, the party was so milked of its promising cadres for government roles that mobilization became virtually impossible. In office, the party could use state patronage as a substitute for organization, and a state decree, instead of promoting popular support. There were parties enough governing in the name of the people, but they did little or nothing to provide the people with the means of participation. On the whole government continued to function much as it had done during the colonial period, as a centralized and hierarchical system of administration.[27] Even in the states of maximum mobilization, where the party grew into a popular institution, it was nowhere really successfully transformed into an effective system of mobilization. Neither Guinea nor Mali had had much of a civil service, so the party emerged by default as almost the sole instrument of rule, responsible for many services normally within the sphere of the administration.[28] Even in Mali the huge network of party organization seemed to spend most of its time relaying directives from the centre; how effective it was at local mobilization it is difficult to say.[29] In Ghana the CPP ceased after some years to be a 'tangibly separate organization'; far from transforming Ghana it came to reflect all the cleavages in the country.[30]

Government and party thus drew weakness from one another. Government was centralized in the capital and fairly rudimentary in the provinces; likewise the party had a large head and under-developed limbs. Because political party, government and power élite were almost indistinguishable, a blow against the one was liable to bring down all three.

The apparent ease of the army coup in Africa must be seen in conjunction with the fragility of the power system. Physical take-over was all too easy. The government had all too few defences. Control of administration and party were centralized in the capital. Government was often concentrated in one man, the president, who was simultaneously head of state and leader of the party. Kidnap the president, or occupy the State House in his absence, as in Ghana, and you captured the state with little more than a single knock-out blow. The military strike for power – given minimum logistical planning and a united officer corps, or at least a sufficient section of the corps, behind the coup – was practically certain to succeed. Army officers would successfully displace the politicians. Their cousins, the civil servants, would manage the state for them. A new partnership of bureaucrats in and out of uniform, the power bureaucrats, would rule triumphant – until it came up full tilt against the complex factors which had triggered a crisis of government in the first place.

Part IV

The Failure of Politics

Many of Africa's new states entered independence, though nominally nation states, more divided than united. Conquest had resulted in the establishment of colonies within artificial boundaries, and diverse societies had been administered piece-meal without any national integrating political system. The test of independence politics was to rest largely on the attempt of the parties and the politicians to devise a unifying political purpose for their countries and peoples.

The Sudan entered independence carrying a double load of disunity. In the North and in the South, two systems of administration had been operated, with the one sealed off from the other. But North–South divisions apart, the Sudan throughout its history had been pawn to the conflict between Britain and the rising nationalism of Egypt. It owed its earlier-than-expected independence to events abroad, in Egypt, rather than at home; and in the years after independence as before them, Sudanese politics were buffeted by conflicting interests, not least those vested in divergent religious sects, which had been inherited from a clash between Egyptian and British – and, later, United States – influences in the Middle East. Little of any significance that happened in Sudanese politics did not have some root in that externally prompted conflict; and few of the political crises in the post-independence years were explicable without reference to it. When the army intervened in the political crisis and took over the government, it, too, acted in the shadow of the same conflict.

Nigeria, the largest state in Africa, was the best-publicized experiment in Western democracy on the continent. But the constitutional structure and political system installed by colonialism filtered all contests, electoral or other, into regional and, inevitably, ethnic or communal channels. When the political system collapsed under the strain of a particularly fierce struggle over the spoils of power, the ensuing conflict took violent communal forms, expressed ultimately in civil war.

In Ghana under Kwame Nkrumah, a policy was enunciated not only for Ghanaian, but for Pan-African unity; not only for the changes that political independence might bring, but for a radical change in the social system, with a commitment to build socialism. Here there was a post-independence strategy and ideology. Yet the regime was put to flight by a whiff of grapeshot in a soldiers' and policemen's coup d'état; and the strategy and the ideology were blamed by Nkrumah's critics for Ghana's 'collapse'.

Each case, sharply different and yet bearing resemblances in the sources of weakness, needs close scrutiny to detect wherein lay the failure of their politics, and the causes behind the intervention of the military.

The Sudan: Pawn of Two Powers

There must be some sort of general control over the soldiers or else they will land us in all sorts of trouble.
Lord Cromer to Lord Salisbury,
December 1898

After the Mahdist revolution, the army led by General Kitchener that marched in to conquer the Sudan was three-quarters Egyptian and mostly financed by Cairo, under Britain's prompting. After the reconquest itself, a formula was then devised for the government of the Sudan which preserved the fiction that Egypt's own had been restored to her, but which gave Britain actual control. This was the Condominium Agreement for joint sovereignty. The governor-general was assisted by officers in the

Egyptian army as provincial governors and inspectors; but since only junior administrative posts were available to them, Egyptians were denied any real share in the governing of the country.

The military cast of government and administration was one of the dominant characteristics of colonial policy in the Sudan. The other was the nightmare of Egypt. Nothing haunted British policy more assiduously than the fear that the nationalist fervour in the lower reaches of the Nile would travel, to incite 'premature' notions about self-government, and even independence, in the Sudan. For the first two decades, Britain grouped Egypt and the Sudan together as one country for administrative and financial reasons. But after the Egyptian revolution of 1919, it was decided to treat the Sudan as a separate and distinct administrative entity, and to wean her altogether from the Egyptian administration. It was also after 1919 that the administration, as though taking quarantine measures against a plague, cut the Southern provinces of the Sudan formally off from the North. The plan was to join the South with Uganda and Kenya, in a greater East-Central African system. The Sudan was nominally one territory, but it was administered as two. The governors of the three Southern provinces – Behar el Ghazel, Upper Nile and Equatoria – did not attend the annual meetings of the governors at Khartoum, but liaised with their opposite numbers in Uganda and Kenya.[1] The South was declared a closed area to all Northerners except government officials. Southerners were taught English, not Arabic, and were deliberately isolated from Arab and Islamic traditions. The region was thrown open to Christian missions, to establish spheres of influence for crusades among the pagans who, if they were not saved for Christ, would at least be lost to Allah. In 1946, the machine was put into reverse. But by then it was too late. When the Sudan became independent, it was as a country with South and North deeply different from one another. Britain's Southern policy had bequeathed a perpetual source of division.

It was the Egyptian revolution of 1919 that alerted Britain to the crucial strategic importance of the Sudan in the imperial management of Egypt. In a letter written a few months before the 1919 revolution burst its banks, Wingate wrote: 'As long as we hold the Sudan we hold the key to Egypt because we control the source of its water supply.'[2] The key was used in 1924, after the assassination in Cairo of Sir Lee Stack, general-in-chief of the Egyptian army and governor of the Sudan. Britain demanded that the Egyptian government withdraw all troops from the Sudan within twenty-four hours, and threatened reprisals, among them that the Sudan would unlimitedly increase the area to be irrigated from the Nile. Though the threat was over-ruled by the British government, it had already served to fortify obsessional but understandable Egyptian anxieties that Britain would go to any lengths in intimidating Egypt, even using the Sudan where necessary to cut off the supply of the vital Nile waters. It was during this crisis, when secret orders were being issued in the Sudan to the governors of provinces to evacuate all Egyptians, civil and military alike, that Egyptian army units resisted, and Sudanese army units mutinied in support. These were momentous times in the Sudan. The first Sudanese nationalist document, *The Claims of the Sudanese Nation*, had been written by Ali Abd al-Latif, a former Sudanese army officer of Dinka origin who had been dismissed from the army after a clash with an Egyptian officer. For this subversive document he had been sentenced to a year in prison. The White Flag League had been formed. Throughout the summer of 1924 it held political demonstrations. Cadets of the Military School, carrying their arms, marched through the streets of Khartoum. The most dangerous moment of the mutiny was the advance of men from the Sudanese 11th Battalion towards the Blue Nile bridge at the approach of the capital. A pitched battle ensued against British troops. But the Sudanese were thrown back when promised support, from Egyptian battalions stationed near by, did not materialize. This failure of the Egyptian troops to come to their aid had a traumatic effect on many of the Sudanese army officers, and on civilians, many of whom had been leading advocates of close cooperation with Egypt. Among those irreparably disillusioned was Abdallah Khalil, then a young officer and a member of the newly formed White Flag League, but subsequently one of the most suspicious and bitter opponents of

Egypt – a factor which played no small part in the military hand-over of 1958 that he master-minded.

The assassination of Stack gave Britain the pretext that it needed to exclude Egypt completely from the Sudanese administration and from any responsibility for the government of the Sudan. Britain had at last a free hand, if ever it had felt tied by the letter of the Condominium Agreement, to decide what was good for the Sudan and for British policy in Africa; what might be favourable to Egyptian interests was irrelevant. As for the Sudanese, they were not consulted, only administered; until, when the moment was judged apposite, some measured, short steps were permitted from advisory to legislative council.

Meanwhile, inside Egypt explosive discontents were soon to erupt in the 1952 revolution and an open confrontation with British imperialism. From 1945 onwards, Egypt presented demands to Britain for the evacuation of its forces from the Canal Zone, and for the 'unity of the Nile Valley' (Egypt and the Sudan together) under the Egyptian crown. In October 1946, the Sidky–Bevan Protocol set 1949 as the date for British troops to evacuate Egypt; but it also provided, in the event of war in the region, for joint defence arrangements which contained a clause on the Sudan so ambiguous that it promptly supplied a fresh source of conflict. Britain interpreted the protocol applying to the Sudan as providing for self-government and self-determination, and for only a symbolic association with Egypt. The Egyptians read the same thing to mean that the development of Sudanese interests would take place within the relationship of the Sudan and Egypt under the common crown, and interpreted this relationship between the two countries as a firm dynastic union. By 1951 relations with Britain had deteriorated so far that the Egyptian government unilaterally abrogated the 1936 Treaty and the Condominium Agreement itself, to proclaim King Farouk king of Egypt and the Sudan. By now, too, Egypt was on the brink of revolution. And it was at this time that United States and British policy on Egypt and the Sudanese question diverged dramatically and publicly. In the interests of a plan for an Allied Middle East Command, the United States was pressing Britain to make peace with Egypt on virtually any terms as long as the Canal was secured. Throughout May and June 1952, Eden records, 'at meetings and in despatches, we continued to be urged by the United States government to recognise King Farouk as King of the Sudan. . . . At one of these discussions I had to say bluntly that we could not keep the Egyptian government alive by feeding the Sudanese to them.'[3]

Britain's obligations were sharply divided between Foreign Office policy considerations and the pull of the Sudanese administrators. Whitehall alone might have acceded to American pressure and acquiesced in the Egyptian demand; but British administrators in the Sudan were implacably opposed to any union with Egypt. Added to the pull by this lobby of administrators in the field, Britain had a considerably more pessimistic – and accurate – assessment of the chances of rescuing the corrupt Egyptian regime. In July 1952, the seizure of power by Egypt's Free Officers Movement overtook Britain's dilemma, for Cairo rapidly negotiated an agreement for self-government directly with the Sudan's political parties. It introduced a three-year transitional period of self-government before independence, and laid down that the first national elections would be for a parliament which would decide on independence or a form of union with Egypt. Britain could no longer, single-handed, determine the basis of the Sudan's future. In this way, Sudanese independence was due directly to Egypt's own seizure of independence; but its form was still to be shaped by influences from both Egypt and Britain, for by now these contrary and conflicting associations had been built into the Sudan's own politics.

For years after the reconquest of the Sudan, Britain feared that the Mahdist movement, though defeated on the battlefield, would sweep the country once again. A safeguard which, if it had not been present, might have had to be invented for classic divide-and-rule purposes, was at hand. This was the existence, among the religious sects or *tariqa*,* of the Khatmiyya, led by

* On the *tariqa* Trimingham writes in: *Islam in the Sudan*: 'The basic idea underlying the existence of the Tariqas is the belief that the common man, to get salvation, needs the guidance of some person endowed with peculiar spiritual virtue who acts as intermediary between him and the deity. Therefore the heads of the tariqas are in exalted position, obeyed absolutely, and are not merely religious but social leaders of their people.'

the Mirghani family. Between the Khatmiyya and the Mahdists there was implacable rivalry. It was deeply rooted in history, and shrewdly manipulated by the administration.[4]

In the 1880s, when the cry of the Mahdi for a rising against foreign rule in the name of the true faith consolidated the Ansar (the followers of the Mahdi), the Khatmiyya and the Shaigia, a major tribe, far from supporting the forces of the Mahdi, co-operated with the Egyptian army against them.[5] The Mahdist state sent the Khatmiyya into eclipse. The reconquest restored them and brought home their head, Ali al-Mirghani, who re-entered the Sudan with Kitchener's forces. While the Ansar and the posthumous son of the Mahdi, Abd al-Rahman al-Mahdi, were kept under tight surveillance, the Khatmiyya were favoured, and their leader Ali al-Mirghani was honoured and promoted.

Then suddenly, with the First World War, Mahdist fortunes changed dramatically, as the needs of Allied strategy over-turned domestic policy in the Sudan. Turkey entered the war against the Allies with a cry to Muslims of the world to rise against their infidel oppressor. This called for a new look at the Mahdists, since they 'were the traditional enemies not only of the Turks, but also of the Egyptians . . . who were held guilty for bringing the British into the Sudan and wrecking the Mahdist regime. . . .' From a Mahdist point of view, therefore, a tactical alliance with the British authorities, who were in any case in control of both the Sudan and Egypt, was for the time being acceptable.[6]

Thus, in an ironic twist hard to equal even in the Sudan's experience of perverse alliances and expediencies, the Ansar, whose armies had martyred Gordon, were turned from Britain's fanatical adversaries into the most dependable allies and, in time, the most expectant wards. Sayed Abd al-Rahman al-Mahdi emerged from obscurity and a modest existence in Omdurman on a government pension of £5 per month to settle, at government initiative, at Aba in the Gezira, the birthplace and strong-point of Mahdism. There he gathered his followers about him in flourishing agricultural enterprises, became the wealthiest land-owner in the country and, the Khatmiyya feared, grew ambitious to be crowned king of the Sudan.[7] The Khatmiyya's deep emotional involvement with Egypt brought them into ever-increasing friction with Britain's policy of forcing apart the two countries of the Nile, while the interests of government and the Ansar coincided ever more closely, inevitably to increase rivalry between the Khatmiyya and the Ansar themselves.

The greater part of contemporary Sudanese political history turns on the axis of these two opposing sects and their opposite orientations. Political party moves and allegiances, seemingly inexplicable, were a mirror of their conflicts. In its turn, even the unity of the army command was rent by opposing sectarian allegiances. Every government of the traditional parties has had to come to terms with, or break under, the all-pervasive influence of the two major *tariqas*.

As the Sudan developed, the communities of the two major sects began to acquire economic interests and roles which further solidified differences between them. Sayed Abd al-Rahman al-Mahdi gathered the Ansar of his father around him on the spreading family estates, combining shrewd economic entrepreneurship with the organization of a tight network of committees that in time of need became a great private army. His support was drawn from the subsistence agricultural sector of the economy and from the tribes of the western Sudan and the south of the Blue Nile province. Organized still on a traditional basis, the tribal leaders were integrated into the administrative hierarchy of indirect rule, and became, through the tax collector, the staff of the native courts and the tribal authorities, the government of the countryside. The Khatmiyya, who drew their support from the Northern province and Kasala, were based mostly on the tribes along the Nile who were settled farmers and became, by contrast, first the village and later the town merchants. These were the first to become integrated in the modern sector of the economy, and who were accordingly first subject to the social ferment that this brought to the town-dwellers.

It was the towns that, as everywhere in Africa, were the birthplace of the independence movement. But, after the defeat of the joint army–civilian rising in 1924, it took time for a new political generation to grow. Disillusionment at Egypt's faltering role led to a long fallow period. Government promoted a system of indirect rule. Armed with Lugard's manuals, it began a search for 'lost tribes and vanished chiefs'.[8] Plans for training Sudanese administrators were thrown to the winds. The Military College was closed down, and the army was modelled on the West African field forces, where commissions were granted only to men promoted from the ranks. In the ten years following 1924, no new schools were opened. There was no national political organization, and no direct political action.

In February 1938 the Graduates' General Congress was founded. (Graduates were those who had completed studies at Gordon College or an intermediate school.) At first it occupied itself with social and educational affairs. The intention, declared a letter to the governor, 'was not in any way to embarrass the government . . . nor to pursue lines of activity incompatible with government policy. . . . Most of us are government officials, fully conscious of our obligations as such.'[9] But in 1947 the Graduates' Congress set out twelve post-war demands. The rebuke of the Civil Secretary, Sir Douglas Newbold, must be hard to equal in its brusque rejection of independence aspirations. Congress had forfeited the confidence of government by the very act of submitting the memorandum, he scolded. The memorandum was returned forthwith. The claim of the Congress to speak in the name of the Sudanese people was especially presumptuous; Congress had to realize that it was the duty and the business of the government alone to decide the pace of development. No sooner had Newbold snubbed the Congress than he was informed 'deviously'[10] that a delegation of 'moderates' craved an interview to prevent an impasse. He received and encouraged them.

Newbold's handling of the Graduates' Congress had important consequences. His blunt rejection of the claims by Congress to speak for the Sudanese drove political leaders to the easiest means of creating a mass movement, a call on the support of the religious *tariqas*.[11] The government tactic of opening private consultations with moderates caused a split into at least two distinct parties. In 1943 Ismail al-Azhari formed the Ashiqqa (Brothers); and the opposing side founded the Umma (Nation). The Ashiqqa had close connexions with the Khatmiyya, and the Umma with the Ansar, the second especially through the patronage of Sayed Abd al-Rahman al-Mahdi. The old dynastic rivalries and religious disputes were rejuvenated. The Graduates' Congress had been an attempt to create a non-sectarian nationalist movement and might have broken from the sects. It came to be racked on the identical issues and along almost the identical lines that divided them.

Through an Advisory Council and a Legislative Council, the government tried to counter the claims of the political groups. The Umma Party took part in elections; the Ashiqqa boycotted these bodies as mere talking shops. But though the Umma Party was inclined to cooperate with the administration in paced constitutional changes, that amity was severely jolted when Britain re-opened negotiations with Egypt over the Canal; it was apparent to the most pro-British groups that the Canal came before the Sudan. Fear of a deal between Britain and Egypt put the spur behind Umma pressures for self-government. Soon only the tribal chiefs in the Legislative Assembly were committed to continuing British overlordship. The Ashiqqa groups looked to Egypt as an ally to displace Britain. The Umma Party pressed for self-government as the first step to independence; its slogan was Sudan for the Sudanese.

New forces came forward to demand an all-party provisional government that would organize elections for a Sudanese Constituent Assembly independent of both Britain and Egypt. Chief among them was the Workers' Trade Union Federation. Organized labour in the Sudan was fired from the outset by a combination of trade-union and political demands.[12] The first conference of the Sudan Workers' Trade Union Federation held in 1951 demanded the immediate evacuation of all imperialist forces and self-determination for the Sudan. Out of this conference and this demand, rose the United Front for the Liberation of the Sudan. It comprised the Federation's affiliated unions, workers' committees and sections of the nationalist movement. Workers' clubs had been formed as far back as 1934 in Atbara and Khartoum. Then, during the war, when without supplies from the Sudan there would have been no Middle East war effort, the unions achieved a national and militant character. Between 1939 and 1953, the number of railway workers alone increased by 10,000 to 25,000. In 1946 the tenants of the Gezira scheme, the foundation of the Sudanese economy, went on strike, all 25,000 of them. On the railways, a management trying to improvise schemes for joint advisory committees found itself bombarded with petitions from workers demanding fully-fledged unions. Fobbed off by the railways management, the workers decided to operate over its head. Within a year, after illegal demonstrations and a strike lasting ten days – which spread from Atbara, the railwaymen's town and birthplace of the labour movement, to Khartoum and Port Sudan – and with the backing of both the political fronts, the railway workers had won recognition. The Sudan's trade unions were quick to draw the conclusion that militancy and strikes were the weapons to use, and that the place of the unions was alongside the political movements. By 1952 the Sudan Workers' Trade Union Federation was organizing peasant cultivators and the share-croppers of Gezira whose landlord was the government. By 1951 there were forty-one unions in existence, although wage-earners constituted only 2 per cent or less of the total population. and wage-earning was largely seasonal. The entry of the unions marked the beginning of popular politics in the Sudan, and gave the political movement new and hopeful dimensions, though it was some time before attempts were made to realize them.

Britain tried diluting pressures for immediate self-government by encouraging the Khatmiyya against the Ansar; and for a while there appeared a last refuge in a new Republican Socialist Party, composed mostly of tribal sheikhs and chiefs. But suddenly a Cairo agreement for self-government was a *fait accompli*, negotiated by Egypt directly with the Sudan's political parties.

In the first elections for a Parliament to decide on the shape of the future – independence or a link with Egypt – the National Unionist Party, which was a combination of the Ashiqqa and other pro-Egyptian unionist groups, emerged victorious with fifty-one of the ninety-seven seats in the lower house; and Ismail al-Azhari became the first prime minister. The Umma Party accused Egypt of interfering in the elections on the side of the NUP; the NUP counter-charged that Britain had interfered in the countryside on the side of the Umma Party. The Umma Party had for too long been too closely identified with the British administration to expect to win the elections; but no parliamentary convention could contain Umma chagrin at defeat, and its anxiety about Azhari's oft-proclaimed pro-Egyptian intentions. When, among other heads of state, General Neguib arrived in Khartoum for the opening of Parliament, some 40,000 Ansar arrived by train and steamer, on camels, horseback and on foot, armed with swords and broad-bladed spears, and waving the black-and-red flag of the Mahdia, to besiege the airport, the streets of the capital and the palace, so that Neguib might hear 'the voice of independence'. Rioting and street clashes forced the postponement of Parliament and the declaration of a state of emergency in Khartoum. This was not the first time the Umma Party had mobilized its private army to besiege the capital and intimidate the *avant-garde* of the towns into compliance with the outlook of the less advanced countryside.

Independence or a link with Egypt? This old battle issue looked like causing political explosion. The Ansar-threatened state of insurrection was a sharp portent of how far the Umma Party was prepared to go in sabotaging any association with Egypt. Yet already the old alternatives had an emaciated air about them. The call for unity with Egypt had been forged as the lever with which to displace British control; but now the lever had done its work, formally at least. The cry of 'the Sudan for the Sudanese' had been a Mahdist slogan, and highly suspect to those who saw it as a cover for continued British supervision; but when the country was self-governing, the slogan expressed the patriotic surge towards full independence. Azhari's formulations of his association-with-Egypt policy had, in any event, grown progressively less precise, in line with a general NUP inability or unwillingness to shape a consistent policy. To the educated in the towns; to the new radical forces of the trade unions and the Gezira tenants' committees; to those secular political forces that Azhari banked on so heavily for his authority, the advocacy of a link with Egypt was no longer necessary to assert the full independence of the Sudan. Azhari accordingly adapted his policy. By the time that the vote on the independence issue was taken in Parliament, there was unanimity in favour. The NUP and Umma Party voted together; and it was Azhari, formerly the leading advocate of Nile Valley unity, who emerged as the prime minister of the independent Sudan in 1956, after short-circuiting the procedural provisions laid down for a transitional period.

After decades of manipulation under contending masters, the about-face on the independence issue was necessary and inevitable. But the NUP could not easily survive the absence of a policy once the unifying issue of association with Egypt was gone; while Azhari's habit of switching policies and partners was to become endemic in his own behaviour, as in that of politicians generally, to make party political behaviour a bewildering series of contradictory and aimless postures in office. Splits in the NUP broke through the paper plastered over them at Cairo in 1952, and spread in several directions. Such splits were indicative of a growing decline in Azhari's prestige, and above all resulted from the total absence of a unifying policy for independence within the governing party or the country. This deficiency was underlined with great urgency by the outbreak in August 1955 of mutiny in the South, in the Equatoria Corps of the Sudan Defence Force.

Only in 1946 had the notion been abandoned of joining the South of the Sudan with East Africa. It was then in the interests of British policy to unite the two halves of the country and to stress the rights of self-determination for the whole Sudanese people, non-Arabs and non-Moslems included, as counter to the claims by Egypt that the peoples of the Nile Valley should unite. The South had long been indoctrinated, however, to believe that its future did not lie with the Arab North. When it knew that independence was coming, and saw what a paltry share of the British-relinquished civil service posts it was likely to get, there was a last desperate attempt to draw attention forcibly to its grievances. Northerners, principally traders and administrators, living in the South were massacred. The Azhari government retaliated by executing 300 of the army mutineers. Later in the year, when Parliament discussed the declaration of independence, it resolved that the claims of the South were to be given full consideration by the Constituent Assembly; but Southerners were never satisfied that this was done.

Meanwhile Azhari himself was becoming estranged from the leadership of the Khatmiyya sect. Despite his call for secular politics, said his critics, he behaved as though he were promoting a third neo-*tariqa*, with himself as leader and patron, and his followers as the faithful believers in his mission, vague as this was in the absence of any social, political or economic programme for the country. By mid-1956 Azhari had lost the premiership; and the patronage of the Khatmiyya was now bestowed on a new party, the Peoples' Democratic Party (the PDP), founded by Mirghani Hamza with the publicly declared support of Sayed Ali al-Mirghani.

The Sudan's next government was a grotesque expedient. The Umma Party, finding itself twenty-five seats short of an absolute majority, formed a coalition with the PDP. Between them these ill-suited partners, headed by Abdallah Khalil, ousted Azhari and what was left of the NUP after the formation of the new Khatmiyya-based party. No coalition could have been more anomalous at this time. The PDP looked to Egypt as the leader of the Arab world in the struggle against British policy in the Middle East. It turned further and further leftwards as Egypt's national revolution promoted the seizure of the Suez Canal, large-scale nationalization and Soviet aid and association. To the Umma Party, Egypt was anathema. The Umma association with Britain was intimate and cultivated. The PDP shadowed the nuances of Egyptian foreign policy. The Umma Party felt itself to be of the West, protected by the West's policy for the containment of Egypt. The PDP suspected the Umma Party of aiming to make Abd al-Rahman al-Mahdi life-president of the Sudan. The Umma Party was alert for every intrigue that might elevate the status of Ali al-Mirghani. Nothing brought this coalition together but their common rejection of Azhari and their ambition for office. Their partnership in government was locked in tension and complete incompatibility of policy. Indeed, the politicians grew nimble at making incompatibles sound plausible and necessary. But meanwhile the government could agree on only the most trivial issues. Ministers of one party ordained policies in their ministries that were challenged, reversed or nullified by their ministerial deputies of the coalition partner. When the political crisis arrived, security chiefs were given contradictory orders by Umma and PDP leaders, jointly responsible for government but tearing it apart in their conflict of purpose.

The crisis itself was precipitated by the Eisenhower doctrine. In 1957 the United States sent Vice-President Nixon on a goodwill tour of African countries. The day after successful negotiations in Ethiopia for American port facilities and an air base in exchange for American aid to the Ethiopian air force, Mr Nixon was in Khartoum, telling the Sudan's prime minister and foreign minister that United States aid under the Eisenhower doctrine was designed to strengthen the independence of new nations. Prime Minister Abdallah Khalil, according to the press reports of the day, made no firm commitment, but emphasized that the Sudan would welcome assistance as long as it placed no limit on Sudanese sovereignty.

Five months later, the United States' president's special assistant on Middle East problems, Mr James P. Richards, who was in the Middle East to give the Eisenhower doctrine a stronger push, announced that he had managed to give out $120 million – half of it in economic aid – which had already brought vast relief to countries of the area, 'especially those on the borders of the Soviet bloc, and *especially to responsible military men*' (my emphasis).[13]

The Suez invasion a year earlier had been intended to bring the Nasser regime to its knees. It had had entirely the opposite effect in Egypt and the Arab world. It ushered in the Iraq revolution and the union of Egypt and Syria. Those that joined the American crusade against Communism in exchange for aid were those regimes apprehensive of their own survival in the wave of enthusiasm for militant Nasserism. In the Lebanon, in July 1958, 5,000 U.S. marines landed, less perhaps for Lebanese reasons than as a warning against the coup d'état in Baghdad, where the Iraqi government had been overthrown for its pro-West policy.

The landing took place as the Sudanese Parliament was in the throes of an acrimonious debate over American aid to the Sudan. It did nothing to calm apprehensions. Nor did Parliament's knowledge that, even while it was debating the Aid Bill, the governments of the Sudan and the United States were engaged in correspondence about an agreement already signed. Furthermore, the prime minister and the Umma Party were known to be giving a sympathetic reception to US proposals for strategic facilities alongside the Red Sea.

Alone of all the countries in Africa and the Middle East pressed to receive the Eisenhower doctrine, the Sudan had expressed reservations. It had decided to postpone a decision 'pending further study'. But this study, and the argument raging around it, had been interrupted by a sudden sharp confrontation with Egypt over three border areas lying near the 22nd parallel, among them a large triangular area bounded on the east by the Red Sea and which included the fishing village of Halayib. (The dispute had its roots in the administrative arrangements of the Condominium.) Troop movements had taken place on both sides of the border, and the issue had been argued before the Security Council. This frontier dispute had dominated the elections which followed; and the ruling Umma–PDP coalition had again been returned. The NUP's defeat was attributed to the frontier dispute with Egypt; Sudanese–Egyptian relations had been rubbed raw once again.

In the new Cabinet, the Umma Party held the major portfolios. And barely a week after the new Cabinet had been sworn in, the Council of Ministers approved and signed an agreement for United States economic and technical aid to the Sudan.* The United States, said the Minister of Finance, had made it clear that the assistance was being extended to economically backward countries, to raise their standard of living as the best safeguard against the spread of international Communism. 'I believe that the agreement does not in any way conflict with the full freedom of our country, infringe its sovereignty, or bind it with any conditions.'

Yahia al Fadli led the opposition attack in Parliament. The

*The Sudan–United States of America Economics Development Co-operation Agreement (Ratification) Bill 1958.

Sudan, he said, had struggled to get its independence without being tied to any pacts or treaties. There were now two alternative courses: to join liberal countries in their struggle for the freedom of Africa; or to lose independence through 'imperialist tricks'. Imperialism was aware that the Sudan was the link between the African belt and the Middle East countries working for the liberation of Africa. The Eisenhower doctrine was meant to fill the vacuum in the Middle East after the disappearance of British and French influence. Had it not been for strong opposition even inside the Council of Ministers, the Sudan might have been prevailed upon to accept the Eisenhower doctrine under the same conditions as Jordan and the Lebanon. That battle lost, the attempt was now being made to bring United States influence in through another door.

Several attempts to adjourn the debate, and with it the Bill, were defeated. The fight went on in committee, with NUP speakers charging that the United States was hoping to find petrol, uranium and copper on the Red Sea coast; that the Americans were interested in the Sudan for its strategic importance; and that a motion during the previous Parliament for the recognition of Peoples' China had been rejected under American pressure. NUP efforts inside Parliament for the rejection of the Bill were followed by a move to stop the government from adjourning the House, on the grounds that this was a time of crisis in the Middle East. The motion for dissolution was passed, however, with a government spokesman felicitously assuring the country that alleged differences in the government were 'no such thing . . . but only a serious search for reality'.[14]

Search or not, the reality was that, while the PDP left it to the NUP to voice opposition, on such issues as US aid, in the House, it was operating an undeclared policy of non-cooperation in the Council of Ministers and in the ministries: breaking quorums; absenting itself from crucial government business; being party to government decisions one day and attacking them in the press on the next. The country was in a state of ferment, both because of the controversy over United States aid and because of the economic crisis. The reserves had dwindled to an all-time low, from £62 million to £8 million, and the country's adverse trade balance was mounting. The 1957 cotton crop had been a poor one and was as yet unsold in the world market, where cotton prices were falling. Severe exchange control and import restrictions had hit the townspeople and the trading classes, already fiercely disillusioned with the ineptitudes of politicians and parties, and especially with a Parliament dominated by career politicians, chiefs, merchants and former civil servants, which showed itself patently unable to tackle the country's financial crisis, but which nevertheless debated the raising of parliamentary salaries from £55 to £120 per month.[15]

By the time that Parliament adjourned, the crisis had spread to the streets. A strike of twenty-four unions, led by the Sudanese Trade Union Federation, brought about an almost total stoppage and the arrest of many demonstrators, including secondary-school pupils. A press conference called by the director of the American aid scheme had to be called off at the last minute for fear of demonstrations, and the American ambassador was mobbed in the street. As a security precaution, all demonstrations were banned. This was, at least, a reprieve for a police and security apparatus harassed by the contradictory orders that issued from the rival factions in government. A senior police officer recounted his dilemma.[16] 'The Prime Minister telephoned me on one occasion. "Why are you sitting at your desk while demonstrators are shouting at me in the streets?" he demanded. I had to reply, "My Minister [the Minister of Interior was the leader of the PDP] told me to stay in my office."'

Meanwhile, army security was known to be visiting regional commands to check on security in the provinces. The campaign against United States aid looked like the issue about to break the back of the crippled coalition. A frantic scuffle for party re-alignments began. Faced with a disintegrating Cabinet, the prime minister tried to prevail on the Speaker and the courts to postpone the reopening of Parliament; but on 11 November the Speaker announced that Parliament would reopen on 17 November. Then, once again, presumably, it would be locked in battle over United States aid, as well as the thorny negotiations with Egypt over the Nile waters, and the economic crisis by now further than ever from relief.

THE ARMY DIVIDED

The army had shown a deep rift a month before the first independence coalition government was formed. In June 1957, a report in *El Rai El Amm* shook the country. 'Arrest of High Officers Preparing Secret Organisation in the Army,' it said, and announced the arrest of thirty-four-year-old Major Abdel Kibaida Rahman of the Signal Corps, recently returned from a study course in England, whose secret activities in the army had been under the scrutiny of army headquarters for some time. Three days later, it was reported that six officers and four non-commissioned officers, as well as five students of the military college, were under arrest. Further arrests were expected within forty-eight hours, among them those of high-ranking colonels. The army command had in its possession a plan of action for seizing control of the army and then the government. A fortnight later, all those arrested were released, except for three officers and three military school cadets, accused of inciting a mutiny and using the army to stage a coup. These were brought to trial before a military court.

The prosecution charged a conspiracy to establish an army revolutionary council and a government of second-ranking politicians, since the first-rankers had disqualified themselves, by 1957, through their year-old independence record. The projected coup was described to the court. Three detachments were to have been used – one for the radio station, one to round up government ministers, and a third to arrest the head of government – after which a press conference would have been held, and contact made with foreign embassies. Administrative and police officers had allegedly promised to make key arrests. The leading members of the new Cabinet would have included Ahmed Kheir, the disaffected NUP leader, and Mirghani Hamza, a PDP minister. It had been planned to make Brigadier Abu Bakr, of the northern Shendi command, commander-in-chief in place of General Abboud.

Kibaida and Omar Khalafalla were sentenced to twenty years' imprisonment; Sergeant Mohammed al-Tayyib to fourteen years'; military college student Babiker Awad to ten years'; and two others to seven years' each. None of the men served his full term. Not long afterwards, the Sudan was taken over by a military junta, and this released the young coup-planners, as though the imprisonment of such was a corrective that army men in office preferred to do without. Two of the men involved in the Kibaida trial were subsequently involved in a later coup attempt, one of three internal army convulsions under the Sudan's military regime.

The Sudanese army was thus split even before the junta took power. The divisions in the army corresponded closely with political, sect and community divisions in the Sudan. The junior and middle officers identified vigorously not only with the nationalist aspirations of the young men in the towns disgusted at the antics of the politicians, but also with Egypt's Free Officers, who had made the independence revolution in their country. The army command – then – had identified with the politicians in power.

Nigeria: The Juicy Morsel

As I stood in one corner of that vast tumult waiting for the arrival of the Minister I felt intense bitterness welling up in my heart. Here were silly, ignorant villagers dancing themselves lame and waiting to blow off their gunpowder in honour of one of those who had started the country off down the slopes of inflation. I wished for a miracle, for a voice of thunder, to hush this ridiculous festival and tell the poor contemptible people one or two truths. But of course it would be quite useless. They were not only ignorant but cynical. Tell them that this man had used his position to enrich himself and they would ask you – as my father did – if you thought that a sensible man would spit out the juicy morsel that good fortune had placed in his mouth.
Chinua Achebe, *A Man of the People*

When, in 1914, Nigeria was constituted a single political unit, the only bond of political unity was the person of Lugard, the governor-general. The only occasions on which the higher officials of two separate bureaucracies, one in the North, and the other in the South, could meet was at the annual session of the

Legislative Council in Lagos. For all the formal act of unification, Nigeria was still run as two colonies. Two distinct administrative centres of power were built: one in Kaduna, the other in Lagos. A frequently heard quip was that if all the Africans were to leave Nigeria, the Southern and Northern administrations could go to war.[1] In administration, in land policy, in a dozen different fields of colonial government, the administration reinforced not the unity of the colony, but the differences between North and South. For a quarter of a century, from 1922 to 1947, there was no representative political structure of any sort that brought the regions together.

In the North, the colonial administration took over intact the system of centralized political power and patronage presided over by the emirs, and used it to rule and collect taxes. In return for helping the British to keep order, the Northern ruling group retained its privileges and was insulated from unsettling influences. In the development of a cash economy and the production of crops for export, the North limped far behind the rest of the country. Social change and Western education came last and least to the North. It was the last region to train its own civil service. Until the 1950s, the North had no vocal and aggrieved educated group; the first, and for some years the only, educated Northerners were the sons of titled families and high-ranking officials whose place in the social hierarchy was assured. Commoners, or *talakawa*, seemed inert under the heavy weight of dynastic, religious and economic overlordship. Rulers were born to wealth, and the ruled to subservience.

Government worked through the Native Authority system, which was embedded in the rigidly stratified social system. And when politics at last started in the North, the traditional elements of authority, government and party were virtually indistinguishable. Of the Northern Peoples Congress (NPC) representatives who sat in the 1959 Federal House of Representatives, one in five was the son of a ruling emir; one in ten was a district administrative head; and seven in ten were Native Authority councillors and officials.[2] When an opposition party did develop (the Northern Elements Progressive Union, known as NEPU), its leadership was drawn from the lower strata in the society:

traders, small farmers and independent craftsmen like tailors, butchers, dyers and tanners.[3] But because government and party were impossible to disentangle, opposition to the NPC was construed as opposition to the Native Authorities, to the traditional social system, and to establishment Islam itself. There were, in any event, decided economic advantages in supporting the system and the party in power. Emirs, chiefs, district heads, Native Authority councillors, regional and federal legislators were the men who dominated the provincial loan boards and the Northern Nigerian Development Board. Credit followed the flag.

The North started to manipulate politics for business later than the South, because an already entrenched leadership, with traditional sources of wealth and patronage, assumed power. Yet it took only a few years for the familiar process, of manipulating government and politics for economic ends, to unfold. The probe into the Northern spoils system ordered after the January coup[4] disclosed how the traditional aristocracy was beginning to build a new economic base in large modern farms, contracting and real estate. A scrutiny of thirty-nine investment and loan projects of the Northern Nigeria Development Corporation showed that the biggest borrowers had been the big men of the government; and that a word from a minister, above all from the Northern premier, had been enough to over-ride the law and the decisions of the Board.

In the South, the colonial administration had made a futile attempt to impose indirect rule; but traditional authority, status and wealth had been overtaken by and integrated with new forces, thrown up by trade and business, economic and social ferment. New classes of entrepreneurs had arisen; of cocoa and rubber farmers, and growers of other export crops; of produce-buyers, traders, lorry-owners, money-lenders. Side by side with them had emerged the clerks, the artisans and the labourers in the employ of the large export-houses, government, transport and trade. Each year thousands of school-leavers besieged the labour market, in the main unsuccessfully; and these young men, led by the thrustful middle classes of trade and the professions – especially the lawyers in Lagos and the Southern towns, groomed in the manners of British law and politics – put the steam behind a rising Southern demand for entry to the political kingdom.

The political parties of the South were built by the aggressive new men of education and money-making. First on the scene was the NCNC. Led by Nmandi Azikiwe, the party dominated Southern politics in both East and West until 1951 and the rise of the Action Group, led by Chief Obafemi Awolowo. Elections were in the offing that year, and there was a prospect of power in the West for a party that could capture the political initiative from the NCNC. The Action Group capitalized on the alliance – already promoted in the pan-Yoruba cultural movement, or Egbe Omo Odudwa – between the traditional leadership of the Obas and chiefs, and the business, professional and educated classes. The leadership of the two Southern parties rose from the same springs of business and professional activity.[5]

In the post-war period, buoyant prices for export crops accelerated enormously the expansion of the farming, trading and business class. Marketing boards, set up to sell export crops at higher prices than those paid to the producer, spawned shoals of new African agents and produce-buyers. The boards also accumulated handsome surpluses which, in 1954, were distributed among the three regional marketing boards, according to the principle of derivation. It was these regional marketing boards that provided the funds for the party in office to dispense patronage and so reinforce itself in power, to manipulate government resources for the benefit of its own political class. Banks were established to break the expatriate monopoly on banking, and development corporations and loan boards set up to supply government capital for development projects in the region. The first hue and cry over the spoils system was raised about the activities, in the Eastern Region, of Dr Azikiwe, the African Continental Bank and the financial and business empire on which the NCNC was built.[6] A government commission laid bare the Nigerian mixture of primitive accumulation and Tammany Hall activity. Not many years later the same pattern was revealed in the Western Region.[7] 'The parties were part of rival business and financial structures which existed to make money for the individuals concerned, and to provide backing for the parties,' wrote Ken Post.[8] The politicians of each region were entrenching themselves by the acquisition of economic interests. At the same time, the political parties that spawned these politicians were consolidating the political control that they had won in their respective regions, and using it to finance their next bids for power, at the centre.

Successive colonial constitutions devised for Nigeria entrenched political power on regional lines. By 1952, there was an NPC government in the North, an Action government in the West, and an NCNC government in the East. In the boom of the 1950s, regional political power was being fortified by economic engagement: largest and most prosperous in the West; catching up fast in the East; and growing more slowly in the North, but embedded there in the traditional social order. Government in Nigeria rested on a tripod of three regions, with the legs of uneven length and fashioning. The time was approaching when a more solid support had to be provided. What was the design to be? From 1951 to 1958 Britain had allowed the Northern demand for half the seats in the Federal House. The 1958 Constitutional Conference rocked this pre-independence balance of control between South and North. With Nigeria about to be launched towards independence, the old British pledge to 'protect' the North – and use it as ballast for conservatism in the old state – had to be honoured. The Federal Parliament, it was laid down, would be elected on the basis of the population figures. The North, with over half Nigeria's population, was thus guaranteed cast-iron political domination of the country.

Thus, at the time of independence, two heirs shared the estate, but they were unequally treated in the will. The favoured child was the traditional ruling oligarchy of the North; the less favoured, the Southern business-political class. The constitutional allocation of power, as Sklar has pointed out,[9] weighted political control in favour of the numerically preponderant, more backward North; in favour of the rural, tied peasantry, as against the urban wage-earners. The region that had achieved self-government last, and had even tried to hold back the date of independence, emerged as the controlling force of the most populous independent state in Africa.

This major divide between South and North – the first, commercially competitive and beginning to industrialize; the second, under the control of an agrarian oligarchy – looked like possessing the potential of an American civil war. But the ultimate contradiction implicit in the economic cleavage did not become determinant in Nigerian politics. The North–South antagonism glimmered and flared, subsided and flamed again from time to time; but the polarities did not remain constant. East, West and North threw up fresh combinations and conflicts. When the political system broke down altogether over the sharing of spoils, and when civil war finally came, it was not between North and South, but followed a different line-up of forces. This line-up may well have looked unlikely from the pre-independence viewpoint; but it developed with cruel logic across six years, in which the political classes of the three regions ground the faces of their competitors in order to get control of the Federation.

From 1958, when the North's electoral dominance was written into the Federal constitution, economic power also swung from the regions to the central government.[10] Buoyant market prices had built regional prosperity; but falling prices for exports, and the rapacity of the political class, began to drain regional reserves and force the regions themselves to turn for aid to the centre. A new banking act gave the Federal government control over the operation of the regional marketing boards, and, through them, the financial policies of the regional governments. The Six Year Development Plan for 1962–8 placed the main initiative for economic growth with the Federal government. The system of revenue distribution to the regions was governed by formulae devised at the centre. And the North controlled the centre.

Faced with the problem of how to operate within a federal system which the North could dominate even when they combined, the Southern parties and politicians were reduced to one of two courses. They could campaign in the North to try and break the NPC monolith, or they could combine with it in the exercise of power. Both courses were tried by one or other of the Southern parties, in a bewildering and wilful round of political compromise, shifting allegiance and incompatible coalitions. Nigerian politics came to be consistent only in inconsistency.

The first engagement in the struggle for control of the political centre and, with it, for sources of national profit and patronage, was fought in the second Federal election of 1959. Both the Action Group and the NCNC subsidized minority parties in the North. The Action Group and the NEPU between them won just under a sixth of the Northern seats from the NPC. This meant that while the NPC was still the largest party, it had to combine with one of the Southern parties to form an effective government: unless, that is, a Southern coalition crystallized. Tortuous and double-dealing negotiations ensued. The NCNC, the oldest independence movement, was determined to achieve a share of federal power, whatever the cost. The Action Group approached the NCNC with proposals for an alliance; but, Dr Azikiwe learned, the same offer had been made to the NPC.[11]* Relations between the Action Group and the NCNC, as between the Western and Eastern political classes, had been strained in early clashes over the control of the political movement, and in the competition for vantage points in the Federal civil service and the economy. In any event, it was obvious to the NCNC that a coalition which included the NPC would be best favoured by the Colonial Office; indeed, as soon as the election results showed that no party had secured an overall majority, the governor had called on Sir Abubakar Tafawa Balewa, the leader of the NPC as the largest party, to form the government. Dr Azikiwe decided, therefore, on an NCNC alliance with the NPC, in a display of opportunism that set a precedent for all Nigerian politics.

Reduced to devising a strategy for effective opposition that promised some real prospect of power, Chief Awolowo switched from a policy of welfare statism to 'democratic socialism'; and the Action Group bent harder to the task, begun in the North

* In *Nigerian Government and Politics*, John P. Mackintosh *et al.* said that some years later Chief Awolowo claimed that that Action Group deputation to the Sardauna had gone without his knowledge.

with the challenge to the NPC in the Federal election, of appealing across regional barriers to the dispossessed of any region or community. This made Awolowo the target not only of both partners in the Federal government, since he campaigned for minority states in both their territorial preserves, but also of the conservative business elements within his own party, which were led by Chief Akintola, the deputy leader. The Akintola group's policy was directed to a settlement with the Federal government based on the old principle of regional security, which meant a tacit agreement that each party would be left to control its own region undisturbed. Akintola calculated on Balewa's acceptance of a national triangular coalition on this basis. Such a pact could, however, have allowed no room for Awolowo himself, and certainly not in the role he coveted as premier of the Federation. The split inside the Action Group widened with deepening ideological (the Akintola group was alienated by all the talk of democratic socialism), internal party and personal disputes. At the party's annual conference in 1962, a majority of official posts went to Awolowo supporters, and his policies prevailed.

The conflict was suddenly carried dramatically from party to government. The Awolowo wing appointed a leader of the Western Assembly in place of Akintola. The first meeting of the House ended in disorder when an Akintola supporter jumped on a table to shout 'There is fire on the mountain'. Police arrived with 'a fine impartiality in using tear gas to clear the whole Chamber rather than remove the disorderly elements'.[12] The Federal government immediately declared a state of emergency and imposed its own Administrator and emergency rule on the region. By the end of this period, the Awolowo group was in restriction, and the Akintola group, swollen by fair-weather elements of the party as well as by NCNC MPs who crossed when Akintola conceded them several ministries, was in office. A minority government was installed in the region: without elections; and virtually by parliamentary coup, with the collusion of the Federal government. And this minority government now settled down to dismantle the structure of Action Group power in the West. The Coker Commission probed the complex Action

Group business and political network, though the Akintola group, once in power, proceeded to use politics for business in an even more flagrant way.

Next spectacular development in the region was the treason trial against Awolowo and other Action Group leaders, on a charge of plotting to overthrow the Federal government. Awolowo, it was alleged, had lost confidence in elections and had set up within the party an inner Tactical Committee to train men in Ghana and import arms from there. The plot was to take Lagos at two o'clock one morning, with a few pistols and torches, and without any supporting action in the region. Was it an Action Group plot; or one improvised by a small group in the party? The defence argued that although military preparations had, indeed, been undertaken, this had been for self-defence against the strong-arm methods of the Akintola government. After a nine-month trial, in which most of the incriminating evidence came from accomplices turned state's witness, all but four of the twenty-five accused were found guilty. Awolowo's ten-year prison sentence proved to be not the prevention of political violence in the West, but its provocation.

Constitutionalism, the idol of the independence generation of politicians, cracked on its pedestal only two years after the inauguration of independence, when the Federal government used its control of the centre to crush an opposition regional government. A state of emergency was arbitrarily imposed though no emergency existed. And when, a few years later, again in the West, an emergency did, patently, exist, the Federal government refused to invoke its constitutional powers against the minority government that was its political ally, even though that government had been reduced to rule by open violence.

In the North, in fact, the NPC was having to call in the army to subdue its own turbulent opposition. The independence constitution had been a majority party settlement, based on the hegemony of the Fulani-Hausa of the North, the Ibo of the East and the Yoruba of the West. In each region, there were minority peoples in opposition to the main parties; but between them, the dominant parties and the Colonial Office had contrived to brush their claims aside. In the North, of course, NPC power was entrenched through the administration. But it never carried with it the Tiv people of the Middle Belt, who clamoured for a separate state. Their United Middle Belt Congress, led by Joseph Tarka, fought elections in alliance with the Action Group and won local landslide victories. The NPC used its control of the regional ministries and the Native Authorities to cut Tiv country off from amenities; to drag opponents through the courts on trumped-up charges; to dismiss UMBC supporters from employment and to bar them from trade. In 1960 there was a 'collective paroxysm of anger',[13] during which armed groups took part in mass arson, and the army had to be used. In 1964 there was an even more serious rising, which the army just managed to quell. Tiv power came into its own only after the collapse of the Federal government, in the wake of the 1966 coup. The two large-scale army interventions in Tiv country, with the rapid decline into chaos of government in the West, were crucial flashpoints for the young officers' coup of 1966.

In the first set of Federal elections of 1959, 'there was no conflict of principles, nor were there any rules of the game'.[14] New-style politicians of the South (in the NCNC) elected to go into partnership with old-style rulers of the North. Differences between them were reconcilable in the interests of sharing power. The next major battle for power at the centre was fought out during the 1964 Federal elections; principles and rules were, again, not discernible; but antagonisms created in the struggle for power now caused a deep crisis of government at the centre.

The NCNC had gone into coalition with the NPC to assert what it had hoped were its superior political and business talents over the 'backward' North. Instead, it found itself outmanoeuvred all along the line. By 1964, indeed, it was in danger of being displaced as a coalition partner by Akintola's government in the West, which the NCNC, ironically, as the NPC's partner at the centre, had helped install by parliamentary coup. When the Western section of the NCNC party organization split off to join Akintola and help him form a new party, the Nigerian National Democratic Party or NNDP, the NPC had found its new federal ally. By the time that the election approached, therefore, the NPC–NCNC coalition was in shreds.

The lines for battle were drawn in the quarrel over the census. The great hope of the South was that it had outstripped the North in population and would automatically get a larger share of the seats in Parliament. The preliminary returns showed exactly this. But a recount, after a storm of accusations about inflated figures, gave the North the same share of the total population as in 1952. It also showed in all regions a population increase so great as to defy biological possibilities, for this time all the regions had inflated their figures! The NCNC called for yet another census. The NPC rejected the demand flatly, and was supported by the NNDP.

Two new alliances formed for the fight over the constituencies. On the one side, there was the NPC with the NNDP and some minor Southern parties, in the Nigerian National Alliance (NNA); on the other, the United Progressive Grand Alliance, or UPGA, composed of the NCNC, the Action Group and the opposition parties of the North, NEPU and the UMBC. A few months of campaigning drained UPGA of any confidence that it could win, a slight enough eventuality in the first place, in view of the grip that the NPC held on the Northern constituencies, and its vigorous intimidation of opposition candidates.[15] In the West elections were fought in what was a state of incipient civil war, with thugs hired by both sides and mounting casualty lists. Beaten back from one constituency after another in the North, and charging bias and improper pressure against its candidates in the West, UPGA called for a postponement of the election. UPGA's lawyers and politicians had hit on a stratagem which they thought would hand them the initiative: if elections were postponed, they reasoned, there would be no lawfully constituted Parliament; and the president, Dr Azikiwe, the last repository of NCNC power at the centre, could assume executive powers in place of the premier, a Northerner.

The UPGA boycott of the elections, announced as the country was already going to the polls, swept a huge majority into the hands of the NNA, and threw the next move to Dr Azikiwe. He had prepared a dawn broadcast that throbbed with vibrant martyred phrases. 'The independence of Nigeria was like a flame that consumed my political ambition. . . . I would rather resign, than call upon any person to form a government. . . . This should release my conscience from the chains of power politics. . . .' The text of the speech was released to the press, but Azikiwe never delivered it; his nerve failed in characteristic fashion during the five-day deadlock that ensued. In the end he announced his decision to reappoint Balewa as prime minister after all – 'in the interests of national unity'. State House in Lagos had been the scene of an attempt by the UPGA leaders to get the heads of the army, the navy and the police to concede their constitutional allegiance to the president, and not to the prime minister. The army declined; its view of its constitutional position was strongly influenced by British High Commission advice. When this constitutional stratagem to use the army failed, Azikiwe's resolve melted, and he called in the police to protect him from his own supporters: UPGA leaders, and the Lagos populace, and not least the principal spirits behind the general strike of a few months earlier, who were incensed by this ignominious retreat from the planned trial of strength. Criticism of the policies pursued by Azikiwe's generation of politicians rumbled among the younger radicals of the South, but it found no organized form. As for UPGA, it had been roundly defeated twice over; in farcical elections; and in a devious legal stratagem, which had tried to manipulate the constitution, but had taken good care not to defy it. For the UPGA politicians had considerable stakes to secure: they were not eager to share Awolowo's sojourn in prison, and there were always fresh rounds of political bargaining in the offing.

Only on one occasion, not long before the Federal election, had the initiative been taken from the quarrelling political class and been given to the urban masses. This was the occasion of the general strike, in June 1964. The government had set up a commission to review wages; but when months went by and no recommendations were announced, various small and previously disunited unions set up the Joint Action Committee and called a general strike. More than a wage strike, this was a symptom of the popular discontent in the towns with the politicians and the political system, and the growing frustration among workers and the unemployed. The Six Year Plan had been launched with a warning to the unions that wages would have to be blocked in favour of profits and investments. 'Our Six Year Plan,' the unions charged, 'cannot plan for imperialistic expatriates, for the Ministers, for the police and the army, for the parasitic élite, and leave out the major producers of the national wealth.' In the end, the government promised to reopen wage negotiations, and the strike was called off. But the workers went back to work without clear gains. The streets were emptied of the demonstrations and the picket lines, but not before Nigeria had been given a fleeting view of a force that asserted itself across regional, ethnic and party barriers. After the strike government and employers were quick to exploit differences between the various unions and union federations, lest this force seize the initiative again. The strike had been spectacular in the history of West African political activity; but its impact was short-lived, and the unions did not take long to lapse again into division and rivalry, while the political parties continued their scramble for vantage points in the system.

A final round remained to be played in the electoral struggle for power. To the West, in October 1965, came the election that ended all Nigerian elections. The Akintola government had used its years in office to destroy the apparatus of Action Group support, and build its own. Chiefs, officials in local government, contractors, business and professional men realized that their livelihoods lay with the patronage dispensed by the party in power; and the toppling of one spoils system had, of course, made room for newcomers. Yet the Action Group remained the party of majority support in the West. This was a time of falling cocoa prices and depressed conditions for farmers. Big men in the villages had crossed to the side of the NNDP, but small men were being squeezed. They pinned their hopes on the next round of elections. This would settle the issue between the parties once and for all. If Akintola's group had to submit to the popular vote, he would not for long remain in office. But elections in the West were marked by the use of blatant and unrestrained thuggery and ingenious trickery. Electoral officers were snatched away before opposition candidates could lodge their nomination papers. Ballot boxes were stuffed with ballot forms that had been distributed to supporters days before the election. Ditches were dug round towns so that the supporters of opposition candidates could not approach the polling stations. In one constituency, an Action Group candidate won the seat; but as his supporters were celebrating victory, they heard a broadcast announcement in which the polling figures of the two candidates had been reversed. The Action Group won fifteen seats out of eighty-eight.

As the full impact of the election was felt, the region seemed to be holding its breath. The NNDP had been keeping an important decision in reverse until the election was over; now it could no longer be withheld. There was to be a substantial reduction in the price paid to cocoa farmers. This news on top of the election fraud pushed the countryside into open revolt. The farmers attacked the big men who had sided with the ruling clique of the NNDP, hounded them from the area, burned their crops, their property and their persons. ('Oba Roasted' said the newspaper headlines.) Telephone wires were disconnected, roads blockaded, taxis prohibited from plying the streets, markets and motorparks boycotted or shut down. One town after another in the West set up road-blocks, manned by Action Group or UPGA supporters, to prevent NNDP politicians from returning with force to intimidate communities that had shown opposition sympathies. The police and the army were brought in to put down the revolt. The security operation terrorized the peasantry to the point of gravely disrupting the harvest and the marketing system. As for government, it had virtually disintegrated. What had begun as political violence to defeat a rival party in elections had grown into a lawlessness uncontrolled and uncontainable.

Nowhere outside the West did the political crisis reach such a total breakdown of civil government; but throughout Nigeria there was a profound disgust with politicians and politics. In the towns, there was a groundswell of popular discontent. Labourer and young professional were equally disillusioned with independence. In six years, Nigeria's political class had staggered drunkenly through a series of crises, each more damaging than the last, using ballot box, parliamentary speech, bribery, nepotism and, where required, thuggery, in the struggle for power. In the beginning, they had been obsessed with constitutional form and legal nicety; then, when occasion demanded, they had scrapped them outright. Burdened with a constitutional form that was faulty and unworkable, the political class had strained it to snapping point. No amount of rearranging could restore the form, only a fundamental reappraisal of national needs, and a different generation of political leaders to try to meet them. But national needs were the last thing that the politicians considered. They built a mass following to win elections, then abandoned their electorates as they devoted themselves to their bank balances and their businesses. Corruption was not back-door and furtive, but flaunted. Big men, men of power, lived on an extravagant scale. For a while, their communities enjoyed the reflected glory and whatever amenities their big men secured for them. But six years of fiddling the coffers to subsidize big men and their parties for the contest of power had wasted the country's economic resources, and the general benefits were drying up even in the favoured areas.

At the bottom of the Nigerian political crisis was the quarrel over spoils. And this took place at two levels. The first was the rivalry of the regions, which competed against each other for a larger share of the federal revenue, and of the export trade; over the location of industries and the allocations of development capital. Federal politics had turned out to be the politics of Northern domination; Federal economics turned out to be the economics of Northern development. In the Six Year Development Plan, 'the bulk of Federal development spending is being concentrated in the North'.[16] When it came to the proposed iron and steel industry for Nigeria, the whole project was held up because the North would not agree to site it in the East, the location recommended by a feasibility study. In the end, three plants were proposed; one for the North, another for the East, and a third one for the West. None has yet been built.

On the second level of the quarrel, there was competition – often called tribalism – for jobs, for promotion, for vice-chancellorships of universities and chairmanships of corporations.

In the beginning, the competition was fought out between Westerners (the Yoruba) and Easterners (mainly the Ibo) in the Southern labour market, professions and public service. Nigerianization and the departure of expatriate officials produced a great spate of openings, but also fierce squabbles.[17] The years just before independence had been boom years; but when commodity prices, especially that of cocoa, began to fall on the world market, and foreign capital did not arrive in the quantities anticipated, the supply of jobs began to dry up, and the élites, the school-leavers, the unemployed and the newcomers to the towns fought desperately for what there was. By the early 1960s, urban unemployment in the South was almost 30 per cent; one in ten of the pupils who held a secondary-school certificate could not find work; and it was estimated that by 1968 there would be 1,000 unemployed university graduates in the area.[18] Northerners, once insulated in their own system, began to assert their claims to the plums in Federal government and employment. Three streams of competitors – excluding minority groups, which were permitted no distinct identity – used their political and community leverage to promote their own interests.

A job affected more than the applicant and his immediate family. Each post, especially the higher ones, benefited a host of kinsmen, a local community, a region. A dispute over a university vice-chancellorship in Lagos, or Ibadan, became an inter-racial dispute. Politics were organized on a regional basis, and politics contrived economic opportunities. Even when the connexion was not so intimate, the habit of ganging-up by region became virtually endemic, except in small uninfluential pockets of the society. The politicians had produced no ideology of national unity which would interpret conflict in social or class terms; and the structure of Nigeria at independence filtered all contests into regional, and so inevitably, ethnic or communal, channels.

THE ARMY INFECTED

The regional cleavages and built-in discord of Nigeria's political system entered, not surprisingly, the army. There, as in politics, it was insisted that regional security and guarantees would cement unity; there, as in politics, far from building a national force and national allegiance, regionalism created fierce strains and divisions. The army became the military counterpart of the contesting regional groups in the country's politics, and finally it went to war with itself.

When coups were breaking out all over Africa in the early 1960s, Nigerians complacently declared that it could never happen to them. There were, after all, the three regions, with three sets of political allegiances (not counting the small, later-established Mid-West). Within them, the army operated under a system of rotating commands and spells of duty, so that a brigade would serve in the West for three months, then be moved to the North, and so on. Nigeria was too big, its political allegiances too dispersed, its army command too diversified, its officer corps too carefully balanced, ever to make a military coup a possibility there.

Before independence, Nigeria's army was woefully inefficient. The relics of Britain's officer corps, transferred out of India but not yet ready for retirement, made up its expatriate command, including the non-commissioned officers. There were some African warrant officers. And the 'other ranks' were totally African. After the war, when the WAFF was broken into constituent national forces, there were slots for West African cadets at Sandhurst; but few were taken up, because the candidates found it so difficult to get past the scrutiny of the selection board. At independence, in October 1960, the Nigerian army consisted of five battalions and certain supporting units organized into two brigades; one at Kaduna, in the North, and one in the South, at Apapa. About one in seven of the officers was Nigerian; and the highest ranking Nigerian officers were three majors. It was planned to treble the number of officers by 1962; then all the subalterns would be Nigerian, together with 5 per cent of the captains and 20 per cent of the higher ranks.

Independence brought an accelerated demand for Africanization. And one month after independence came the decision to send a Nigerian contingent to the Congo, for which a Third Brigade was rapidly raised. 'For political reasons,' said a British army observer, 'of course they wanted it to be as black as possible.' In the Federal Parliament there were pressures for speedier Africanization. 'Our army in the Congo is being looked after by an officer who is not Nigerian,' protested Mr C. O. D. Eneh.[19] But the Minister of Defence, Alhaji Mohammed Ribadu, warned against Nigerianizing so fast as to produce another Mobutu! 'I appeal to both sides of the House,' said the minister, 'not to bring politics into the army. Because one has a brother in the army, he should not stand up and say "Nigerianize the armed forces".'

But politics had already been introduced into the army by the Federal government. One of its first acts – under British pressure – had been to introduce a quota system for the recruitment of officers and men, which was intended to reproduce in the army the dominance of the North in the political system. The Northern region was to have 50 per cent of army recruits, officers and men, with the Eastern and Western regions 25 per cent each. This principle of regional balance was also applied to the selection of candidates for training schemes abroad, as Nigeria added to the old connexion by establishing defence links with other parts of the Commonwealth, like Canada and India, as well as Ethiopia, the United States and Israel. Recruiting of ground troops was supposed to be based on provincial allocations, to prevent a particular region from being over-represented, or certain traditional areas of army enlistment from outweighing others. This was of particular Northern concern, since the Middle Belt was just such a traditional area, and the emirates of the far or 'true' North were not. In practice, however, army recruitment in far Northern centres like Sokoto, Katsina and Kano was virtually nil. The bulk of the riflemen in the army – some say as many as 75 per cent[20] – were Northerners, but mostly from the Middle Belt. There was also heavy enlistment among men from Bornu, and from Niger and Chad, who crossed the border into Nigeria so as to join the army. Some recruits from areas considered over-represented in the army took on Hausa names and gave their origins as some centre in the far North. Others bought themselves places. In certain places, it was said to cost £10, and later £20, to persuade the recruiting officer. In the Middle Belt the army had become a traditional avenue for employment, and even in many Southern towns there was strong competition to be enlisted: army pay was steady and three or four times the national average wage. The army did not publish regional statistics; but it was clear that the system of 'balanced' regional representation was not working in practice.*

If the ground troops were predominantly Middle-Belters, the officer corps was dominated by Southerners, especially Easterners. For until the operation of the quota system, officer corps selection had been by open competition, with entry by educational qualification. By the end of 1961, the great majority of tradesmen, technical and transport staff, signallers and clerks were Southerners. In the ranks of major and above, Southerners outnumbered Northerners by about five to one.[21] Three-quarters of the officers were Easterners, the majority of them products of schools round Onitsha (during the 1950s, incidentally, there were more schools in this region than in the whole of the North).[22] Easterners had taken advantage of the pre-independence British-initiated scheme to enlist university graduates for officer training, and about half the Sandhurst generation commissioned between 1954 and 1960 were Ibos from the East and the Mid-West.[23] The quota system was devised to speed the intake and training of Northerners; and with it went a concerted effort to promote Northerners more rapidly, especially into the middle-level officer group where Easterners were so dominant.

By 1965, when the army was totally Nigerianized, about half the officer corps was Ibo. In the highest levels of command, there was a careful sprinkling of regional representation: two of the five brigadiers came from the West, two from the East and one from the North. Among the battalion commanders, there were two Northerners, a Westerner, a Mid-Westerner, two Easterners (one of them Ojukwu) and a Rivers man, with the regions more or less equally represented in headquarter and special branch posts.[24] The quota system began to show results at the level of the junior officer ranks. Ibo officers still predom-

* In April 1963 a Senator asked the Minister of Defence how many men had been recruited into the army from each region since 1960. 'It will not be in the public interest to divulge this information,' was the Minister's reply.

inated in the middle ranks, especially at the level of major. But Northerners were being favoured for promotion and pushed upwards faster than their Southern counterparts. It was plain that redressing the balance through the quota system meant favouring the North. There were many Southern officers eligible for promotion; but they had to stand by and watch Northerners of shorter service and less experience being promoted over their heads instead.

Far from controlling regionalism, therefore, the quota system only inflamed it. Southerners were quick to notice that, like the weighting of the constitution, the army quota was calculated to guarantee the hegemony of the North. It was noted, too, that the Minister of Defence was invariably an influential NPC politician – first Ribadu, then Inuwa Wada; and that the military academy, the air force training school and the ordnance factory were all sited in the North. Surely, Southerners argued, the most equitable national system for the army, as in politics and the civil service, was not to weight the system in favour of any one region, but to pin access on the basis of merit. The quota system was, in fact, abusing the army for the purposes of Northern politics. To the middle-rankers in the officer corps, the political disabilities of the South and their own professional disabilities in the army converged only too glaringly.

Promotion blockages caused by the rapid Africanization of the army took on the same political and regional overtones. The rush to localize the army had meant rapid promotion for the senior command. The ranks below had to wait on the death or retirement of relatively young men. And the way that Northerners were being favoured for promotion looked like meaning that Southern middle officers would be largely passed over. This promotion jam after the rapid upgrading of the officer corps was, of course, not exclusive to Nigeria; it was experienced by every African army that Africanized with the onset of independence: but in the Nigerian army it was one more source of stress inside an officer corps already rumbling with regional discord.

There was also, of course, the usual tension in African armies between the different educational generations of officer. Ironsi and the most senior officers had risen steadily through the ranks.

The younger officers had graduated from secondary schools at least, some from a university, and had then won their commissions against stern competition. They openly despised the inferior intellectual showing and narrow professionalism of their seniors. But more than the cleavages between men from different army backgrounds and generations, with a jealous eye fixed on the weighted system of officer-recruitment and promotion, it was the political crisis in the country that threw the army into politics.

Middle-ranking Southern officers identified with their equivalents in civilian life. They had been to school – a few of them, to university – with their equivalent age group in the civil service, the professions and politics. They associated the fixing of Northern control in the army with Northern dominance in politics; and the top brass in the army, who connived at this system, with the corruption and incompetence of the political class. When it came to filling the place of the British army head who withdrew in 1965, it was obvious to the whole country that each of the contestants – Brigadiers Maimalari, Ademulegun and Ironsi – had his backers among the political bosses. It did not endear Ironsi to the discontented young officers that the Federal premier, Sir Abubakar Tafawa Balewa, backed him, against even the opposition of the Sardauna, Sir Ahmadu Bello, the Northern premier, who wanted Maimalari. After this, Ironsi was regarded as 'Balewa's boy'. Then, the corruption of politics began to infect the armed services. Three Nigerian naval officers embezzled nearly one-tenth of the 1964 navy vote.[25] There were leakages about the ingenious system of perks used by Minister of Defence Ribadu to ensure the loyalty of the army's top officers: he had been Minister of Lagos Affairs before he took on the Defence portfolio, and was admirably placed to influence the allocation of building sites in the capital. It was said of Brigadier Ademulegun, a Westerner in command in the North who had taken to polo with verve so as to hasten his acceptance in the region's social and political hierarchy: 'The Sardauna dashes him with ponies.'

By the constitutional crisis at the end of 1964, when Dr Azikiwe charged that the elections were not free or fair and found himself in a showdown with NPC power, the army was politics-ridden and divided into pro-Balewa and pro-Azikiwe groups. At the height of the crisis, when the army had been paraded round Lagos in battle order, Dr Azikiwe[26] summoned the heads of the army, the navy and the police to State House, so as to assert his presidential control over the services. The legal advice obtained by the service chiefs contradicted this assertion. The UGPA feared that the NPC would remove Azikiwe, for someone who would obediently nominate Balewa as premier. It was at this point that a group of lieutenant-colonels in the army, with Ojukwu prominent among them, offered intervention by a section of the army on the president's side. The go-between was Azikiwe's eldest son, who was a close friend of Ojukwu and arranged a private meeting between the president and the officer in State House. Ojukwu urged Azikiwe to take seriously the rumours of his impending arrest and protective custody by the army. He advised him to assume emergency powers and form a provisional government. The army, Ojukwu assured the president, would not arrest him, and some of his officer colleagues would back a provisional government.

One version has it that the plan came to nothing because Azikiwe wanted to know its details before he gave the go-ahead, and the officers' attitude was, 'You leave that to us'.[27] When Azikiwe disclosed the incident in 1966,[28] he maintained he had assured the young officers that he had no political ambitions, and had throughout his political life always advocated an orderly change of government. (He, had, however, taken the scheme for the assumption of emergency powers and the setting up of a provisional government to lawyers, six in all; they, of course, had advised that the Constitution gave the president no such powers.)

The incipient rebellion against the senior army command in 1964 evaporated with the crisis itself. One significant feature of the plot was that among the lieutenant-colonels whom Ojukwu approached to join him were Yakubu Gowon, a young Middle Belt officer, and David Ejoor, from the Mid-West. (Both rejected the scheme.) The officer coup was thus conceived as an intervention against NPC power and Northern dominance, in which opposition elements from both North and South would join. The president was an Easterner, but that was incidental to his role as figure-head of the political opposition to the Northern ruling group. Significantly, too, planning was done at the rank of lieutenant-colonel, and initiative was preserved at that level. Two years later, when the 1966 coup took place, it was organized at the level of major, and no lieutenant-colonel was included in the inner group. There were, accordingly, strong cleavages inside the army between officer ranks, and a repeated tendency, when officers acted, for them to do so within their particular army 'generation'.* When they did act, however, it was not for reasons, primarily, of intra-army conflict, but in response to political challenges outside into which, they felt, the army was being drawn.

Nine months after the country-wide constitutional crisis, the Western region began to erupt. The 4th Battalion, stationed in the West for the better part of nine years before being transferred to the North in 1966, was used, inevitably, as an extension of the Akintola administration. Many young officers resented this use of the army. The battalion commander, Colonel Largema, was publicly exposed for giving 'secret' military support to the NNDP.[29] A soldier was court-martialled, and in the course of his trial he announced that he had listed his commander's acts of partiality: these included harbouring Akintola in his official

*A. R. Luckham, *The Nigerian Army* (paper presented to a post-graduate seminar of the Institute of Commonwealth Studies, London 1968), commenting on the phenomenon of the January coup being led by majors, the July one by lieutenants, and the fact that a group of lieutenant-colonels had contemplated intervening in the crisis over the Federal elections of 1964, says: 'This reflects a well-developed tendency in the Nigerian army for interaction and friendship to cluster within groups of military peers, a tendency which is represented in its strongest form by the solidarity that develops between "course mates", those who have been through the Nigerian Military Training College and Sandhurst, Mons or other cadet training schools together.... Yet although peer groups provided a pattern or frame for cleavage ... conflicts in the army drew their dynamic from elsewhere and created new conflict groups that transcended the lines between the ranks. The Majors of January did have their grievances against their seniors, but these were definitely secondary to their main political objectives; and it was the strategy of the coup more than feelings of direct antagonism which dictated the murder of the army's senior officers ...'

quarters; bringing politicians into the army barracks to sign for the issue of self-loading rifles, and inviting them to practise firing at the forty-five yards range. Colonel Largema, he claimed, had personally supervised Chief Akintola's target practice. In the week after the fraudulent election, army units and armoured cars were widely deployed in the region. But the presence of the soldiers – many of them UPGA supporters – only added to the tension. Eventually, at the insistence of the general officer commanding, Major-General Ironsi, the troops were withdrawn from the West, and mobile police from the North were brought in to replace them.[30]

After three months of unrelenting violence, the NNDP found itself driven out of almost all areas in the region except Oyo in the North. Its administration was collapsing and being ousted by local improvisations in the Action Group strongholds. NNDP 'refugees' had crowded into Ibadan, the capital, which was close to open warfare. Akintola himself was reported to be moving through the city in an ambulance for safety, and to be ordering a total blackout of the city's street lights when he was travelling from one point to another. An £8,000 bullet-proof car was on order from Germany, the first such to be imported into Nigeria.[31] Yet when the Federal government was pressed to deal with the emergency in the West, the Federal premier and the premier of the North echoed one another in declaring that there was a legally established authority in the West, and 'no reports of any breakdown of law and order'.[32] The Western House of Assembly opened with armed soldiers and police standing shoulder to shoulder round the House and inside the Chamber.

Early in 1966, the Northern premier and Chief Akintola met at Kaduna. It was the week that the Commonwealth prime ministers assembled in Lagos for one of their sporadic conferences. Security arrangements were tightened along the ten-mile route from Ikeja airport to Lagos, where cars were being burnt and thugs were active in broad daylight. Balewa, said his critics, was debating whether violence should be used against a white minority regime in Rhodesia, while turning his face from the violence in his own country. By now there was a widespread belief in the South that, with the failure of police and spasmodic army operations to stamp out opposition, the army was to be thrown into the West for drastic action to prop up the Akintola regime. The operation, it was said, was timed for 17 January. Legislation for preventive detention was to be placed before the Federal Parliament the day after the army moved in. A list of Action Group activists for liquidation or detention was said to include a judge, renowned for the fearlessness of his decisions in cases against Akintola supporters, and leading Action Group intellectuals. The rumours were becoming too persistent to ignore. There were also suspicious moves afoot to change the army and police command. It was suggested to General Ironsi (without success) that he take his accumulated leave at this time. Changes in the police command resulted in a Northerner, Alhaji Kam Salem, stepping up to become acting head in the place of two Eastern officers senior to him.[33]

To UPGA politicians, the operation began to sound more ominous than just a move to crush resistance in the West. There were suggestions of a simultaneous declaration of emergency in more than one area. Powerful Northern voices interpreted the violence in the West as instigated by the Eastern regions.[34] There was the curious case of Isaac Boro and the Niger Delta Congress, which claimed to speak for the minority Rivers people in the Eastern region. It was alleged that the NPC was encouraging Boro, an undergraduate of Nsukka University, to start an insurrection in the Niger Delta, so as to provide a pretext for moving Northern soldiers into Eastern Nigeria.* This was how the Action Group had been toppled in the West: why not the same fate for the NCNC in the East, since it had gone into opposition?[35]

In some circles in the capital, the rumour was current that the plans for declaring an emergency in the East had gone so far that there was already rivalry for the job of administrator.

*Boro was brought to trial in 1966 and condemned to death for his part in stoking rebellion and setting up a 'new' government. He was condemned to death, but released by the Gowon government, and given a commission in the Nigerian army (*West Africa*, 14 October 1967, p. 1331; *Daily Times*, April 1966).

But even if political gossip was improving on schemes actually laid, it was apparent that the Sardauna and Akintola were planning a final assault to entrench the NNDP in the West. It was after the meeting of these two politicians in Kaduna on 14 January, and in the conviction that the army was about to be used for the repression of the West, that the young majors jerked into action.

Ghana: Heirs Jump the Queue

I believe it is true of any country to say that the soldier is a much better proposition to deal with than, for example, the politician, whatever the colour of his skin.

General H. T. Alexander, *African Tightrope*

For many years in Ghana, the Colonial Office had been juggling a power balance of the traditional chiefs-cum-administrators with the propertied middle class and Western-trained intellectuals in the United Gold Coast Convention. But in the social and economic upheavals of the post-war years, new aspirants jumped the queue to usurp the position that the older élite regarded as their own. During the war, the West African territories had been closely tied to the Allied economies; Ghana, perhaps, most of all. Then, after the war, there was a steep decline in terms of trade; import prices soared because of shortages; and there was mass discontent, linking towns and villages, over rising costs of living. The towns of West Africa were flooded with work-seekers and members of a fast-growing urban petty-bourgeoisie. The UGCC leadership had been essentially an African business lobby, seeking to capture the trade of European merchant-importers and the Lebanese trading community. In 1949 Kwame Nkrumah, having returned from abroad to become the Convention's secretary, led a militant breakaway from the UGCC, which became the Convention Peoples' Party (CPP).[1] It attracted in opposition to the worthy of the professions and academics in the UGCC, elementary school-leavers, teachers, clerks, messengers in government and commercial offices, petty traders, artisans and transport workers, small-scale contractors and small businessmen, urban wage-earners and ex-servicemen. The CPP's organizational base was provided by the network of youth, workers' and farmers' associations set up, or linked together, by Nkrumah when he had been UGCC secretary.

Discrete élitist representations gave way to processions by ex-servicemen, strikes and other militant activity. The year 1950 saw the launching of the first 'positive action', the Gandhian-type tactic devised by Nkrumah. Once launched, these positive action campaigns were brief and poorly sustained; but they took Nkrumah and other party leaders to jail and to political prominence. The CPP became Africa's leading mass party. In municipal elections held in Accra, the capital, a few months after the first 'positive action' initiative, the CPP won every seat; and it emerged triumphant in the first general election of 1951. The governor and the Colonial Office had to recognize that the party was the most representative and influential political force in the country. Less than two years after its formation, Nkrumah was Leader of Government Business in Ghana. For the next six years, from self-government to independence, the CPP was a partner in government with the colonial power.

It was during this period, a critic has written,[2] that the character and orientation of the CPP, as the movement of a petty bourgeoisie seeking to entrench itself, were indelibly fixed, notwithstanding Nkrumah's later efforts to change both party and policy. The initial post-election period was one of tactical action to mark the transition to full independence. The CPP would work through colonial government to liberate Ghana from colonial rule. The party had, at one and the same time, not to forfeit electoral support and yet give colonial officials evidence of its moderation and responsibility in government.

Above all, this was the period when CPP economic policy served to keep colonial economic interests intact. For the first ten years of CPP government, the party made no structural changes of any kind to the economy. A symbiotic relationship between Britain and Ghana in the marketing of cocoa, Ghana's chief export, preserved old colonial ties and, at the same time, helped the CPP cement itself in power. Two young analysts have shown[3] how, at this time, it was the funds of Ghana's Cocoa Marketing Board, and those of other African colonies with similar produce-marketing machinery, which primed the pump of Britain's post-war economic recovery. Ghana supplied Britain with more capital than any colony except Malaya. The Board was the country's sole buyer, grader, seller and exporter of cocoa; and a reserve fund was built up by setting the price paid to domestic growers at a lower level than that prevailing in the world market. A large part of the country's economic surplus was thus accumulated by one body, and in London. By the end of 1955, Ghana's overseas reserves stood at £208 million. These blocked sterling balances were invested in long-term British government securities: the colonies were lending money to the colonial power. The practice was indispensable to Britain's economic interests. It was also invaluable to the CPP, which used it to undermine political and economic opposition among the developing or aspirant bourgeoisie of rich cocoa farmers and merchants, and to promote support through the dispensation of benefits and patronage. In 1952, the CPP founded the Cocoa Purchasing Company (as a subsidiary of the Cocoa Marketing Board), to become Ghana's largest cocoa-broker. The vigorous growth of a Ghanaian bourgeoisie had been stunted by the monopoly of the UAC and other foreign firms, which dominated the import–export trade, and controlled prices, import licences and wholesale credit. The effect of the CPP's cocoa policy was to undermine this class further still, for government went into direct competition with local cocoa-brokers. Determined to prevent the growth of a Ghanaian capitalist class, Nkrumah deliberately brought under attack not only the policies of the embryonic Ghanaian bourgeoisie but also their economic foundation. And into the vacuum caused by the absence of a matured bourgeoisie and entrenched political class, stepped the CPP, the party of the petty bourgeoisie. The Cocoa Purchasing Company provided the party with large supplies of credit, and business openings with which to consolidate its own support. Big farmers and chiefs in the rural economy were by-passed or assailed; in their place the CPP assisted poorer farmers, especially those who joined the CPP-sponsored United Ghana Farmers' Cooperative Council. Party leaders, parliamentarians and party supporters acquired contracts, commissions, loans and licences. CPP rank-and-filers were favoured for jobs. Funds made available for welfare projects consolidated community support. In the hands of the CPP, political authority was translated into control of state resources, which in turn dispensed party patronage as elsewhere in West Africa by a not dissimilar process.

The CPP's cocoa policy consolidated its echelons of support; but the cocoa farmers with whom it had entered into business competition, the businessmen worried by the threat of state buying in timber as well as cocoa, the chiefs, and their allies within the established middle class and professions, were being fast antagonized, not least by the pegging of the cocoa price well below the world price. Antagonized, too, were certain elements inside the CPP. Some defectors joined the opposition, especially in Ashanti country; but in time it was the opposition within the party itself that was to prove more destructive than the opposition outside.

Outside opposition mustered in the National Liberation Movement, which was a party based on the Ashanti rulers and land-owners, cocoa farmers and traders – both the traditional leadership and embryonic bourgeoisie in the richest part of the country – and which was reinforced by regional interest groups like the Northern Peoples' Party and the Togoland Congress, among others. The strategy of this old-style alliance was to delay the granting of independence, and to demand a federal constitution from which regions would have the right to secede. Hedging its bets for the last time, the Colonial Office insisted on a fresh round of elections in 1956 – though there had been elections only two years earlier, in 1954 – and the attainment by the winning party of 'a substantial majority'; how substantial was never defined. The Colonial Office, influenced by the NLM leader Dr Busia, and by commercial interest in London which consistently overstated the strength of the Ghanaian opposition to the CPP,[4] was at cross-purposes with its governor-on-the-spot in Ghana, Sir Charles Arden-Clarke, who anticipated that the CPP would sweep the polls and calculated his strategy for the transfer of power accordingly.[5] In the elections, the opposition won most of the seats in Ashanti and the North; but, overall, the CPP emerged with a handsome majority. (It was, however, an abysmally low poll; in fact, only one in six Ghanaians eligible to vote actually supported the CPP, on the very eve of independence.[6] This low level of popular mobilization was to dog the CPP in this and subsequent elections.)

By 1957 the National Liberation Movement and other opposition groupings had consolidated in the United Party; for government had passed a law requiring that all political parties should be nation-wide, with membership open to all, irrespective of tribe or region. Now firmly in the saddle, with independence at last, the CPP proceeded to concentrate power at the centre and to weaken the potential opposition of the regions. The regional assemblies, protected by the independence constitution, were curbed, and then abolished; the powers of the chiefs were circumscribed; and entrenched provisions on the judiciary and the civil service were revoked. Opposition immediately after independence had been open and expressed, and on occasion even spectacular, as with the troubles in Trans-Volta Togoland, and in Accra itself where the urban unemployed and the Ga petty-bourgeoisie demonstrated against the CPP government. The CPP began to stamp out resistance with the apparatus of the state. The Preventive Detention Law was passed in 1958; and strikes were made illegal at about the same time. The assets of pro-opposition state and local councils were confiscated; and opposition MPs themselves were arrested.

Ghana's experiment in socialism failed, it has been argued,[7] because the attempt to break with Ghana's colonial past was not made soon enough, and because, when it was made, it was not complete. There were two distinct periods in Ghana under Nkrumah and the CPP. The first was the pro-Western period from 1957 to 1961. During this Ghana operated as a neo-colony within the British sphere of interest. It looked to the British pound as its anchor of safety. It kept its external reserves in London instead of in Accra, and allowed the British banks systematically to deflate the economy. Cocoa dominated (from 1950 to 1962, it accounted for from 50 to 75 per cent of total exports). In 1958 manufacturing contributed only 1·8 per cent of the gross domestic product.[8] The export–import enclave linked to the foreign overseas market was monopolized by foreign firms, and a major proportion of the country's surplus flowed out of the country.

Development strategy was orthodox and passive, with a total dependence on foreign capital for any projected industrialization. This policy, guided by W. A. Lewis, the eminent West Indian and later Princeton economist, was seen by the early 1960s to have failed. Ghana experienced a rapid deterioration in its balance of payments, lost huge amounts of its external reserves and failed to attract anywhere near the amount of foreign capital on which it had counted for industrial development. From 1957 to 1961, indeed, there was a net *outflow* of private capital. And by 1961, Ghana's balance of payments deficit was £53 million, or 12 per cent of the national product.[9] It was, in fact, a conventional development plan inspired by orthodox economists in the pro-Western period, and not primarily the extravagance of the regime in its flirtation with 'socialist' planning, which depleted Ghana's foreign reserves between 1957 and 1961. A second development plan introduced in 1959 was informed by the same strategy of reliance on foreign capital, and of government activity in a welfare state direction only.

In 1961 this plan was abandoned. In its place came the Seven Year Plan for Work and Happiness. Ghana was to attain self-sustaining industrial growth by 1967, it was proclaimed, and the state was to play the major role in economic development. The Plan would try for the first time to alter Ghana's rigid export orientation and, in an internal economic breakthrough, to exploit some of the surpluses previously leaked overseas. Ghana, Nkrumah decided, was to be a socialist state.[10]

Five years later, the Seven Year Plan was floundering and Ghana was eye-deep in debt, with a balance of payments crisis that bonded her to external – mostly Western – creditors. A cabal of army officers and policemen was able to use the falling growth rate of the economy, among other things, to justify its armed seizure of power.

Yet Ghana had made attempts, however limited and ill-conceived, to chart a development course towards industrialization. There had been an unprecedented growth in the necessary infrastructure: the deep-water harbour at Tema; the improved railways; the new roads built and maintained; the Volta dam project, which generated a vast increase of electricity, even if it did not meet the other demands of the Seven Year Plan; and the moves to establish a national shipping line and airways. There had been what were, for Africa, unprecedented programmes of constructive social welfare, with the spread of benefits not to a closed élite circle, but beyond, to the village. Great strides had been made towards free and compulsory primary and secondary education; new universities had been built, and university education made free; a beginning had been made in the establishment of a free health service, and the first steps taken towards a social insurance scheme, including unemployment benefits and pensions. But the debts *were* rocketing; and, in its crucial purposes, the Seven Year Plan *was* failing.

In the decade between 1955 and 1965, the gross domestic product doubled; but the import–export sector continued to dominate, and cocoa and cocoa products still accounted for 66 per cent of all exports, with very little processing done inside Ghana itself. The Plan was to balance the economy between agriculture and industry to support secondary industry on the products of agriculture; and to provide, meanwhile, sufficient cheap food for the people. But foodstuff production was almost stagnant; the price of locally grown food rose between 1963 and 1964 by as much as 400 per cent in some regions (the national rise was 36 per cent), and the state farming ventures were disappointing if not outright failures, having produced food in quantities which did not justify anything like their capital and current investment.[11] Manufacturing remained a tiny share of the gross national product: it was 3·8 per cent in 1962, and 4·4 per cent in both 1963 and 1964. There had been heavy government outlay on consumer and capital goods factories, but industrialization had been spasmodic and ill-planned, and had relied heavily on short-term financing by suppliers' credits.* Ironically, as has been shown,[12] foreign investment was plainly unimpressive during the period of *laissez faire* and state inactivity in industrialization; while, during the period of 'socialist' experiment after 1961, foreign capital poured in, relatively speaking. By 1964 Ghana had received £168 million-worth of medium- and short-term credits.[13] But of this amount, £157 million consisted of suppliers' credits, with the bulk of repayments concentrated within four to six years.[14] Ghana's economy was fast drowning in cumulative debt; and as early as 1964, the mounting repayment commitments were beginning to disrupt the economy.

Nkrumah, up to the fall of his government and even after, refused to recognize the nature or the magnitude of the crisis in Ghana's economy. ('Of course the Ghanaian economy was not without its problems, but is this not true of all national economies, and particularly of those of developing countries in the context of the growing gap between rich and poor nations? Our imperialist critics would be better employed examining the economic situation in their own countries, many of which are in grave financial difficulties.')[15]

It has been suggested[16] that the Nkrumah government in its last years began to lose control, and even knowledge, of Ghana's external debt.

Certainly, the government's financial system was in a state of virtual collapse, a critic[17] deduced from the auditor-general's

*'The system of suppliers' credits is one in which individual foreign firms undertake to complete a "development" project under an agreement guaranteed by the firm's government. The firm then advances the credit for the cost of the project to the African government, generally at terms above the prevailing rates, with the principal to be paid in four to six years. The debt is in turn guaranteed by the African government. Consequently one of the main points about these foreign "investors" is that they do not invest. They neither risk any of their own money nor wait for the project to pay before they take their profit.' (*West Africa*, 26 March 1966, p. 341.) Furthermore, as the bulk of these debts were contracted in foreign exchange, repayment worsened Ghana's balance of payments position, at a time when no additional foreign exchange was forthcoming from other sectors of the economy.

annual report of government accounts in the last year of the Nkrumah regime. Complete records of several contracts and suppliers' credit agreements did not exist in the government's official files. Estimates of expenditure in the final accounts were found not to include credit committed and utilized by the government, with the result that Ministry of Finance control became a game of blind man's buff. And apart from major breakdowns in the country's system of financial regulation there were scores of minor irregularities, some due to corruption, but many to

> the disturbing gap between the increasing complexity of government operations and the fall in standards of integrity and in the level of technical competence. . . . A substantial portion of the taxpayers' money sustains little more than the unmistakeable incompetence of some civil servants.

At the beginning of 1964, Finance Minister Kwesi Amoako-Atta laid a twenty-six page memorandum before the Cabinet, in an attempt to draw attention to Ghana's precarious financial position. But the memorandum received short shrift from Nkrumah, who was notoriously impatient with unfavourable reports. Two days before the 1966 coup d'état, the Budget speech acknowledged certain economic difficulties; but it attributed them, in the main, to the catastrophic drop in the price of cocoa. The CPP had, indeed, come to power in the post-war period of soaring cocoa prices, and had built its regime, as it had drawn its development plans, on the politics of cocoa prosperity. In 1954, the price had been £350 a ton. The Seven Year Plan had been drafted on the basis of an average £180 a ton, and on the assumption that increased output would ensure an average annual foreign currency income of £86 million. (The cocoa monopolies had, in the post-war years, urged Ghana and other West African countries to increase output, and had pledged that a fair and stable price, of at least £200–50 a ton, would be forthcoming.) By the 1960s, however, the cocoa boom was over; and by August 1965 cocoa was selling for as little as £90 a ton. Ghana's cocoa production had doubled, but its export earnings had fallen to below pre-1957 levels. As foreign exchange problems worsened, the government's first recourse had been to employ the reserves; then, to depend on supplier credits. If the world cocoa price had not crashed, Ghana's economic crisis would undoubtedly have been cushioned, at least for a time. But the economic crisis was not encompassed by the cocoa price.

Ghana under the Seven Year Plan achieved an impressive state-enforced rate of capital accumulation; the envy, indeed, of many a development planner. The trouble was that the mobilization of capital was nowhere matched by any similar mobilization of human resources, in political, administrative and technical commitment or even enthusiasm for Ghana's economic goals. The paradox was, an economist has suggested,[18]

> that in the period when the rate of investment was being increased, the rate of growth of the economy as a whole was slowing down. In other words, while additions to the stock of capital were growing, the average output obtained from a unit of capital was declining.

Chaotic administration of import controls was one of the reasons; poor planning, another. 'The unthinking proliferation of hastily conceived state enterprises used up large amounts of foreign currency, but resulted in absurdly poor levels of economic performance. In 1963–4, for instance, the output of State enterprises was just over a quarter of the amount they were intended to produce.' Above all, the Seven Year Plan had become entirely dependent for its success on 'an inflow of foreign capital on a scale completely without precedence in the recent history of the country'.

This was puzzling in view of Nkrumah's consistent denunciation of the diabolical role played by foreign capital. Foreign investors, the Seven Year Plan had laid down, were to be welcomed in a spirit of partnership, for they would help Ghana in developing its full industrial potential. There was to be no partnership between local and foreign private capital, however, for this would encourage the growth of a Ghanaian capitalist class; it was to be a partnership between foreign investors and the Ghana state. Nkrumah remained confident that foreign capital could be attracted and yet regulated in its operation. The Volta River project was one of those partnership projects;

but the Ghana state proved a very junior and subservient partner indeed. At the opening of the Volta project, Nkrumah talked of a 'dual mandate'[19] on the part of a power like the United States to increase its own prosperity and at the same time to assist in the prosperity of developing countries.* The Volta project did not, in practice, do both. Nkrumah and Ghana staked heavily on the hydro-electric dam and the aluminium industry at a period of rising aluminium prices. But by the time that the United States firm of Kaiser had amended the project as originally conceived, it was at sharp variance with the purposes of the Seven Year Plan.[20] Nkrumah's theory in welcoming foreign capital was that the state sector of the economy would be dominant. But the CPP lacked the popular political base, and the state economic control, to secure this primacy. The notions that foreign private capital would let itself be used to lay a foundation for socialism and that a state dependent on financing by private capital could retain the initiative, proved equally deceptive. Nkrumah wanted Ghana to contract out of the capitalist world, and yet hoped to develop his country's economy

*On 27 April 1964, before the Committee on Appropriations of the U.S. House of Representatives, William Kling, economic adviser of the Department of State's Bureau of African Affairs, and Otto E. Passman, Democratic Congressman from Louisiana who was chairman of the subcommittee on foreign appropriations, discussed the Volta River project:

KLING: 'Of course, Mr Chairman, I think in approaching this situation we have to realize that we have made a very substantial investment in Ghana so far. I think the consensus of the American businessmen that I have visited when I was in Ghana was that the Volta River Project was a force for good in the country.

'I think we do have an interest in having the Volta Dam in Ghana. I do think we do have an interest in trying to preserve the very valuable resources of Africa for the free world. Africa does have a considerable amount of bauxite, electric power.'

PASSMAN: 'Do they also have a demand for aluminum?'

KLING: 'We have the demand for aluminum.'

PASSMAN: 'Do the African countries have a need for aluminum?'

KLING: 'They consume very little aluminum.'

PASSMAN: 'Do they have a need for aluminum?'

KLING: 'Yes, a potential need, but I agree there is an element of risk involved here. We certainly considered this very carefully, and it gives us sleepless nights, too.'

PASSMAN: (*Discussion off the record*)

with its aid. Far from laying a basis for full independence, let alone socialism, what was really happening in Ghana, it has been suggested, was 'a re-negotiation of terms with foreign capital (with accompanying re-distribution of surplus).'[21]

In the last two years of the CPP regime, while there was little searching scrutiny, there were some sidelong glances at policy. Agriculture was not developing, and there was a marked decline in the production of major export crops like coffee and timber, and even, in 1966, of cocoa. While the public sector accounted for some 38 per cent of all wage employment, this was largely unproductive. Inflation was rampant, with a flow of wages out of all proportion to production and thus a critical shortage of goods. During 1965 the Cabinet tried to tackle the problem of foreign exchange, and appealed for help to the International Monetary Fund. The IMF, however, made assistance conditional on a reshaping of Ghana's development goals and means. Ghana rejected all the IMF conditions but one: that the price paid to cocoa producers should be cut so as to bring it into line with world prices. (This price cut was announced two days before the coup d'état that toppled the government.) There was another way out. This was to lessen dependence on the West by strengthening already growing economic links with the socialist states. Trade was being stepped up with such countries, and more and more development projects were handled by Soviet, Chinese and East German experts and technicians. Towards the end of 1965, a crucial mission, led by Finance Minister Amoako-Atta, set off for the socialist states, to negotiate the expansion of cocoa exports there. On its return it reported that it had secured guaranteed prices for a fixed quantity of cocoa in the remaining years of the Plan period. Part of the payment was to be made in sterling. If the deal went through, it would go a considerable way towards solving the foreign exchange crisis. The precise guaranteed price for cocoa was still being negotiated when the army and police coup struck at the government. There was no time to test whether the Soviet Union would have done for Ghana's cocoa what she was doing for Cuba's sugar exports. There had, however, been time enough for the significance of this swing in direction to be measured by the opposition, both outside and within the CPP, as well as by Ghana's traditional trading partners.

THE STATE OF THE PARTY

When Finance Minister Amoaka-Atta set out on his mission, the then Minister of Trade, Kwesi Armah, was due to go with him; he opted out of the assignment because its ends were inimical to his own. Some in the CPP were committed to Ghana's declared goals, but they were greatly outnumbered by those who were not.

There were two essential political conditions for the success of Ghana's Second Revolution, it has been suggested.[22]

> First, the political structures had to be fully democratised so as to draw the mass of the people into the reconstruction of the economy and the state. Secondly, as a precondition of the first, the CPP . . . had to be turned into an instrument for socialist transformation; in fact it turned out to be the major obstacle in the way of that transformation.

The CPP had been organized essentially as a vote-gathering machine, and it never really changed. It had no body of cadres at the grass roots to stimulate popular support; instead the state, and with it the party, used patronage and coercion. Above all, the party had no grasp of the problems involved in constructing a socialist economy.

Castro said, and Nkrumah echoed ruefully after his own fall, that socialism cannot be built without socialists. After 1961, Nkrumah's political commitment – though not necessarily his theoretical grasp – changed radically; the CPP's could not. It had never been an ideologically cohesive party, let alone one committed to socialism, even within its leadership. It was, from its formation, an omnibus party. It combined elements of the old Gold Coast intelligentsia, who left the UGCC when Nkrumah offered the prospect of power, with trading interests, mostly small contractors and the market mammys, middle and small farmers, all of whom had a basically free enterprise outlook; with the petty bourgeoisie of the towns and larger villages, clerks, secondary and primary school-leavers; with urban wage workers, and the unemployed. Many of Nkrumah's closest lieutenants did not share his view of the need for Ghana's Second Revolution, from political to economic independence. They had been the life and soul of the 'positive action' campaigns; but once the CPP was in power, they had reached journey's end. They calculated on settling in office to enjoy the spoils. It was not always a matter of ideology. Ideology and ideologists were thin on the ground in the CPP. Views of socialism ranged from Krobo Edusei's description (no doubt influenced by his wife's gold bed and other finery): 'Socialism doesn't mean that if you've made a lot of money, you can't keep it',[23] to the finer definitions by a minute group of Marxists that was divided against itself in doctrinal polemic. The real differences within the CPP, certainly in the early days of power, were manifestations of the tug-of-war between different groups for authority and advantage. Intrigue and manipulation asserted personal, family, business, clan, community or other vested interests. The CPP became an unmanageable lobby of different pressure groups, with the tussles for power carried on at the university, in the press, in Parliament and in government ministries, as well as in the party itself.

Early-comers, the old-guard politicians, men such as Krobo Edusei, Kojo Botsio and Gbedemah, all Nkrumah's colleagues of the 'positive action' days, had built popular support in their constituencies and had their fortress in Parliament. Then there were those who entrenched themselves in bureaucratic office when the CPP began to run the Ghanaian state, with their armaments in the press. During 1961 Parliament and the press joined issue, as a spirited round in the battle for ascendancy was fought out.[24] In April of that year Nkrumah's dawn broadcast warned against the high living of MPs and ministers. A national call went out for an end to corruption and self-seeking. (In the event, manipulation only became more subterranean, and the proclamations of the party more glaringly incompatible with the deeds of its big men.) The dawn broadcast was the signal for an attack on the old political guard. The purpose was to undermine it, but not to annihilate it altogether, for Nkrumah doubted whether he could survive the backlash of its supporting factions. The old guard lost ground temporarily, but by the following year it had recaptured the initiative. For meanwhile there occurred, in August 1962, the attempt on Nkrumah's life at Kulungugu. Several within the newer ranks of leadership, among the party managers and controllers – men like Tawia Adamafio, the former CPP secretary-general – were arrested for suspected involvement in the plot, tried for treason and thus removed from their positions of power. After Kulungugu, many of the old political guard were restored to office. They had lost the battle in 1961, but won the war in 1962. They had office if little power, but this was sufficient for their needs, especially as the new economic administration, devised in order to push the country towards socialism, and abounding in state corporations and controls, was prolific in opportunities for commissions and grants.[25]

Over the years, the struggles between the CPP's parliamentary and bureaucratic élites were inconclusive. But their effect on the CPP was to render it totally ineffective except as a battleground between the factions. Politics in Ghana became the harangues of Nkrumah and the factional disputes. The factions themselves were never really reconciled. Their differences were never openly, let alone exhaustively, debated. Once the single party system removed the need for elections, the CPP, essentially a vote-gathering machine, rusted. There was no forum for thrashing out policy, and no instrument for popularly promoting such policy as there was.

Nkrumah himself, whether out of sentiment for his old colleagues or in fear of isolating himself from them, or both, avoided confrontations like the plague. They were not his style of work. Now and then, in the later years of his government, he confessed to intimates that he discounted the old CPP political generation for Ghana's Second Revolution. But he could not, and did not wish to dispense with it, and he calculated instead on neutralizing it. He became a past-master at balancing opposites to try to cancel conflict. He played off one faction against another, one veteran political operator against another – even combining within a single delegation or work party quite irreconcilable opposites – till the futility of it was apparent to almost everyone but himself.

Careful, thus, not to force a break with either the old-guard politicians, or with the younger but equally acquisitive bureaucrats in power, Nkrumah calculated during the later instalment of CPP government on developing new bases of support among still younger, ideologically trained cadres. These would be committed to socialism, and exercised in the skills of planting and watering the grass roots. The Winneba Ideological Institute (staffed in the main by expatriate teachers who were well versed in the European classics but had a very superficial knowledge of Ghanaian society) was to be the forcing house of the new political generation. And soon it was supplying candidates for office in party and ministries. Many of these had distinct theoretical commitments, if little practical experience, as a result of the Winneba courses; but their entry, far from immediately strengthening Nkrumah's radical arm, alerted the conservative old guard to counter-attack with accusations of plotting and subversion against the Nkrumah regime by the new men.

By 1965 the CPP was in an unmistakably run-down state. Nkrumah, receptive to highly coloured accounts, substituted security reports for contact with his people, party and country. The old guard close round him made sure that only they had his ear. Back-bench and party branch officials had no access to the president; and if they could not reach the president, they reached nowhere at all in the power structure. The party's national executive had long lapsed into oblivion. A crisis was created by a demand from some of the new men that the membership of the party's central controlling committee be announced. Manipulation of the factions was no longer enough. An attempt was made to revive the party, at least the national executive, which was enlarged to 240 members, including local party officials (as long as they were not MPs), and officials of the trade unions, the farmers' cooperative councils, the young pioneers and the workers' brigade. The machinery was being overhauled at last. But by then, it was already late in the day. (The first meeting of the new national executive took place on 18 December 1965.)

It was one thing to train new activists in the theory and strategy of socialism. It was quite another to produce cadres who were not only adepts at talking ideology, but also in positions of mass leadership. For instance, a year after the programme for socialism was adopted, the CPP's trade-union support, which had played a leading role in the early CPP campaigns, was broken, with the smashing by government of the 1961 strike among railway workers at Sekondi and Takoradi. The strike had been sparked by the compulsory deduction of workers' savings from pay packets. (Independence had brought a temporary increase in real wages, but within a few years these had fallen heavily.) The strike gave Nkrumah the pretext for dismissing some of the old-guard politicians, like Gbedemah, but it also alienated permanently the trade-union support of the CPP. The strike was denounced by both CPP and TUC as counter-revolutionary; the workers were expected to subordinate their needs to those of the national economic plan. The unions lost their independence and were integrated into the state apparatus.

This had become inevitable. In 1960 Ghana got a new constitution; two years later, the CPP got a new programme for Work and Happiness, and a new structure to fit it for its role in the Second Revolution. The new constitution gave Ghana a highly centralized state. In the CPP there was an elaborate arrangement of bureaux and departments to tone up party organization and discipline. And Nkrumah himself exercised personal power wherever he thought it unsafe in the hands of associates. Under the pretext of mobilizing CPP supporting bodies, like the unions, the farmers' cooperatives, the youth and the women, these were assimilated into the CPP. Nkrumah thought that he was creating a new instrument for the country's changed needs. The result was not to galvanize popular initiative, but to stifle it. The trade unions came to be supervised by the Ministry of Labour, for the TUC was not much more than one of its sub-departments. The pioneer movement was run by the Ministry of Education. The farmers' organizations were controlled by the Ministry of Agriculture. The mass movements no longer had any independent existence, but were absorbed by the party, which in turn blurred with the administration. Nkrumah, as secretary-general of the CPP, had power to appoint not only the members of the central committee, but the district commissioners, the pivot of local government. In time the party's committees no longer even met, and policy-making and discussion came to a dead stop. The Preventive Detention Act, first used to stifle the opposition when this had turned to violent resistance, was now used to silence rival factions in the party and government hierarchy.

Nkrumah paid lip-service to the need to re-tool the CPP for its new tasks of economic development. In reality, however, the CPP was left much as it was and simply by-passed more and more for the machinery and methods of the state administration. The party bureaucracy never really took root.[26] From the outset it was little more than Nkrumah's personal court. In the absence of open discussion and activity, there was soon little to unite the different factions of the party but allegiance to Nkrumah. The mystique of the leader, the regime, the party and the programme was not ideological, but a substitute for ideology. If all were united in their adulation of Nkrumah and took good care that this was constantly demonstrated, intrigues could proceed apace below the surface.

For the most part, Nkrumah functioned in splendid isolation, except for subordinates. (And the more inept these were, the more sycophantic to the Osagafeyo.) He took more and more decisions personally, controlled more and more functions of state, built around him the party and government, especially the African and foreign affairs departments, as great appendages of his presidential role: till, elephantine, administration lumbered slowly through its routine bureaucratic procedures, and was prompted into swifter action only by the personal intervention of the president for some special project that made his own office more encumbered and labyrinthine than ever. Petty corruption and chicanery abounded; but more damaging by far were the sheer muddle and incompetence. CPP appointees kept their jobs not because they were efficient or trained (there had been little time or opportunity for that) but because they were CPP appointees. They were elevated because they alone were politically trustworthy and because, beside, it was *their* government. Many a ministry with sound enough schemes was assiduously undermined by sheer foolishness and mismanagement on the part of its underlings – or its chiefs. When the army–police government later, for its own purposes, opened the records to scrutiny, it found corruption, true, though not approaching the scale or polish of the big grafters in Nigeria; but more, by far, it uncovered evidence of sheer bungling in the management of the economy and the state.

Intrinsic to the failings of the CPP was Nkrumah's own character, with his limitations as a theoretician and a leader. He saw socialism, and economic development, as a process to be promoted by edict, from the pinnacle of government, by himself, a strong man and charismatic leader. Changing Ghana's social system was a matter of his power and authority. He undertook no close analysis of Ghanaian society and instructed no one else to do so. He published descriptions of imperialism, and of neo-colonialism, and thought that, having identified their purposes, he could prevail against them. His domestic development projects were predicated on the deliberate suppression of an indigenous capitalist class, yet he made his whole economy vulnerable to its infinitely more powerful international counterpart. He lived in a world of paper plans, ministerial and presidential instructions, diagrammatic schemes for Pan-African unity, African high commands, the clandestine sponsorship of radical groups in neighbouring countries addicted to more conservative policies than his own. Many of his schemes were exactly what Ghana and Africa did need; but between the scheme and its execution was a world of woolly thinking. Even where his strategies were sound, he depended on subordinates for their implementation; and, with exceptions here and there, these subordinates were pathetically unequal to their tasks, or reluctant to perform them. As the gulf between presidential purpose and practical execution yawned, till the two resembled one another hardly at all, Nkrumah's estimates of what had been and still could be done grew fiercely unreal. He was physically isolated from life in Ghana; psychologically resistant to unfavourable reports, or even accurate ones; and, towards the end, incapable of making a sound assessment. He dismissed with impatience reports of accelerating economic setbacks. Those around him were given to pessimism of outlook; setbacks were the work of hostile external forces. Analysis was replaced by a sophisticated form of demonology. Ghana was ringed round by imperialist hostility and intrigue, which alone accounted for failure. Firm revolutionary fervour would defeat them. Meanwhile Nkrumah took no close look at the forces inside Ghana which were ranged against his purpose; and it was these, ultimately, warmed in a climate of general international encouragement, that brought him down.

The fact is that, for all his faults of understanding and leadership, he was less a jailer than a prisoner of the forces around him. He had a very restricted range of political choices. Nkrumah, it has been said,[27] had to work within the limitations imposed by the actual character of the party as well as those imposed by the actual character of the state and its institutions.

By the spring of 1965, there was a feeling inside the CPP, and among the social strata it had favoured, that Nkrumah might no longer lead on their terms. New echelons were beginning to join the ranks of the earlier rejected. Inside the party and government, the products of Winneba, in the more assertive role of the 'socialist boys', now that they had reinforcements, were arguing for less adulation of the president and more discussion of the policy. The debate took the form of Nkrumahism versus scientific socialism. Differences seemed at last to take on more ideological forms, and the balance began to tip slightly in favour of the left wing. There were proposals to clean out the TUC and to sweep the party and the ministries with new brooms. Simultaneously the country's economic situation, not least the chaos of the import licence and marketing system, demanded measures that would clearly undermine the entrenched. A commission[28] was appointed to scrutinize irregularities in the import licensing (and traders' pass book) system, the havoc in the state-run trading corporations, the soaring costs of local foodstuffs and allegations of racketeering. The findings of the Abrahams Commission were edited out of all recognition to shield big men (and their trader-wives) in party and government who were implicated in speculation and racketeering, but it did publish a list of guilty men and women, and criticized the activities of the 'Queen Mothers' of the food markets. The commission proposed strict supervision of traders, and their eventual displacement by consumer cooperatives. It proposed the tightening of income tax assessments and collections.

In the rapid capital accumulation required for Ghana's Seven Year Plan, cocoa farmers had borne the main brunt in the expropriation of the surplus. They had become more and more unwilling to postpone immediate consumption to swell state savings. And the urban middle class and the traders felt exactly the same. Post-coup accusations of corruption were all very well. But discontent among the middle class was caused not so much by the presence of corruption, as by the absence of opportunity. The traders and other nascent members of the bourgeoisie fiercely resented the sealing off of certain kinds of profiteering. A tough but frustrated propertied and trading class had always been impatient at the barriers to its growth. By the sound of the new policies, Nkrumah was preparing to contain them even tighter. Nkrumah himself had, after all, risen to power on the fervour and the collections of the traders, especially the market mammys. State shops were not yet driving them out of business, but they were threatening to do so; while the shortage of essential supplies, thanks to the chaos in the system of import licensing, and the need to husband foreign exchange from the import of luxuries, was almost doing the job meanwhile.

When, in 1965, the cold war began to blow through Ghana's trading sector, Ghanaian free enterprise protagonists and Ghana's old-established Western trading partners found themselves close allies. Nkrumah was said to be trying to ease the balance of payments position by switching a third of Ghana's trade – not only cocoa – from West to East. Western interests were alarmed, and not least influential firms like UAC, which envisaged with growing revulsion the prospect of Ghanaian stores stocked high with Bulgarian and Polish canned goods instead of their own. Their counterparts in Ghanaian society were equally agitated. Would the same cuts and commissions operate? For how long would the system of retail trade survive in its old form? What would altered trade patterns do to the trader's opportunity for speculation and profiteering?

By now administrative muddle, speculation with import licensing, trader panic at the prospect of anti-corruption measures and the reduction of trade with the West, began to play havoc with the markets. When news leaked (many of the biggest traders were eminently well connected with ministers) that Ghana's wheat order was to be switched from Canada to the Soviet Union, the traders hoarded overnight, and the price of bread shot up to 5*s*. a loaf. Matches, and matchets, were at times unobtainable. The soaring cost of living soured memories of the benefits dispensed by the regime. By 1965 it could not yet be said that the CPP excited active opposition in the populace at large; but the trouble was that it found few protagonists or defenders. It was not the masses that toppled the regime at last; but they did not come to its aid.

When it came to organized resistance, there was little to see. The old opposition had been jailed, exiled or reduced to political impotence; its conspiracies had grown very spasmodic. The traders were alienated from the CPP, but they took no organized action. There were, however, other important members of the middle-class élite who, if they lacked a party, nevertheless dominated the state in the higher ranks of the administration: civil servants, diplomats, the judiciary, the higher ranks of the army and the police. The tight centralization of government after 1962 made civil servants more important than politicians in many of the secretariats that replaced ministries. Finding socialism, non-alignment, and the single-party state equally abhorrent, the civil service made its opposition felt in silent ways. Leading men abandoned Ghana and sought jobs abroad, to become members of international bodies like the ECA, FAO and others. Others dragged their feet inside the administration. They were not wholly to blame. Most of the ministries were in the hands of incompetent politicans preoccupied with ensuring their stake in party and government. The honest and conscientious administrator was lost in a jungle of precipitate top-level decisions and intrigues. If this was socialism, it should be firmly rejected, they felt. Meanwhile, one could ignore instructions by being negative – like losing directives in a morass of paper.

While the mismanagement of the economy affronted their standards of professional performance as much as the official ideology affronted their background and beliefs, the civil servants, unlike their uniformed colleagues in the army, felt that there was not a great deal they could do. Or was there? Two years before the coup d'état, a journalist had a revealing conversation with a leading Ghanaian civil servant. He was lamenting the fact that no new enterprise had been started with foreign capital after 1963, and he was convinced that the present state of affairs could not be allowed to continue.

'But what can you do?' the journalist asked. 'You cannot get rid of either your present government or your president in a general election, so long as there is only one party?'

The official smiled broadly, rose, went to the window and looked out in both directions – they were on the ground floor – and returned. 'You must understand, Mr Fergusson,' he said quietly, 'that there are more ways of getting rid of a president than by holding general elections.'

The civil servant was Mr Emmanuel Omaboe, whose appointment as head of Ghana's National Economic Committee was announced the day of the coup.[29]

In the civil service and commercial circles, it was rumoured that Britain was about to cut off all commercial credit after 1 April 1966. Perhaps it was a lever to stop the shift to new trading partners? Perhaps it was only a rumour? When the soldiers struck it was not a month too soon for Ghana's middle class, traders and civil servants, or for its champions abroad.

THE ARMY INJURED

At independence, Ghana's army consisted of three infantry battalions under a British officer corps, with some thirty Ghanaians in the lower ranks. Major-General Henry T. Alexander was appointed chief of defence staff in January 1960. His predecessor, Major-General A. G. V. Paley, had prepared a plan for Africanization of the army by 1970. By the time that General Alexander was relieved of his command in 1961, the terminal year for complete Africanization was 1962, eight years ahead of schedule. By 1966, there were some 600 Ghanaian officers in the army, the navy and the air force. The Ghanaian army was the largest in West Africa and the eighth largest in all Africa.

Officer cadets were recruited from the secondary schools. And to make the army an attractive proposition, the Nkrumah government raised the pay and fringe benefits of officers to approximate parity with the civil service.[30] Thus, by 1961, a newly commissioned second lieutenant received £663 a year; and a college graduate entering the civil service, £680. Two strains of conservatism fused in the officer corps. It identified in attitude and ambition with the upper and middle groups of Ghanaian society; and it was steeped, via Sandhurst, Mons and Eaton Hall officer cadet schools, as well as Hendon Police College and the Royal Naval College at Dartmouth, in traditional British army attitudes. Africa's blazing Sandhurstphilia ('I entered Sandhurst as a boy and left a soldier.... I loved the companionship of people of identical calling, and the English breakfast.... I look back with nostalgia ... it is one of the greatest institutions in the world')[31] was abnormally exuberant. But the stereotypes held: armies and politics do not mix (a military coup d'état is the result of the other side mixing the two); a soldier takes his stand on matters of honour and fair play; British-type armies are best, and events in the Congo and Rhodesia had nothing to do with Ghana, for it was only Nkrumah's ambition and appetite for foreign adventures which committed his country on the side of Lumumba or against the declaration of independence by a white settler minority.

Nkrumah has written[32] that he always knew the army was not only conservative but potentially disloyal and counter-revolutionary. The ideal course would have been to abolish it, and build instead a people's militia of armed peasants and workers, as in China and Cuba. In fact, Nkrumah's army policy went through the same somersault as the two distinct political phases of Ghana before and after 1961: first leaning heavily Westwards; then trying, though fitfully and largely unsuccessfully, to pull free.

Immediately after independence, Nkrumah maintained the British-commanded, British-type army he had inherited for two reasons. Without an army, he argued, Ghana would have no influence with other African states. Secondly, he calculated that it was sound security to have an army officered by Britishers: 'The individual loyalties of such officers and their training, combined with the political complications for Britain which would have resulted in their joining a revolt, would have made it unlikely that a military take-over could take place.'[33] The British chief-of-staff would act as a buffer between army and state; and the continued inculcation of British army tradition would inhibit military excursions into civilian affairs. It was a convenient thesis to encourage at the time.

This prescription for Ghana's internal security did not, however, make at the same time for an effective pursuit of Nkrumah's Africa policy. The Congo episode proved this conclusively. Nkrumah believed that the Congo was a turning point in Africa; and that the defence of Lumumba as the head of that country's legitimate government was crucial for the unfettered political independence of the whole continent. It was to defend Lumumba's government that Ghanaian army and police contingents went into the Congo. But once there they fell under United Nations command; and as UN strategy unfolded, it was plain that this would not reinforce but displace Lumumba's government. Ghanaian forces found themselves blocking Lumumba's entry to the radio station in the capital after his dismissal by Kasavubu; and Lumumba wrote bitterly to Nkrumah, renouncing the help of Ghana's troops 'in view of the fact that they are in a state of war against our Republic'.[34] Ghana's ambassador in Léopoldville blamed their expatriate commander, General Alexander, for the plummeting of Ghana's popular prestige in the Congo; the Ghanaian military blamed the confused, erratic, and at times ludicrous activities of the Ghanaian diplomats, especially after the Mobutu take-over, for the mounting antagonism of the Congolese. Ghana and its associates in the Casablanca group of African states eventually decided to withdraw their contingents from the Congo, so torn were they between the conflicting purposes of their own and UN policy. Nkrumah, with Alexander's fervent approval, left his contingent at the disposal of the UN.[35]

The Ghanaian army contingents found the Congo operation a searing experience. They watched the political system of another independent state break down into chaos, Congolese soldiers go on the rampage, and the people whom they had come to the Congo to protect and help boo and hoot at them. The Ghana army there itself experienced serious casualties in one battalion, a mutiny in another, and saw its equipment badly run down. To Afrifa,[36] the Congo political operation was 'an unbridled adventure by Nkrumah. . . . We lost lives in struggle which was not ours.' General Alexander could have handled the situation, if only Ghana's politicians had left him alone. Military operations were simple enough; it was the machinations of politicians which led to trouble. General Alexander was frank about his own conflict of loyalties. Was it possible, he asked, for a senior expatriate to hold a high post without finding himself in an impossible position?[37]

It was not only the operation inside the Congo that produced the conflict of loyalty. Instructed to strengthen the army intelligence system, General Alexander was disturbed to hear that a consignment of Soviet arms had been unloaded at Takoradi port. His uneasiness was nothing to the consternation of the Americans and British, who were immediately apprehensive that the arms were destined for Gizenga in Stanleyville. Alexander found himself quizzed by a UN representative in the Congo. He made clear that he had tried to dissuade Nkrumah from any such action on Gizenga's behalf: subsequently to discover that Nkrumah had received a report of the conversation via New York. 'Had I been disloyal?' Alexander asked himself.[38]

It was after the Congo operation that Nkrumah made up his mind to dispense with General Alexander and eighty of his fellow British officers. The army command was also deeply hostile at this time to Nkrumah's decision to diversify his sources of arms and training methods, so that Ghana should not have to depend on a single major power for military assistance. During his 1960–61 visit to various socialist states, Nkrumah sent an instruction to General Alexander to select 400 cadets for officer training in the Soviet Union. Alarmed British officers were emphatic that mixed arms and mixed training made for military nonsense. Said Alexander: 'From the British point of view it was unpleasant to think that a lot of good little Communists were being trained to take their place in Nkrumah's army.'[39] On the day that General Alexander wrote to Colonel Ankrah,[40] then on service in the Congo and later head of Ghana's army government, that the affair of the cadets might mean that he could not continue to help the Ghanaian army, Nkrumah summoned the general to hand him his letter of dismissal. Alexander left the president's office walking side by side with his successor, Brigadier S. J. A. Otu, who turned to him and said: 'General, excuse me for bothering you at this time, but can you possibly lend me some major-general's insignia?' Otu took over the insignia, and, with his fellow-members of the officer corps, allegiance to the customary ways of the British-trained army. (Eventually only sixty-eight cadets were found for the course in the Soviet Union; the cream of the year's complement of eligible school-leavers had already been skimmed off for Britain and the military at Teshie.) There were other sources of discord between government and army. The new constitution of 1960 made the president also supreme commander, chairman of the Defence Committee and the Chiefs of Staffs Committee, with powers to dismiss or suspend military personnel; to call up reserve forces and integrate them in to the regular forces and generally to control the army. In 1962 the officer course at the military academy was shortened in order to produce more graduates; this may have offended the military's sense of professional standards.[41] There was government intervention in the selection of personnel to be sent abroad for military training. In 1962 an Armed Forces Bureau was opened, as part of a civic education programme, to engage the officer corps in discussions on current affairs and the military's role in economic development. The military was unenthusiastic about the project, if not visibly resistant. But the Bureau soon became moribund.

It was after the assassination attempts – the bomb explosion at Kulungugu in August 1962, followed by the Flagstaff House attempt and several bomb incidents in Accra – that Nkrumah began to take drastic steps against army and police. The assassination attempts inaugurated internal struggles within the CPP, and also loyalty probes in the party and police. Nkrumah came to believe, and Police Chief John Harlley is only too ready these days to confirm, that the police chiefs were actively plotting counter-revolution.[42] At least, if they were not fellow-conspirators, they were allies by inefficiency, the evidence seems to show. How else explain the trail of police and intelligence incompetence running through their investigation of successive plots ? In the Kulungugu attack, directed by United Party conspirators operating from Togo, an army sergeant suspected of providing the grenades died in a fall from police headquarters. In the January 1964 assassination attempt on Nkrumah's life, Police Constable Amatewee had been newly appointed to guard duty at Flagstaff House; who was responsible for the posting, and who promised him £2,000 if he got his man ?[43] None of this was ever revealed. Nkrumah used the Flagstaff House attempt to lop off the heads of the police force. Within a week, the nine most senior police chiefs had disappeared into preventive detention. This drastic surgery resulted in the promotion of John Harlley as Police Commissioner. Harlley now claims that he had been plotting Nkrumah's downfall for years, and that he escaped detention largely because he was promoted to a better vantage point for subversion and his private counter-security. Was it coincidence alone that Harlley, as head of the Special Branch, had investigated the January 1964 affair; and that while the evidence he gathered implicated the top nine senior police officials, it was Harlley himself who, as tenth senior officer, then found himself head of the force ? After 1964 there were far-reaching security changes. The police force was disarmed; the Special Branch was removed from police control; the customs and border guards were put on a para-military basis but also removed from police control. Military intelligence was organized in such a way that while not cut off altogether from the army, it was integrated in the security services run from the president's office.[44] It was during this period that Harlley illegally established his own secret intelligence apparatus, with Anthony Deku as one of his operators.[45]

At the same time the army was being inflamed by the reorganization of the Presidential Guard. Originally the President's Guard Regiment had been established by General Alexander as a relief tour from duty in the Congo, for old soldiers no longer fit for the field. Its members were drawn from regular army units and had at first been under army command. In 1963, under Soviet security advice, Nkrumah transformed the force into the President's Own Guard Regiment (POGR) and laid plans to extend it to two battalions for ceremonial duties, but also for security work. In 1964 the order was given to raise the size of the Guard by another regiment. ('By February 1966 it was fortunate for us that only two companies had been raised for the new battalion.') At the time of the coup the POGR had grown to fifty officers and 1,142 men, armed in part with Soviet weapons and assisted by Soviet security advisers.[46] By then the POGR had been detached from the army command, and made directly responsible to Nkrumah, under the command of Captain Zanlerigu. This was the so-called 'private army' which, more than any other single grievance, ignited the military into coup d'état action. Immediately after the coup, General Ankrah broadcast the vastly overstated plaint:

> Massive sums of money were spent every month to maintain an unnecessarily large force of so-called security officers whose duty is ostensibly to provide for the security of the state but really to secure Nkrumah's own personal safety. He established a private army of his own at annual costs of over £500,000 in flagrant violation of a constitution which he himself had foisted on the country to serve as a counterpoise to the Ghana Armed forces.[47]

Major A. K. Ocran echoed it in even more alarmist terms: 'The obvious intention was that the army would die off in course of time and be replaced by the POGR.'[48]

By 1963, there was wrangling over protocol between the Guard Regiment and the regular army. The Guard Regiment commander maintained that he received his orders direct from Flagstaff House. The commander refused to pay compliments to the Chief of Defence Staff on one occasion – when China's Premier Chou En-lai was seen off at the airport – and Ocran wrote the letter of complaint. 'In a country where there is only one Major-General, it does not look nice in the public eye for him to be ignored completely by troops on parade.'[49] In January 1966 staff officers were summoned to Flagstaff House to a meeting to work out conditions covering the Guard Regiment. It was made final that the Chief of Defence Staff should have nothing to do with the Guard Regiment, 'which had for all purposes become part of Flagstaff House and of the Household'.[50]

Army hackles rose next at the retirement of Major-General Otu, Chief of Defence Staff, and his deputy, Major-General Ankrah, in August 1965. Ghana, complained Afrifa, was informed that they had been retired, but most in the army knew they had been dismissed – this was not the way to treat generals.[51] In their places, were appointed Generals Aferi and Barwah. Subsequently, the Ankrah–Otu dismissals were explained by the fact that a coup had been timed for Nkrumah's absence at the Commonwealth Premiers' Conference in London in 1965. The attempt had to be called off at the last minute when Brigadier Hassan, director of military intelligence, got wind of it. It was when rumours of the abortive plot began to reverberate round Accra that Nkrumah got rid of the two generals. In the reshuffle that followed the installation of new commanders, Major Kotoka, who was to be principal army coup-maker soon afterwards, was made a full colonel and sent to Kumasi in the North, to replace Aferi as commander of 2 Brigade.

By this time, there was a state of general unease in the officer corps. There was admiration for the soldiering qualities of army commander General C. M. Barwah, but resentment that he was in Nkrumah's special confidence, and was used for special assignments (though the post-coup charge that he alone knew of the existence of training camps for freedom fighters is patently false; top police officers knew of them, too). There was suspicion that he saw no conflict in serving both Nkrumah and the army, for Barwah cooperated with the scheme to introduce political education into the army. Kotoka himself felt that he had no future under Nkrumah. It was common talk that he and army commander Barwah did not get on with one another. The monthly intelligence report in November 1965 accused Kotoka of a deliberate attempt to transfer Ewe officers into 2 Brigade. The accusation was later formally withdrawn, but the suspicion of Kotoka's favouritism towards the Ewe persisted. Afrifa has disclosed that he sensed Kotoka was in danger of being removed from his command, for a senior officer of the Military Academy and Training Schools who was married to the daughter of an important official of the National Council of Ghana Women. ('Fortunately this was not to be.'[52])

Army shortages were blamed not on balance of payments difficulties, but on the preferential treatment of the POGR. 'The pride of the regular soldier was hurt,' wrote General Ocran. 'There was no boot polish available; of the armoured vehicles only four in ten were roadworthy by 1966.'[53] By Christmas 1965, Afrifa wrote in his account, the troops lacked equipment and clothing, things essential for the pride, morale and efficiency of the soldier. Shortages were said to be due to a rash expansion scheme to meet the challenge of white Rhodesia's UDI in November 1965. Afrifa wrote, 'I personally knew that Her Majesty's Government was quite capable of dealing with the Rhodesia situation. I felt that Nkrumah was making too much noise about the whole issue, especially by raising the people's militia. . . .* Furthermore I do not know why we should have been fighting.' Ocran has written: 'Why did Nkrumah want to send troops to Rhodesia? The Africans there should fight their own battles as a first step, or risk being treated like the aborigines of other countries. Fighting your own wars is a cleansing experience through which our brothers south will have to go.'[54] By the end of 1965 and the beginning of 1966 it was by no means certain that Ghana would commit herself to any Rhodesian action – Chief of Defence Staff Aferi was still to go on an OAU reconnaissance mission, but it was already becoming obvious that African belligerence on this issue would evaporate into hot air. It was merely a convenient pretext for an army that acted to preserve its own status, and that made a

*The People's Militia started to be formed in December 1965. It was more talked about than seen. It was said to be on Chinese advice that the militia be formed.

case for the legitimacy of its action out of prevailing political and economic currents of discontent.

For all its declarations in defence of liberty – and the economic growth rate* – and against tyranny, the Ghanaian army struck only when it itself was affected by the regime. The coup was an act of self-defence by members of an army and police command under suspicion and fearful of having their powers stripped from them. The army as a corporate body felt under attack; but so especially did the leading participants in the coup, and their role in defence of their individual professional careers was probably paramount.

The failure of politics in Ghana was a failure on the part of Nkrumah to elucidate a strategy for the social changes which would have made a breaking of Ghana's dependency possible. But of no less importance was his related failure to consolidate forces around him and his regime for necessary social change. Military coups in Africa succeed less through the power they muster than through the power that popular indifference fails to muster against them. The CPP was ineffective except as a battleground for opposing factions. Nkrumah himself was solitary in government. Castro in Cuba, subjected to an even tighter external containment, consolidated about him young Cuban activists who enlivened the party and its contact with the people. In Ghana, the regime alienated those who hoped to improve their personal and political fortunes by independence; but it did not disarm them, or displace their influence.

Ghana's social structure was not basically different from that of Nigeria – and other West African states or indeed African states in general – and the middle-class élites which acted not to

* It was unthinkable, said General Kotoka on take-over day, that Ghana's economy had developed in the previous three years at the rate of only 3 per cent per annum. In phrases like 'The myth of Nkrumah has been broken' the NLC statement sounds to some ears very non-indigenous; some said it had been drafted with the help of a British information officer, a former district commissioner who was much in evidence on coup day, but this has not been substantiated.

assert but to impede Nkrumah's purposes were the very forces in Nigeria which, in their scramble for office and privilege, strained the political system to breaking point. Army officers, once again, acted to conserve the independence, or the 'neutrality' of the army; but because the army, far from being neutral, was infected by the country's larger divisions, its intervention in politics was bound to sharpen them.

In the Sudan, too, the army reflected the country's divisions: on the one hand, between the parties and religious organizations of the traditional rulers in the countryside, and the commercial interests of the towns; and, on the other, between the political parties of both these groups and younger Sudanese, who expected independence not to further the interest of the privileged groups and politicians, but the country as a whole. When the army command struck to defend particular men in power, the action was bound to divide the army.

Part V

The Soldiers Invade: Coup Casebooks

A Coup Inventory

How should one differentiate between coups? Coups in Africa, no less than elsewhere, do not fall into ideal types. Seeing that it is the first intervention in politics that tends to set up a coup trajectory, by breaking the previously accepted convention that government is for politicians and parties, it is useful to examine coups by the trigger at the start. But the typing of the coup d'état has limited efficacy; they are often born in a muddle of motives, and they displace their own motives midway as they switch from one type to another and back again in the course of the action.

The simplest and occasionally the initial stage of the coup d'état cycle is the army strike, or the pay mutiny. Pay strikes are classic instances of class action by the poorest-paid in the army; armies, when they act as trade unions, have the power to hold the state, their paymaster, to ransom. In 1964 in *Tanganyika* (now Tanzania) and the neighbouring East African states of *Kenya* and *Uganda,* the regulars of all the three armies were chafing at service conditions and the slow pace in Africanization of the officer corps.

At the time that Tanganyika achieved independence, there were only three African commissioned officers in the army. (A further fifteen were on training courses.) A request for a crash training programme, a few weeks before the mutiny, produced a scheme by the British commander to have the army Africanized in ten years. But a State House circular shortly before the mutiny announced a slowing down of Africanization, in an attempt to accommodate non-Africans who had opted for Tanganyika nationality under the citizenship provisions of the independence constitution. 'The nation,' the circular had read, 'must use the entire reservoir of skill and experience. It would be wrong for us to distinguish between Tanganyikan citizens on any ground other than their character and ability. We cannot allow the growth of first and second class citizenship. Africanization is dead.' It was a sharp statement; and among the men preoccupied with promotion prospects, it had a sharp impact. Anonymous letters of grievance had been emanating from the army for some weeks, but they were considered no cause for alarm by the British command. When the mutiny broke, it was men of the First Battalion, Tanganyikan Rifles, who sounded a general alarm at Colito barracks, where they arrested all their officers. Later in the day the Second Battalion mutinied at Tabora, several hundred miles to the west, and there were incidents at a third barracks, in the south. The mutiny was treated as an industrial dispute. Negotiations were opened with the men – led by a sergeant – who were demanding more pay, quicker promotion, the removal of their British officers and complete Africanization. On the third day, the mutiny was considered settled. President Nyerere had broadcast an appeal for calm; and the Cabinet was resuming its functions.

During the next two days, mutiny broke out in the Uganda army barracks at Jinja, and among Kenya forces at Lanet. Both mutinies were put down by British troops, still present in some force in Kenya. Then, when it was thought that the mutiny in Tanganyika was all over, the army men there were seen to stiffen their terms. Evidence came to light of contact between them and a group of political dissidents, reported to have met with a former Opposition leader and several trade-unionists who had emerged as strong critics of the government. Tanganyika requested and received British troops. In Uganda and Kenya the pay strikes had been in no danger of escalating into anything else. In Tanganyika the pay strike was on the verge of becoming a coup that might have brought down the government. The mutineers were court-martialled; the Tanganyikan leadership called on the TANU (government party) Youth League to build a new army; and the government improvised army representation on the national executive committee of the party, alongside similar steps aimed at politicizing the soldiers in support of its policy.

By contrast with the three East African countries, where pay and promotion grievances provoked a mutiny that fell short of a coup, and foreign intervention was invoked to discipline the soldiers, there was *Congo-Kinshasa*, site of Africa's first coup d'état, which was ushered in by a pay strike.

Independence was in fact not five days old when the army mutinied. The immediate cause was the obduracy of the Belgian army commander in refusing to permit any speed-up in Africanization; after the mutiny, discipline in the army shattered, with bands of armed soldiers becoming instruments for any politician or group that could use them. But the Congo's first army intervention in government shortly afterwards was not locally improvised; nor, for that matter, was the second in 1965. (Little in the crises of the Congo since independence has been.) Mobutu's ascendancy was made possible, when different political groups were advancing their claims through antagonistic forces of armed men, by two decisive acts of outside intervention. The first was when, four days before he acted against the Lumumba government, five million francs were handed over to him by the United Nations, so that he could pay the army.[1] Then Mobutu was helped to create around himself a small but intensely loyal force of paratroopers, through the agency of the Moroccan General Kettani – who had served for many years in the French army – and who headed the United Nations military group charged with assisting in the reorganization of the Congolese army.[2] It was this force that made Mobutu the arbiter of all subsequent political crises in the Congo. Auxiliary power structures were the security and police apparatus, and the College of Commissioners run under Belgian and American aegis.[3] (Incidentally, in the first year of independence, the army's pay increased by 450 per cent.) The army stayed in the background during the political developments of the next five years, and then climbed firmly into power in October 1965 – during the disputes for control between Tshombe and Kasavubu – to install Mobutu as President and Minister of Defence, with Brigadier Leonard Mulamba, the army commander, as Prime Minister, and to announce that the army would rule for five years so as to get the country off on a new start.

The first of the West African coups took place in *Togo* in 1963, in the third year of independence, and was also triggered off by a pay strike. The immediate cause was the demobilization of veterans in a major French defence re-orientation. When President Sylvanus Olympio refused to take 626 Togolese, who had been serving in metropolitan regiments, into the Togo army, then 250 strong, a group of these ex-servicemen, led by a former master-sergeant, Emmanual Bodjollé, surrounded his house and shot him. The army installed a civilian government, presided over by Olympio's political rival, Nicholas Grunitzky. Bodjollé made himself colonel, commander and chief-of-staff, while a former sergeant in the French army, Étienne Eyadema (who, it is widely believed, fired the shots that killed Olympio)[4] became a major in an army expanded to 1,200 men. Two years later Eyadema ousted Bodjollé, to make himself colonel and commander, and subsequently to become Togo's head of state.

The pay strike was the trigger for the army coup, but it was not the only source of crisis in Togo. Olympio had built the Comité de l'Unité Togolaise (CUT), as French Africa's first nationalist party. And this he used to score the overwhelming electoral victory which put him at the head of the country's first independence government, in opposition to the party of Nicholas Grunitzky, who had been held in power previously with French support and the backing of Northern chiefs. Just before the army coup, CUT's youth movement split away from it to form the Mouvement de Jeunesse Togolaise, on the grounds that Olympio's policies were entrenching '*les vieux*' among the politicians; were abandoning the party's radical youth and militancy; and were displacing French interests by tying Togo to other foreign interests, particularly American and West German. The replacement of Olympio by Grunitzky, with French-army-oriented and Northern soldiers as his support, won that initial round for France. The North–South conflict was also significantly coincident with the uneven distribution of benefits and government positions. The coup installed a Northern president, who ruled for a predominantly Northern army, with the civil servants – Southerners, mainly Ewe – manning the ministries in truculent though unexpressed opposition to the real rulers of the land, the army commanders.

In November 1966 there was an attempt to overturn the junta. It came not from a section of the army, but from within the administration, and it was led by Noël Kutuklui, Lomé's leading lawyer and secretary-general of Olympio's former party, renamed Unité Togolaise. This was an attempt to seize power by civilian rather than military means. Some of the government's most senior administrators were involved. Leaflets calling for the toppling of the Grunitzky government were printed on the government's presses; the daily government paper came out for a change of government; and the radio broadcast anti-Grunitzky statements. Kutuklui and an aide occupied Lomé's radio station to call for anti-government demonstrations, and claimed, falsely it seemed, that the army was 'behind the rising'; in fact it was the army that cleared the demonstrations off the streets at gunpoint, though with no casualties. French military officers serving as advisers to Togo's army seem to have been mainly responsible for defeating the plot, while American connexions with the anti-French group in CUT had spurred the attempted putsch. A few months after the abortive 'administrator's coup', the army removed Grunitzky, abolished the civilian ministries and took direct control. Eyadema, the former master-sergeant, became President. The Togo cabinet is now a combination of military, police and civilian members; and it is difficult to say in what measure it is military rule: but whoever takes decisions, it is the army that enforces them.

The experiences of the three coups d'état that started as pay strikes suggests that it may take a foreign intervention on the side of government to stop an army pay strike from escalating into a military seizure of the state. Tanganyika, Kenya and Uganda used foreign troops surgically to terminate the coup before it could develop into something worse; Togo, with some evidence that French defence advisers inclined not to government but to its antagonists, fell victim; and in the Congo, foreign intervention secured the army command and political control of the state for a chief-of-staff who was, in time, to constitute the most strongly entrenched army-backed regime in Africa.

If pay strikes can topple governments, the military often intervene in politics to reinforce regimes. These are not army take-overs, but hand-overs to the army, when the army is used as a political sheet-anchor.

In the *Sudan* a simultaneous government, foreign policy and party crisis provoked the Prime Minister, formerly a brigadier in the Sudanese army, who also held the Defence portfolio, to ask the army commander, an associate since the Gallipoli campaign, to rescue the government from its opposition, by suspending Parliament and banning the parties. The result was not a reinforcement of the governing party by the army, but its displacement by a military junta. The junta ruled for six years, during which the army was rocked by three attempted coups within the officer corps, and was finally brought down by a combined assault of popular opposition and a fissure in the officer corps. In 1969 the same forces that had toppled the military junta used the coup d'état to install themselves in power, with the proclaimed aim of using government to build a popular base of support.

In *Sierra Leone*, likewise, the army commander was called upon, by the prime minister defeated in an election, to impose martial law before the opposition leader and party could assume office. The Sierra Leone People's Party (SLPP) had won the post-independence elections of 1962 under Sir Milton Margai's leadership; but after his death and the accession to the party leadership of his brother, Sir Albert Margai, the party declined in influence and in reputation, and was seriously challenged by the All Peoples' Congress (APC) of Siaka Stevens. As in the Sudan, the prime minister feared not only the defeat of his party, but with it his own political eclipse. As the elections approached, he tried various stratagems, including the proposal to establish a one-party state, and other constitutional changes which would have increased his executive powers; he also appointed as chief justice – the man who hears election complaints – a political associate. The polling was manipulated, just as the economic system had been, for the politicians in office; but the voting results still showed a majority for the APC. The governor-general had no sooner sworn in Siaka Stevens, than Sir Albert's friend and supporter in the army, Brigadier Lansana, tried to prop him up. This was a sheet-anchor action in the making; but inside the army, several of the brigadier's officers arrested him. Then, instead of installing the APC, with Stevens as prime minister, the officers of the new junta dissolved the constitution, banned the parties and assumed power themselves, as the National Reformation Council (NRC). The move against Lansana had army, not party political, causes; but it soon enough produced political consequences.

Thirteen months later, the NRC was removed from office by a pay-strike type of coup from the ranks, with non-commissioned officers as spokesmen for the men. Apart from the Council's failures in government, the army itself was seething with discontent, directed at the officers as a whole, and at the ruling NRC in particular. The grievances were over pay and conditions and the inequalities between officers and men. Such are the discontents that stoke a pay strike, and when the soldiers acted it was exactly that; but it coincided with a countrywide resentment of the military junta, and a demand for the return to civilian rule. A group of perhaps a dozen, mostly privates but including a few non-commissioned officers, struck simultaneously at the Wilberforce barracks in Freetown and at Daru near the frontier, where there was a battalion detachment. The Anti-Corruption Revolutionary Movement emerged, to announce that it had arrested the entire officer corps, and that there was to be an immediate return to civilian rule, followed by an army pay increase. Not long after, Siaka Stevens was invited to form a government. In Sierra Leone a pay strike had ended the coup trajectory – that one, anyway – and led not to the installation of a military junta, but to a civilian regime.

In perhaps the largest number of coups, the army has extended its normal police-security function (for African armies are glorified para-military police forces) and has stepped down, as from Olympus, to settle conflict between parties and politicians and resolve a government crisis. But having entered the action as referee – or, in Nigeria, because army officers feared that the military would be used as sheet-anchor on the wrong side – it has often remained in power for itself or on behalf of the groups it espoused.

In *Dahomey* there was an intense struggle among three political groups, organized round three political leaders, and with their political bases reinforced by regional–ethnic divisions between north and south and, in the south, east and west. By 1963 two of the three politicians, Hubert Maga and Migan Apithy, had managed to arrive at some sort of accommodation, but the third, Justin Ahomadegbe, was in detention for alleged plotting against the regime. Dahomey's economic position was precarious. Unemployment was endemic, and growing at an alarming rate, especially among civil servants and teachers. The civil service was swollen by the enforced repatriation of Dahomeyans from other African states and the cutback in France's African armies. Ahomadegbe had allied himself with the trade unions in the port of Cotonou, who deeply resented the political predominance of the capital, Porto Novo. (By 1957 there were estimated to be 22,000 wage-earners in Dahomey, of whom 7,000 were administrative employees in Porto Novo, and 13,000 employees in Cotonou factories or workers in the country's four oil mills.) The crisis was caused initially by the arrest of trade-union leaders, for demonstrating against the government, and especially against its attempts to control the unions. General Soglo, the army commander, stepped in to referee a government re-shuffle; but as the strike continued he felt impelled to assume executive responsibility himself, over a new triumvirate government comprising Apithy, Ahomadegbe and Maga. The general remained at the head of the provisional government for a few months and then formally withdrew in January 1964, handing power jointly to Apithy as president and head of state, and Ahomadegbe as vice-president. The unions had instigated the fall of one government, but they had to watch the army intervene because they themselves could not constitute any other. Two years later, at the end of 1965, the heads of government, working under a system of dual executive, were in fresh deadlock, and the army stepped in again. This time, in the face of growing restiveness among the young intellectuals, and among civil servants – the civil service itself had grown from 12,000 in 1960 to 18,000 in 1965 – who were faced with salary cuts in the interests of austerity, the army set up a nine-man government of army men, technicians and one or two politicians. This was overseen by a National Renewal Committee of the military, technical experts, representatives of the unions and the youth and other interest groups. The leading politicians were in exile.

By mid-1967, however, the Soglo government was being criticized for the same deficiencies as its civilian predecessors. Soglo enjoyed the confidence of France, but the unions were once again organizing resistance to austerity cuts, and the budget deficit was larger than ever. In December 1967, during another bout of strikes, the army stepped in for the third time. Younger army officers dissolved General Soglo's government. The unions immediately presented their demands, among them the refund of a 25-per-cent reduction in their salaries. The middle-rank officers, who had mounted this latest coup, installed as head of state Colonel Alphonse Alley, formerly Soglo's chief-of-staff. A return to civilian rule through elections proved a fiasco, owing to a boycott, but the regime found a civilian head in a former politician, Dr Émile Zinsou. One of Zinsou's first decisions was to retire Colonel Alley and promote Major Kouandete to his post. In October 1969 the trial opened in Cotonou of Colonel Alley and others, charged with an attempted abduction of Major Kouandete. Successive referee actions had set off a pattern of military cannibalism in the army, where one commander devoured another.*

In *Upper Volta* the army has been immune to inner-army strife. There, too, the army seized power during a showdown between the government of President Maurice Yameogo and the trade unions, and after conflict between political factions representing different regions. This was in January 1966, and the immediate cause of the discontent was a cutback in civil service salaries. The army was to hold the ring while the politicians negotiated a new coalition. But within a year Colonel Lamizana

*On 10 December 1969 a group of officers deposed President Zinsou. Lt.-Col. Maurice Kouandete, chief-of-staff and military commander of Cotonou, Dahomey's commercial capital, was believed to be behind this coup.

announced that military rule would continue for four years. Government was composed of seven military men and five civilians, with Lamizana as president and prime minister.

In the *Central African Republic*, Colonel Jean-Bedel Bokassa, army commander-in-chief, used the army to adjudicate the conflict between himself and the president, David Dacko, a close relative. Bokassa claimed as his justification for the seizure of power, the existence of a coup against the president and himself, and a Chinese plot against the country. The army government, he said, would 'abolish the bourgeoisie'. The political reasons for action, among them the need to pre-empt a radical coup, were extravagant; the effect of the coup was probably more minimal in the Central African Republic than anywhere else.

In *Burundi*, the young king Ntare V dethroned his father Mwambutsa IV through a military coup in July 1966, and installed himself as head of state, with Captain Micombero as prime minister. Three months later, the premier deposed the nineteen-year-old king for his failure to keep his promises. A National Revolutionary Committee of army officers was created until a new government was formed. There had been a sequence of cabinet crises, political assassinations, plots and political executions over three years.

In *Nigeria*, too, though the reform declarations of the coup-makers suggested otherwise, the first coup of January 1966 cast the army essentially in the role of referee. The young officers were convinced that the army was about to be used by the politicians in power to reinforce their hold. The effect of throwing soldiers into the Western region, which was in a state of incipient civil war, would have been to strengthen a federal government based mainly on Northern power; the young majors intervened to adjudicate the contest in favour of the harassed opposition. The soldiers would have imposed an interim authority to bring Awolowo to power, they subsequently disclosed. Their declarations of reform were vague, if sincere, and though they admonished a class of corrupt politicians, they expressed no real alternative. (It was not the system that was wrong, but the men in power, one of the coup-makers later declared.[5]) In any event, the coup lasted barely a week-end, not long enough to produce any alternative. It failed in a bid to take over the country and was smothered in a sheet-anchor counter-move by the army command under Ironsi. The army was then rapidly affected by the contagion of political division in the country, so that trends which had once resulted in constitutional, electoral and government deadlock became, in the hands of the soldiers, counter-coups for control – such as the coup from which the Gowon government emerged in July 1966 – armed clash and civil war.

Whether it enters as arbitrator or guardian of government, the army is liable to become a competitor for power. Sometimes the habit of power grows upon it in office; at other times its intervention in politics is immediately inspired by this purpose, especially if it sees its interests as coinciding with those of other groups that do not feel satisfactorily accommodated within the political system.

In *Congo-Brazzaville*, there was no military participation, only that of the police commander, in supplanting the government of Youlou by that of Massemba-Debat in 1963. The initiative appeared to lie in the hands of the politicians backed by militant and radical-sounding youth and trade-unionists, organized in the union federations, in the youth section of the party, the National Movement of the Revolution (MNR) and in a civilian militia as a counter to the army. In 1966 an attempted army mutiny against the government was suppressed only with the help of Cuban army officers on secondment to help train the civil defence organization. Apart from this incipient conflict between army and party youth wing (throughout, the French retained their influence in the army; but the party and the youth section were forging links with Cuba, with China and the Soviet Union), there was another rift that ran through politics in Congo-Brazzaville. This was the division between Northern elements, strongly represented in the army (like the Kouyou people, from whose ranks rose young officers like Captain, later Major, Alfred Raoul, and Major Marien Ngouabi: alongside, incidentally, General Mobutu of Congo-Kinshasa, and General Bokassa of the Central African Republic); and the Bakongo, especially the Lari, people of the South, round the capital, of which Massemba-Debat was a representative, as he was of the élite in the capital itself. In August 1968 the arrest of several leading supporters of Massemba-Debat was a prelude to the army take-over proper.

For some weeks there was a prolonged tussle for control of the capital between the party youth and the army. Massemba-Debat was eclipsed, first temporarily, and then permanently. The army emerged victorious. A new provisional government was established under the National Revolutionary Council, in which the army held three key positions, with Captain Alfred Raoul as prime minister, and Major Ngouabi as representing the real power of the army. Brazzaville Radio announced communiqués setting up committees for the defence of the revolution, and suspending the party, its youth and women's organizations, and the trade-union federal councils. Soon, at the beginning of 1969, Ngouabi emerged formally as head of state, while remaining head of the armed forces. Pay increases of up to 40 per cent were announced for low-grade, and up to 20 per cent for middle-grade, civil servants. A cabinet reshuffle dropped the most important remaining Bakongo members of the government. A thousand members of the youth wing were officially incorporated into the regular army.

In Congo-Brazzaville, as in Algeria, the army saw itself as the more reliable revolutionary force. If Western-trained army officers are traditionally pro-West, not so Ngouabi, whose government was the first in Africa to recognize the government of the Viet Cong. Time will tell whether the radical pronouncements correspond with internal structural changes.

Algeria's road to independence, with the origins and inspiration of its army, was unique in the African experience. Algeria raised peasant-based forces that fought a gruelling war for seven years, setting a record for liberation by armed struggle without African parallel in the phase of decolonization. But after the crisis in the summer of 1962, post-independence Algerian politics resembled not the models of China, Vietnam and Cuba – of armed struggle from a guerrilla base liberating the rest of the country – but those of other newly independent states on the continent. The war had produced not a unity between politics and the army fighting for liberation, nor even a united army, but several divided centres of power. The political leadership and the military were never integrated, as the guerrillas of Guiné-Bissau insist that they must be, as an essential pre-condition of building not a professional, coup-making army, but a political movement of armed militants.[6] The FLN was the party for Algeria's liberation, embracing patriots of every political hue from moderate liberals to radical socialists. But when the government-in-exile was formed, it was reformist old-style politicians who negotiated the settlement with France, not the representatives of the militant forces in the interior. For these, in the *wilayas,* were cut off from one another at the height of the war, and from the army held in reserve over the frontier in friendly Maghreb countries; and no unified guerrilla base or leadership was ever built. By the time that independence was achieved, the army of the exterior was highly cohesive and organized; it not only absorbed or disbanded the *wilayas,* but was the force that backed Ben Bella to head the government over other contestants, and thus ruled, without coup d'état, behind the scenes. The issue in the ensuing years remained the locality of political power in the new state. The FLN grew no grass-roots organization, and attempts to articulate the meaning and policy of the independence government floundered between contesting claims and vagueness of purpose. The primary cause of the coup d'état led by the army chief-of-staff, Colonel Boumedienne, in mid-1965 was the attempt by Ben Bella to form a people's militia and solidify his political base as a counterpoise to the strength of the army. The principal justification of the army was the failure of government and the economy. After the coup, the role of the FLN was re-defined as one of elaboration, orientation, animation and control, but not of supremacy in the state. It was the army, through the Council of the Revolution, that was to be supreme.

Most of these coups d'état have been 'palace' or political establishment revolutions, not social ones. They have changed personnel, shifted the balance in governments, arbitrated the claims of interest groups. The re-shufflings have been between groups pivotal in the conduct of politics and the administration, but they have made no substantive changes in the direction of the economy, or the government's policies of social management. Between the army acting as sheet-anchor or as referee, there is a fine, barely visible line. The sheet-anchor action is generally initiated not by the army itself, but by government; by contrast, the coups which start as referee actions, to replace or to reprimand governments, are often staged by middle and younger officers (the young majors of Nigeria; the abortive attempt of the young lieutenants in Gabon). The army command tends to identify itself with the government ushered in to office with independence; the younger officers question the record of such government, and champion other aspirants, and their own army grievances often coincide with political discontents. In the coups where the army acts as a competitor for power, it often proclaims more revolutionary purpose than the government shows ability to pursue; yet the test of its purpose lies not in the proclamation, but in the army's ability to formulate alternative strategies and corresponding social instruments.

There are coups d'état that serve as levers for change, or against it. In *Egypt*, now the United Arab Republic, the Free Officers destroyed a corrupt and failing palace-aristocracy; and although the initial action had not calculated on far-reaching social change, or even the continuance of the officers in government, they soon felt themselves impelled, for domestic, social and foreign policy reasons, to institute land reform and nationalization, alongside an endeavour to build a popular political base. And in this last, Egypt's army has revealed most glaringly the intrinsic limitations of professional armies in politics and government.

In *Libya*, in September 1969, the army removed a feudal monarchy and promised a passage to the Egyptian model. In the *Sudan* the young officer coup of 1969 wrenched power not from a feudal-based aristocracy but from traditional political parties enmeshed in sectarian religious politics. These armies pledged a transformation of the economic and social structures in their countries, through state action dominated by themselves.

In both *Ghana* and *Mali*, the army – together with the police force in Ghana – acted to reverse reforms that the Nkrumah and Modibo Keita regimes had tried, however unsuccessfully, to set in motion. The coups revealed in one stroke the fatal weaknesses of these regimes: while they were committed to initiating economic undertakings that would break with the old colonial dependence, and would induce far-reaching changes in the social structure, the changes themselves had been insufficient to alter the fundamental character of the state or the political party. These systems showed no more resilience under attack from their armies than have half a dozen feeble, divided élite-run states. At the same time, changes induced by the army junta and its civilian base, certainly in Ghana, as soon as power was seized, were sufficiently removed, in declaration and purpose, and in long-term effect on the economy, to characterize these coups as levers to reverse change. Nkrumah had not found a strategy for African development, let alone for socialism; but the Ghanaian coup d'état – like the one to come in Mali – was calculated to prevent any such prospect.

Coups that Failed

In *Ethiopia*, the coup that failed in 1960 has been called both the first real attempt at social revolution there,[7] and a typical palace putsch.[8] The principal conspirators were the commander of the Imperial Bodyguard, Brigadier-General Mengistu Neway, and his younger brother, Girmame, an enlightened provincial governor; and they were joined by the head of the security service and the police commissioner, and supported, once the coup was under way, by demonstrations of university students (although, from among the graduate élite of four to five hundred in Ethiopia, only a handful were known to be fully committed in the preparation of the coup).[9] The coup reflected the conflict between the traditional nobility and the newer, larger Western-educated groups 'whose initiatives were blocked in a palace world of court political intrigues'.[10] The coup-makers proclaimed a reform government; yet they failed signally to find a firm base of support, and they fell back on traditional ones –

the crown prince, in whose name their proclamation was announced, noblemen, the military leadership – in order to justify and confirm their seizure of power. The coup was defeated militarily because it was staged by the Imperial Guard alone; and countervailing military forces, in the shape of the army, the territorial force and the air force, were mobilized, with the help of United States military and diplomatic advice,[11] until the dynastic power bases of the imperial regime, not least the Church, could re-assert themselves.

In *Senegal*, in 1962, a long-standing political conflict between President Senghor and his prime minister, Mamadou Dia, led to an attempted coup by the latter. The army was divided. The commander-in-chief supported Dia; the paratroop commander, Jean Diallo, threw his forces behind the president. The support of the paratroops was decisive. Senghor frustrated the coup and had Dia and his supporters arrested. The paratroop commander became head of the armed forces.

In *Gabon*, in 1964, French army intervention restored the government of President Léon M'ba, after a coup d'état had achieved power for just under two days. The coup-makers were young lieutenants, who constituted themselves the Revolutionary Committee. They had begun to install a different government, headed by the former Foreign Minister, Jean Hilaire Aubame, whom the former United States Ambassador to Gabon is only too willing to describe as pro-American,[12] and were broadcasting in the streets of the capital, Libreville: 'A peaceful revolution has just been accomplished. We ask foreigners, including the technical advisers, not to worry.'[13] The French Ambassador bent to the task of trying to negotiate the release of M'ba and a compromise government that would accommodate all factions. The French government had other plans. General Kergaravat, commander of the French Forces of the Second African Zone, had been alerted at his headquarters in Brazzaville. ('A group of Frenchmen sent the appeal to de Gaulle,' according to one observer.)[14] A French troop airlift went rapidly into action. Forces were called in from the Central African Republic and from Dakar in Senegal, until there was a build-up of some 600 French troops. According to the American Ambassador, from the time that General Kergaravat arrived in Libreville until he left Gabon forty-eight hours later, the French Ambassador was out of touch with his government; the Elysée was communicating directly with the general. In Gabon, after the restoration of President M'ba, crowds stoned American cars and accused the CIA of instigating the coup to put their protégé Aubame in office.[15]

After the French Cabinet meeting at which the Gabon intervention was discussed, M. Alain Peyrefitte, Minister of Information, declared: 'It is not possible to leave a few machine-gun carriers free to seize at any time a Presidential Palace, and it is precisely because such a threat was foreseen and foreseeable that the new-born states signed agreements with France to guard against such risks.' The Minister disclosed that France had intervened ten times under these agreements since 1960.

I. THE SUDAN

The General Changes Hats

The Sudanese Parliament had been precipitately adjourned in November 1958, at the height of a crisis over the acceptance of United States aid. The morning it was due to re-assemble, the country found itself under the control of a military government – the second, after Egypt, in Africa. 4,000 troops had been moved into the capital on the authority of the commander-in-chief, General Ibrahim Abboud. The country, he said in his first broadcast, had been in a state of degeneration. Chaos and national instability, which prevailed among individuals and the community alike, had spread into all government machinery and public utilities without exception, as a result of which the nation was gradually being dragged to disaster. 'Praise be to Allah that your loyal army has today . . . carried out a peaceful move which it is hoped will be the turning point towards stable and clean administration.'[1] General Abboud, as Prime Minister and Minister of Defence, headed a Council of Ministers of eight army men and five civilians, and a Supreme Council of the Armed Forces, of the same eight army men together with five others.

Nine years later, Abdallah Khalil had a touching if unconvincing version of his last day as prime minister. The afternoon before the coup, he told me, he had been due to give a lecture at the military college. 'My subject was "The Spirit of the Soldier". I went to deliver the lecture, but no officers came. Perhaps they were too busy preparing for the next day.'[2] This defiance of army regulations was dismissed with surprising lightness by the man who had lived his life by army discipline. Abdallah Khalil had spent thirty-two years and two world wars in the army. He was commissioned in the Sudanese battalions of the Egyptian army after joining in 1910 and serving at Gallipoli, and in 1967 was still able animatedly to recall the

Dardanelles campaign. In the Second World War, he saw action in Ethiopia, and by his retirement in 1942 was the first Sudanese to reach the rank of brigadier or Miralai. 'I like the army,' he confided. 'You know what you're doing. You know where you are with the army.' This was a strange statement from the man who eased the army into power in the Sudan when he could not impose his policies and his premiership in any other way, only to find that his army-holding rescue operation developed overnight a power structure of its own, which jettisoned his place in the post-coup government, and, subsequently, even imprisoned him.

For, after a decade, several governments and much probing and reconstruction of events, it is clear that the coup in the Sudan, far from being a take-over of power by the army, was a hand-over to the army. It was a coup by courtesy, set afoot by an army commander and his senior aides in response to the demand for emergency measures by the head of government. The premier was losing his grip on his coalition, his party and his office as premier. He used his post as Minister of Defence to assert military compulsion where political solutions had not worked. Abdallah Khalil's various public and private explanations were inconsistent, where they were not patently shifty, as in the evidence he gave before the official Inquiry into the coup.* The account that he gave, whitewashing his own role, squared not at all with the evidence of the army participants in the coup, or with the sequence of events.

The coup was a talking point in the Three Towns† several weeks before it occurred. Abdallah Khalil made it clear that he regarded the rejection of United States aid by MPs as mutiny.‡

* *Inquiry into the Causes of the 17 November 1958 Coup, conducted by the Attorney-General's Office under the Sudan Penal Code*, January 1965, hereafter referred to as the Inquiry. The report of the Inquiry is in Arabic.

† The Three Towns comprise Khartoum, Khartoum North and Omdurman, all contiguous.

‡ Abdallah Khalil's evidence to the *Inquiry into the Causes of the 17 November 1958 Coup*. Among those questioned about their part in the coup were Generals Abboud, Wahab and Hassan Beshir, as well as Zein Abdin Salehm, a retired army officer. For the most part the examination was not searching nor intensive enough to prevent evasion and vagueness on the part of witnesses.

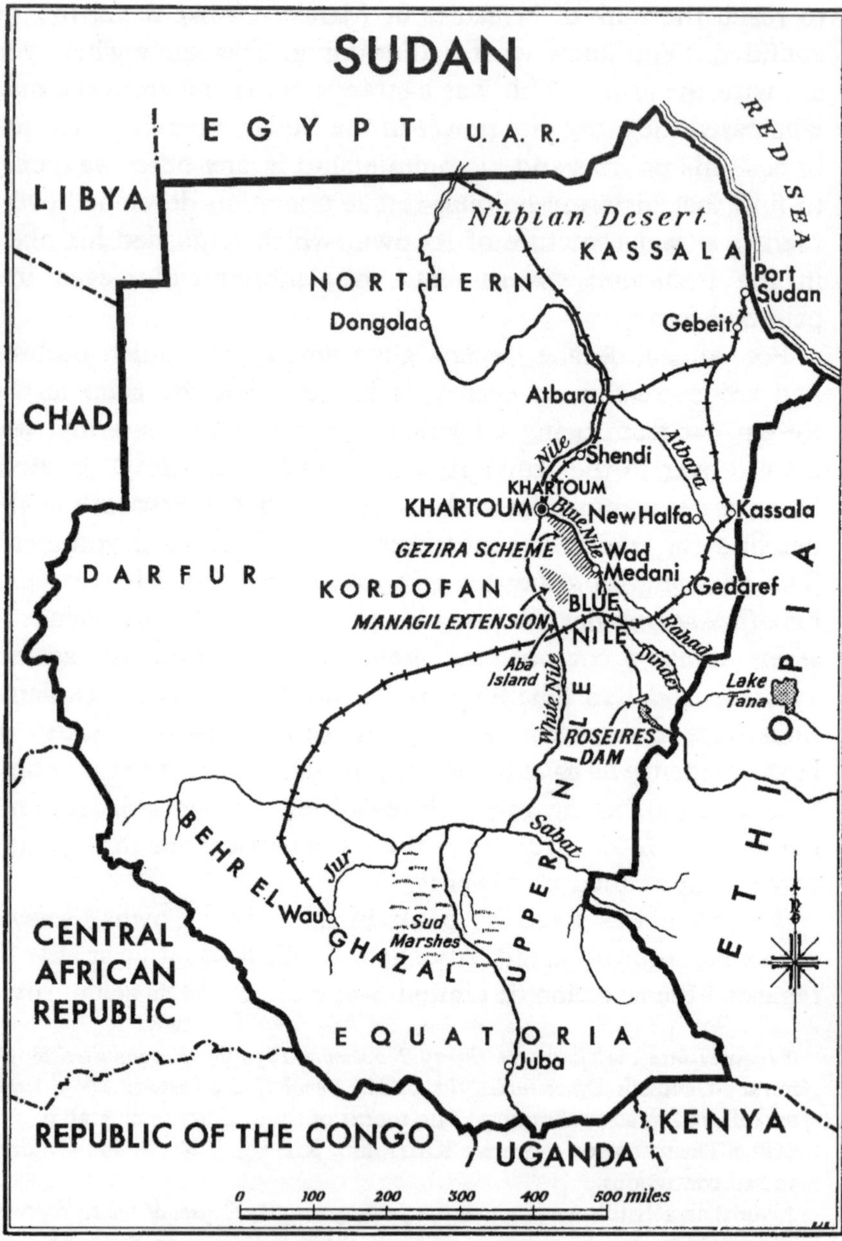
SUDAN
EGYPT U.A.R.
LIBYA
RED SEA
Nubian Desert
KASSALA
NORTHERN
Port Sudan
Dongola
Gebeit
Atbara
CHAD
Atbara
Nile
Shendi
KHARTOUM
KHARTOUM
Blue Nile
New Halfa
Kassala
GEZIRA SCHEME
Wad Medani
DARFUR
KORDOFAN
Gedaref
BLUE NILE
MANAGIL EXTENSION
Rahad
Aba Island
Dinder
White Nile
Lake Tana
ETHIOPIA
ROSEIRES DAM
UPPER NILE
Sabat
BEHR EL GHAZAL
Jur
Wau
Sud Marshes
CENTRAL AFRICAN REPUBLIC
EQUATORIA
Juba
REPUBLIC OF THE CONGO
KENYA
UGANDA
0 100 200 300 400 500 miles

He threatened that if the politicians failed, he could resort to other forces, and rumour was rife that he was planning to call on the army.* He sounded out the Speaker of the House a month before the coup about proclaiming a state of emergency, but was advised that neither Parliament nor the Supreme Council would allow it.[3] A Communist Party leaflet circulated a fortnight before the coup warned that 'democracy is in danger and might be replaced by a military dictatorship'. *Al Ayyam* columns were voicing disquiet at suspicious developments behind the scenes. The day before the army acted, Abdel Khalek Mahgoub, the Communist Party secretary-general, urged Azhari to issue a public warning of an imminent military intervention, but the NUP leader refused. Diplomatic wires were also humming with official and unofficial reports that an army coup was on the way in the Sudan. Abdallah Khalil confided in Haile Selassie,[4] his friend and associate from Second World War field-campaigns in Ethiopia; the news travelled on the diplomatic grapevine from the Emperor to the British embassy in Addis Ababa, and thence to the British and Ethiopian embassies in Khartoum.

It was clear that the Umma–PDP coalition was too far eroded to survive the forthcoming session of Parliament. The PDP tactics of non-cooperation endangered the working of the United States aid agreement to which the Umma Party was

*Under cross-examination at the Inquiry, Abdallah Khalil said: 'After some time there was the latest rumour that the army was planning a coup, and I heard this rumour like others did, by hearsay and not in any formal or official way. I did not investigate the rumour although I was the Minister of Defence. For one thing, I did not hear officially . . . and anyway it wasn't possible for me to stop the army because the coup was ready.'

P. M. Holt, *A Modern History of the Sudan* (London, 1961), p. 184, reports a conversation which Abdallah Khalil is said to have had with General Abboud on 20 November and a statement after 26 November that he was aware of what was going on in military circles.

Abu Rannat, Chief Justice under the Khalil government and one of the civilian pillars of the Abboud military regime, told the writer: 'Tacit agreement for the army to step in had been reached in discussions over some weeks. The matter had been ventilated. It was known from discussions that the army would be welcome. The error of the army was not to plan exactly how to intervene, and at what point to hand over again.'

committed. Umma leaders also made no secret of their ambition to have Sayid Abd al-Rahman al-Mahdi declared president of the Republic; the PDP calculated that an UMMA–Ansar president would make them very much the junior partner of the coalition both in fact and in the eyes of Egypt, so it was scarcely surprising that the PDP obstructed more energetically than ever. The Umma Party saw this as urgent, for Abd al-Rahman al-Mahdi's health was reported by his doctors to be failing; but Umma eagerness to settle the issue was rivalled only by PDP perversity in prolonging it. The alternative was for the Umma Party to find a new partner in coalition. But to Abdallah Khalil, whose hostility to Egypt and Egyptian influences had first been incited during the Abd al-Latif mutiny and had not subsided in thirty years, an association with the NUP and an accommodation with Azhari were unthinkable. The coalition with the PDP had been possible only because Abdallah Khalil had a working relationship with Sayid Ali al-Mirghani, whom he had tried, unsuccessfully, to prevail upon to dismiss Ali Abd al-Rahman as party leader, and because the two Sayids had produced a common declaration of purpose in their mutual desire to break Azhari.

Other events added to the pressure on Khalil. Government had been rendered unworkable by the conflict inside the coalition, and now the same problem provoked a split inside the Umma Party itself, with Abdallah Khalil and Siddiq al-Mahdi, the son of Abd al-Rahman al-Mahdi, in heated contest over whether the NUP was acceptable as a coalition partner. The dispute was taken for mediation to Sayid Abd al-Rahman al-Mahdi who, on constitutional grounds, threw his support behind Abdallah Khalil as leader of the party in government and its secretary-general.[5] In fervent disagreement but unwilling to challenge his father's authority, Siddiq left the country for Switzerland. By then, however, Umma negotiations with the NUP had already been initiated; and among important members of the party, there was every expectation that, when Parliament assembled, it would be controlled by an Umma–NUP coalition, without Abdallah Khalil. The Umma Party leader who, on the afternoon before the coup, took the prime minister a copy of the plan for a new partnership in government, found him closeted in his office with the Chief Justice, Abu Rannat, who was to be one of the two civilians on whom the military government would lean. The NUP–Umma coalition was ready, men of influence in the Umma Party said, 'but Abdallah Khalil betrayed us'.

Azhari, himself, was meanwhile engaged in a double set of calculations. He was negotiating a coalition with the Umma representatives on the one hand, and on the other was taking soundings with the PDP. Azhari and a small group of party associates had travelled to Iraq during the parliamentary recess, to congratulate General Kassem on his successful coup. On the way there and back, they had spent brief periods in Cairo. Also in the Egyptian capital at the time had been the leader of the PDP, Abd al-Rahman. In Umma circles, Azhari's visit to Iraq was seen as a way of being innocently in Egypt at the same time as the leader of the PDP. The latter asserted that he had gone to Cairo because Sayid Ali al-Mirghani wanted the way prepared for a settlement of the Nile waters dispute. In the course of this mission, the PDP delegation was received by Nasser, Zakariah Mohieddin and the Egyptian Minister of Agriculture. Azhari denied emphatically[6] that the simultaneous presence in Cairo of himself and the PDP leader – and the arrival of Sayid Ali al-Mirghani – was anything but coincidental. At the time, however, Yusuf Mustafa al-Tinay, the Sudanese ambassador in Cairo, and one-time editor of the Umma Party organ, was drawing his own conclusions. Intelligence reports submitted to Khartoum and press coverage of Sudanese comings and goings in Cairo could be relied upon to play on more than only Abdallah Khalil's deep-set fears of Egyptian intervention. Less personal but scarcely less crucial were the susceptibilities of United States foreign policy, with its penchant for military men and military machines as more malleable and understandable than Third World political forces, and its revulsion for both NUP and PDP policies, with their hint of Nasserist influence.

The Umma Party, up to now undivided, began to develop schisms. Some members of the party's parliamentary group expressed public dissent with Khalil's policies, and a meeting of youth activists and some MPs passed a vote of censure on the prime minister. The Umma group that opposed US aid was accused by the traditionalists in the party of being Egyptian agents. Popular pressures were rising to the point where none of the parties and no new government could totally discount the demand for a rupture with existing foreign policy commitments. National Front committees were being formed in the provinces, on the initiative, chiefly, of the Communist Party (which was illegal, but operated more or less openly as the Anti-Imperialist Front) for a swing to the left,[7] with cooperation of all left forces inside and outside the parties. The politicians were still preoccupied with manoeuvres at the top; but rank-and-filers, especially in the PDP, in the trade unions, among the students and the Gezira tenants, were campaigning for more fundamental political realignments. They demanded the 'regaining of sovereignty by the abrogation of the American aid agreement' and the 'abolition of the feudal system and its economic base', as well as a 'national democratic constitution that guaranteed the full participation of patriotic forces'. The surge of popular pressure was prompted by the spreading conviction that the politicians and the parliamentary system had squandered the country's independence hopes.

By 13 November, United States policy-makers in the area appeared to have convinced themselves that an Egyptian take-over of the Sudan government was imminent. This was based largely on a cannily timed announcement by a prominent NUP leader that an NUP–PDP coalition was certain. This had deliberately been leaked to speed the still slow progress of Umma–NUP negotiations.[8] But this news had exactly the opposite effect to what had been intended, for it prompted Abdallah Khalil to execute his own contingency plan. By now, any objection from Britain or the United States to an army action had been either neutralized in the interests of achieving government 'stability', or enthusiastically dropped in the interest of containing Egypt and its conspiracies, real or imaginary, against the Sudan. When the time came for the army to play its part, there was the reasonably sound assurance that, even if they indicated no public approval, the two major powers with interests in this area of Africa would look kindly on the actions of the military.[9]

Abdallah Khalil had begun sounding out close army associates two months before the army stepped in. A few days before the move, General Abboud, army commander-in-chief, convened a meeting of the senior army officers in Khartoum to discuss the premier's request that the army intervene to ensure stability in the country. The army attitude varied. Major-General Abd al-Wahhab, the army's strong man and second-in-command, was Abdallah Khalil's relative, had also been his ward and protégé since he had been enrolled at cadet school, and was a strong Umma supporter. If one crutch of an Umma coalition fell away, the army would make an alternative prop. General Abboud took the same conveniently confused view as did his head of government. Of course, an army move meant that he who had been badgering the Ministry of Finance to finalize his pension had to postpone his imminent retirement; but he accepted this with the good grace of any well-trained army man. Others of the generals felt that the army had to act to pre-empt a move by more junior officers.[10] But whatever they thought at the time about their intervention, the army commanders subsequently explained themselves as having responded to a military command that had to be executed without question. It had been issued from head of government to commander-in-chief of the army, and so on down the command structure.

The inside planning of the army move looked very much like the work of General Wahhab and Brigadier Hassan Beshir Nasr. The latter said that he had three weeks in which to prepare army dispositions in the Three Towns.[11] The declaration, on the prime minister's orders, of a twenty-four-hour state of emergency for the re-opening of Parliament pointedly set the timing of the operation, and gave the army the cover that it required under army regulations for emergency standby. The official excuse was that security forces were being alerted in case of rioting on the resumption of Parliament. In fact, this was the screen that the army used to assemble in barracks on the night of 16 November, guns at the ready. They moved into action at 2 A.M., according to careful pre-arranged headquarters planning.

Ali Abd al-Rahman, the PDP leader,[12] paid a courtesy, or curiosity, call on Abdallah Khalil immediately after the coup. Khalil said, to the considerable consternation of Umma associates present: 'Don't worry. Nothing has changed. Politics will go on as they are. Tomorrow you will hear on the radio that there will be a new government, and a new Council of Ministers. Azhari and I will be in the Supreme Council, and some of our big officers in the Council. The parties and Umma politics will continue.' To Abdallah Khalil, the coup was to be the continuation of his politics by other means. It was some days before the irony of the situation sank in. Abdallah Khalil, the pillar of British establishment traditions in the Sudan, pioneer member of the advisory council, of the legislative council and then of Parliament, who had climbed all the carefully placed rungs to self-government and independence, had used a British-trained army to dismantle the whole structure – and with it the generally accepted British army tradition that soldiers do not meddle in politics. And all this had been done only to have his own army then evict him from the new authority that he had himself tried to establish.

Whether or not there was a formal or gentlemen's agreement among Generals Abboud, Wahhab and Hassan Beshir on the one hand, and Abdallah Khalil on the other, it was unquestionably a shock to the deposed premier when he learned, on the day of the coup, that far from acting to reinforce his authority, the army was distributing ministries to army officers, and setting up a Supreme Council of the Armed Forces that would consist of army men alone.

Not that the army on the day of the coup gave the impression that it knew where it was going. The operation itself went off without loss of life, with almost ostentatious politeness, and without round-ups at all; there were only letters of dismissal from office and a brief period of house arrest for the leading politicians. Within hours of the take-over, the army was brandishing a message from the head of each of the two sects 'blessing' the new government. From Sayid Ali al-Mirghani, the blessing came with some warmth, probably because Abdallah Khalil had given him some prior inkling of developments, and because his PDP, like Abdallah Khalil, stood to lose from an Umma–NUP coalition. Sayid Abd al-Rahman al-Mahdi's message implied certain reservations, but a strong hint that acceptance would be the smoothest path to civil peace.

At army headquarters, a flurried series of consultations began, as the generals cast about for their course of action. No senior civil servant appeared to question the authority of the new masters; and, indeed, for some while after the coup, it was not certain who they were. At least one important member of the army senior command did not know that the army had taken power: when a civilian reported to Major General Mohammed Talaat Farid, in charge of the Southern Command at Juba, that he had heard the broadcast of an army take-over from Radio Omdurman, Farid had the man thrown into jail for spreading rumours and undermining confidence.

In the period between the troop movements a few hours after midnight and the broadcast of the military take-over, Generals Abboud and Wahhab had been paying urgent calls. One of their visits was to Abu Rannat, the Chief Justice, who agreed to continue in that post. The second philosopher-guide of the army command was Ahmed Kheir. A lawyer like Abu Rannat, he had been one of the founders of the Graduates' Congress, and much admired by the independence student generation. But quarrelsome and hypercritical of his fellow-politicians who had excluded him from office, he had broken with them and retired from active political life. General Wahhab called on Ahmed Kheir for a legal consultation. What would he advise, he was asked, about the dissolution of Parliament and the installation of a new regime? These, Ahmed Kheir replied, were matters not of procedure, but of policy. His impression of this first consultation with the army general was that a civilian Supreme Council was about to be nominated which would include Azhari, representatives of the Mahdi and Mirghani families, a Southerner and Abdallah Khalil.[13] But later in the day, when the generals returned for a fresh bout of advice, they had changed their plans. The military alone were to comprise the Supreme Council.

Twelve officers, under General Abboud as president, were decreed the supreme constitutional authority in the Sudan; and to General Abboud were formally delegated all legislative, judicial and executive powers, as well as the command of the armed forces. The army invited Ahmed Kheir to become one of five civilian ministers who, together with seven army men on the Supreme Council, would comprise a Council of Ministers. He was appointed Minister of Foreign Affairs. Among the five civilian ministers, two had been Umma members of the Khalil cabinet: Ziada Osman Arbab, the Minister of Education; and a Southerner, Santino Deng, the Minister of Animal Resources.

The Brigadiers' Mutiny

The initial popular reaction to the coup was relief that the politicians were at last out of the way. For many people, military rule evoked the examples of Egypt and Iraq, where radical officers had removed corrupt politicians at gunpoint. But as the months passed, and the country and the army took a closer look at the shape of the new authority, there was serious disquiet.

The seizure of power by the small group of senior officers in Khartoum had been swift and effortless. Organized political opposition on a number of fronts under the leadership of left-wing forces would in time pierce the myth of the army regime's invincibility, but this needed time to gather strength. What the top army command did not bargain for were the fissures in its own ranks. These opened in the inner circle that was the Supreme Council of the Armed Forces, through the hostility between Abd al-Wahhab and Hassan Beshir; and in the army at large, following the exclusion from the inner circle of several important members of the army hierarchy, who suspected political reasons for their being kept out. Combinations of career rivalry, the cleavage in sect allegiances and the conflicting politics of different army generations made for a turbulent first year of army rule;

and helped, in the convulsive last days of the regime, to topple the army government from power.

The NUP–Umma and Ansar–Khatmiyya conflict soon rose to the surface. From its beginnings, the army and the police force had been largely Khatmiyya-based. Among the Khatmiyya, the Shaigia, whose military prowess had given the Egyptian Khedive some considerable trouble, were particularly well represented in the army, and in its top command, through General Abboud himself and Hassan Beshir.

The army take-over had been managed by a small group of officers in Khartoum. Suspicions that the army was being used for Umma political ends stirred in Brigadier Mohieddin Abdallah, the commander of the eastern area, who was a strong NUP supporter; for he was neither consulted about the coup nor included in the Supreme Council of the Armed Forces, although senior in rank to one of its members. Abdallah Khalil's role in the master-minding of the coup, and the dominating heights held in army and government by Abdallah Khalil's protégé, Abdul Wahhab; the presence among the five civilian ministers of two members of the former Umma cabinet; and the pro-Umma imbalance in the Supreme Council of the Armed Forces, combined to alert Mohieddin and his friend Brigadier Abd al-Rahim Shannan, commander of the Northern area, and a strong PDP man. Not four months after General Abboud and his Council had installed themselves, these two senior army commanders staged a march on Khartoum, followed by a second, two days later, and yet another, two months later. Brigadier Abd al-Rahim Shannan of the Northern Shendi command stormed the capital with a company of fresh recruits, not one of whom had yet fired a rifle, though he could have drawn on two well-equipped and seasoned battalions. This gesture of bravado was intended to humiliate Abboud, and was said to be typical of an officer known for his reckless panache. The troop moves on the capital were ordered under cover of movements from the Northern and Eastern commands to take up active service in the South. The insurgent troops cordoned off army headquarters and arrested General Wahhab, together with two of his supporting colonels, whose place in the Supreme Council was viewed as a token of their Umma political allegiance and not of their army seniority. Sensitive of his precarious hold, General Abboud sought the mediation of Abdallah Khalil and of the two sect leaders. Mohieddin and Shannan released Wahhab and the colonels after having secured a promise that their forceful representations would be considered. They then took their troops back to their commands.

Two days later, on 4 March, they were back in Khartoum to reinforce their case and to avert action against them. Claiming to speak for the young officers, and playing on the Neguib–Nasser parallel, they alleged a conspiracy against Abboud by Wahhab, and maintained that their 4 March movement was to 'protect the gains achieved by the revolution of November 17'.[14] Shortly after, it was announced that all the members of the Supreme Council of the Armed Forces had resigned, and that a meeting of officers was in progress in the Ministry of Defence, summoned for consultation.[15] Fifteen commands took part in an unprecedented election of a new Supreme Council. Mohieddin, always a popular officer, polled fifteen votes; Abboud, fourteen; Hassan Beshir, number two man of the Supreme Council, only nine. Wahhab, too, was re-elected; but he refused to join a Supreme Council with rebel members, whose troops had not returned to their bases, and he was dropped from both the Council and his ministerial office, to retire with a pension and a grant of 3,000 acres of state land.[16] The day after his resignation, the press carried a delicately framed news item – 'It is officially announced that all troops from provincial units who stopped for a few days in Khartoum have now returned to their posts.'[17]

As a member of the Supreme Council, Shannan demanded the release or trial of trade-unionists held in prison, among them four officials of the Sudan Federation of Trade Unions. He also pressed for the reinstatement of nineteen officers dismissed from the army following the Kibaida coup. But his advocacy of these causes was to be of brief duration. By the second half of May, the army was in fresh convulsions. The supporters of Shannan and Mohieddin in the provincial commands – chiefly the heads of Gedaref and Shendi, their own previous commands – felt that the March victory against the old-guard officers had not been carried far enough. Hassan Beshir was their main target. This time, however, Mohieddin and Shannan did not move in concert, and Shannan's followers appear to have precipitated him into an action about which he was dubious. The Eastern command moved, but not the Northern. When a new commander was sent to Gedaref, he was arrested by the acting commander, who moved two battalions to Khartoum; but Hassan Beshir acted promptly to send the troops back to Gedaref and to arrest the chief organizers. By 1 June, Shannan and Mohieddin were themselves under arrest. Three weeks later, they and fourteen other officers faced a court martial, charged with inciting a mutiny.

During the trial, Shannan developed a vigorous defence of what he called the aims of the 4 March movement. They were, he said, to ascertain that Abboud would continue to be president; to stop foreign interference, through Wahhab, and thwart a plot to make the Sudan depart from her policy of positive neutrality; to solve the outstanding issues between the Sudan and the United Arab Republic; to achieve close cooperation of the government with the people; to promote the standard of living in the Sudan, and to make national welfare and prosperity a reality. He told the court of the occasion in May 1958 when he had been at Halayib on the north-east border with Egypt, and Abdallah Khalil had arrived in the company of two Americans to inspect an air strip. Snatches of their conversation had been overheard by Shannan and had aroused his suspicion – reinforced by an instruction in December 1958 to build a road in the area – that Abdallah Khalil planned to allow foreign military bases in the Sudan. The plot which the 4 March movement had been designed to stop was the forced retirement of General Abboud, to allow Abdallah Khalil's protégé and Umma colleague Wahhab to take over. 'We found ourselves driven by patriotism to save the Sudan. Hence the March 4 movement.'[18] Shannan and Mohieddin were sentenced to death; but this was commuted to life imprisonment. (They served barely more than five years; their punishment was interrupted by the events of October 1964.)

The two coups caused a major change in the structure of army and government. After May, all the members of the Supreme Council, with the exception of Generals Abboud and Hassan Beshir, received their army pensions and were retired from active service and command. Army officers were prohibited from calling on ministers in their government offices. Rather belatedly, thus, an attempt was made to stop members of the Supreme Council from using their army commands in bids for power.

The next blow struck from inside the army against the army command came from the ranks of the junior officers. Numbers of young officers had been expelled from the army in the wake of the Shannan–Mohieddin coups and, further back, after the Kibaida attempt; others, not yet exposed for their participation in any of these actions, were increasingly critical of a military regime that, far from curing the country of the disputes and divisions of the politicians, was inflicting them on the Sudan in an intensified form. By the second year of the military regime, the paint of the army's promises to bring stability was peeling fast. The officers who met in secret to plan the next coup, though unclear about ways and means, talked of the return to civil rule: but not a return to power of the former discredited parties and politicians; rather, a government of selected politicians that would be committed to work within the framework of a national charter, with both government and charter to be supported by the army. It would have to be a reformed army, of course. And who were the politicians to be? Some members of the group plumped for independents. Others found some leaders of the parties acceptable, among them the former Minister of Foreign Affairs, Mahgoub. Others had confidence in – and, indeed, the leader of the group was himself related to – Mirghani Hamza. The name of Dardieri Mohammed Osman was also mentioned. Both Osman and Hamza were men of considerable influence in the country, loyal to the Mirghani house and its leaning towards Egypt. Aims and planning were still at an early, tentative stage. In the course of two months, several dates were fixed for action and then, for one reason or another, cancelled as unsuitable. In Khartoum garrison and the infantry school at Omdurman about thirty officers were involved in the planning of the coup, as well as others in the Central, Eastern and Western commands, and in the tank corps.

The defeat of this coup was unwittingly prepared in an early approach made by the leader, Colonel Ali Hamid, to two young non-commissioned officers of the Western command in charge of a company at Omdurman. 'If,' Ali Hamid asked them, 'we were one day to send an officer to move the company for an operation unknown at headquarters, what would your reaction be?' 'We would agree,' the NCOs said.[19] But one of them reported the conversation to Deputy Commander Hassan Beshir at headquarters. Ali Hamid was watched. He was also called before Hassan Beshir and warned that his involvement in a conspiracy was known. A meeting of the planners held immediately after the warning discussed the seriousness of the leak. The majority concluded that, while Beshir knew something was afoot, he had very little detail and no inkling of the plan's dimensions. They agreed to persist. A final date for the coup was fixed.

The night before the action, Ali Hamid addressed the officers of the infantry school at Omdurman and the battalion as a whole. He needed their help, he said, in a plan to bring down the Abboud regime. Soldiers were Sudanese citizens whose country and army were being dragged through the mud by corrupt generals. The army had to act to restore its own reputation. Those, he said, who wished to restore the reputation of the army, 'Take three steps forward'. The entire battalion moved forward.[20] It was to provide the manpower for the following day's action, under the leadership of Captain Hamid Abd al-Magid, who happened to be a son-in-law of coup-maker Brigadier Shannan.

The plan was a simple one. Ali Hamid's infantry school battalion was dispatched with orders to capture the two bridges commanding the entrance to the capital, to take the broadcasting station and to arrest the members of the Supreme Council. Ali Hamid himself went to mobilize a company of the Khartoum garrison. But instead of joining in the action, the sergeants and other non-commissioned officers of this company placed the coup-leader under arrest. This was not known for several crucial hours by the other members of the conspiracy. And the plan misfired fatally in another direction, too. Hoping for a swift seizure of control, the planners relied on arresting the members of the Supreme Council. But perhaps as a result of noticing abnormal movement in Khartoum garrison and the infantry school, perhaps in a state of general alert as a result of the earlier tip-off, the members of the Supreme Council had gathered secretly at headquarters on the night of the coup to plan their own moves. With the failure to round-up the Supreme Council and in the absence of Colonel Ali Hamid's leadership, the conspiracy began to flounder. Though some of its command was hesitant, the tank corps had been expected to join in the coup; but the Supreme Council, through General Awad Abd al-Rahman, acted to prevent this. Several officers suspected of sympathy with the coup, as a result of previous association with the Shannan–Mohieddin actions, were arrested. When the tanks moved on Khartoum that night, they came not to make but to break the conspiracy.

The court martial that followed a week later placed eleven officers on trial. Five of seven officers convicted were sentenced to death; among these were Ali Hamid and Abd al-Hamid Abd al-Magid, the son-in-law of Shannan.

The execution of the Ali Hamid conspirators did a good deal to dispel the illusion that army rule brought 'stability' in its wake. Most susceptible to the notion that a strong arm gets things done had been the civil servants, so close to the generation of politicians who had proved so inept and unprincipled. Military men were expected to be plain but decisive, to import army precision into government business, and to give due weight to the specialist advice of civil servants frustrated by the squabbles and irrelevancies of previous governments. To many in the service, the prospect that they would at last come into their own, with the rulers ready to rely on the only élite really trained to govern – their assumption being that government consisted of nothing more than efficient administration – was definitely cheering. If there were any doubts over whether armies were fit to rule, they were not expressed in the early days. It was a relief to get rid of the politicians; and, where there might have been misgivings, it seemed judicious not to provoke armed men. In any event, the civil service seemed unaware that in the early shaky period of this, or any other, army regime, the military needed the civil service more than the other way about.

The service was newly entrenched: 800 posts had been filled when senior British civil servants were displaced in the independence rush to decolonize. The new men basked in a pre-independence salary rise, instituted for the benefit of expatriate officials on their way out, which swallowed practically the entire surplus of the independence year cotton crop. Impatient to get on with their well-paid jobs, the civil servants accepted the new heads of government without question, and by their uninterrupted working of the administrative machine, put the seal of authority on the coup. Governors in the provinces with provincial armies at their command; the permanent secretary at the Ministry of the Interior, with power to summon the security council to confront the army; the Department of Justice which controlled the police: none of these seemed to have any conception of, or were willing to exercise, their ability to challenge the legitimacy of the take-over. Nor did they question the powers of the Supreme Council of the Armed Forces which, from the outset, monopolized the formulation of policy and made the Council of Ministers a mere cipher. The ministers, the five civilians among them, were heads of departments; but any issues of importance – and many of apparent unimportance – were decided by the Supreme Council,* without reference to the Council of Ministers. This was left to handle routine duties, like the consideration of departmental memoranda. Government in the Sudan, it was generally believed, was conducted by four men – General Abboud and General Hassan Beshir, and lawyers Ahmed Kheir and Abu Rannat – with other rulers, whether military or civilian, as mere executors.

At first the civil service hope that clean and efficient administration would come into its own seemed to be realized. Memoranda were handled with greater speed, decisions taken with less

* Even scholarship awards had to be approved by the Supreme Council.

procrastination. But 'after a while,' said a leading civil servant, 'the army gave us their back'. A state of conflict between junta and civil servants was formally recognized by the amendment of the Civil Service Pensions Act in 1962. It provided for the retirement of any civil servant, 'if recommended by the Minister concerned as being in the interests of the service, and approved by the Council of Ministers'. Several top administrators were forcibly retired under this section 32b, among them a provincial governor. But civil service conflicts with the military reached crisis in only a small minority of cases. In the main, the attitude of the civil administrators was one of smug passivity, of letting the army men commit blunders on their own. It would not be for too long, after all. Had the junta not promised a return to barracks in six months, a year, perhaps two years? By its own declarations the military government was guarding the national interest through a difficult period, when it was necessary for some force to hold the ring until a return could safely be made to a reformed parliamentary system. Meanwhile, the civil service would carry on.

It had little option, it supposed. The army had seized control of the power to command. Indeed, what civil servants principally resented was interference with the administrative chain of command. Reverting to the days of Kitchener and Wingate, the junta appointed provincial military governors as their direct representatives. Two systems were expected to function side by side: the military administration taking instructions direct from the Supreme Council of the Armed Forces; and the civil administration functioning under the Ministry of Interior. Depending on the assertiveness or self-effacement of the particular civilian governor, the operation of two parallel but separate systems of control produced conflict or hesitancy, and underlying paralysis on the part of the civilian system. In fact, said one governor, the military had scrapped the civil administration without knowing it. The parallel system dismantled the authority of the civil administration, interfered with a working system and atrophied any civilian initiative. 'Whenever something went wrong,' said one governor, 'I would telephone the military governor and say "Come and shoot".' The final authority of the military administration lay in its capacity to use force. In the Sudan, as elsewhere, the army regime was to show that it could not build a civilian base without civilian participation. Such participation was impossible without political organization. And political organization was illegal.

With nostalgia for the mechanical perfections of the old authoritarian colonial system, the army regime improvised its variation of indirect rule. This was after August 1959, when Abu Rannat was appointed as head of a commission to consider 'the best ways for the citizens to take part in the government of the country', with emphasis on 'quick' decision-making, and on efficient and unified administration.[21] The commission's recommendations resulted in three ordinances,[22] redolent with colonial 'native' administration associations. The Sudan was returned to stage-by-stage introduction of partially representative institutions, in small doses as and when the regime judged fit. Under local government democracy, the country was divided into eighty-four local councils (eighteen urban and fifty-six rural), two-thirds or one-half of whose members were elected, 'depending on the degree of maturity', and the others nominated. Above the local councils were provincial councils, composed of heads of departments, as *ex-officio* members to represent the government, with two-thirds of the remaining members elected from local councils, and one-third nominated. The chairman of the provincial council was in practice the military governor. Above the provincial councils was the Central Council, composed of the ministers and seventy-two members, six each elected by the nine provincial councils, and eighteen nominated by the president.[23] A striking feature of the first elections to the local councils at the beginning of 1963 was the large number of unopposed candidates, one-third in all. 'What prompted many a candidate to stand for election was the prospect of an easy victory in the absence of people with a political background – who boycotted the election – as well as the allowance or salary he would receive as a member of the local or higher councils,' commented one critic.[24]

Control was exercised from the top. The Council of Ministers could disqualify anyone from membership of a provincial council, or at any time suspend a provincial council altogether and exercise all its powers. Each minister had power of supervision and inspection over provincial administration in anything concerning his ministry, and he could annul any decision taken by a provincial council, by merely notifying the provincial authority not to execute it. At no level did elected members command a majority; at every level, any nominee could be excluded from a council 'for the sake of the public interest'. Throughout, the president and the Council of Ministers could act as though there had been no delegation of authority at all. For, in fact, there had been none. The Central Council was a dusty and fly-blown shop window, and all that the councils were effectively doing was extending military control deep into the ordinary lives of the Sudanese. On 17 November 1961, the third anniversary of the army take-over, General Abboud declared the aim of his government to be the reinstatement of a parliamentary system based on general elections. But nothing in the council system operated by the junta hinted at this. Once again, as under the colonial system, indirect elections and local councils were screens for the power of an authoritarian centre, with politics and parties treated as extraneous to the raising of popular participation.

The first acts of the military junta had been to outlaw all political parties, ban demonstrations and place the press under severe restriction. The Defence of the Sudan Act of 1958 provided for unlimited detention without trial, the transfer of civil cases to military courts and increased penalties for a wide range of activities considered hostile to the government. In May 1959 alone, fifty-six activists of the Anti-Imperialist Front were arrested and detained without trial until the end of the year. Newspaper proprietors and editors, called to a conference addressed by General Abboud, were warned that the government would tolerate no opposition or criticism, and that no reference should be made in their columns to the political parties or the sects. The Minister of Interior gave notice that he would close down any newspaper or arrest any editor casting doubts on the intentions of the government. Banned topics included news of the armed forces (except for official hand-outs), criticisms of United States aid or diplomatic facilities extended to experts under aid plans, court proceedings in the trials of political accused, news about workers' or students' strikes, peasant demands and the activities of the ex-politicians.

Not that the ex-politicians were active. They seemed to accept at face value the assurances of the army that it would hold the reins for two years at the longest. They effaced themselves from political life with a sense of relief that they were invalided out of government with no more than bruised reputations. They abandoned the country to the military as lightly as they had previously indulged in carpet-crossing in the House, or in wildly illogical party alignments, as though it was after all only the luck of the draw. The exception was the Communist Party. First organized in 1944 but never allowed the luxury of public campaigning, it had adjusted to a state of illegality under the Condominium and the Republic and was organized to operate underground, without a parliamentary presence, and with precise short- and long-term programmes. It issued protests and rallying calls against the junta in its own name and in association with the trade unions, students and Gezira tenants. It kept up a battery of pressures on NUP, President Azhari and others to declare open opposition to the army regime. It took part in the junta's council system to express opposition from within; but it also advocated a national front of political leaders against army rule.

Not until two years after the military take-over did a memorandum reach General Abboud over the signatures of some twenty politicians.[25] Among these were Siddiq al-Mahdi, who had succeeded his father as head of the Ansar when Abd al-Rahman al-Mahdi died in March 1959, Azhari, Abdallah Khalil and Mohamed Ahmed Mahgoub, the former Umma Foreign Minister who was to become prime minister in 1967. The memorandum urged that the army should once again concentrate on the country's defences, that the emergency should be lifted and that a national government be set up to write a constitution and hold elections. The National Front memorandum was delivered two days after General Abboud announced the system of provincial councils as a stage in the army's plan for guided democracy. 'You told us in your first proclamation that your regime was transitory,' the memorandum declared. The people had been 'decent enough' to wait 'in spite of their conviction that armies were not made to rule indefinitely.' Why had there been no mention in General Abboud's latest statement of the promised return to full parliamentary government?

The next shot in what became an extended battle of memoranda was fired by the declaration of the 'Honourable Citizens', sponsored by Sayid Ali al-Mirghani, with PDP support. This one, unlike its predecessor, was published in the press and repeatedly broadcast, because it fully supported the regime. By now it was plain to see that, while the military take-over had been mounted to pre-empt the fall from power of an Umma premier and the Umma party, the predominantly Khatmiyya-based and led army had deflected this course. The Shannan–Mohieddin coups were inspired by a combination of radical and Khatmiyya motives, and made the army, once General Wahhab had been removed, a force against and not for the Umma Party. General Abboud was the moderator and conciliator of the factions inside the junta, but he himself was a dedicated follower of the Khatmiyya leader Sayid Ali al-Mirghani; through Abboud himself, Hassan Beshir, Abu Rannat and Ahmed Kheir, all four Shaigia and Khatmiyya, the sect was the core of the government. In the traditional pendulum politics of the Sudanese sects, Ali al-Mirghani's statement of unequivocal support sent the Umma–Ansar forces even further over to the side of the growing opposition.

Concurrent with the lodging of the politicians' petitions were Siddiq al-Mahdi's attempts to conduct private negotiations with the junta. He met General Abboud, and then Generals Magbul and Talaat Farid,* to protest at the favoured treatment meted out to the Honourable Citizens' memorandum: 'You are favouring supporters and fighting opponents. This is nepotism.'

* Siddiq's negotiations started in February 1961 and consisted of one meeting with General Abboud and two with Generals Magbul and Farid. Both meetings were minuted. There were also several written memoranda.

Siddiq said that he would have no objection to the continuance of the Supreme Council, provided that some civilians were grafted on to it; but that the Council of Ministers, as the executive government, should be composed exclusively of civilians. Such a reconstituted government should lift the emergency, and hold general elections for a constituent assembly to write a permanent constitution. The two generals pointed out with some firmness that the army had taken over by force, and would not return to barracks except by force. The two generals would convey Siddiq's representations to the Supreme Council, but they were sure what the outcome would be, 'because we are united as a bundle of sticks'. The negotiations were suspended, and then finally aborted by the death of Siddiq in October 1961, only two and a half years after that of his father. Both leaders of the Ansar, though the son proved considerably more outspoken than his father, accepted without question that the onus for keeping the peace lay with them; for the private army of the Ansar, once roused, could prove a formidable adversary of the regime.

Attempts to get concerted anti-junta actions by political leaders in an opposition front were faltering and inconclusive. They were undermined by the support that the PDP and Sayid Ali al-Mirghani lent the regime, and by the hesitancy and passivity of the traditional parties. When in July 1961 twelve political leaders, among them a number who had signed the petition to General Abboud, found themselves arrested and deported without trial to detention in a Juba prison in Equatoria, this was a response not so much to the impact of their representations as to the popular ferment, largely under left-wing leadership, brewing in the country. The twelve men sent into exile for a year* were a strange bag of Umma, NUP and Communist politicians. Among them were Azhari, Mohamed Ahmed Mahgoub, Abd al-Khalek Mahgoub and Advocate Ahmed Suleiman of the Communist Party, an Omdurman merchant whose arrest was later admitted to be an error, and Abdallah Khalil. The immediate cause of the deportations was a telegram sent to General Abboud protesting at the torture by the military

* They were released in January 1962.

police of a witness in a political case, Hassanein, a member of the Communist Party. This became a *cause cèlèbre* when the military court took over the case, blocked the access of lawyers to the victim and the evidence and arrested the defence counsel. The arrest of the politicians, whether they calculated on it or not, was for a while a rallying point of popular opposition to the junta, but the National Front of the parties collapsed in 1962. (The Communist Party had withdrawn from it earlier.) It had produced no coherent programme, no rallying point for sustained opposition. The politicians were as ineffective in opposition as they had been in government.

Insurrection

One advertised achievement of the military government during its first year of office was the conclusion of the Nile waters agreement with Egypt. Pre-coup discussions had probably paved the way, but the army regime claimed the credit.* An allocation of water was agreed upon, as well as the sum of compensation for the land in the Wadi Halfa region which would be flooded on the completion of Egypt's High Dam. This created the problem of removing and resettling a population of 50,000 in the area. Officially-initiated consultations with the Wadi Halfans were suddenly interrupted during 1960 by the government decision. It had chosen as resettlement area the one site which the Wadi Halfans had been unanimous in rejecting out of hand. Demonstrations ensued in Wadi Halfa, supported by others in Khartoum and other towns openly challenging the junta. Three ministers who went to Wadi Halfa to intervene were kept imprisoned in a hotel for three days by protesting demonstrators who were finally dispersed by police armed with tear gas and whips. In the face of opposition, the military attitude hardened; the resettlement project was one on which the prestige and authority of the regime, not to mention the interests of certain contractors, would rest. The price of prestige helped to cripple

* Although the agreement gave the Sudan only about half the compensation demanded by the previous government.

the central treasury. As for the authority of the regime, the myth of its invulnerability had been challenged by the act of Wadi Halfa defiance, and would never be the same again. The Wadi Halfa protests injected spirit even into the timorous politicians, and initiated bold, supporting demonstrations by students and the trade unions.*

The following year, 1961, the workers on the railways went on strike for higher wages. Trade unions had been declared abolished a month after the army take-over, 'till present laws are revised and a new law enacted';† and penalties for illegal strikes had been stiffened. The railways workers' union, the pioneer of militancy in the Sudan, ignored the ban, brought its 27,000 workers out on strike for an increase equivalent to almost half as much again of their existing salaries and crippled the railways for a week until the union was dissolved by the junta. Next, the students of the University of Khartoum came out into the streets, as they were to do each year on the anniversary of the army take-over. The University of Khartoum became the open target of the regime: the students' union was declared dissolved; student meetings were consistently interfered with by the police, who also removed any wall newspapers put up by night; campus demonstrations were dispersed. Eventually, irritated beyond endurance by yearly student strikes and demonstrations, the regime altered the dates of the academic terms so as to keep the university closed during November, when the army celebrated the anniversary of its coming to power. The student response was to demonstrate in September, at the convocation ceremony. The government amended the university act to control the institution directly, putting it under the Ministry of Education.

Towards the end of 1963, a general crisis in the cotton-growing schemes, caused by the falling price of cotton and rising production costs, roused the Gezira tenants, already incited by the refusal of the regime to permit them to hold their annual

*The Wadi Halfa demonstrations were at the end of October 1960. The first memorandum by twenty politicians went to General Abboud on 29 November 1960.

†New trade union legislation was passed in 1960.

elections for their committees. The Gezira scheme is the pivot of the Sudanese economy. The tenants demanded that their share of the cotton proceeds be raised and that the costs of picking should be included in the joint account of state and tenants. When the regime refused, the Gezira farmers responded with a strike of all picking and agricultural operations on the scheme's two million irrigated acres. The government threatened to bring in the army to pick the cotton; but probably because it knew that this would only produce an armed clash, avoided such a step, and capitulated. The tenants' share of the proceeds was raised; the costs of ploughing, though not of picking, were borne by a joint account; and elections were permitted. (These returned to the leadership Sheikh al-Amin, the prominent Communist leader of the Gezira tenants.)

Protests were in most instances, however, more submerged and suppressed than successful. Acts of dissent were often isolated and easily dealt with by the regime; but they were indicative of a decisive turn in public opinion. In the towns, the army was rejected with unconcealed contempt; in many parts of the countryside, especially in the Umma areas, it was barely tolerated. Tribal heads worked the council system, but they were government servants on the government payroll. If the masses of the people were not yet demonstrating in the streets against the regime, they were certainly not working its machinery, as the low polls in elections under the council system showed. Both the Umma and the NUP boycotted the elections. The Communist Party contested them in order to use the councils as instruments with which to attack and undermine the regime. In general, though, the membership of the councils reflected Khatmiyya participation and the PDP policy of support for the regime, even if the party, not officially legal, did not officially say so. The army had managed to commandeer a civilian base of a sort; but this was only in some areas, while in others it was rousing open antagonism. The state of emergency in the country showed no sign of being lifted. The atmosphere of repression had become all-pervading.

Even the much-vaunted economic progress turned out to be exaggerated and distorted. Much was made of the seven-year economic plan; but this was in greater part the development designed by the British administration before independence, and any economic policy pursued between 1958 and 1964 was a continuation of previous plans and targets. All these schemes and projects were lumped together and, with the impressive-sounding cost label of £250 million, presented afresh. The problem of the Sudan, no different from that of any independent African state, had always been to find money for development. The soldier's government fell – or was helped – out of the right side of the bed. 1958 was the height of the cold war. The Sudan, after Egypt, was the first newly independent country in Africa and occupied a region where investment offered strategic influence if not scintillating economic stakes. The foreign policy announced by Ahmed Kheir[26] sounded like all things to all powers, and achieved a crafty amalgam of ideas to suit both Umma and NUP propensities. There were obeisances both to the Charter of the United Nations and to the Arab League; affirmations of support for the Rights of Man, alongside the specific claims of Algeria, Cyprus and the Cameroons; declarations of non-alignment with military pacts and a rejection of the arms race and nuclear tests, but also expressions of firm ties with the Arab world and the Arab-Islamic countries, with the countries of Africa, and especially 'our sister neighbour Ethiopia'. As if this range of friendship was not catholic enough, the statement added:

> We will endeavour to further political, economic and cultural co-operation with all, as no nation can afford not to exchange ideas, trade and expertise with other countries . . . we welcome foreign capital and its investment in our country whether it comes from government or private enterprise . . . we are in need of foreign loans and aid; we shall therefore do our best to create a favourable atmosphere to attract them. In our commercial relations we shall deal with *all countries of the world* on the basis of mutual interest.

As a ringing finale to this bounty of goodwill, the declaration embraced the principles of the Bandung conference and, in conformity with these, recognized forthwith the Peoples' Democratic Republic of China and its six hundred million inhabitants.

The Sudan took aid from West and East. It signed the Nile waters agreement with Egypt, but absented itself from the ceremonial opening of the High Dam. Lip-service was paid to its allegiances with the Arab world; but in practice, under the manipulative touch of Ahmed Kheir, the emphasis was more on the Sudan as part of Africa, so that it could afford to stand at a distance from the forces competing for leadership of the Arab world. This looked like the ideal middle-of-the-way policy, an attempt to be friends with everyone, and to take whatever aid was offered.

United States assistance at last came into its own. Less than a fortnight after the take-over, Ahmed Kheir announced that the original aid agreement concluded by Abdallah Khalil would stand, and that the restrictions imposed by Parliament would be deleted. A government statement declared that the Sudan would use the $15 million made available in foreign currency to finance imports from external markets, mainly the United Kingdom. The following year, the British government announced that it had agreed to make large export credits available to the Sudan. The regime found itself the recipient of aid from many sources – the World Bank and West Germany among them. But then the economic projects embarked upon by the junta entailed a heavy expenditure of foreign currency. Over the three years 1959–61, the deficit on current account was £8·3 million, with an additional £31·1 million drawn from foreign loan allocations. Repayment and interest charges on loans contracted in 1961 amounted to £19·1 million during 1962–5. An economist commented that the interest to be paid on the loans for the Roseris Dam made the water conserved there more like Coca-Cola. In six years of fierce concentration on dams, roads, bridges, street lighting, all of which involved large capital outlay and monumental physical projects – prestige expenditure, for the army lives by shining brass – a national deficit of more than £75 million was accumulated. Expensive schemes misfired when factories were wrongly sited or too hastily planned. The costs of administration soared. Embarked upon with abandon, as though totally indifferent to the fact that in the long term aid accumulates liabilities, the junta's economic projects succeeded in plunging the Sudan deep in debt.*

They also levered a significant new economic group into view, which in turn was to produce changes in the country's political forces. Business had previously been in the hands of small town and country traders. New men were now to be seen, working as contractors and agents, wholesalers and company directors, their first opportunities provided by the need for Sudanese middlemen on the sites being erected by foreign states and firms, and their first capital, in many instances, by lump sum pensions paid to civil servants and retired army men, commissions and rake-offs.

Corruption, never before entirely absent but never present on a dramatic scale, thrived under the military in a variety of ways: new roads were routed past the homes of senior army kin; new homes sprang up for their relatives; huge real estate plots were registered in their names. General Abboud, the once reluctant ruler, grew to enjoy the parades and the public ceremony. Many of his fellow-officers were attracted by the more sordid but remunerative rewards of office. There were accusations of favouritism in the granting of import licences, and unauthorized acquisition of government land. Younger brothers and nephews began to benefit from scholarships abroad, and other relatives from expensive medical treatment there. A spate of prosecution for scandalous sex and embezzlement crimes† gave the public a distinct impression that men in high army places were being protected. Members of the junta were having to live down suspicions of direct corruption, immorality and attempts to manipulate the system of justice.

The junta was failing as a government; in the South it was also failing as an army. After the army mutiny of 1955, the South had never been quiet for long. And the short-lived independence governments of Azhari and his successors had

*Over-estimated revenue and under-estimated expenditure had resulted in a deficit of more than £75 million in five years (News Service, No. 44).

†There was the Nuweila Embezzlement Case 1962–3; and the trials that came popularly to be known as the 'Omdurman Girls Case', the 'Suitcase Case' and the 'Dustbin Case'.

failed to solve problems considerably less knotty than those of the South, where they had disastrously under-estimated the crisis. The politicians and the parties had treated the three Southern provinces as an extended electioneering field, for drumming up support in the periodic conquests of majorities in the assembly. Now the army regime proceeded as armies do and decided that the only solution to the Southern problem was a military one. At the end of 1962, there was a prolonged strike in the schools of the South against forced integration of Southerners into the Arab cultural stream. By the end of 1963, the Southern protest had taken the form of organized rebellion headed by a guerrilla force, the Anya Nya. Led by some Southern officers and NCOs who had deserted the army, it was backed by the Azania Liberation Front, a movement in exile or operating in the bush. It was armed and assisted, Khartoum charged, by West Germany, Switzerland, Israel and the Vatican for reasons of their own. The war became intense around April 1964, with strikes by the rebels westwards from bases in Ethiopia along the Upper Nile. Well-trained fighters in a favourable terrain were tying down huge forces and had brought the administration, especially in Equatoria, to the verge of collapse. Tax collections had come to a stop, for there was no agricultural production to tax and little administration to organize the collection. Schools were closed or moved to the North. Thousands of villagers were restricted to camps, and the South experienced a rigorous and repressive army occupation. In turn, the prolonged emergency in the South was debilitating the general economy.

It was also stoking tensions inside the army. The men on dry rations in the swamps and the young officers in the field railed against the incompetence of the top brass, sitting comfortable and safe at army headquarters. Service in the South was supposed to average two or three years, but some officers did duty for considerably longer and knew of officers never posted to the front at all, thanks to the pull that they and their families exerted in Khartoum. As the much-vaunted military solution turned to stalemate or defeat, the military unexpectedly confirmed for a perceptive public its own frailty, uncertainty and sense of failure. It appointed a twenty-five-man commission on the

South, and opened the issue to public discussion. The army's final justification lies in how it conducts a war. This one was being lost in full view of the country.

Public opinion was voiced with uninhibited frankness. It disassociated itself with expressions of shame and anger from the excesses of the armed offensive in the South. The Southern crisis needed a political, not a military solution; and this depended of necessity on a return to parliamentary government in the Sudan. Such was certainly not what the junta had wanted to hear. It placed a ban on public meetings. But it was too late. At the University of Khartoum, student actions were beginning to trigger off events that were to bring the army regime in the Sudan to an end.

During September 1964, a student meeting made outspoken attacks on the government. On 10 October the security authorities banned a discussion circle, and the police dispersed a meeting in the science faculty. Eleven days later the students met in defiance of the ban. For hours beforehand, the police had been taking up positions on the university campus, which – appropriately enough for the events that followed – had formerly been the British army barracks. As the meeting opened, the police used loudspeaker hailers to order the students to disperse. Nobody moved. The police read the riot act warning and then hurled their tear-gas bombs into the gathering, chasing the students into the hostels where they ran to wash the tear-gas from their eyes, and then interfering with the water supply. During a running battle between students and police which lasted the better part of an hour, rifle shots were heard.

'I went into the room where a body lay, covering the mattress with red blood,' a student participant said; 'and as we carried the wounded out, the police were using their batons on us.'[27] In subsequent rueful mitigation of the police shooting, officialdom explained that the student troubles had broken out on a night when the police commandant had been in bed with a broken leg, and the commissioner of the police and General Irwa, the Minister of Interior, away from the capital. The request of panic-stricken police for support from the police post in the vicinity had accidentally brought reinforcements armed not with anti-riot sticks, but with fire-arms.[28]

Ahmed al-Gurashi was shot dead that night; a second student died in hospital the following day; and several dozen students and police were injured. When Ahmed's body was taken to the morgue at the hospital, students flocked there in droves. The next morning the newspapers carried no report of the shooting. 'It was as though nothing had happened,' the students said. 'No one in the Sudan knew.'

A procession from the hospital that started with some thousand participants swelled to a massive 30,000 in the Abdel Moniem Square. Throughout the morning, crowds of students and secondary-school pupils were joined by people from all walks of life in the capital. The afternoon of the giant gathering and that evening, enraged crowds were overturning and firing police vehicles in the streets. The following day, Friday, was one of sporadic shootings, as crowds formed in spite of police warnings and an early curfew imposed for two in the afternoon. There were incidents, scattered and spontaneous, throughout the capital; and behind the scenes, organization was forming.

Another great procession began to form on the Saturday morning. Jittery police, and behind them the army, ringed round the building of the Judiciary in the centre of the capital. Vast crowds milled about outside; and inside, judges, lawyers, university academics, others from the professions and representatives of the trade-union movement prepared statements to be carried at the head of a procession to the palace. Several of these statements demanded an immediate investigation into the shootings; the university academics went much further, to demand the return of the army to barracks. The police refused to permit the procession to move; they would allow six citizens to present the petitions, but no more. The leaders of the procession, prominent among them the Deputy Chief Justice, Judge Babiker Awadalla, were conducting urgent negotiations on the telephone with General Abboud in the palace, when shots were heard from the vicinity of the great milling crowds. Negotiations on the right of the procession to march were still under way, but it seemed that the police were forcibly dispersing the crowd. One of the judges, Abdel Magid Imam, came striding out of the Judiciary towards the police officer in charge. 'I am a Judge of the High Court,' he said. 'I order that you, the police, leave.' The police officer saluted and dispersed his force. The army reinforcements standing by were immediately summoned, and no procession moved that day; but state authority had evaporated in the public challenge to it by representatives of the law. The police had acknowledged that they should act only with judicial sanction, and the armed power of the junta was being steadily emasculated by popular defiance in the streets.

In 1961 the underground Communist Party had posed the weapon of the political general strike as the way to bring down the military regime. The day before the shooting at the university, members of the party, meeting illegally, had studied an appraisal of the political situation which characterized the country as not yet ready for a strike, and the leaders of the other parties as obstacles rather than allies in opposition. By the afternoon of the banned procession, the general strike was on the agenda. Meetings of academics, lawyers, teachers, doctors, students, together with leaders of the trade unions and the Gezira tenants, were turning what had been a footloose and spontaneous unity of protest into the Professionals' Front. This new body, called into existence and fashioned by the October events, would also be ultimately destroyed by them: until it rose phoenix-like from the ashes of a still later crisis of government in 1969.

The Professionals' Front arose in reaction to the incidents of the day; but as it solidified, it changed its nature. The social reforms required by its radical core (like the demand for nationalization of the private cotton schemes, of foreign banks and firms, and for a state monopoly of foreign trade, that issued from the Gezira tenants); the solid base given it by the masses of the Three Towns, the Gezira farmers and the unions; and the feel of street power at its feet: all this made the Professionals' Front far more than a reflowering of the intellectual leadership given by the Graduates' Congress during the independence awakening of the 1930s.

The general strike was announced the afternoon that the

procession was banned; and when the Deputy Chief Justice threw his weight behind it, he and another leading High Court judge were dismissed from their posts, and placed under arrest. Meanwhile in Omdurman, the political parties had been stirred from their torpor and were at work to form a combined front of the Umma, the NUP, the PDP and the Moslem Brotherhood, whose leader Hassan Turabi had been a voluble orator at the student meetings. The two Fronts of politicians and radical 'professionals' were to hold their first joint meeting by the following week.

The general strike ground the towns to a standstill. It halted all internal communications, emptied the administration of its civil servants, cut the army in the South from its supply lines and reinforcements, and drew massive popular demonstrations up and down the country. The towns were rising in slightly slower sequence than the capital, but they were rising all the same, at Port Sudan, at Medani, El Fasher and Atbara. Kasala, some 500 miles to the east, sent two trainloads of citizens to join the insurrection in the capital. At Gezira, delegates of sixty organizations, watched by a continuous audience of 3,000, held a conference for the duration of the strike to hammer out new policies for the country.

By now the Supreme Council was in almost continuous session. A strong whiff of grapeshot might have sustained a rigorously united and self-assured army government for a while; but at the height of the crisis, the army itself fell apart. Hassan Beshir, the strong man of the Supreme Council, was preparing a ruthless crackdown on demonstrators, but he was alerted that an officers' revolt was imminent. By Monday evening, a torn and fractured Supreme Council, that had lost confidence in its ability to govern, decided that it had no option but to dissolve itself and the Council of Ministers. General Abboud would retain legislative and executive powers pending the formation of a transitional national government. The radio broadcast to this effect emptied the houses of the Three Towns: with a great roar, the populace piled into the streets to welcome the end of six years of army rule.

The débâcle was caused by the combined assault on the junta

from within and from without. The street barricades and the general strike, the emergence of a militant leadership, drew the Sudanese in the towns and on the Gezira into direct action of the sort that shakes Cabinets, but does not necessarily dislodge armies. It was the splits in the army command and in the officer corps at several levels that toppled an already shaky junta.

The Kibaida, Shannan–Mohieddin and Ali Hamid coups inside the army had been snuffed out, and their supporters removed in careful and regular purges. Yet a Free Officer tradition and even an organization, the *Dubat Ahrar*, had persisted in the army. During 1961–2, *The Voice of the Armed Forces* had circulated secretly, though spasmodically. When the crisis came, junior officers, mostly second lieutenants and captains, were debating among themselves one of two courses: a coup within the army to install 'an honest man' at the head of a reformed military government; or the return to civilian government under the young educated rather than the traditional old-guard politicians. The October convulsions threw the middle-ranking officers, majors and lieutenant-colonels into the mess and barrack-room arguments of the junior officers. The latter had decided in favour of a civilian government as long as it was headed by an army man: to conserve the prestige and the influence of the army, but also to shore up a regime of young politicians. The 'honest man', these junior officers determined, should be Colonel Mohammed al-Baghir Ahmed. But Colonel Baghir proved to be a reluctant candidate. He asked for forty-eight hours in which to make up his mind. In that time, news of the plan reached Mohammed Idriss, third in command of the army after Generals Abboud and Hassan Beshir, and then Hassan Beshir himself. Hassan Beshir had his own intrigue. He was planning to assume command in place of General Abboud. The young officers' plot, he considered, called simply for the accommodation of Colonel Baghir as the representative of the junior officers, under his own supreme command. The plot came to a head at the final Monday meeting of the Supreme Council. Several diehards were refusing to surrender authority. The members of the junta and their advisers who had been talking about transitional steps to civilian rule insisted that the army should continue as guide, allowing progress in its own time, in its own way. Hassan Beshir, making his own bid for control, tried to convince General Abboud that he had no option but to cede power; the army was against him. When his argument failed to carry conviction, he called on General Mohammed Idriss for confirmation. Junior officers provided their own; for at this juncture, troops were seen to be taking up positions in the vicinity of the palace. It was a motley collection of non-commissioned officers and men drawn from the Engineers' Corps at Omdurman, but it made its point to General Abboud, who not long after made the radio announcement dissolving the Supreme Council.

While the Sudan celebrated this, General Hassan Beshir alone among the members of the junta was not under house arrest, and troops called to Khartoum from Shendi were under the command of a close relative and confidante of General Mohammed Idriss, Brigadier Mohammed Mukhtar. Now junior officer plans for a final strike to wipe out all remnants of the old army command became an open secret. Rules of conspiracy were thrown to the wind. The army and the Three Towns hummed with news of imminent young officer action against the intrigues of the generals. By mid-week General Beshir's proffered leadership in a reformed command was decisively rejected by a meeting of the army commanders of the Three Towns. Beshir had hoped to sweep the young officers behind his bid for control of the army, and then of the government. He had calculated on the force of their rebellion against the junta; but not on their identity of political conviction with the graduates of 1956 and of the independence years, who were storming the army's citadels with another objective than to install one more general at the head of government.

Two rebel streams of the Sudan's independence youth looked as though they were about to converge and change the face of the country's politics. The young officers who had political conflicts with the old army command were teaming up with the young radicals of the professional organizations, the unions and the Communist Party. They had already succeeded in bringing down the army junta. The crucial issue for the Sudan was the shape of a successor government. On the day after the dissolution of the Supreme Council, the first official contact took place between the Professionals' Front and the United Front of the political parties. While the meeting was in progress, two of the generals from the Supreme Council attended as negotiators, to establish the first formal contacts between the Professionals' Front, the political parties and General Abboud, who was waiting to cede power. But how and to whom was the power to be ceded? The Supreme Council had no sooner resigned than it seemed likely that the army command and the parties would negotiate a settlement between them. To prevent this, the word went out for a mobilization of the Three Towns in a renewed phase of popular demonstration. The young officers began to see themselves as armed caretakers of a government more radical than any the political parties could produce, and built from the support that the Professionals' Front had mustered. Suddenly the two streams of young radicals were diverted, and dammed, by an unpredictable and tragic incident. When a crowd began to form outside the palace on the Wednesday morning, to demonstrate against rumours of the Beshir play for power, and against a compromise between army commanders and politicians, a panic burst of fire from an armoured car killed close to a score of people. In the wave of anti-army feeling that swept the country, the young officers opted for the army's complete return to barracks, and the handing of political power back to civilians in whatever form they could negotiate.

However loosely coordinated and haphazardly organized, the young officers' movement had defeated the designs of the generals to resurrect the army junta. For, from the moment that they had seized the initiative, the army had not been united or reliable enough for its command to exert authority. Conversely, the sudden abdication from the political arena of the young officers enfeebled the forces that between them brought down the army regime, since a popular movement for political reform was already meeting the opposition of the traditional parties.

The negotiations at army headquarters were carried on jointly by the representatives of the Professionals' Front and the parties; and by the eighth day after the shooting at the University, they were concluded. The two groups combined to form, for 103 at first exhilarating and then uneasy days, the Transitional government. The old guard and the new militants were prisoners of one another. They were in control of a power that had been partly seized, partly negotiated. Together they steered a policy that went too far for the parties, but not far or fast enough for their partners in office.

The old-style politicians found the Professionals' Front a suspicious animal. It was compounded of intellectuals and radicals, townsmen and agitators all (not least, the well-known members of the Communist Party, who belonged to the Front in their own right as leading professionals or as veteran leaders of organized labour and the Gezira tenants' union). These were men who had initiated action before and without the political parties, and action of a kind that the parties had carefully eschewed in the past. It was the presence of the Professionals' Front and its leadership of the mammoth strike which killed any prospect that the parties might have entertained for negotiating a transfer of authority directly with the junta. Both parties and army knew well that the politicians had no command over the course of the strike and could not hope to call it off or cut it short as a token of their strength in any play for power.

During the feverish days of the insurrection, it was dangerous to quarrel over the aims of government, for the means of governing were not yet fully wrested from the generals. But even as the Professionals' and United Fronts began to discuss terms for the liquidation of the military regime with General Abboud, what had started as a revolutionary seizure of power was diluted during the process of bargaining into a negotiated compromise. It was agreed that there would be guarantees of basic freedoms; a lifting of the state of emergency; the guaranteed autonomy of the judiciary and the university; the release of all political prisoners and detainees; a foreign policy of opposition to colonialism and military pacts; the transfer of the Chief Justice's powers to a five-man High Court of Appeal; and the formation of a commission to draft laws 'consistent with Sudanese traditions'. On these points there was no dispute. When it came to a policy for the South, however, the army insisted that the state of emergency should not be lifted there. From the start, therefore, the October government was infected with the same weakness, the Southern crisis, that had promoted the military collapse. The North felt that, 'by their bare hands tearing down the military regime they accomplished a great act of apology and atonement to which the Southerners should have responded with equal magnanimity. The mere overthrow of the military was sufficient in their view to call for acceptance by the South that the North were of the same kith and kin.'[29] It was a failure of imagination and of policy not to perceive that the euphoria of October had not permeated Southwards; that the crisis in the South was too endemic to be conciliated by half-measures; and that to the Southern provinces, living under uninterrupted martial law, the administration and the army run by Khartoum did not look very different.

Out of the October rising came a Cabinet of fifteen members. It was headed by Sir al-Khatim al-Khalifa, a former Director of Education, chosen because he had a civil service and not a political background, and was a conciliatory figure acceptable not only to all partners in government but also in the South. Each of the five political parties – Umma, NUP, PDP, Communists and the Moslem Brotherhood – had one representative in the Cabinet. Seven posts were filled by the Professionals' Front, to represent the workers, peasants, lawyers, engineers, teachers, academics and students. Two seats allocated to the South were filled by Clement Mboro, as Minister of Interior, and Ezbon Mundiri, as Minister of Communications, on behalf of the Southern front; but less in the spirit that North and South should work together for changed policies, than that Khartoum was showing signs of weakness and could be worked against from within.

Not that the Transitional government was free from its own inner dissensions. The October victory was claimed by all forces; but they had conflicting ideas of how to use it. The parties could contain neither their alarm at their minority position in a sinisterly radical government nor their impatience for elections to a new assembly. The Professionals' Front insisted that the gains of October were not yet secure; that the failures of parliamentary democracy in the hands of the traditional parties had precipitated the country into military rule; and that October had been a popular mandate for social and political reform to prevent all this from happening again. This spirit fired a series of edicts by the October ministers to sweep clean the house vacated by the junta. A purge was ordered of guilty men in the army and civil service (twenty senior officers who had actively supported the military regime were pensioned off). Newspapers that had accepted subsidies from the junta were suspended. One commission was appointed to advise on agricultural reform, and another to probe the forces behind the hand-over to the army. This last was empowered to question and arrest civilian and military personnel and any other person who had 'participated in the destruction of democratic life'. It was strongly opposed by the Umma Party, as violating the guarantee given by the politicians during their negotiations with General Abboud before the installation of the October government. But in the streets the cry was 'Hang the Generals'; and with them Ahmed Kheir and Abu Rannat, the second of whom excited particular hostility for his collaboration with the junta.

A committee was set up to replace 'native' administration with local government. An Illegal Enrichment Court was established to prosecute charges of corruption and suspect economic deals. (For the most part its findings were inconclusive.) Women other than graduates were given the vote for the first time in the history of the Sudan. A quarter century of fairly cordial relations between the governments of Ethiopia and the Sudan, inaugurated when Sudanese troops helped reinstall the Emperor on his throne after the war, was disturbed by a declaration of support for the Eritrean insurgents. This may in part have been a reaction to reports that reached Khartoum on the eve of the junta's collapse that the Emperor of Ethiopia had offered General Abboud the services of two battalions.

Such reforming vigour was deceptive, however, for within the government the Professionals' Front was struggling to survive under a bombardment of charges of Communist domination, and a demand from the Umma Party for its outright dissolution.

Bitter and unresolved arguments about what the basis for elections and the character of a new constitution should be, throbbed in a partnership trying to reconcile the irreconcilable. Irresistibly the government began to disintegrate into its component parts. The Umma and the NUP explored an alliance, their old conflict relegated to the background in the need to unite against forces to the left of them both. The Gezira tenants demanded that half the seats in any new assembly be reserved for workers and tenants. Sadiq al-Mahdi gave notice that the parties would never tolerate this, and insisted that a new government should be formed in proportion to the results secured by them in the previous parliamentary elections.

Black Sunday, on 6 December 1964, brought the Southern conflict to Khartoum. In church congregations throughout the capital, Southerners were exhorted to assemble at the airport to meet Clement Mboro, the Minister of the Interior, on his return from the South. The plane did not arrive as scheduled. Enraged crowds of Southerners stormed through the capital, smashing and burning cars, and attacking passers-by. By the end of the day scores of people were dead and many more injured; and the cause of conciliation with the South – along with the ability of the Transitional government to effect it – had been dealt a grave setback. The round table conference a few months later at Khartoum went some way towards propitiating a section of the Southern leadership; but despite the unilateral cease-fire declaration by Khartoum and the attempt to solve the problem of Southern refugees, the Southern conflict became even more intractable as Southern secessionist leaders read the signs of conciliation as evidence of weakness. The conflict continued to drain the country's material resources, erode the unity of the state, and, immediately, block the way to national elections and a permanent constitution. The army, dislodged from central power, still ruled the South.

In mid-February 1965, the Ansar massed at the capital in a show of force against the Transitional government. The Prime Minister resigned; chosen for his acceptability to all sides, he was unable to resist pressures from one of them. 'Cooperation is now impossible with the party leaders,' he said: but his resignation was effected so quietly and confidentially that the Professionals' Front complained it had not had notice of it. For five days the country was without a Cabinet – during the vacuum, it was suggested that resort be had to a government of civil servants – and when one was produced, the political parties were once again in sole command. Elections held three months later installed an Umma–NUP coalition. (The PDP boycotted the elections ostensibly because of the crisis in the South, but more probably because it feared to reveal its weakness in the country after its collaboration with the junta; it was now trying to erase this record in a wild swing to the left and an alliance with the Communist Party.)

The Sudan was back in the familiar but fatuous round of Cabinet reshuffles, assembly crises and coalitions, governments falling and struggling to their feet, rumour of party alliances and mergers and internecine disputes. But the disputes seemed to be about the lesser, not the more important, issues. All the major parties that juggled government amongst themselves for the ensuing years held much the same view on economics, foreign relations and the South. They advocated no significant change from the Gezira-type mixture of private enterprise and state concerns; nor hazarded any solution to an economy stunted and limping, to low cotton sales, and balance of payment crises. The professional politicians continued to seek the purpose of independence in the pursuit of political office. Policies and programmes to formulate what the country required from independence were irrelevant, indeed distracting, to the manipulation of party alliances.

The Sudan was a country that had embarked on independence with elation and verve. It suffered less than most from the psychological hang-over of colonialism: partly because the British withdrawal was sudden, and the intensive drive for Sudanization made it complete; partly because Islamic culture and a secular education system resisted any notion of a superior alien culture and pressures for Anglicization; and partly because the educated, who had been suspected and rejected by the British administration, embraced the independence cause with fervour and militancy. This was not a nation only semi-conscious at independence. In the towns and on the Gezira the young men sparkled with ideas; political controversy was animated; and the independence generation not only judged the politicians and the military, to find them wanting, but acted in consequence to bring them down. Perhaps uniquely in independent Africa, the Sudan has a revolutionary intelligentsia with close links with a vital trade union, as well as student and peasant movement, and a seasoned marxist party. The October events demolished the military regime in a popular surge rarely seen in Africa. But the aftermath bequeathed a sapped resilience, a sense of missed opportunities and lost causes, that fitted only too easily into the continent-wide pattern of post-independence setbacks.

The six years of army rule had convinced the Sudan that military efficiency was no better able than political rhetoric to grapple with the country's problems. In the hands of the parties after, as before, the military regime, the political system grew tired and flaccid. The mass enthusiasm of the cities was dissipated; the passivity of the country, left undisturbed. For once, in October, the contest had been over a real issue: the site of popular power. And that contest had been lost to the discredited professional politicians. The conflicts within the Transitional government expressed the lasting deadlock of Sudanese political life: the impulse for social change coming from the towns, from the young educated, from the unions and from the only organized ranks of the peasantry, is smothered by the deadweight of the countryside and the sects, which are invoked for religion but deployed for politics. The Ansar, the private army of the Umma, can lay physical siege to the capital; but even when the swords of the faithful are sheathed, under an electoral system of one man, one vote, the countryside engulfs the state. Constituency delimitation in the 1953 and 1956 elections shows the added weight given to the countryside from the Sudan's first election in 1953 to the second in 1956:

	Size of urban constituency	*Rural*
1953	43,000	120,000
1956	53,000	60,000

Transitional government proposals to provide reserved seats for graduates, workers and Gezira tenants were attempts to weight the parliamentary system in favour of the independence generation in the towns, and against the stagnant countryside, where a vote is traditionally an act not of political but of religious or communal faith. This, above all, was what the traditional parties feared from the Transitional government, and so they destroyed it.

For a while after the elections of spring 1965, the NUP and the Umma Party served together in government, with Sadiq al-Mahdi at the head. But party politics based on sect allegiance seemed to reveal its anachronism in the split that broke the Umma Party wide open. This was during 1966, when Imam al-Hadi, the religious head of the Ansar, challenged the leadership of his nephew, Sadiq al-Mahdi. Sadiq, thirty-year-old Oxford graduate, hailed by the Western press as the student-prince of the Sudan and its last remaining hope, had helped defeat the forces of October, but he was not entirely impervious to them. The country was changing, and the parties had to change with them. To the Imam, the Mahdi House was an ideology and a creed based on the Book of Allah and the Traditions of his Prophet. Sadiq's wing of the Umma Party wanted to refashion the party as an instrument of 'national reconciliation' between traditional and modern, including the urban intelligentsia and the students, and even sections of the labour movement.

For the greater part of its life, the Umma leadership had been drawn from the tribal heads of the Ansar living on subsistence agriculture, mostly in the west of the Sudan. The Gezira Scheme, under part-state ownership and direction, and the irrigation provided by the Sennar Dam, nurtured a landed peasantry in close alliance with the Ansar leadership; for it was Abdel al-Rahman al-Mahdi, with his sons and kinsmen, who acquired first one agricultural licence, then another, on the private estates of the White Nile, south of Gezira. From the 1930s, but especially after the Second World War and the 1950 cotton boom, a new class of landed proprietors grew on the vast estates carved out of the 630,000 acres. There the pump-scheme owners, with a turnover of £13 million a year, are responsible for the cotton production of the country and are the pillars of the Umma Party. The estates of 10,000 to 40,000 acres each are divided into holdings of ten feddan* for cotton and five for millet; and the tenants of these holdings, bonded in semi-feudal relationship to the big proprietors, constitute a fertile recruiting ground for Umma votes and Ansar mobilization. After October, the Tenants' Association of the White Nile started a demand for nationalization and the conversion of the schemes into cooperatives. Personal and political fissions in the Madhi family and the Umma Party were aggravated when, in response to the pressures for nationalization, the Sadiq group initiated an agrarian reform project, providing for the nationalization of the Blue and White Nile schemes for which the fifteen-year pump licences had expired. The cotton boom was over; many of the schemes were already running at a loss; and compensation for nationalization would have provided a landed group with ready capital resources to invade other sectors of the economy. To the wing of the Umma Party not ready to make any adaptation to the demands of the modern sector of the economy, the agrarian reform project was an ominous attack.

It began to look as though the NUP and the Sadiq wing of the Umma Party might draw together; and though they could not banish the old *tariqa* allegiances, they might in part displace them. Could political alignments swing from the fulcrum of Ansar–Khatmiyya, Umma–NUP competition? The Umma Party was changing in some measure. So, too, was the NUP. Once it had been the birthplace of the independence movement and its vanguard; but in office it had refused to recognize a body like the Sudan Trade Union Federation, and it had passed the Subversive Activities Act to curb the unions. The party of small traders, villagers, shop-keepers and young nationalists had become the party of an expanding commercial group. This group had been fertilized by the military regime and was growing in the shadow of foreign investment. Many of the party's energies went on cornering, in any government, the Ministry of Trade and other such key posts; for control over the distribution

* 1 feddan = 1·038 acres.

of import licences, tenders and contracts, and the judicious use of these, could build personal fortunes and party influence. Both the NUP and the Sadiq wing of the Umma Party were steered by leaderships set on acquiring interests in the modern sector of the economy, whatever their earlier traditional base had been.

The Sudan had been a more egalitarian society than many. Poverty and religious piety have combined to give the country a spare and ascetic aspect. In Khartoum there has been little of the frantic conspicuous consumption of, say, West African capitals; nor the vast gulf between rich and poor (though the gap is growing; the *per capita* national income is still only £27 a year, but an MP, for example, earned £1,200). In the mud-brick city of Omdurman, Azhari's bizarrely over-ornamented mansion, and one or two others almost as dizzy and ostentatious, are pointed out with derision as trophies of the military period and certain other 'opportunities'. But even if off to a slow start, government and business, political and administrative office and economic pull have been growing as parasites one upon the other, and the Sudan, like the rest of Africa, has been acquiring that new political–administrative élite that uses office to turn itself into an economic class.

In the towns near the agricultural schemes, a new élite of the civil service has developed. Its average income is perhaps ten times that within the rising middle group of farmers. The *nouveaux riches* merchants and the politicians angling for business aim to displace the weaker of the alien groups like the Greek and Armenian merchants. The owners of the private agricultural schemes have surplus capital and ambitions in industry. These groups are swirling about in all the traditional parties, which would tend, one might think, to bring them closer together. The old tendencies persist, however, in negating neat categorizations. The one is the *tariqas*; dead, many charge, as religious inspiration, but still with a hold on mass political allegiance. The other is the tenacity with which the politicians play the old game of expediency.

Azhari, leading the NUP, watched the split in the House of the Mahdi widen until he was certain that it had reached a point beyond bridging, and that Sadiq al-Mahdi's political influence had been deeply undermined by the flocking of the faithful to the Imam. Then he forged an alliance with his old enemy, the PDP. When Sadiq's government collapsed under a two-pronged attack from the Imam's wing of Umma and from the NUP, Azhari formed a government coalition with, of all groups, the Imam-led Umma, under Mohammed Ahmed Mahgoub of the latter as premier. (The NUP and the PDP merged formally as the United Democratic Party in December 1967.) Had the Sudan ever seen a stranger coalition? It had, once again, no meaning beyond the enjoyment of power. The issue of a permanent constitution for the country remained to be settled. Was a presidential or a parliamentary system to be preferred? Azhari was leaving no move untried to secure his accession in any system, though a presidential one seemed the most likely.

At the beginning of 1968, the Sudan went through yet another constitutional crisis. Elections, the third since independence, had been promised for February 1968; but the wrangling over the constitution had been prolonged, and because it was not complete, the group in the Assembly headed by Sadiq dug in its heels against the dissolution of the House. The Sadiq group, for all its talk of modernity, had staked its political future – as had the Imam's faction – on an Islamic Constitution which, if it did nothing else, would destroy any hope of a solution in the South and irreparably harm secular politics as a whole. (In alliance with the Sadiq group and campaigning for the Islamic Constitution was the Moslem Brotherhood. Its call for a return to the fundamentalist purity of the faith made attacks on radicalism acts of Islamic revival rather than of political persecution, and gave the Brotherhood a sinister access to the coffers of kingdoms in the Middle East.)

The constitutional crisis seemed insoluble, with no single party able to command a majority in the Assembly. At this juncture Azhari showed all his old mastery at manipulation. He prevailed on a majority of the Assembly to resign. This gave a majority of the Supreme Council a justification for dissolving the Assembly, which needs a two-thirds membership to function. The opposition MPs, led by Sadiq, refused to recognize the dissolution. Parliament's buildings were closed, but not the lawns near by, and there the opposition MPs assembled. They accepted the resignations of those who had not convened; declared themselves to be the country's lawful government; and took urgent case on the unconstitutionality of the dissolution to the Court of Appeal. Their championship of a thoroughly unpopular Parliament roused no answering echo in the streets. As for the Court, it was in no mood to treat the legal points with urgency, since the Assembly, under Sadiq's own leadership, had previously refused to abide by a court judgement against a constitutional amendment banning the Communist Party.

The army found itself in a dilemma. Would it, in this newest political crisis, once again be called upon to do its duty by the state, and support government? Which *was* the state's lawful government: the MPs and party leaders who had resigned; or the minority that continued to convene itself in an Assembly? Army headquarters addressed an urgent official note to the Chief Justice, with copies to Azhari, Mahgoub and Sadiq, asking for a statement on the constitutional legalities and declaring that, as custodians of the constitution, the army would support only the duly constituted government.

The crisis evaporated when the Sadiq group could make no more than a token protest. In the elections a few months later, the United Democratic Party of the Azhari and PDP groups won 101 of the 218 seats, to be joined in coalition by the Imam's faction of the Umma Party, with thirty seats. Sadiq's party won only thirty-six seats, while the leader and several of his executive members lost theirs. The Moslem Brothers won three seats, and their leader, also, was defeated. The Communist Party polled a fifth of the vote in the fourteen towns of the Sudan (it elected two MPs to the House) but insignificant support in the countryside.

Another of the Sudan's governments of expediency was in power and a new cycle of intrigue and careerism began. The form of the constitution remained unresolved. The economy stumbled on. The troubles in the South continued raging. The Southern parties commanded thirty seats in the Assembly and had been variously aligned with the others in electoral politics;

but the nub of the crisis remained the demand of the Azania Liberation Front for the 'liberation' of the Southern Sudan, and the inability of government to grapple with the issues there short of sending its army in to pacify the area when turbulence made this necessary.

A popular insurrection joined by the young officers of the army had interrupted this circuit before. Young radicals and clamorous townspeople had brought down a military government, but they had not been able to make government in its place. As for the army's own entry into politics, this had not evolved into revolution, as in Egypt. It had been a mere holding action, reforming nothing, initiating no change except backwards, into the colonial administrative past. When the military had been eclipsed, the country had returned to the same dilemmas of poverty and political deadlock; with these rendered, if anything, more intractable by the six years of the military regime.

A Putsch with a Popular Front

On 25 May 1969 the government of the Sudan was toppled once more by coup d'état. Any line of inheritance linking 1969 with 1958, however, ran back not to the military usurpers of power, but to the forces which unseated the junta only five years earlier. In 1964 radicals of the Professionals' Front and young army officers had converged to force the dissolution of the Abboud government, but they had failed to hold power. Five years were spent by the revived Free Officer movement in the Sudanese army assimilating the lessons of the October failure. It had been weak, and had finally been destroyed, not only because it was a compromise with the traditional political parties, but also because it had needed the protection, even the assertion, of a reformed army under Free Officer leadership. The plan in 1964 to place an armed striking force at the disposal of the new government thrown up by the events of October had been doomed by the unpopularity of the army after six years of military rule. This time the officers would seize power, but they would not withdraw to the barracks once this was achieved; they would ride in tandem together with the civilians they placed in power. Their claim to legitimacy would be that the government of the political parties they displaced had itself usurped power from the Transitional government, formed after the downfall of the military regime in 1964.

A National Revolutionary Council was created, presided over by thirty-nine-year-old Colonel Jaafer al-Nimeiry, the leader of the coup, and consisting of ten members, all young army officers except for the former Chief Justice, Babiker Awadullah. The latter was appointed prime minister, and presided over a twenty-one-member Council of Ministers. This itself included several members of the Transitional government and several who had been executive members of the Professionals' Front during 1964; two prominent Southerners, one of them the well-known Communist Joseph Garang, and the other an ex-Southern Front MP; several members of the former Socialist Party, and several Communists like Farouk Abou Eissa, who had been secretary of the Professionals' Front; two former NUP MPs; a number of intellectuals and university academics, a few of them with a reputation as independent marxists; the editor of *Al Ayyam*; an ex-army colonel from the Nuba Mountains; a former Professionals' Front member who was the manager of the country's largest textile mill; and the conservative deputy-manager of the Sudan Commercial Bank.[30] The regime looked like an October type of coalition, without the parties and with young army men standing by to stiffen the mixture; though also with a clear commitment from the outset to find a political formula that would tilt the political system away from the control of the traditional parties and the sects with which they were linked. It was disclosed after the event that secret negotiations had been opened with Sadiq al-Mahdi, testing his attitude to the new regime in the light of his conflict with the more traditional Umma forces led by Imam al-Hadi. Sadiq had offered to support the men of 25 May on condition that Communists should be excluded from the government; he was detained not long after. 'You see,' explained Major Farouk Osman Hamdallah, Minister of the Interior, 'it's impossible to introduce socialism without the help of the Communists as individuals and the workers as a class. Those who try to separate us from our natural allies refuse to accept the transformation of society and are probably seeking to destroy us.'[31]

Immediately after the coup, the constitution was annulled, and all political parties dissolved. It was announced that no political leader of any dissolved party would be allowed to join the government in his capacity as such a party member. A new political movement was to be formed of workers, farmers, intellectuals, soldiers and those 'who work with national capital that is not tied up with colonialism'. The revolution had become necessary, Nimeiry declared, because the Sudan's independence had been crippled by successive governments which had no ambition other than that of power. 'Our political parties moved in the circle of imperialism and acted according to its will.'[32]

By the time of the 1969 coup, the country's debts were beating all records, at double the figure for 1964. The worst of it was that these credits, obtained at high rates of interest to finance development projects, had been used chiefly to meet a budget deficiency caused by waste, lavish expenditure and inordinate increases in administrative personnel. By 1969 internal borrowing had soared to over ten times the figure of 1966. Faced with this catastrophic situation, the World Bank, Khartoum's main creditor, and Western powers had become more and more reluctant to listen to the appeals for aid from the Sudanese government. When the new regime came to power in 1969, it announced that it would expand economic and trade relations with the Arab and the socialist states; extend the public sector to replace foreign investment; encourage national capital that was unconnected with imperialism; and protect this capital so that it could compete with foreign capital under the supervision of the public sector. The Sudan would be 'democratic, socialist and non-aligned'. It was a decision prompted by both necessity and conviction. How far internal structural changes in the economy would go, it was early to say.

The coup had been made by fourteen officers who comprised the inner circle of a Free Officer movement inside the Sudanese army. This body had worked clandestinely for ten years, according to the new regime's Minister of the Interior and member of the Revolutionary Council, Major Farouk Osman Hamdallah.[33] Nimeiry himself had a long political record within the Sudanese army. He had been dismissed after the Kibeida affair of 1957, but had been permitted to re-enlist in 1959. That was the year of the Ali Hamid coup, and though Nimeiry had been involved, he had eluded detection. During October 1964, when Colonel Baghir had been put forward as spokesman of the young officers, Nimeiry was said by the initiated to have been the real leader of the Free Officers.

During an amateurish coup attempt of trainee soldiers led by Khalid el Kid in 1966, Nimeiry had once again fallen under suspicion and been detained; but this had been one coup attempt in which he had not been involved, and he had been released. Posted to the training centre at Gebeit in the Red Sea hills, he had concentrated on the recruitment into the Free Officer organization of the young officers who flowed through the training courses. In May Nimeiry was on leave from Gebeit in Khartoum; it was during this fortnight that he organized the coup.

At least fourteen of the army's senior commanders were out of the country, using the unbearably hot Sudanese summer months for technical assignments abroad; delegations were negotiating arms purchases in both Cairo and Moscow; another three top army men happened to be in London for medical treatment. It was a swift and bloodless take-over. Two groups of soldiers under Free Officer command were sent for training to Khor Omer, at the base of the Kerrari hills north of Omdurman (the site of the famous Omdurman battle of 1898). They returned to the capital in relays, at half-hour intervals after midnight, to disconnect the telephone system, the second to take over army headquarters and arrest the army command as well as the politicians, prominent among them Azhari and Mahgoub. Then the bridges straddling the Nile were secured, and the radio and television centre occupied. In all, the coup-makers commanded two parachute units, an infantry unit and 424 soldiers deployed around the capital on training manoeuvres. It was a tiny force, and very thinly spread.

Then, the day after the coup, the regional commands, all of which had Free Officer cells working within them, declared their support for the Revolutionary Council. The only minister who had been contacted beforehand by the army officers was the new premier, Babiker Awadullah. All the other ministers learnt of their appointments over Radio Omdurman.

Not that the Sudan was altogether surprised to find itself once again in the midst of a coup d'état. There had been coup speculation for months. There was on all sides a total disillusionment with the parties and politicians. Government was drifting aimlessly, virtually at a standstill in many ministries. The parties were unable to govern together or separately. The reunification of its two factions, which the Umma Party achieved in April 1969, was threatening the governing partnership between one of its factions and Azhari's party, which was itself threatened by new internal splits. One government marriage of convenience was breaking up in violent mutual recriminations; but what would replace it? Al-Hadi and Azhari had agreed that the Islamic Constitution be promulgated by year-end, and that, if the formal drafting was not complete, its remaining articles be taken to referendum. A presidential system of government, which would have placed considerable power in the hands of al-Hadi or Azhari, whichever of the two was successful, excited much alarm, as did the Islamic Constitution, with its final block to any solution of the Southern troubles. The army was apprehensive, and in all probability divided. The judiciary had been alienated from the government in a long series of manoeuvres by politicians to outlaw the Communist Party and unseat its MPs. Babiker Awadullah had resigned the Chief Justiceship in a last stand on principle over this issue, when a parliamentary motion prejudged a case taken to the High Court for decision. Above all, the cost of living was soaring, the economy was stagnant and the politicians utterly discredited.

As the year opened, Ahmed Suleiman (who had been the representative of the Communist Party in the Transitional government), wrote a series of articles in *Al Ayyam*, in which he dissected the October 1964 experience. The only way out for the Sudan, he argued, was a similar coalition, but under army protection this time. Others on the Left warned against adventurism at a time of ebb and not flow in the radical movement of the Sudan. The coup was initiated by the non-Communist members of the Free Officer Movement. The Communist Party's response to it was cautious on the first day; but by the third, the party threw its weight behind the mobilization of popular forces in defence of the new government. Committees in Defence of the Revolution started to take form, though they were subsequently ordered to dissolve by the government: no political formations of any type were to be permitted independent of Revolutionary Council initiative. A week after the coup, gigantic demonstrations marched through Khartoum in support of the Revolutionary Council. Of the popular enthusiasm in the towns for the new regime, there was no doubt. Several dozen politicians were taken into detention, among them Azhari and Mahgoub, and Sadiq al-Mahdi; but support for the new regime was growing among the rank and file of the former NUP and PDP. Imam al-Hadi and his leading men, however, placed themselves on Aba Island, the base of Mahdism in the White Nile. The whole country was aware that the principal source of challenge to the new regime lay with the Ansar, and with Umma Party followers who had enlisted in the army for just such a confrontation as the one now looming. The new regime would be seriously threatened, if there were any signs of relapse in the army. Its top command layer, the generals and brigadiers, were pensioned off; and, with them, some middle-ranking officers who had been associated with Free Officer action in 1964 but not in 1969. The highest ranks of the police force were purged; then the civil service and the judiciary. Side by side with the lists of officers removed from command, was a shorter list of officers reinstated after dismissals in previous years intended to 'weaken the armed forces'. This time the army was taking no chances of Trojan horse activities from within. Alone among the nine officer members of the Revolutionary Council (seven of whom were under the age of thirty-two) Nimeiry accepted promotion; the others publicly declined. As the new regime proclaimed its general policy, it also addressed itself directly to the army with a ten-point soldiers' charter.[34]

Inside the new government among the soldiers of the Revolutionary Council, and outside in the movements of the Left there were insistent pressures for the speedy launching of a new political movement. Unlike their counterparts in Egypt's Free Officer Movement, they wanted this sooner rather than later. This, they were adamant, would be the only way to guard the Sudanese revolution.

After the first excited but nervous weeks, the threat of an immediate counter-move seemed to recede, and the new government bent its back to the tasks of running the country. Three tests would be all-decisive: the revival of an economy dangerously undiversified and stagnant; the unity of the army, and its alliance with its civilian allies for a programme of social revolution still to be elaborated in detail; and the Southern crisis, for this had been the test of each of the Sudan's successive governments, and each, in turn, had failed it.

A fortnight after the new regime had taken power, the Revolutionary Council and the Council of Ministers held a joint meeting to recognize the right of Southerners to regional autonomy within a united Sudan. The official announcement recorded that the past had left historical differences between North and South; but the government believed that unity could be built. Southern leaders had contributed to the crisis by seeking alliances with reactionary Northern politicians; with a revolutionary government in power new prospects for real independence for the peoples of the South, and in all the Sudan, were now at last open.

The Sudan's May 1969 revolution was consolidated in the counter-revolution. The defeat of the Ansar rising led by Imam al-Hadi opened the way to the re-distribution of the private estates of the White Nile among the peasantry. This policy, and that of the nationalization of banks and foreign trading firms which was announced on the first anniversary of the Nimeiry government, was to break the economic power of the traditional political parties. The key to the Sudan revolution remains the site of popular power: will it lie, essentially, in the army or in the forces of the Sudan's organized Left? The coming period will decide.

2. NIGERIA

The Coup of the Young Majors

Then Major Nzeogwu threw a smart military salute. 'I will be back in time for polo on Saturday,' he said as he climbed into his car – a vehicle still carrying the familiar crest of the former Governor.

New Nigerian, 20 January 1966

A senior Northern expatriate civil servant saw Major Chukwuma Kaduna Nzeogwu at his headquarters the day after the coup. The desk before the military commander, he said, was bare of papers; there were no incoming telephone calls and the major made no outgoing ones during the interview, and he appeared to have no idea of what was involved in the take-over of government. What were his instructions to the civil service? Were they to report for duty on Monday? the expatriate administrator asked. Were the schools to open as usual? Yes, yes, of course, the major said, all was to run as normal. He listened attentively when told that if he wanted the administration to continue as it was, he should instruct it accordingly. It was only after this that Northern civil servants were summoned for instructions, and Major Nzeogwu held a press conference at brigade headquarters to announce that permanent secretaries – among them the head of the service, who had feared for his life the night before, in the conviction that his name was on the coup-makers' extermination list – would assume the duties previously held by the ministers of the old regime. In Kaduna the coup, led personally by Nzeogwu, had been swiftly effective by contrast with the bungling of the young majors in the South; but throughout most of the critical first day after take-over, Nzeogwu acted as though the plans of the coup-makers not only for seizing, but for holding power, had been very far from adequately conceived, or were in suspense pending developments at Lagos. There, however, the coup had failed.

It had begun to unfold under cover of several army parties in Lagos on the Friday evening of 14 January 1966. The main party was given at the Ikoyi house of Brigadier Maimalari, for staff officers going on postings; and another was on board the Elder Dempster mailboat *Auerol*, then in harbour at Apapa, for which Major-General Aguiyi-Ironsi left the first party early. Major Mobalaje Johnson saw a group of junior officers converging on the house of Major Ifeajuna towards midnight, but he thought nothing of it at the time;[1] thirteen young officers, some of them members of the inner planning circle, and others selected to take part, were about to receive their last-minute briefing, it subsequently appeared. The coup-makers operated in several detachments in the capital: some were detailed to round up and shoot the senior army commanders; others, to arrest the prime minister and the Minister of Finance, Chief Festus Okotie-Eboh; others, to occupy police headquarters control room and the telephone exchange. According to Major Emmanuel Ifeajuna, who was in charge of the Lagos operation, the plan was to kidnap the Federal prime minister, Sir Abubakar Tafawa Balewa, and compel him to broadcast his resignation, with a transfer of power to the young officers,[2] so giving the new regime a spurious legitimacy. Chief Awolowo would then have been released from prison to head an interim government.[3] A flat in Lagos had been selected to record the prime minister's announcement. The broadcast, the signal for which Nzeogwu was waiting that week-end and for which he delayed his own radio announcement that Kaduna had been seized, was never made.

The Lagos coup-makers went into action two hours after midnight. They used service troops from Apapa barracks, but intended to rally the Federal Guard which Major D. Okafor commanded; and they hoped that once the coup was under way, 2 Brigade at Ikeja, where Ifeajuna was brigade-major, would declare for them, or at the least stay neutral. But their operation was barely launched when General Ironsi began to mobilize a counter-action of the army. He had returned from his Apapa

party after an armed group had called unsuccessfully at his home to arrest him. And he had no sooner entered his house, when he was alerted by a telephone call from Lieutenant-Colonel Pam's wife, made moments after her husband had been taken away by soldiers. Less than an hour and a half after the coup-makers had gone into action, General Ironsi arrived at police headquarters. He entered the lobby holding a pistol in his hand and demanded to know from the two soldiers on duty what they were doing there; he then ordered them to return to their barracks immediately, and added that he was turning out 2 Battalion to attack the men then engaged on unlawful operations in Lagos. At Ikeja, Ironsi roused the regimental sergeant-major of 2 Battalion, had the alarm sounded and the troops fall in, and then cleared this with the commander of the battalion,

Colonel H. Njoku. Troops from Ikeja were immediately posted outside key points in the city. General Ironsi then moved on to the barracks of the Presidential Guard, and after bringing the Guard out on parade, took a detachment of soldiers to Apapa for duty. Not long after Ironsi's instructions to the Guard, Major Okafor arrived at the barracks and tried to rally them for the coup. He was confronted by the regimental sergeant-major who told him that Ironsi had already been there, and had instructed him to shoot Okafor if he came; since Okafor was his senior, however, he was giving him a warning.[4]

In a few hours of frantic activity about the capital, the coup-makers had secured several of their targets. Troops under the command of Ifeajuna had arrested the Federal prime minister in his house at more or less the same time that Chief Okotie-Eboh, the wealthy Finance Minister who more than any other figure of the regime personified its corruption, was 'brought from his house close to hysteria and screaming "Don't shoot me", and was flung into a fast car like an old army sack'.[5] Both men were murdered the same night. Brigadier Maimalari had escaped the first attempt to kill him; but, on his way by foot to the Federal Guard headquarters at Dodan barracks, he had seen the car of Ifeajuna, his brigade-major; had shouted to him to stop; and had been shot by him on the spot. Ifeajuna had also burst into the Ikoyi Hotel to kill Lieutenant-Colonel Largema, commander of 4 Battalion stationed at Ibadan, who was in Lagos on a special mission, assumed to be connected with the Sardauna–Akintola planned army action in the Western Region. But as the hours flew by, it had become obvious to the young majors, speeding frantically about the capital to complete their assignments, that the operation had failed. Ironsi had escaped their net and was organizing 2 Battalion at Ikeja; their plan to move armoured cars of the Reconnaissance Squadron from Abeokuta to Lagos, so as to seize the airport and the barracks of 2 Battalion, had patently misfired. The coup-makers decided to take over. Ifeajuna made a hurried trip to the Eastern Region where, according to the coup plans, he was to arrest leading politicians. But it was already too late. After midnight, when the coup was getting under way in Lagos, Kaduna and Ibadan, the adjutant in charge of 1 Battalion at Enugu, a Northerner, received a signalled message that he was to arrest the ministers. When he tried to confirm with headquarters in Lagos, he found that communications were not working. Wrestling with an instruction that he found incredible but which he was unable to have confirmed or contradicted, he decided to do the minimum and throw a restraining cordon round the houses of the ministers. When they woke on Saturday morning, they found their homes under guard. But it was not long before Major David Ejoor arrived from Lagos to take command: Ironsi had commandeered a plane to carry Ejoor to Enugu, thus forestalling Ifeajuna and Okafor who were still on their way, travelling by road in a Mercedes.[6] Ifeajuna stayed briefly in Enugu – where he is said to have had a conversation with the Eastern premier, Dr Michael Okpara; though by the Saturday afternoon of the coup week-end, the ministers and the politicians had begun judiciously to melt away from the capital, to homes or friends in the country – and then travelled back to Ibadan in the West. There he lived under cover for a few days, before travelling on to Accra in disguise via Cotonou and Lomé. In Ghana he asked for and was given an interview with Nkrumah. His request was for arms and a hundred men to finish off the coup. But Ghana, the first country to do so, had recognized Nigeria's new government three days after the coup. By then the army's counter-operation had succeeded, and Nkrumah is said[7] to have calculated that an army government could not but be an improvement on the old regime; besides, recognition by Ghana, and other African states, would forestall any British attempt to reinstate the previous Cabinet, or what was left of it.

At Ibadan, in the Western Region, on the night of the coup, Chief Akintola had put up a spirited fight with an automatic rifle until shot dead. The soldiers drove off with his deputy Chief Fani Kayode in their car; but by the time that they reached Lagos and Dodan barracks, the army had taken control. The soldiers were arrested, and a badly frightened Fani Kayode was released.

No plans seem to have been laid for carrying the coup into

the Mid-West, the smallest of the regions, where no troops were stationed.

In Kaduna, Major Nzeogwu, instructor at the Military Academy, had been mounting exercises for men of 3 Battalion for fully a week before the night of 14–15 January. To the brigade commander, Brigadier Ademulegun, these seemed merely routine; as they seemed to people in Kaduna town and its environs, who grew used to the sight of armed soldiers moving about the area in broad daylight, and sometimes by night. There was not the least suspicion that Major Nzeogwu was staging careful pre-coup rehearsals. During one of the manoeuvres, the Sardauna had been seen watching the soldiers from a window.[8] On the evening of the coup, Nzeogwu left the Academy with a detachment of soldiers and on the road some distance from barracks told them, for the first time, of the night's assignment. 'Any man had the chance to drop out. More than that; they had bullets. They had been issued with their weapons but I was unarmed. If they disagreed, they could have shot me.'[9] There were four targets: Government House, where the governor, Sir Kashim Ibrahim, was put under guard; the Northern premier's residence; the house of Brigadier Ademulegun; and the house of Colonel Shodeinde, his deputy. At the Northern premier's house, Nzeogwu and his men met resistance, and a gun battle ensued before the Sardauna, one of his wives, and several members of his security guard and personal staff lay dead. Perhaps because they were short of personnel, the coup-makers did not synchronize their attacks on all four targets, but moved from one to another, so that the operation took several hours. Even while it was still in progress, the news began to leak out. A visitor in the Sardauna's guest house saw the main building ablaze and rang the head of the civil service, who alerted the commissioner of police. At police headquarters they spent some time trying to decide who could be behind the trouble. Soldiers had been seen at the premier's house: could Brigadier Ademulegun, a Westerner in command in the North, be staging a coup? By the time that police headquarters decided to check with the brigadier, he had already been shot, and his wife beside him. A telephone call was made to alert Colonel

Shodeinde. But as he replaced the telephone, the coup-makers burst in and shot him.* In the North, unlike the South, the coup was going according to plan. Even members of the Air Force training squadron at Kaduna were alerted on their side. A young second-lieutenant of the air force undertook to ensure that none of the senior officers would be in a position to use aircraft against the coup-makers; three senior officers were detained in guard-room cells for several days until released on the orders of Major Nzeogwu.

Nzeogwu broadcast over Radio Kaduna just after noon on Saturday 15 January. He spoke in the name of the Supreme Council of the Revolution of the Nigerian Armed Forces, to declare martial law over the Northern provinces of Nigeria.

> The constitution is suspended, and the regional government and elected assembly are hereby dissolved [he said]. The aim of the Revolutionary Council is to establish a strong, united and prosperous nation free from corruption and internal strife. Our method of achieving this is strictly military, but we have no doubt that every Nigerian will give us maximum cooperation by assisting the regime and not disturbing the peace during the slight changes that are taking place. . . . As an interim measure, all permanent secretaries, corporation chairmen and similar heads of departments are allowed to make decisions until new organs are functioning, so long as such decisions are not contrary to the aims and wishes of the Supreme Council. No minister or parliamentary secretary possesses administrative or other forms of control over any ministry, even if they are not considered too

* The fifteen casualties of the coup included the prime minister of the Federation; his Finance Minister, Chief Okotie-Eboh; the premier and most powerful man of the North, Sir Ahmadu Bello; the premier of the Western region, Chief Akintola; and seven senior army officers. Of these, four were Northerners: Brigadier Z. Maimalari, commander 2 Brigade, Apapa, Lagos; Colonel Kuru Mohammed, deputy-commandant Nigerian Defence Academy, Kaduna; Lieutenant-Colonel A. Largema, commanding officer 4 Battalion, Ibadan; and Lieutenant-Colonel Yakubu Pam, the adjutant-general. Two were Westerners: Brigadier S. A. Ademulegun, commander 1 Brigade, Kaduna; Colonel S. A. Shodeinde, commandant Military Training College, Kaduna; and one an Easterner (Ibo): Lieutenant-Colonel Arthur Unegbe, quartermaster general at army headquarters in Lagos, who was shot when he refused to hand over the keys of the armoury to the coup-makers in the early hours of coup-day.

dangerous to be arrested. This is not a time for long speechmaking, so let me acquaint you with the ten proclamations of the extraordinary order of the day which the Supreme Council has promulgated. These will be modified as the situation improves. You are hereby warned that looting, arson, homosexuality and rape, embezzlement, bribery or corruption, obstruction of the revolution, sabotage, subversion, false alarm and assistance to foreign invaders are all offences punishable by death sentences. Demonstrations, unauthorized assemblies, non-cooperation with the revolutionary troops are punishable in varying manner up to death.

Then followed a long catalogue of diverse other offences, from spying, doubtful loyalty, shouting of slogans, loitering and rowdy behaviour, smuggling, or attempts to escape with documents or valuables or state assets, to wavering or sitting on the fence and failing to declare open loyalty for the revolution.

Our enemies [said Major Nzeogwu] are the political profiteers, the swindlers, the men in the high and low places that seek bribes and demand ten per cent; those that seek to keep the country divided permanently so that they can remain in office as Ministers and VIPs of waste; the tribalists, the nepotists; those that made the country look big-for-nothing before the international circles; those that have corrupted our society and put the Nigerian political calendar back by their words and deeds. . . . We promise that you will no more be ashamed to say that you are a Nigerian.*

Two hours after Nzeogwu's broadcast, Lagos went on the air to announce that the prime minister had been kidnapped by 'a dissident section of the army', but the bulk of the army was loyal, and the 'ill-advised mutiny' would soon be at an end. The Federal Parliament held a brief and jittery session on the Saturday morning, attended by no more than thirty-three of the 312 members, mostly NCNC; it adjourned for lack of a quorum. Several senior Cabinet members and the attorney-general were

* Text of broadcast taken from a tape of the speech by Major Chukuma Nzeogwu over Radio Kaduna on 15 January 1966, starting at about 12.30 P.M. Apart from remarks made at press conferences and another sketchy interview from Calabar prison in *Drum*, September 1966, this was the only public statement of the aims of the coup made by its organizers, until in May 1967, over a year after its defeat, Major Nzeogwu gave an interview to *Africa and the World* from Enugu.

summoned to a meeting with senior police officials at the Obalende police headquarters, where General Ironsi had taken up command: the police had just recently installed a new communications system, and it was on reports coming over the police wires and on British High Commission sources that Lagos was relying at this stage. The British High Commissioner, Sir Francis Cumming-Bruce, sat in on that emergency consultation and was privy to various crucial decisions that week-end: notably, the decision to hand over to the army, a course probably advised by High Commission personnel. The news of the coup had split the Cabinet into two factions, on UPGA–NNA lines, which caucused separately during most of the two days after the coup. Then, when these met together in several emergency sessions, the Cabinet dissolved in indecision and finally – under British High Commission, army and police security pressure to let the army handle a dangerous situation – was eclipsed, altogether. An American visitor to Lagos at the time of the coup watched photographers get a picture of the British High Commissioner's Rolls-Royce outside police headquarters where Ironsi had established his command post, and quoted a visiting British journalist's remark: 'They still depend on us, you know, even when they are sorting out a private revolution of their own.'[10]

When Ironsi officially broke the news of the army revolt to the rump of the Cabinet, 'he appeared genuinely shocked'.[11] And 'We (the Cabinet) were in confusion'. Through police channels, if not officially (the British High Commissioner denied to newspapers the existence of any official request), the Cabinet members asked the British government for assistance. This, they were informed, would have to be put in writing over the signature of a head of government. The prime minister was missing, and the president, Dr Azikiwe, had been on extended convalescent leave in Britain since October 1965. A worried acting president, Dr Orizu, spent the week-end on the telephone trying to get clear instructions from Dr Azikiwe; and the rest of the Cabinet caucused over their respective candidates for prime minister. The NPC–NNDP men wanted Dipcharima, a former Minister of Transport and the most senior minister available, while the NCNC was pushing the candidature of Mbadiwe, Minister of Trade. The attorney-general suggested that the best course would be to appoint the most senior minister as successor to the missing premier. The Cabinet was due to assemble on the Sunday evening to make a decision. By the late afternoon, however, Major-General Ironsi had told several senior ministers that the army considered the situation so grave as to warrant a take-over. It was reported that Major Nzeogwu was preparing to march on Lagos, while Colonel Ojukwu, in charge of the Kano garrison, was accusing the general of losing valuable time and was urging that the army act.* Three hours later, at a brief Cabinet meeting attended by Major-General Ironsi, Admiral Wey and Police Commissioner Kam Salem, with perhaps half the thirty-two members of the Cabinet (the rest could not be found and had probably left Lagos by then, in considerable apprehension at the fate of politicians), it was decided to hand over the administration of the country as a temporary measure to the army and the police under the control of Major-General Ironsi. The Cabinet meeting was presided over by Dipcharima, and the handing-over document was signed by Dipcharima and Mbadiwe. The decision was broadcast to the nation ten minutes before midnight, when Major-General Ironsi, as Supreme Commander of the Military Government, announced decrees for the suspension of the office of president, prime minister and Parliament, and a military government in each region responsible to the Federal military government. The Cabinet members were divided and demoralized. Arguing from hindsight months later, they attributed sinister motives to Ironsi; but at the time they were slow to rally in the face of crisis. And

*Klaus W. Stephan, in *The Nigerian Misunderstanding* (Bavarian Broadcasting Corporation, 11 September 1967), says he has a tape-recorded statement by Ojukwu to the effect that he had requested General Gowon to crush the coup.

Ojukwu said, in an unpublished interview with Suzanne Cronje, in Enugu, 8 April 1967: 'On January 15 I was the one who advised Ironsi to stand at the Head of the Army, call for support and then organize the various units that would immediately support, so that the rebels who were bound to be few and already committed would suddenly find that the whole thing was phasing away.'

it is exceedingly doubtful whether a refurbished Cabinet of politicians would have been accepted by the country at large; for even before the position had cleared and it was known who was in control, the news of the attack on politicians had unleashed a wild mood of celebration.

At the time of Ironsi's broadcast on the military assumption of power, however, Nigeria had not one, but two army governments. In Kaduna, his arm bandaged from injuries sustained in the mortar attack on the premier's house, Major Nzeogwu had given his press conference at brigade headquarters on the Sunday morning. He was adamant that the operation he had led in Kaduna was not a mutiny. 'In a mutiny you have undisciplined troops,' he said;[12] 'there is no indiscipline here.' On the execution of the coup in the South, Nzeogwu was explosively angry. They had bungled the whole thing, he said. If he had had his way, he'd have killed the Eastern premier, Dr Michael Okpara, and Osadabey, the premier of the Mid-West; and he would do so still, if he could. Asked his opinion about Dr Azikiwe, he replied, 'Zik is a rogue.'[13] Apart from the press conference, he had spent the morning consulting with the North's top civil servants. The first matter they raised was the detention of the Northern governor, Sir Kashim Ibrahim, who was under army guard in State House. Was it necessary to hold him? Nzeogwu agreed immediately that he be released. The governor had been 'a complete gentleman', Nzeogwu said, and had received honourable treatment while under arrest.[14] (It did not enter Nzeogwu's mind that holding the governor hostage would be a trump card in negotiations with Lagos and army headquarters.) At the press conference, too, Nzeogwu announced that government would be administered by the permanent secretaries. 'We have experts to do the job rather than profiteers,' he said. Sir Kashim Ibrahim had signed a declaration transferring all powers previously held by him to the commander, and this made the proper appointment of a government possible. Top administrators who the week before had manned the Sardauna's administration, offered no resistance to being co-opted into the administration of Nzeogwu's Supreme Council. At the press conference, Nzeogwu said that it was not the intention of the military to remain in office permanently. They were simply dedicated to the efficient administration of law and order.

Nzeogwu was establishing a government, but he was only partly in power; he had already partly lost control, not only because of the Ironsi-headed government take-over in Lagos, but also because of complications within the North itself. In Kano, Lieutenant-Colonel Chukwuemeka Odumegwu Ojukwu, the officer commanding 5 Battalion, seized the airport as soon as he had news of the events on the night of 14–15 January. By mid-morning on the Saturday, he had sent for the heads of the administration and had had the Emir of Kano brought to his headquarters to rally and consolidate his authority in the city; but not for the coup. If he was watching and waiting to see the outcome of the Nzeogwu seizure, he said and did nothing that conveyed his support of it. When Ojukwu sent a group of soldiers to the emir's palace, they came not to arrest him but to serve as escort to army headquarters. There the emir found Ojukwu trying to contact Lagos and Kaduna for the latest news of the situation. 'My impression,' said the emir,[15] 'was that he was not part of the coup. He said he would take no orders from the young majors. He explained that he had had me brought to his headquarters so that he could tell me personally what he knew, and I would not have to depend on rumours. I was not under arrest. He told me that there had been an army coup, and he wanted my help in keeping passions down. He was trying to get up-to-date reports on the situation.' At the suggestion of the provincial secretary, the emir broadcast an appeal for calm and order. Later in the week Major Nzeogwu, still in control of Kaduna, though his removal was imminent as authority in Lagos began to move, had a serious problem on his hands. The following Thursday was army pay day; and to meet the large cash requirements, the administration had to draw specie from the Central Bank in Kano and transfer it to Kaduna banks. The Kaduna banks were worried that the soldiers would literally leap over the counters for their pay. (When banks opened on Monday, they restricted general withdrawals of cash to £50.) The problem was raised with Nzeogwu at the meeting he had on Sunday at 11 A.M. with the permanent secretaries. 'Oh,' he said, 'there's no problem; just bring it.' Would he order the road-blocks to let it through? No need for orders or explanations, he said; 'I am in control.' In Kano, however, Lieutenant-Colonel Ojukwu refused to permit the banks to send the money through. From Kaduna Major Nzeogwu sent an air force plane with an official on board to explain and negotiate; the plane was impounded by Colonel Ojukwu. The money did not reach the Kaduna military administration until General Ironsi was fully in control, and the new military governor of the North, Colonel Katsina, had been installed.[16]

Nzeogwu's Supreme Council of the Revolution of the Nigerian Armed Forces remained in effective government barely three days. By the end of the week-end, Lagos had rallied an alternative central authority; and, on receipt of information that Nzeogwu's forces were likely to march south, had deployed the Ibadan garrison across the main road to the north in a ring of mortar positions. It looked as though the Nigerian army was about to go to war with itself. But as the new week opened, army headquarters in Lagos and the young major in Kaduna started negotiations, and terms were hammered out on the army communications network for a surrender of authority by Nzeogwu. At midday on the Tuesday, Nzeogwu announced that he would accept the authority of the Ironsi regime on five conditions. These were: (1) a safe conduct for himself and all his officers and men; (2) a guarantee of freedom from legal proceedings now or later; (3) an assurance that the politicians whom they had fought to remove would not be returned to office; (4) compensation to be paid to the families of officers and men killed in the uprising; and (5) the release of all his officers and men arrested in Western Nigeria. At a press conference in Kaduna at which acceptance of these terms was announced, Major Nzeogwu said:

> We have pledged allegiance to General Ironsi on behalf of all the men who were, for some unknown reasons, referred to as 'rebels'. We feel that it is absurd that men who risked their lives to establish the new regime should be held prisoners. We wanted to change the government for the benefit of everybody else. We were concerned with what was

best for Nigeria. Our action made the Supreme Commander, and he should recognise us.[17]

The major said that five men in the inner circle had planned the action. But most of those concerned in the revolution were Northerners. 'It was a truly Nigerian gathering. Only in the army do you get true Nigerianism.'

At one of his last public appearances, Major Nzeogwu appeared side by side with the newly appointed military governor of the North, Major Katsina. They told a curious tale of reversed fortunes in the three days since the coup. It was after the attack on the Northern premier's house, said Nzeogwu, that he had called on Major Katsina and demanded: 'What side are you on? Are you with me, or are you with them?' Major Katsina had replied: 'Don't bother. I'm on your side.' Major Nzeogwu said that he would always remember how, at the crucial moment, Major Katsina had been on his side. Major Katsina returned the amiability. Waving his hand towards Major Nzeogwu, he said: 'As you see, I am still alive. I will be here for many years yet. I am proud to have a chance to help save my country. We respect each other. I have been able to help Major Nzeogwu with some of his problems during the past few days. I am his good friend and I am sure he will now help me. We will work together for the betterment of our country.'[18] The new military governor and the man who led the army coup shook hands outside brigade headquarters; Katsina was bound for Lagos to meet the newly appointed military governors.

Sent to escort Nzeogwu to Lagos under a guarantee of safe conduct from General Ironsi was Lieutenant-Colonel C. D. Nwawo, flown to Nigeria from London the night before. He had been Major Nzeogwu's superior officer at the Military Training College. 'I don't think he would have left Kaduna with any other man at this time,' said Lieutenant-Colonel Nwawo. Nzeogwu said that he had no worries about the repercussions from the coup. 'My only worry is that I did not have time to tell my men that I was leaving. I would have liked to have said a proper goodbye.'[19] Major Nzeogwu was seen in Lagos for a few days thereafter. Then he disappeared. He and the other participants in the attempted coup, including Major Ifeajuna, whose return to Nigeria from Ghana Colonel Ojukwu helped to negotiate,[20] were arrested and detained in eight different prisons throughout the country. Their fate while in detention was one of the several issues that racked and finally broke the Ironsi government.

AN IBO PLOT?

An Ibo plot? Propaganda, then credibility, and at last Nigeria itself fragmented on the issue of the January coup. The army regime headed by General Ironsi began in a burst of popular euphoria that the rotten past was gone for ever. That illusion was dispelled within a few months. The country ranged itself into two hostile camps, each with a totally incompatible view of the January coup. Much said and done over the ensuing year and a half drove the two camps to open breach and then to war. As the country tottered from one crisis to the next and more serious one, so the different official versions of events solidified and justified all done in the name of each. The January coup was the departure point for disaster, for – it was said in the official Nigerian version – it was an Ibo plan for Ibo domination. After the initial 'Ibo' conspiracy, the coup seven months later in July, directed against Ibos, was 'the natural course of events'. (More than one senior civil servant, as well as young army officers in the Federation, used this precise phrase.) What Ibos did or are supposed to have done that week-end in January became, in time, justification for eliminating them: first in the army; then in the North; and finally as the enemy in war.

The full story of the Nigerian coups will probably never be known. Two opposite official accounts have grown,[21] and with them a tangled undergrowth of popular belief.* Gossip and rumour, eye-witness and circumstantial account have become legend in the telling, and legend has calcified into war propa-

*One instance, current among Northerners, but not exclusive to them: Brigadier Maimalari escaped assassination on the night of the coup and went into hiding in Dahomey. From there, a fortnight later, he telephoned General Ironsi, and then returned. He was then shot down in cold blood, and the autopsy showed forty-seven bullet wounds. This rankled deep among his men and an act of revenge became inevitable. The fact is that Brigadier Maimalari was killed on the night of the coup.

ganda. Rumour should be brushed aside as evidence, but in an atmosphere both rancorous and gullible, it becomes reality: what people believe, regardless of hard evidence, becomes cause for action. How is one to separate fact from legend and propaganda? Every member of the Nigerian élite – civil servant, university lecturer, engineer, Lagotian socialite – and every student in London and New York, not to talk of Ibadan and Ife, Nsukka, Zaria and Lagos, has an elaborate version of most incidents. Each version is impressive in the telling: until you hear the next version, and the contradictions glare. Few who recount the events of January will admit any doubts of the full facts, or any gap in the sequence of cause (Ibo plotting) and effect (Ibo domination, which was thwarted seven months later by the counter-coup).

There exists, in a government safe at Lagos, a draft White Paper on the January coup, of which only a few pages have ever been published. It was ordered by decision of the Executive Council under the Ironsi regime. It was drafted on the strength of intelligence and security reports, after the young majors and their associates in the January coup* had been exhaustively interrogated during the months that they were held in detention by the Ironsi government. Apart from the investigation conducted by the Ironsi regime, the Gowon government undertook to issue a White Paper on the events leading to the change of

*Almost all the leading figures of January are now dead. Nzeogwu died in the battle for Ubolo-Eke, near Nsukka. His body was given full military honours by the Federal forces though, report or legend tells, not before Northern soldiers had plucked out his eyes so that he 'would never see the North again'. Major Okafor, who was detained at Benin, was buried alive by Northern troops during the July coup. Major Anuforo was also killed in the July coup. Major Ifeajuna, the vacillating hero, was later shot as a traitor in Biafra after the invasion of the Mid-West. Major Chukuka died in prison in the Mid-West when Northern soldiers held the warders at gunpoint during the July coup. Captain Oji was killed in action on the Biafran side in February 1968. In August 1968 it was thought that Major Ademoyega was serving in the Biafran army. Nzeogwu talked freely to friends who visited him in prison during 1966 and again when he was in Enugu, helping at Abaliki to train the army of what would soon be proclaimed Biafra, but no systematic account of his version exists in writing. He made no bones of his opposition to secession and, for some while during 1967, was put under restriction by Ojukwu.

government in both January and July.[22] This White Paper has not appeared to date. As the Federal version was put out only after the July coup had taken place, it is not surprising that it served to justify that second coup. Publication of the full report was stopped at the insistence of the Eastern region, when it looked as though agreement might emerge from Aburi and other negotiations at the beginning of 1967. The Federal government agreed that an account of the January coup would reinflame old wounds. (Though, curiously, when wounds were bleeding freely in the fighting and the propaganda war that accompanied it, the White Paper revelations were still withheld.) But in January 1967, enough of the report was published by the Gowon government in *Nigeria 1966* to show that it interpreted the coup as an Ibo plot, and treated events going back to 1964 as part of that plot.

> Certain officers in the Nigerian army sought to use the army created for the defence of the fatherland and the promotion of the citizen to attain purely political ends. . . . As far back as December 1964, a small group of army officers mainly from the Ibo ethnic group of the Eastern region began to plot, in collaboration with some civilians, the overthrow of what was then the Government of the Federation of Nigeria and the eventual assumption of power in the country.

Booklets published by the Northern regional government and another by the Current Issues Society[23] went considerably further on the subject of the Ibo plot. Claiming to be a dispassionate and forthright account of how the Ibos, 'through their devilish determination to dominate or break up Nigeria, plunged the country into crisis', this version asserts that the 'North's record was one of restraint and compromise in the face of unprecedented acts of provocation which eventually did succeed in momentarily stretching beyond breaking point the monumental imperturbability of Northern Nigerians'. The January mutiny was no mutiny,

> but a premeditated and carefully projected plan by the Ibos to impose themselves on the other tribes of Nigeria. It was the culmination of an effort, the fulfilment of a dream and the realisation of a hope long entertained by the Ibo tribe in Nigeria.

Countless elaborations of this version exist. The general assumption is that every Ibo is guilty, if not by act then by association with his ethnic group. Azikiwe, Ojukwu, Ironsi, Nzeogwu are all Ibos: therefore, whatever overt acts they committed, they must all have been privy to the plot; and if their behaviour should appear to have deviated from the purposes of other conspirators, this is either because the enormity of the plot was not at first fully revealed, or because their behaviour was deliberately calculated to confuse those of other tribes. So, it is said, General Ironsi tricked the Cabinet into ceding power to the army under his command. (This ignores the fact that the Cabinet was too divided and demoralized to hold the government together.) If Ironsi's actions were loyal during the three crucial days following the coup attempt, this was because 'the role assigned to him was to appear to be taken by surprise'. Supporters of the government find it hard to understand why 'the government has not released the information it has. The Northern Government has a tape-recording of Ironsi's voice outlining the plans for the coup. It's incredible to me that Gowon has not released the proof he has of civilian involvement in the coup planning.'[24] Never mind that it was General Ironsi's rallying of the army that smothered the Nzeogwu-led coup; the fact that the general emerged at the head of the military government made it an Ibo coup. Colonel Ojukwu was also part of the plot.* In Kaduna top-ranking security officials spread the report that Ojukwu was in the city while the coup was being executed in the early hours of Saturday morning. Some embellish the account by saying that he personally led the attack on the Sardauna's residence; others, that 'Ojukwu pushed the young men into action'. But why, if Ojukwu was privy to the coup, did he prevent Kaduna, under Nzeogwu's control, from making withdrawals for army pay from Kano banks? Ah, said Major Hassan Katsina, who conceded Ojukwu's obstruction of

*The *New York Herald Tribune* of 19 October 1966 reported: 'Before Major Nzeogwu surrendered his three-day control of the Northern region . . . he declared flatly that if Colonel Ojukwu had joined him, the take-over would have succeeded.' Instead, the report added, Ojukwu remained loyal to Ironsi who put down the mutiny, jailed the plotters and named Ojukwu military governor of the East.

Nzeogwu that week: 'They had fallen out by then.' Why, if it was an Ibo plot for domination, did General Ironsi appoint Colonel Katsina military governor of the North and not Ojukwu, the commander of the Kano garrison and the obvious choice for strong man? 'Oh, you don't know the Ibo – man.' Above all else, the Federal version insists, the coup must be judged by 'the pattern of the killings'. No Ibo died apart from Lieutenant-Colonel Arthur Unegbe, who was killed trying to guard the keys of the armoury; and his death was clearly an incidental casualty, which did not alter the planned pattern of the killings.

The first press suggestion that January was an Ibo coup open to Northern reprisals was made by the BBC correspondent, who beat the news blackout on coup day and mentioned that all the young majors seemed to be Ibo.[25] A week after the coup, the *Sunday Times*[26] asked 'Can Ironsi Hold Nigeria?'

> According to reliable evidence, Major-General Aguiyi-Ironsi, head of the military government, has a list of seventy further notables (apart from the Sardauna of Sokoto and the Prime Minister) who have disappeared, largely Northern leaders again.* Ramadan, the Muslim fast period, closes at the end of the month with religious celebrations which could easily lead to violence. And the Northerners would have plenty of Ibo targets . . . for despite Nigeria's sharp geographical divisions, the Ibos, the most adaptable of the tribes, have spread through the nation as workers, traders and officials.

Perhaps some of the toppled politicians were thinking such things in the jubilant weeks immediately after the coup; but none of them dared to say so publicly. Only when the wound inflicted by January turned septic in the Nigerian body politic did this version of events catch the old tribal infection. Every event, every individual action, had to be fitted into a grand theory of conspiracy. The trouble was that all did not fit easily; for there was more than one conspiracy, and more than one level of commitment within any one conspiracy. The fact that there were Ibos among the lieutenant-colonels of 1964 who contemplated intervening in the government crisis, and among the majors of the 1966 coup, does not make this a continuous thread of conspiracy. An army intervention in 1964 would have

*This was quite inaccurate – *author*.

been aimed at entrenching President Azikiwe in power; the 1966 action was to topple him along with the rest of the government. The 1964 plot was initiated by Colonel Ojukwu; the 1966 one, he helped to crush.

The Nzeogwu coup was launched in an atmosphere of anti-government intrigue, in which blows against the Federal government might have been planned, if not executed, by several groups. President Azikiwe, in Britain ostensibly on convalescent leave, was demonstrably confused. He put out prompt feelers to General Ironsi about whether his return home would be welcome. He told the press that he would be going home. But he did not leave Europe for several months. In an unpublished interview,[27] he admitted that – like many Nigerians – he was expecting the government to be brought down by some act of political opposition. But from which quarter had it come? He delayed his return until he could be sure that he would be accommodated, or at least left alone. For several plots were in the making by the beginning of 1966, and the Nzeogwu-led coup seems to have been only one of them. The army was divided against itself so far that, when the coup started in Kaduna, high-ups in the civil service suspected that Brigadier Ademulegun, a Westerner in command in the North, might be behind it. Civil servants were widely said to be hatching their own plot; though this, said a young Northerner, 'was a coup that melted away'. In Nigeria, as in other African states, what young members of the élite would have liked to have done, only their counterparts in the army succeeded in doing.

To some observers, the young majors' coup was the outcome of planning, or at the least prompting, by UPGA politicians. Frustrated and embittered in opposition, UPGA might have had most to gain from a toppling of government. But if there was an UPGA plot brewing, it was not the one that chose as principal initiator Major Nzeogwu, who derided all politicians of the establishment equally. UPGA would, in any event, have been most unlikely to have tried initiating an army action at only the middle level of the officer corps. If the young officers had any direct political links, they were with young radicals scattered in the trade unions, the civil service, at the universities and inside the Nigerian Youth Congress. This was a diffused and amorphous pressure group, with some members inside UPGA and others not; with associations both among young intellectuals and in the army among the young officers, especially Nzeogwu. As far as is known, only one of these young radicals was entrusted by Ifeajuna with the task of drafting the proclamation of the young officers' coup for broadcasting; and he could not be found on the crucial night.[28]

The genesis of the plot apparently goes back to August 1965, when Majors Okafor and Ifeajuna and Captain O. Oji confided in one another their dissatisfaction with political developments in Nigeria and the impact of these on the army; they then set about searching for other officers who held similar views and might be prepared to act on them. Next to join the conspiracy were Major I. H. Chukuka and Major C. I. Anuforo, who brought in Major Nzeogwu. By early November, the inner circle seems to have comprised the above six men plus Major A. Ademoyega – a Yoruba officer, incidentally. Major Chukwuma Kaduna Nzeogwu was a Mid-West Ibo but, as his middle name shows, had made the North his home, spoke fluent Hausa, and made all his closest friends among Northerners, who admired and respected him; though, unusually in a soldier, he was a puritanical man and a book-worm. He was a practising Catholic, of rebellious temperament. While at St John's College in Kaduna, he had clashed with the school authorities and been suspended from school so that he had had to write his West African School Certificate examination from home. His posting in the North had been a form of reprimand, after he had beaten up an expatriate major in an incident in Lagos. Ifeajuna and Ademoyega had been students together at Ibadan University. Ademoyega had been an Action Group official and possessed perhaps the closest links with politics. Ifeajuna was probably the best-known of the coup leaders, as Nigeria's Commonwealth Games gold medallist at Vancouver in 1954 (after which athletic victory he was fêted and, said his critics, 'had his head turned'). Of all the coup-makers, apart from Nzeogwu, Ifeajuna had the closest connexion with the young Ibadan intellectuals and radicals. But his student record was not unblemished, and his contemporaries in a student strike, of which he had been one of the ringleaders, never forgave him for having produced a forged medical certificate to get himself off the hook with authorities. In all, 200 men were arrested for their part in the conspiracy, of whom sixty played more prominent roles: among them, a Yoruba captain, an Ekoi captain, and two Yoruba second lieutenants.

Planning for the execution of the plot started in earnest in early November 1965, at a meeting of the inner circle which took place at Ifeajuna's house in Lagos. Nzeogwu does not appear to have been present. Captain E. Nwobosi, who was entrusted with the Ibadan coup operation, was drawn in only forty-eight hours before. What coordinating was done largely accompanied Ifeajuna's mobility as adjutant-general to Brigadier Maimalari. This emerges from Ifeajuna's version of the coup, written white-hot in Ghana where he sat out the immediate aftermath of 15 January until persuaded to surrender to Ironsi.* The version suggests some divergence of purpose among the planners. They could not agree, for instance, on the list of victims for their assassination list, and so it was left to the commanders of the various operations to make their decisions on the spot. Nzeogwu said:[29] 'It was agreed that the three Regional Prime Ministers should be seized and shot.' There had been no plans to harm the Federal premier. Commenting subsequently on the fact that the Eastern premier, Dr Okpara, had been left untouched, Major Nzeogwu said: 'We all started with the same spirit, but some got faint-hearted on the way.' Ifeajuna put the failures of the coup down to reliance on too small a group.[30] 'We were rushing from one assignment to another, instead of being able to pull them all off simultaneously.' The

*The Ifeajuna manuscript has not been published and may be lost. At one time there were plans to publish it in Enugu, but Chinua Achebe, who was associated with this publishing venture, pronounced the manuscript worthless when he read it. Some of Ifeajuna's friends in Ibadan and Lagos had the manuscript briefly and nervously, and hastily got rid of it as the atmosphere in Nigeria turned against all versions Eastern and Ibo. But not before one reader, in his words, had ascertained that the manuscript was 'the nut without the kernel' for, beyond what was already known about the events in January, it disclosed little. I have spoken to three persons who read the manuscript.

same factor probably explains why Nzeogwu, who abominated Ojukwu, nevertheless had no option but to leave him in control of the Kano garrison.

Among the January coup-makers and coup-breakers – though not necessarily among all Ibo members of the Ironsi government – loyalties were not inherently tribal, but political and army-institutionalized. The young majors included in their planning group no officer above the rank of major, for fear that such colleagues, whether Ibo or even potentially sympathetic to their aims, would have been dangerous to the security of their plan and might have meant their surrender of control. For his part, General Ironsi's loyalties were to the regime he served. There is incontrovertible evidence[31] that some weeks before the coup, General Ironsi had wind of talk in the officers' mess that the army should act to end the crisis in the West. He reported this incident to the Federal prime minister's secretary and, at his suggestion, to the attorney-general. Ultimately the report reached the Minister of Defence and the prime minister himself. But the report was discounted, perhaps because too few details were known, and because the men in charge, General Ironsi among them, thought that a coup could not succeed in Nigeria.

The January coup was not an Ibo coup with motives of tribal domination. It was a coup inspired by widespread political grievances, yet lacking a direct organizational link with UPGA or any other political group. The coup grew out of the angry but confused political purposes of young officers, who shared the disgust of their generation at the iniquity of the politicians, not least their use of the army to further their purposes, but who, when they did decide to act, lacked the mass support that clearer political aims and preparation might have provided. The planning of the coup was defective both militarily and politically; the more so because of the need to bring the date forward so as to pre-empt the use of the army in the West.

More men and a longer period of preparation might have improved the logistics of the coup operation. It is doubtful if it would have made much difference to the post-coup politics of Nigeria. The soldiers would have released Awolowo and installed him as head of an interim government. 'I would have stood by,' Nzeogwu said.[32] (He added that three-quarters of the police and more than half the judiciary would have been eliminated, because they had permitted themselves to be used for political purposes.) But the shape of an alternative Nigeria was nebulous to the young officers, and would in all probability have been left to Awolowo to decide. It was one thing to remove men who were pillars of a rotten political system, but quite another to get the system working any differently. On this, the young majors appear to have had little to offer, except a rather brutal vengeance against those whose moral and political purpose they had found so deficient. They planned their coup in a small, closed group of school and army course class-mates, never giving a thought to the charge that because five of the six inside planners were Ibo, this would be seen as evidence of an Ibo coup.

The Army Brass Takes Over

Quite honestly, I don't feel like a governor, I still feel like a soldier. I would be much happier in the barracks with my men than in this Government House.

Lieutenant-Colonel Fajuyi, *West Africa*, 19 February 1966

The coup was greeted with more enthusiasm than independence itself had been six years before. 'Here in Ikenne and Shagamu you can feel the streets sighing with relief today,' wrote a school teacher. Nzeogwu and the young majors were heroes. In the West, the thuggery stopped almost overnight; the region veered from chaotic banditry to jubilant expectancy with astonishing speed. Within a fortnight, the police mobile contingent from the Northern provinces was withdrawn. Ministers vacated their official homes and returned their official cars. The politicians slunk out of sight; those who ventured into public places had to face open derision. The big men in the black cars excited not envy but contempt. Never was the venality of the old regime more despised than at the moment of its ignominious collapse. Nor was the mood of celebration confined to the South. The

North, too, experienced a week of exhilaration. The houses of Northern ministers were looted, by Northerners. While the Sardauna was alive, conducting government like a medieval court, holding all authority in the palm of his hand, and dispensing largesse or peremptory instruction, it seemed impossible to contemplate any other order. A strong North, it was believed, needed a strong Sardauna. But whether they were prepared to say so or not while he was alive, the younger civil servants and the younger levels of the NPC were restless under his tyrannical dominion, and they found welcome release when he had been removed. Those who had been the pillars of the old order were shocked and stunned into inactivity in the period immediately after the coup. But the ease with which the old order had been toppled was deceptive; and if NPC power, in the shape of Federal ministers and politicians, local big-wigs and their retainers, did not immediately react to the coup, this did not mean that there would be no reaction. It was a matter of time.

Nigerians were slow to grasp what had actually happened. The week-end had seen not a coup to break the old order, but a coup of reformers defeated in a holding action manned by the regular army command. Nigeria was in the hands of a military government; military governors had replaced the discredited political heads; but it was a military government that derived its legitimacy – and, minimal though this was, it was considerably greater than that of its successor would be – from a decision of the Cabinet to call in the army to restore order. In the general relief at the dislodging of corrupt politicians, army declarations of intent went unexamined. Nigeria watched Ironsi replace Nzeogwu, Nzeogwu bow out of Kaduna under military escort, and Nzeogwu disappear from the public eye, without realizing that this was the counter-action in progress. The political parties, the trade unions, the students, the Nigerian Youth Movement, traditional leaders like the Emir of Zaria, the Oni of Ife, the Alake of Abeokuta, the Sultan of Sokoto, all fell over one another to announce their enthusiasm for the new regime. The country was expecting radical changes to prevent the resurgence of the old order. But Major-General Ironsi and his four military governors – Major Hassan Katsina in the North, Lieutenant-Colonel Ojukwu in the East, Lieutenant-Colonel F. A. Fajuyi in the West and Lieutenant-Colonel Ejoor in the Mid-West – were not reformers of the Egyptian Free Officer type. If Nzeogwu had been inspired by Nasser, Ironsi was more comparable with Neguib, who became head of a military government despite himself. In Nigeria, unlike Egypt, Neguib removed Nasser, not the other way about, and the reforming zeal of the young officers was snuffed out by the senior army command. The political representatives of the old order had gone, but the order itself was intact.

Nigeria's principal investors were not slow to record their confidence. 'Under Ironsi,' wrote a researcher for the Aero-Space Institute, in a US Air Force document, 'hope returned. There seemed to be a chance of finding a moderate middle of the road solution for problems of political administration in Nigeria.'[33] President Johnson told the United States Congress that despite the recent 'painful upheaval', Nigeria was one of the five countries which together accounted for nine-tenths of the $665 million deployed in development loans. (The other four were Congo-Kinshasa, Ethiopia, Morocco and Tunisia: all countries that, in the view of the United States, were determined to help themselves.) On the same day as the US president's speech, the British High Commission sent personal letters to the heads of all British firms operating in Nigeria, assuring them that all was calm throughout the country, and that reports in the British press about the military take-over had 'exaggerated the seriousness of the situation'.[34] The major donor countries led by the World Bank increased their development aid to Nigeria, on the strength of a Six Year Development Plan which had one more year to run, but which was already far behind target and unlikely to catch up. Twice in its first week of office, the Supreme Military Council issued the assurance that there were no plans for nationalizing private industry, and that foreign investors would be 'fully free' to continue operating as they had done prior to the new government.[35] When probes were begun into the shady deals of the politicians, these did not touch the workings of expatriate firms. One of the first delegations that

General Ironsi received was from the unions, to urge on them that no strikes be called while the military regime was in power. Strikes were 'wasteful rivalries', he said. All labour organizations should 'work as a team in the national interest'. One of the last statements of the Ironsi regime dealt with trade unions,[36] on the day that Ironsi himself was kidnapped by the July mutineers. The National Military government, it declared, was considering: (*a*) the introduction of compulsory arbitration and the establishment of industrial courts, to facilitate a speedy settlement of trade disputes which might otherwise result in strikes; (*b*) the banning of all existing labour unions, since these were a source of disunity in the country.

Into the power vacuum created by the toppling of the politicians stepped a new ruling group. This was the bureaucracy: the army and the civil service in close alliance, with the civil servants doing most of the thinking for the military. Hovering behind them were the academics. Ironsi made a tentative move to combine in government the forces of military men, civil servants and academics; the idea was debated for forty-eight hours non-stop, in the early stages of setting up a government machine. Some of the civil servants objected to the academics on the grounds that their inclusion would destroy the non-political character of the civil service. Ultimately two bodies emerged at the centre, the Supreme Military Council and the Federal Executive Council, with the second performing the functions of the former Council of Ministers. Both were all-military in composition; General Ironsi was head of both. The individual ministries, however, were run by the permanent secretaries; and while there was a clean sweep of ministers and legislators, of political appointees to corporations and of elected councillors in the South, the civil service remained intact. Accordingly, for instance, the attorney-general's office was still headed by the man who had drafted the emergency regulations for the West and who was widely regarded as the hatchet of the old regime.*

The theory was that a military government would operate

* Some two months after the Ironsi government came to power, protests resulted in his being dropped from office.

without politics. Politics and politicians had been at the root of the evil old regime. The military cabinet, being non-political, needed no political heads, only technical and administrative experts. At long last the civil servants had obtained their release from the professional politicians, whose activities they had always regarded as an impediment to good government. The trouble was that the technocratic thinking of army men and civil servants alike led to an over-simplified notion of politics and the political process. It was assumed that the faults of the old regime had been due to the politicians, not to the political system; so that if, under the military regime, there were no politicians in government, the sources of political dissension would also have been removed.*

Even as this antiseptic partnership of public servants, in uniform or out, went virtuously to work, however, 'politics' was growing underground, in the regions, within the army and the civil service, to thrust its way through the surface later. This was so especially in the North, where political power had been most firmly rooted in a more solidified social class. In the South, politicians were detained, some for longer periods than others. In the North, the old political class was at liberty, and the Native Authorities, the real source of NPC power, were intact;† it was not long before the politicians were at work exploiting the apprehensions of Northern civil servants and students, and the frustrations of the unemployed.

Ironsi, a man of the old order, with the reflexes of the old regime and the pace of a staid senior administrator, filled his office with vagueness and procrastination. This was the failing of a military governor, but also of a government which had no clear purpose, made no statement of aims beyond immediate ones and, when it decided on a policy, acted by administrative fiat, without consultation or any attempt at mobilization in the country. Two main challenges faced the new regime: the ending

*In May, eighty-one existing political parties were dissolved and the formation of new ones prohibited.

†At one stroke, reported the *New Nigerian*, 8 July 1966, three ex-ministers of the Federal government and two former Northern ministers were made Kano Native Authority Councillors.

of the old regional divisions, with the building of national unity; and the eradication of corruption. General Ironsi and the four regional military governors issued declarations of policy in varying degrees of moderation or flamboyance. What pronouncements of reform were made were unexceptionable. But without clear proposals for the shape of the new political system, let alone any concept of long-term social and economic policy, the declarations amounted to little more than a vaguely stated commitment by soldiers and civil servants to honesty in public affairs, order and regularity in government. The Ironsi regime had no policy for reform when it began; and it had not found one by the time that it was brought down six months later.

In the absence of firm policy and direction from the government at the centre, the old regional interests began to reassert themselves; and the regional military governors, like chameleons, began to take on the colourings of the political system they had displaced. In the West, Fajuyi's broom swept cleanest, as the furniture of NNDP patronage and pressure was removed. More or less the same had happened when the Action Group split in 1962. But the old animosities were not deeply buried, if buried at all, in the region. In the North – by contrast with the West, the East and the Mid-West, where probes of the activities and interests of the politicians were initiated – the military governor was silent or defensive on the subject of corruption. The Northern Nigerian Marketing Board was investigated, but only strong pressure on the governor resulted in the report of the inquiry being published. The NPC and NNDP were drawing courage from the inaction and indecision of the regime and were waiting their opportunity to test their strength. Among young Southerners, there was a growing disillusionment with the regime. By the time that Ironsi's government was caught in the crossfire of the old regional conflicts, the forces of the old order had rallied; whereas the regime had knocked any possible support from underneath itself by demoralizing or antagonizing the reformers.

The touchstone of the conflict was the fate of the young majors. In the South, the Ironsi regime stood condemned for its failure to release Nzeogwu and his fellow coup-makers. In the North and in the army, the regime was under constant pressure to court-martial the young majors for insubordination, perhaps treason. By July the minutes of the Supreme Military Council recorded that the young majors were to be court-martialled not later than October. The proceedings would be open to the public.[37]

Ironsi's instinct was all along to placate the Northerners. Thus, as his regime opened, he appointed Major Hassan Katsina, son of the emir of Katsina, as military governor of the North. This soothed the traditionalists temporarily. Similarly, Ironsi's open reliance on Northern officers in the army (he appointed Lieutenant-Colonel Gowon chief-of-staff over Ogundipe, giving him virtual command of the army; placed young Northerners in charge of ordnance and signals; was guarded only by Northern soldiers) and the state visit to Lagos arranged for the Sultan of Sokoto were gestures of conciliation. But they did not resolve his government's mounting dilemma in the face of conflicting pressures. For fear of antagonizing the North, the regime did nothing to mobilize support for itself. The most obvious step was the release of Chief Awolowo, Chief Anthony Enahoro and their associates of the treason trial in the West. General Ironsi three times set a date for their release. The first date was in March; but Ironsi told Peter Enahoro of certain rumours that he himself had taken part in plotting the January revolt: 'To allay fears that the South had conspired against the North, he decided to defer. . . . Another date was fixed in May. At the discussions in State House, the Governor of the North said vehemently that Chief Awolowo's release at that time would cause furore in the North . . . though Fajuyi pressed, as he had done for many months, that contrary to exciting rebellion in the North, Chief Awolowo's discharge would rally civilians to the banner of the military regime.'[38] The final release date was set for 1 August 1966. By that date Ironsi was dead.

Ironsi temporized in the same way over Tiv demands. He claimed to be impressed by their arguments for Middle Belt autonomy; but nothing happened. He received deputations from J. S. Tarka, the Tiv leader, on six different occasions; but then reports circulated that he was about to have Tarka arrested.

Government was already being run largely by rumour and

intrigue. Those who could not reach General Ironsi's ear through committee or formal proceeding, buttonholed him at drinking parties. The coup had done nothing to remove old antagonisms between the high-ups of the civil service; for the service, no less than the government of the politicians, had been a tug-of-war between contestants of different regions for office and promotion. Under the Balewa regime, Southerners argued, Northerners had been elevated to senior posts because they were Northerners, not necessarily because they were qualified; now, with its destruction, Northerners were apprehensive about their future. The bitter power struggle that had been going on for years between Ibos and Yorubas in the federal service, where Yorubas had entrenched their monopoly as the first arrivals and earliest qualified, was now given a sharper bite. It was an open secret in Lagos that old rivalries among the country's top civil servants who had enjoyed different sources of patronage under the old regime, far from being forgotten, had flared again. Ironsi, an Ibo, it was said, was going out of his way to further Ibo power: did he not depend on an inner clique of Ibo advisers, whose instrument he was? and when key appointments were made, as of the new attorney-general and several heads of crucial commissions, were they not Ibo?

It was the report on the future of the civil service from one of these commissions that precipitated the crisis. The study groups* set up by the regime were the long-awaited preliminaries to reform. A number had been appointed: one to deal with the constitutional review; one to function as an economic planning advisory group; one to report on different policy aspects. Mr

*National Study Groups were set up by edict on 28 February 1966. The first group of seven members was to consider a number of related subjects in the context of national unity: Mr Justice S. P. J. O. Thomas (judicial services), M. O. Ani (statutory corporations), F. C. Nwokedi (public services), J. O. Udoji (education), A. I. Wilson (information services), Yusufu Gobir (police and prisons), O. Bateye (administrative machinery). The second group of nine members was to deal with the constitutional review and was composed of Dr T. O. Elias, Chief Rotimi Williams, Dr Essien Udom, Dr Okoi Arikpo, Alhaji M. Buba Ado and four administrative officers. The third group of nine members composed the National Planning Advisory Group and included Chief S. Adebo, Dr Pius Akigbo, Mr Godfrey Lardner, Professor F. A. Oluwasanmi and Dr I. Abubakr.

Francis Nwokedi, former permanent secretary for external affairs and one of the most senior Ibo federal civil servants, was to make proposals for the public services, 'in the context of national unity'. The outcome of his inquiry was Decree 34 and, accompanying it, an announcement by General Ironsi that Nigeria had ceased to be a federation, that the regions were abolished and that the public services were to be unified. Decree 34 was promulgated on 24 May. Five days later there were fierce mob killings of Ibos in Northern towns. The North struck against its loss of power at the centre and at what it believed to be the real purpose of the Ironsi regime, the abandonment of the federal constitution in order to consolidate Nigeria under Ibo domination. After the May killings there came, at intervals of two months each, the revenge coup of Northerners in the army, which brought down the Ironsi regime and installed the Gowon government; and the September–October massacre of Ibos in the North, after which the word *pogrom* became part of the Nigerian vocabulary.

The Nwokedi recommendations were in reality not as climacteric as the furore surrounding them. They changed less in fact than in Northern fear. The regions were to be known as groups of provinces, and the governors were to be heads not of regions but of provinces; but they were to govern under the same arrangements as previously. The public services were to be unified under a single public service commission; but provincial commissions were to make all appointments to the unified service except for the top-ranking posts (group 6 and above in the civil service list, which meant salaries of £2,200 a year and over). It meant that the provincial services would have more patronage to dispense than the regional ones had had previously, when all federal posts from the highest to the lowest had been dealt with by the Federal public service commission. But top Northern civil servants stood to lose from the fact that seniority in the federal service was to be calculated on salary; for civil service salary grades were lower in the North than elsewhere. Above all, the North was fearful at the sight of power at the centre in the hands of Ironsi and a close group of civil servants from the East.

It was, of course, stupid and provocative to appoint civil servants to tackle on their own the most taxing problems facing the country, before the regime had formulated on overall policy of reform and the main outlines of a new political structure. Only when these principles had been decided, could civil servants constructively be asked to pad out these proposals. If provinces were to displace regions, and a unitary state a federal one, what would the functions and powers of the provinces be? What political and administrative structure was to be devised for the unitary state? How would the system of revenue allocation operate? Such questions were left wide open. Civil servants had been instructed to search for unification formulae as though this was a purely technical exercise.

General Ironsi's announcement of the decree[39] was a measure of his regime's confusion. The new arrangements for the civil service, he said, were 'without prejudice' to the commission still at work on the new constitution. But if the overall lines of the new constitution had still to be considered, why the unseemly haste to push through the Nwokedi recommendations? One of the most influential of the Federal permanent secretaries complained that he had first heard of the decree on the radio as he came off the tennis court. There had been two months of argument for and against a unified public service; suddenly it was law. The Supreme Military Council had been divided, with most of its members opposed. At the meeting immediately before the decree was promulgated, Ironsi heard the governors out after they had lodged their objections in writing, and then said, 'I'm committed.' Colonel Katsina flew from the meeting of the Council to announce at Kaduna airport, 'Tell the nation that the egg will be broken on Tuesday. Two important announcements will be made by the Supreme Commander.' These, he added with characteristic accommodation, would be for the betterment of the nation as a whole and 'a very good thing'.*

*Lieutenant-Colonel Fajuyi had written a five-page memorandum setting out the difficulties and problems that he envisaged. He added a concluding paragraph stating that if these objections were taken into account he agreed with the tenor of the document. The governor of the North telephoned Fajuyi. 'Why the last paragraph?' he asked. 'Out of courtesy,' was Fajuyi's reply.

In all, sixty-four of the country's most senior civil servants – seventeen of them expatriates – were directly affected by Decree 34. But the civil service is the main outlet in all regions for Nigeria's too rapidly growing educated élite, and young Northerners, fearing displacement in open competition within a national bureaucracy, felt themselves directly in the line of fire. Significantly, the incident that set off the killings in the North was a demonstration, in Zaria's old city, of students from the Institute of Public Administration. They carried provocative placards: 'Avenge the Sardauna's death' and 'Northern unity'. Decree 34 was precipitate; and the unification announcement that accompanied it, ill-considered and ambiguous. But neither the decree nor the speech was judged by what it said or meant, except, perhaps, by those who were immediately affected. Decree 34 was not the cause of the trouble but the occasion for it. It was announced in an atmosphere polluted by propaganda that behind every policy emanating from the Ironsi regime lay an Ibo plan for domination. The first step in the Ibo plan to colonize the North would be the Ibo take-over of the civil service; and the word spread that Ibos were about to migrate northwards in droves to take over all competitive posts. In the North, where Ibo immigrants had always been resented as alien, incitement by a small group of plotters flared only too fiercely into a mob violence that, once provoked, was self-generating. The cry of the killings was '*Araba*' (Let us part). Northern secession was the watchword. Ibos in the North were attacked as the embodiment of the Ibo-run government in Lagos. In Zaria the rioters began to identify themselves as 'the army of the North', ready to repulse so-called Ibo attacks; for rumour had been assiduously spread that Ibos were preparing to retaliate. This had the calculated effect of setting off fresh violence. The May killings showed that the old order in the North was ready to fight back. And by then it was also clear that the Ironsi regime had thrown together in the North forces previously incompatible, even hostile, to one another. Northerners, whether NPC or NEPU, Hausa–Fulani ruling class or Middle Belt, closed ranks in the belief that, if Northern power had been broken at the centre, the alternative was an Ibo domination that threatened all Northerners.

The May killings were barely reported in Nigeria. The *New Nigerian* of 30 May 1966 appeared with four of its eight pages blank and the announcement: 'Within fifteen minutes of this edition ... going to press a telephone message was received from a government official instructing that no reference be made to the subject that formed the basis of the reports and pictures which should have occupied this space....'

The month after the killings was spent in trying to pick up the pieces. Ibos who had fled to the East were persuaded, by Ojukwu himself, to return under promise of protection. Northern emirs and chiefs met in conference with the Northern military governor, to hear him discourage all acts of lawlessness and to insist at the same time that there be no permanent changes in the constitution without consultation. From that meeting a memorandum listing the demands of chiefs and emirs, and threatening secession if they were not accepted, went to Lagos. The contents of the memorandum were never disclosed, but the reply of the Supreme Military Council incensed the North. 'The Military Government is not an elected government, and should not be treated as such,' it said. 'It is a corrective government, designed to remove the abuses of the old regime and create a healthy community for return to civilian rule.'[40] The constitutional review group, the statement added, was still weighing the merits and demerits of a unitary or federal form of government; but 'while in office, the military government can run the government only as a military government under a unified command. It cannot afford to run five separate governments and separate services as if a civilian regime.' Less than a week later, in an address at police headquarters, Ironsi announced a scheme for the rotation of military governors, and for the creation of military prefectures – responsible for carrying government policy to village level – which, like the governors, would be rotated from one group of provinces to another. The military government had begun to take more power to itself.

But the May killings had shown that General Ironsi could not lean on his army to control disorder, let alone to unify the country.* Anti-Ibo and anti-Ironsi feeling had been fermenting inside the army as inside the regions. Of 4 Battalion, it has been said that[41] 'the barracks were trembling' during the January coup, and men in the ranks wept at the deaths of their Northern commanding officers. Suspicion and antagonism probably mounted more slowly and unevenly than this, for 4 Battalion reaction does not seem to have been general throughout the army so soon. There is evidence that the army basked in the general acclaim at having been instrumental in bringing down the old regime. But by May there was explosive junior officer and other rank (overwhelmingly Northern) hostility against an officer corps more than ever dominated by Ibo officers, since the elimination of the most senior Northern officers in January, and after a batch of promotions almost all Ibo, especially at the rank of lieutenant-colonel, by the Ironsi regime.

The Revenge Coup

The July coup was not war between North and South, but a misunderstanding between members of the armed forces.
Lieutenant-Colonel Hassan Katsina

In July the army turned to slaughter the Ibos within it, as the North staged its counter-coup. Plotting had been going on for months. The NPC and, in the West, the NNDP had been at work subverting the army. Former Minister of Defence and NPC treasurer, Unuwa Wada, was ideally placed to do this. He had close contacts with Northern officers, having been responsible for the promotion of many of them; he was related to the most aggressive of the Northern army hawks, Colonel Mohammed Murtala, who was the NPC's instrument among the military; and he had at his disposal large funds, from both the NPC treasury and his personal fortune, with which to buy influence. The process of subversion could be seen at work

* In Zaria where some eighty people were killed at the end of May the army barracks adjoin the *sabon gari*, but no soldier was mobilized to help the victims, Dr James O'Connell points out in his article in *Race*, p. 99 f.n.

among the young lieutenants and captains sent on a training course in Kaduna from April till early July. Politicians and their contact men made a dead set at these twenty-five young officers, drawn from all five battalions and some training units; indeed, after the May killings, little trouble was taken to conceal the fact that the leading disaffected Northern officers were making a concerted bid to contact their counterparts in other units at Kaduna, and that a plot was in preparation. A rumour circulated during the course that the Ibos had been given live rounds of ammunition (by an Ibo officer, of course), while all others had received only blanks. But specific acts of provocation apart, the general talk was of imminent bloodshed to avenge the officers killed in January. Several men on this course subsequently figured among those who played a prominent part in the July coup.[42]

Cover plan for the Northern mutiny of 29 July 1966 was the spreading of the alarm that the Ibos themselves were preparing a second coup; in August, some said. One version claimed that this was 'to finish off the North'; others believed that young radicals were to remove Ironsi by force because he was not carrying through tougher policies. Ibos were among those who believed and spread the rumours. But no hard evidence of any such planning has been produced; and it is difficult to see why Ibos, already accused of being too firmly in control, would need to take such drastic actions; or, if Ironsi was to be the target because he was too conservative, what forces were being mustered to remove him. Rumour of the so-called Ibo coup that would 'finish off' Northern officers added urgency to the planning and incentive to the by now fiercely embittered groups of Northerners, especially in 4 Battalion and 2 Battalion, which Mohammed Murtala commanded at Ikeja and from where he was to seize the airport.[43]

General Ironsi's visit to Ibadan – up to now his only journeys outside Lagos had been to the North – became the occasion for a several times delayed assassination plan. (During a visit to Kano, only the intervention of the Emir had prevented it.) Intelligence sources had wind of the plan forty-eight hours before; but either Ironsi discounted their reports, or they did not reach him. In the event, the first shots fired in the revenge coup were aimed not at the head of state, but at three Ibo officers in the mess of the Abeokuta barracks. The gun battle in the mess grew swiftly into a manhunt through the barracks by armed Northerners for Ibo officers and men to kill. From Abeokuta the news of the killings was transmitted to 4 Battalion at Ibadan and to 2 Battalion at Ikeja which, under Colonel Mohammed Murtala, seized Ikeja airport. By midnight General Ironsi's bodyguard had been removed and disarmed. Northerners among them were reinforced by a special contingent of Northerners from 4 Battalion under the command of Major T. Y. Danjuma – who, with Colonel Mohammed Murtala, was one of the two prime organizers – which placed Government House under siege. But it was not until the following morning that Major Danjuma confronted the Supreme Commander, ordered his arrest, and had him led into the police vehicles waiting outside.

It looked very much as though the North's counter-coup went off at half-cock before it was quite ready. The operation was a combination of conspiracy and spreading combustion. Like January, it did not synchronize in all centres: the kidnap party arrived at State House, where Ironsi was staying with Fajuyi, to take away the general only some hours after the mutiny flared at Abeokuta; and the killings of Ibo officers began in the North only some twenty-four hours after the Abeokuta attack. In the Mid-West and in the East, the plan aborted, as in January. At Enugu reports on trouble in Abeokuta were received in time for the governor to order action to forestall it. On the other hand, the killings revealed not only a fanatical fury, but high ingenuity and some considerable organization, too: as in the use of army signals for the ambush of Ibos ostensibly being ordered to special duties.

Legend has grown round the last hours of Ironsi, and of Fajuyi,[44] who is said to have murmured 'John, it's not our day', and to have insisted that if the soldiers were removing the Supreme Commander, they should take him, too. Ironsi's air force aide-de-camp was witness, as co-prisoner, to the kidnap; but he managed to escape from the spot ten miles from Ibadan where Ironsi and Fajuyi, after being stripped and flogged, were finished off with a few rounds of machine-gun fire.[45] In the evening of the same day, Northern soldiers returned to the spot and covered the two bodies with earth scraped from the ground around them. As the killings spread, they followed a pattern. Soldiers of Southern origin were disarmed; the armoury and magazines were seized by Northern troops, and an alarm sounded: when Easterners responded along with others, they were arrested, thrown into the guard-room or some other place of captivity, and shot, often after torture. The Eastern version of the July coup is the only one available. The Federal government ordered no investigation into the events. A guarded government spokesman at State House in Lagos told me, in an unexpected burst of candour, 'Some of the people involved may be at the helm today.'

The Eastern version contains lurid descriptions of terrible killings. In some instances, eye witnesses appear to have survived and escaped to the East; several of the accounts appear to be based on their experiences. The version is replete with names and details of time, place and particular incident. It must be read for a sense of the horror and fury and fear that rose in the East after the July coup. In the rest of the Federation, the press reported virtually nothing of the July events. On one day before the week-end, Nigeria knew Ironsi as head of government; one day after the week-end, Gowon had taken his place. What happened over that week-end itself, inside the army, in the frantic, shifting cliques of king-slayers and king-makers, is barely known.

In the absence of other accounts, it is impossible to test conclusively the accuracy of the Eastern version. Some descriptions are convincing enough: as, for instance, the account of how Ibo officers at Ibadan were locked into the tailor's workshop and then systematically wiped out with hand grenades and rifle and machine-gun fire; twenty-four corpses were buried in a mass grave that night. There is also an account of the spot near the intersection of the Jos and Kaduna roads which was turned into an execution ground. There are details of such cryptic instructions to kill Ibos as: 'Send him to the Eastern House of Chiefs.'

Where the report does strain, though, is in its determined identification of every single Northern officer with the plot; even, as in the case of General Gowon and Lieutenant-Colonel Akahan, where there is evidence that they themselves were pushed into action under duress by their men and NCOs,[46] or when links between them and events were tenuous in the extreme. The compelling feature of the July mutiny, indeed, was the initiative taken by NCOs, and the pressure put by them on their officers. This is not to discount the role played by Lieutenant-Colonel Mohammed Murtala and Major Danjuma; or the existence of an inner group that deliberately incited and planned the killings. But once the killing had begun, the NCOs and other ranks took over; and if authority rested anywhere, it was at the rank of young Northern lieutenants.

Within three days of the July outbreak, every Ibo serving in the army outside the East was dead, imprisoned or fleeing eastward for his life. The death toll is thought to have been in the neighbourhood of 300.* Army clerks and technicians of Eastern origin were kept at their duties under duress; but with the army officers who fled to save their lives, went a number of civil servants and ordinary people. For, as the news of the killings in the army leaked out, there was no knowing if the violence would stop there. Chinua Achebe left his radio job in Lagos at this time, hours before armed soldiers called to fetch him from his house.

For the best part of August, it was touch and go whether the army, or Nigeria, would hold together at all. For four days there was not even a nominal government, as two forces in the army struggled for control. July was the North's revenge coup; but the North consisted not only of the old NPC Hausa–Fulani power bloc, represented in the army by Colonel Mohammed Murtala, but also of the Middle Belt, which commanded 80 per cent of the army's rifle power. The two forces in the North had coalesced to mount the revenge coup, but they diverged immediately it was successful. Akahan for the Middle Belt elements in

*The Eastern account lists forty-three officers and 171 other ranks killed. The evidence for the incidents at Ibadan and Ikeja barracks was kept in the military archives at Umuahia, Biafra.

the army and Mohammed Murtala for the old North jostled for control. It was out of this contest that Gowon emerged on top.

By army practice, Brigadier Ogundipe, a Westerner, should have succeeded to the command after Ironsi's removal. He spent a nightmare week-end trying to take command. When he heard the news of the mutiny, he set up an operations room from where he tried to reimpose discipline. The telephone conversations he had with Colonel Akahan, commander of the Ibadan battalion, convinced him that Akahan was not his own master, but that there was a gun, or some other pressure, behind him. Ogundipe ordered all soldiers to remain in barracks, but forces of mutineers had already moved off to set up road blocks on the airport–Lagos road. He decided to clear the airport of the mutineers, but he could muster only a scratch force of non-combatant troops and one headquarters unit, which was ambushed along the road by the mutineers and retreated in disorder. A column managed to reach the Ikeja barracks, but the troops, largely Northerners, refused to take orders from their officer, a Mid-Westerner. This, the brigadier told himself, was no longer an army. From the airport, a spokesman of the mutineers telephoned the brigadier. They had decided to go North, they said, and had detained a VC-10 at the airport to carry their families home.

'You take over command,' they said. 'We want to go.'

'I'm a soldier, not an administrator, you obey my orders.'

'What orders?'

'Back to the barracks. Return your arms to the armoury. Then we'll talk.'

'No,' they said.

Around Ogundipe, in nominal but transparently ineffectual command, there fluttered that week-end a series of consultations in Lagos sitting-rooms. The Chief Justice, the former attorney-general, a former Minister of Education, and the secretary of Lagos' Institute of International Affairs discussed how to fill what they called 'the political vacuum in the country'. The peace-makers, as they saw themselves, were in touch with Ogundipe, and he with Admiral Wey and the military governors, so that there was a network through which, for instance, the Northern governor's adviser could be reached. Up and down this line went proposals for a new army head and the countering of the secession cry raised by the Northern army mutineers. For by then it was plain that the seizure of the VC-10 was not an isolated step; that the cry of the July coup was '*Araba*', and that the Northerners were preparing to pull out. If Ogundipe was acceptable at all as Ironsi's successor, it would be to preside over the division of the country's assets, the 'peace-makers' argued among themselves in Lagos. But the army would not have Ogundipe; and Ogundipe, after eighteen years, decided that he would no longer have the army. The one constructive course that could be followed by this group, therefore, was to get Ogundipe out of the way. He was convinced that he was to be the mutiny's next victim. He left his headquarters, his pistol at the ready, as troops were taking up position. The problem of where to find him a new posting was knotty. 'We don't have any colonies', mused one of the group wittily. In time he emerged in London as Nigeria's High Commissioner.

The core of the crisis was being probed not in these rather peripheral areas but inside the Ikeja barracks. Most of the day on which the mutiny broke out, Ogundipe had been waiting for Gowon, his chief-of-staff, to join him in his operations room; but nothing had been seen of Gowon since his arrival at Ikeja barracks, where he had gone to have a look at the trouble. There 2 Battalion's other ranks had taken over and ordered their officers aside as they went about their business of killing Ibos. Gowon had been placed under guard on Colonel Mohammed Murtala's orders; but as the coup got under way, he graduated from hostage to nominee of the NCOs as commander-in-chief. Murtala might have been the evil genius behind the coup; but it was executed by the NCOs, largely Middle-Belters; and it was Gowon, not Murtala, who had their confidence and who emerged to speak for them. Ogundipe's last contact with Gowon was on the telephone. Just before leaving his headquarters, he rang Gowon to say: 'Jack, I'm fed up. There was a gentlemen's agreement there would be no shooting [referring to his telephone attempts to persuade the Ikeja mutineers to return their arms to the armoury].' And Gowon answered, 'Well, sir, if you hear the reason, they were justified.'

Before he left the scene altogether, Ogundipe referred an anxious group of permanent secretaries to 2 Battalion barracks. 'Talk to the boys Iatkeja,' he said; 'they're in control.' When a group of them arrived at the barracks, they were stopped by the soldiers on guard who called to their escort, 'What tribe?' The answer came, 'Civil servants'. 'That's okay. They can come in.'[47] The Northern coup-makers were set on secession. Through the mutiny, they had achieved their act of revenge; this done, the North would go it alone. The mutiny had no sooner broken out, indeed, than large numbers of Northern civil servants quit Lagos for home; and the exodus was not stemmed for several days. But a compact group of permanent secretaries, which was to emerge after the Gowon take-over as the strongest pulse of that government, set desperately to work at trying to stop the Northern secession movement. They were joined by a group of influential young Northern civil servants, who were in constant telephone communication with the Ikeja mutineers, urging them, 'For heaven's sake, don't leave, stay there.' If there was to be any withdrawal, went one argument, 'it had to be done on a systematic and agreed basis'; and the time was not yet come. Northern secession, went another argument used in Lagos, would mean 'Our money will fly away. Foreign bankers will lose all confidence.' It was the pressures of British and, above all, United States diplomats that drove this latter argument forcibly home, for the influence of the two powers converged decisively on the permanent secretaries and thus on Ikeja during these shaky days. Mohammed Murtala remained adamant for secession; but Gowon represented the group of Middle-Belters who saw in Northern secession the danger that they would be a perpetual and vulnerable minority in the North. Thus it was that Yakubu Gowon – thirty-four years old, and a member of the tiny Angas tribe of the Middle-Belt plateau – emerged as the North's compromise candidate for head of government, to be later confirmed as Supreme Commander by majority decision of those in the Supreme Military Council who still survived.

The conflict between the two wings of the army, and the hair-breadth victory of the anti-secessionists, comes out starkly in the broadcast address delivered by Gowon on 1 August to announce his assumption of command. 'I have now come to the most difficult but most important part of this statement. I am doing it conscious of the great disappointment and heart-break it will cause all true and sincere lovers of Nigeria and of the Nigerian unity, both at home and abroad, especially our brothers in the Commonwealth,' he said. The basis for unity was not there. It had been badly rocked not once but several times. 'We cannot honestly and sincerely continue in this wise as the basis for unity and confidence in our unitary system has been (unable) to stand the test of time.'[48] (The official version in *Nigeria 1966* inexplicably, for the sense of this sentence, leaves out the negative.) Then followed an undertaking to 'review the issue of our national standing', but no announcement of secession. Clearly there had been a secession announcement in the original draft of the statement; it had been cut at the last minute, and whoever had tried to rejoin the remaining pieces had left the stitches showing. It had all, in fact, been done at inordinate speed. Last-minute British High Commission arguments persuaded Gowon to excise the critical paragraph.

The threat of Northern secession, so narrowly averted, showed through even more seriously inside the Supreme Military Council. Ojukwu announced over the Eastern Nigeria Broadcasting service[49] that the only conditions on which the 'rebels' (the July mutineers) would agree to a cease-fire were: (1) that the Republic of Nigeria be split into its component parts; and (2) that all Southerners in the North be repatriated to the South, and all Northerners resident in the South be repatriated to the North. This, he said, had emerged in discussions with Brigadier Ogundipe and the other military governors, and with Lieutenant-Colonel Gowon as army chief-of-staff. Although, continued the Ojukwu broadcast, the only representations made at these 'cease-fire negotiations' were those of the rebels and their supporters in the North, and notwithstanding that the views of the people in the Eastern provinces had not been ascertained, it was agreed to accept these proposals to stop further bloodshed. Ojukwu announced that he would shortly call a meeting of all chiefs and organizations in the Eastern provinces to advise him on the future of Nigeria. In the meanwhile, chiefs and leaders should stop any retaliation, 'in the hope that this was the final act of sacrifice of Easterners'.

Ojukwu's statement appeared in the Lagos press on two successive days; on the second, the same paper also carried a short report of an interview with Colonel Hassan Katsina: 'At no time did the government consider the repatriation of people from one part of the country to another.' In the same issue there was a statement by Lieutenant-Colonel Gowon, whose attention had been drawn to the Ojukwu broadcast, that the 'National Military Government was not aware of any arrangement or agreement in the terms outlined in the statement'.[50] Both the Ojukwu–Ogundipe–military governors' exchanges along the army communications network and the Northern secession move had been overtaken by events in which the Eastern military governor had no part. He was going by the last official contact he had had with what was to him the last recognizable army authority. But in the meanwhile authority in both army and government had changed hands. Easterners, decimated in the army officer corps, and for all practical purposes dislodged from the Supreme Military Council because it was considered unsafe for the Eastern governor to leave the East for Council meetings, found no way to reconcile the Eastern region to this change.

In the first week after the July coup, Nigeria seemed to hang by a thread. It was a small group of Federal civil servants (most of them, significantly, Mid-Westerners or Middle-Belters, and thus from the least viable of the states or from the areas agitating for separation), stiffened by the regular if not always formal exchanges with British and United States diplomats, that knitted together new strands of support for the Gowon regime. Two days after his assumption of power, Gowon released Chief Awolowo, Chief Anthony Enahoro and other jailed Action Groupers. Indeed, Gowon went personally to the airport to tell Awolowo that his wealth of experience would be needed. It had taken a Northern coup to release Awolowo; now, in one move, the Gowon regime propped itself up in the West and drove the first wedge between any potential alliance of the Action Group radicals and their counterparts across the Niger in the East. Two weeks later, Gowon amnestied 1,035 Tiv who had been imprisoned for their part in the rioting in Tiv Division between 1960–64. 'So we are really free,' remarked one as he was released. 'God bless the National Military Government.'[51]

'There will be a return to civilian rule very soon,' said General Gowon, 'and I mean it. Very soon is very soon.'[52] In the regions, 'Leaders of Thought' meetings were held to prepare the way for a constitutional conference. In Kaduna, Leaders of Thought, picked by the governor and his advisers, walked hand in hand into the hall where they were to deliberate. Political labels were anathema, but most of the old figures were there. The lawyers with degrees and the lawyers with guns instead set to work. Federalism or confederalism? Which powers to the centre? What constitutional formula? The old faith in the constitution reasserted itself: with the right constitution, all else would fall neatly into place.

The army, however, was still in turmoil. The killings had not ended with the emergence of a new military commander and head of state. Colonel Mohammed Murtala was pressing for a march on Enugu. Armed groups of soldiers were taking gun law into their own hands and committing new acts of vengeance. Army headquarters played events down by denying them. 'All Army Officers are Safe in the North', read a government press release.[53] Persistent rumours that a number of army officers in the North had been taken away to an unknown destination or had been killed had been personally investigated by the Supreme Commander and found to be false.[54] On 9 August the decision was taken to divide up the army and repatriate troops to their regions of origin. On the telephone Gowon told Ojukwu: 'Honestly my consideration is to save the lives of these boys (Easterners), and the only way to do it is to remove the troops back to barracks in their region of origin.' In the West, this was to mean virtually a Northern army of occupation; for there were few Yorubas in the army, and those were mostly tradesmen.[55] But for all the apprehensions of Westerners, the army was not looking in their direction; it was still going about the unfinished business of the July revenge coup. On 12 August, there was the mass round-up of Eastern NCOs in the Apapa units. On 19 August, Northern soldiers from Ibadan converged on Benin prison and seized Eastern detainees – among them one of the January majors, Okafor – to beat and torture five of them to death. (Okafor was buried alive.)[56] Among Ibos the fear grew that Northerners were intent on a final solution. Who, after May and what was to happen in September, could say that their fears were unfounded? Throughout August there was a panic exodus of Ibos eastwards. Many took their families home and then returned; but shuttered houses in the *sabon garis* of the North and a stream of applications for leave from work bore testimony to a flight which was reckoned to have involved half a million by mid-August.[57] The Federal government treated it as a disciplinary problem. Throughout August and September, Enugu radio broadcast reports of how soldiers were interfering with convoys of returning Easterners.* Government officials in Kaduna described the allegations as false, but said that all Native Authorities had been instructed to prevent such occurrences. The incidents of July were confined to the army, insisted the Federal government,[58] and it was mere rumour-mongering that was causing civilian panic. In Lagos and Kaduna, police, in combined operations with soldiers, recovered official army uniforms on sale in the open market.[59] Ojukwu in the East called for a day of mourning; Gowon in Lagos said that the call was unconstitutional and unhelpful to attempts at keeping the country together.

Already it was as though there were two Nigerias: in the one, bitterness and rising panic; in the other, a dogged refusal to admit that anything untoward had happened, and a dogged search for constitutional forms. The national conference to discuss Nigeria's future form of government opened on 12 September. Lieutenant-Colonel Gowon ruled out both a unitary form and a complete break-up of the country. The conference was to consider four possibilities: (1) a federal system with a strong central government; (2) a federal system with a weak federal

*About sixty trucks bringing home refugees were held up about six miles from Lafia in Northern Nigeria. All male passengers were being asked to pay a tax of £2 8*s*. The operation was carried out by a combined team of Native Administration and Nigerian police in the North. (ME/2245, 19 August.) There was organized gangsterism against Easterners at Makurdi where trains were held up by armed soldiers and the men ordered out. At Oturkpo the food of the travellers was seized. (ME/2248, 25 August.)

government; (3) a confederation; or (4) an entirely new arrangement perhaps peculiar to Nigeria and which had not yet found its way into any political dictionary.

Civilian figures [writes Martin Dent] were being asked to do too much, to produce an all-embracing blueprint for the future Government of Nigeria, at a time when the crying need was for some immediate reconciliation between North and East, for some working agreement on the question of secession, to produce acceptance of the head of Government throughout Nigeria, and for some way to assuage the grief and anger of the Ibos for their loss in May and in July. The 120-page document of the proposals for the final constitutional conference reads a little sadly – a collection of PhD theses on an ideal constitution at a time when the chance of any of the recommendations being implemented was slight indeed.[60]

Constitutions and Killings

I have looked around the country to find just one person who is human, to whom I can speak or write, and who would not betray me. I can hardly find any for fear that humans are no longer human – you can never say what happens next – they turn round against you.

For six months I can hardly sleep, eat, no rest, can't sleep an inch from my room, have lost my parents, brothers and deprived of my wife and property, my good friends have either been killed or kidnapped. . . .

. . . I agree we and I are a cursed tribe, we are infidels and criminals, we are traitors, we are braggarts and everything. I agree entirely. If you dare enter public transport, in the offices and elsewhere, and hear how we are being talked about, your ears will bleed to death. They ask what we bastards are still doing here – can't we go home? . . . I want to tell you categorically that I am an Ibo man, a Nigerian, opposed to secession because I cannot afford to lose my many good friends all over the country. If I had wanted to go back to the East I could have done that long ago, but I bluntly refused to go in spite of persistent persuasion and force by my people. The Federal Government promised us protection of life and property. Every Ibo man is so frightened to go to the North, Lagos is worse than a concentration camp, we are beaten daily and killed. To go home is a problem because the fight has been carried even to our homes. Where else do we go? Back to God? I have seen Ibos mercilessly beaten up and killed. I have seen soldiers go from room to room collecting every known Ibo and dumping into the landrover. I have seen Yorubas beaten up for not disclosing Ibos. I have seen a Hausa man, a big man for that matter, being tortured for refusing to surrender an Ibo friend. I have myself been tortured in a public place but lucky to escape death, to my greatest surprise my Yoruba friends around and others started to weep, knelt down, begging me to forget and leave everything to God. Why is all this happening? simply because we are Ibo, just that name alone.

Every Iboman is regarded as a security risk.

. . . The other day a Yoruba friend of mine ran frantic to me, after seeing for the first time what it looks like torturing an Iboman (a Nigerian) by a soldier (a fellow Nigerian) and said 'When they come to you don't admit you are Ibo. I have seen some mid-Westerners do the same. And please put on a Yoruba gown.' I looked at him and sobbed. Though I am of Ibo parentage my foot has never stepped in the East.

Letter from an Ibo in Lagos
9 September 1967, sent to Tai Solarin

At the constitutional conference that opened at Lagos in September, the memoranda of the delegations dilated on the powers to be enjoyed by the head of state: cabinet procedure; banking; common services; copyrights, patents, trade marks; weights and measures; the borrowing of money inside and outside Nigeria; for all the world as though it were a British-style Marlborough House constitutional conference, and a new state was about to be born. On the matter of new states, the East said nothing initially; the Mid-West wanted twelve states in a tight federation; the official Western delegation advocated eight instead of the existing four states, and Awolowo, speaking for himself, advocated his own pet scheme of eighteen states; and the North wanted a confederation of four autonomous states, each with its own army and police force, civil service and judiciary, but sharing common services through an organization centred in the capital.[61] After several days of proceedings, there was an adjournment moved by the Mid-West for delegations to consult with their regional governments. When the conference reopened four days later, the North had somersaulted on the issue of states. It now definitely favoured the retention of the Federation and the creation of new states, even to the extent of splitting the North itself. When the state scheme subsequently became part of the war effort against Biafra, Northern spokesmen represented their *volte-face* as a far-sighted compromise for the sake of Nigerian unity. A compromise it was, but not out of statesmanship. On the day that the conference adjourned, Tiv rifle power, that had wrenched the July coup from the old Northern power groups, nudged the constitutional conference into line. A Tiv petition, rough and ready, but with a map attached to it that divided the North into four states, and signed by two Middle-Belt politicians, reached the Mid-West delegation. The Tiv petition move had actually started outside the conference hall, among Middle-Belters of the Federal Guard in the Lagos barracks; it was their suggestions for their own Middle-Belt state that the two politicians had collated.

Over the week-end when the conference was adjourned, the Northern delegation had been in crisis. Once again there had been a showdown between the two forces in the North: with Tiv pressure insisting, change your policy, and the 'old' North capitulating. Once the petition was in the hands of the Mid-West delegation, there was forged a combination of minorities from two states, one official, the other emergent. And this combination became formidable with the backing of the Middle-Belters in the army, who could account for well over half the riflemen as well as a large proportion of Northern officers and NCOs. It was thus the army once again that shifted the centre of power inside the Federal government, where a knot of minority permanent secretaries that had emerged from the July coup already dominated the key ministries.

It followed that if, in the interests of the new states, the inviolable North were to be divided, the same had to be done to the East. During the conference, indeed, a petition had been lodged for a Calabar–Ogoja–Rivers state.[62] By the time that the proceedings resumed, the East was faced with a *fait accompli*. The East argued that, to save the country before it was too late, immediate constitutional arrangements for Nigeria as a whole should be made on the basis of the existing regions, and new political arrangements to suit minority problems should best be settled within the regions themselves.[63] The Eastern delegates, protesting that they were not plenipotentiaries but delegates, and that they had to consult their region, talked to an unresponsive conference. All the other delegations pressed for an immediate public release of conference decisions. The talking was not yet over when the fury broke, or was unleashed.

The Ibos in the North of Nigeria, it has been shown[64] – like the Jews, the Armenians, the Dahomeyans in the Ivory Coast and Niger, and other minority groups at other times in history – were ready targets for a pogrom. For decades they had spread out through Nigeria: as wage labourers, lower-level administrators, railwaymen, policemen, post office clerks, technicians in state corporations and as fiercely competitive and successful traders. They had lived as a minority in a traditional and static society, resented as pushful intruders. A pogrom requires both a particular social situation and the exploitation of that situation by a politically organized group. In the North, social change had begun to produce a group of Northern entrepreneurs who were ready and eager to take over the businesses of the Ibo, the alien and successful minority on which could be projected odium and guilt for any state of crisis generated by change. The violence of a pogrom in the making can be contained where a government is strong or willing enough; in Nigeria the government proved that it was neither.

The killings were horrible enough, but even more horrible was their organization; for there is no doubt that, as in the May killings, there was deliberate and systematic organization. The organizers were the ex-politicians of the NPC, Native Authority functionaries, contractors, civil servants; their agents were unemployed thugs, provocateurs and rumour-mongers, but also young journalists and careerists who could manipulate information media and skills.* The occasion was the shock of the con-

*A government statement on the massacres (*New Nigerian*, 22 October 1966), says: 'Meanwhile in the North local petty contractors and party functionaries whose livelihood depended solely on party patronage became active. Most of them, like their political counterparts in other regions, were indebted

stitutional conference proposals to divide up the North. The opportunity presented was to drive the hated Ibos from the North once and for all.

The planning was not done overnight. There had been ominous signs of preparation for some while. The expatriate police officer and provincial secretary from Kano who, with help from the Emir, had stopped the May killings in the area very rapidly, were transferred, inexplicably and unexpectedly, in the weeks before September. There were the leaflets that made their appearance: 'You Northerners must help yourselves. Get up from your sleep'; and the messengers who brought the instruction that the leaflet would be the signal for action the following day. There was the duplicating machine brought by a group of four young men, used in the bush and then buried; so that days later when the police raided the Gaskiya Corporation, where one of the young men was employed, they drew a blank. There were collections to buy the wherewithal for the North to 'defend itself'.[65] Depending on the area, provocative rumours were slanted to incite local panic. The Tiv were told that Tiv students at Nsukka University in the East had had their eyes gouged out so that they could not learn; the Idoma were told that the Idoma Federal Minister in the former government had been killed in Enugu; the Birom were told that a train-load of Birom corpses had been delivered to Bukuru station.[66] A foreign correspondent in Kaduna was handed an eye-witness account of mob action outside the mosque and the house of the late Sardauna (the account was written in the past tense) an hour before anything happened in the town.* In Bauchi a top civil servant had a list of Ibos in his hand, and was seen ticking them

* *Source:* One-time editor of the *New Nigerian.*

---

either to the Northern Marketing Board or the Northern Nigerian Development Corporation. They were the hardest hit by the change of government, especially all those indebted to the Marketing Board and the NNDC who were made to pay up their arrears. They resorted to whispering campaign, rumour-mongering, incitement, aided and abetted by other factors. They are the elements most close to the ordinary people and they have utilised that to create a public opinion which is very strong and potentially dangerous . . .'

off as their deaths were reported; this was the one centre where several senior Ibo civil servants were killed. A district officer checking on the killings in his area asked a village head at Kandedun sugar plantation how many had been killed, and how many refugees there were. 'Did you kill any Ibo?' he asked. 'No,' was the reply. 'We did not get the message in time.'[67]

Not that there was any single cohesive inner planning group with squads of provocateurs and executioners. In a general atmosphere of diffused anti-Ibo provocation, it needed only a few inspired organizational touches, and a sense that authority would condone, even abet, attacks on Ibos, for the molestations of August and September* to become wholesale butchery, especially when 4 Battalion cut loose at the end of September and soldiers went side by side with armed thugs on the rampage. The battalion which had started the July coup was not only transferred north to Kaduna after July, but, by hideous design or ineptness, it had a general post around its units. Wherever these went there was a spate of killings within hours of their arrival. They joined armed civilians in attacking Ibo areas indiscriminately, but also in making for special targets. From 4 Battalion the infection spread to the 2nd and later, in Kano, to the 5th, which mutinied on the parade ground when told that it was being flown to Nguru in Bornu to stop trouble there. It was this battalion that wreaked havoc, and the largest casualties of all, in the town and at the airport where Ibo refugees had gathered to be flown to safety.

There had been periodic attacks for some weeks on Easterners in various places in the North, but the worst killings occurred during the last week of September and the first week of October. One of the first major trouble spots was Minna. The *New Nigerian* received an eye-witness account from its own correspondent. That report was suppressed, and instead the paper published a brief Ministry of Information hand-out which

*Apart from the reports of molestations broadcast by Enugu radio, incidents were recorded by persons living in the North. Some examples: On 5 September an Ibo contractor was killed in Kano; on 24 September the chief warder of Kaduna prison was killed in his house during the night by soldiers.

played down the incident. Two days later the paper received an editorial from the same ministry with instructions that it be published in full. *Genesis of the Exodus* it was called.

The historic exodus of the Ibos from some parts of the Federation has been misinterpreted to mean that this pre-planned exercise is confined only to Northern Nigeria. This is untrue and wicked. Why should we not summon courage to admit the fact that those so-called refugees have decided to migrate home *out of their own volition* [my emphasis], and that the North, as well as the West, the Mid-West and Lagos have witnessed this abnormal social phenomenon.[68]

On the day that the editorial appeared, the killings started up in Bauchi. Jos began to blaze the same afternoon; Zaria and Kaduna, the following day.

Curfew was imposed for the first time on the sixth day of the killings. Only with enormous difficulty were the authorities persuaded to organize the evacuation of Ibo civil servants. The press in the North, inhibited by official attitudes made only too clear, was censored or tongue-tied; during the first wave of killings, it carried not reports of the killings, but denials that they were taking place at all.[69] In the very week that they were reaching their peak, Gowon issued an instruction to all government staff who had 'deserted their posts' to return by a given deadline.[70] The day after the killings in Minna, the Northern military governor said publicly that the staff absences were a deliberate plan to paralyse the efficiency of the public service:

Assurances have been given that all living and working in the region are safe. In spite of assurances, employees in government service have found it necessary to desert their work on flimsy excuses of exaggerated allegations of threats. The plans are shortsighted in failing to observe that desertion by staff of their posts only causes hardship . . . and this affects the economy of the country, and the people as a whole.

Not only the killings, but official callousness seared the Ibos indelibly. Gowon's remonstrance – belated, provocative in its pointed reference to himself as a Northerner, almost half-hearted in its measured caution – did little to mollify them.

You all know [said the Supreme Commander], that since the end of July God in his power has entrusted the responsibility of this great country of ours into the hands of yet another Northerner. I receive complaints daily that up till now Easterners living in the North are being killed and molested, and their property looted. I am very unhappy about this. We should put a stop to this. It appears that it is going beyond reason and is now at a point of recklessness and irresponsibility.[71]

By the time that the appeal was made, the storm had receded.

The official Federal version of the massacres explains that the disturbances in the North were reprisals for attacks on Northerners in the East; and that it was an inflammatory news report of these attacks carried by Radio Cotonou that had incited Northerners.* The broadcast said: 'Travellers returning from Enugu have reported that many Northern Nigerians resident in the Eastern region were killed during the last weekend....'[72] The incident to which it refers appears to have been the arrival of a lorry of refugees from the North who had been attacked and stripped at Makurdi; the news of this spread like wild-fire, and several Hausa men were set upon. (They were subsequently escorted by the police over the border; and by Ojukwu's orders, provincial secretaries were made directly responsible for the safe evacuation of non-Easterners.)[73] The Cotonou broadcast was delivered in French on 27 September. A monitored version found its way – presumably from the United States-staffed and operated Foreign Broadcast Information Service which does monitoring in the region by arrangement with the Northern authorities – to Kaduna's Information Ministry. There the item was transformed from a monitored news report into a government press release. Kaduna Radio broadcast it several times.† It was issued by the Ministry to the *New Nigerian*.[74] The

**Nigeria 1966* says on p. 10: 'There were certain disturbances in both Eastern and Northern regions after 1st August 1966. The first one started in some principal towns in the East around September 23.... The report of these incidents in the East were carried by radio stations in Cotonou and later at Kaduna and by some papers in Lagos and Kaduna. These radio and newspaper reports were soon followed by other disturbances in the North with Northerners retaliating with attacks on Ibos living in the North...'

† See the letter to *Nigerian Opinion* No. 8/9 August–September 1967, by M. O. Raji: 'The pogrom of September 1966, and a pogrom it was, might not have been but for the propaganda launched by Radio Kaduna.... The news item [was] relayed over the network of Radio Kaduna several times on 28 and 29 September...'

decision to release the Cotonou report under government information auspices was taken by a caucus of top Northerners, among them Ali Akilu, head of the civil service; the military governor cleared it. This was the week that the constitutional conference in Lagos issued its press release. It was apparent to the Northern traditionalists that they were being out-manoeuvred in Federal politics. The timing of the Kaduna repeats of the Cotonou broadcast suggests that this was their riposte; and they could scarcely have been unaware of the effects it would have in a region already launched on an anti-Ibo pogrom. When it was all over, the *New Nigerian* announced: 'No truth in Radio Cotonou report.' The paper's special correspondent in Port Harcourt had investigated and found nothing to substantiate the Radio Cotonou statement. In Lagos the government took into custody the young Nigerian newsman presumably responsible for a report, similar to the Cotonou item, which appeared in the Ibadan *Daily Sketch*. Thus the government officially nailed the Cotonou broadcast, which it called an 'unfounded rumour' in its announcement of a military inquiry into the Kano mutiny.[75] Yet by the following year, in *Nigeria 1966*, the 'unfounded rumour' that the government itself had denounced had become the official Federal version of the massacres in the North.[76]

Government – and, at its injunction, the press – had played down the full horror and magnitude of the killings. Once again the facts were shadowy, and propaganda could assume the substance. The version grew that the Ibos had run away from the North. When there could no longer be any reasonable doubt that massacres had indeed taken place, the response was: little wonder, since the Ibos had struck first. And by the time that, too, became an untenable excuse, it was an academic point. In the Federation, attitudes varied from a strange sense of perverted joy in some – not only in the North – to a blasé indifference in others.[77] As for Easterners, after September they despaired of finding safety and security out of their own region. Close on two million people fled their way back into the Eastern region.*

* By the end of December the Eastern Nigerian rehabilitation commission estimated the number of refugees at 1,175,000. (*West Africa*, 26 December 1966, p. 1497.)

The panic exodus of May had been stemmed just in time for Ibos to receive the full impact of the September holocaust. Hardly an Ibo lineage had escaped unscathed; but if the scale of the disaster was hard to bear, the conviction that the rest of Nigeria neither knew nor cared was unendurable. At Kaduna, in the North, over one thousand unemployed thronged the Department of Posts and Telecommunications Training School, in response to an announcement over Radio Kaduna of two hundred vacancies, 'created by workers of Eastern Nigerian origin who had deserted their posts for home as a result of the present situation in the country'.[78]

'Old Boys' at Aburi; and at War

There will be no war because the two old boys will meet at the frontier and tell each other – Old boy, we are not going to commit our boys to fight, come on, let us keep the politicians out – and that is the end.

General Ankrah at Aburi

The constitutional conference was resumed at Lagos in late October. No Eastern delegates attended. Ojukwu was also not present at the meeting of the Supreme Military Council, the first since the death of General Ironsi, at which it was decided to take political leaders into the government. Since they felt unsafe in Lagos, the Easterners insisted that Northern troops should be withdrawn from the West, and the police, not the army, have charge of security in the capital. 'Gowon is not in control,' said Ojukwu.[79] The impasse between Lagos and Enugu was punctuated only by bouts of verbal sharp-shooting. Each side accused the other of gun-running.* Both sides were undoubtedly

*Towards the end of October a DC-4 carrying a thousand sub-machine-guns crashed in the North Cameroons. For the Lagos case see *Sunday Times* Insight report, 23 October 1966; for the Eastern version see *Africa 1966*, No. 21, 29 October 1966, p. 5.

This did not include more than 45,000 refugees absorbed by the Mid-West. (*New Nigerian*, 15 December 1966.) The number of dead was estimated at 30,000.

stock-piling arms, and reorganizing their armies. The East by September had been left with almost no arms, merely the shreds of an officer corps, and hardly any riflemen (only general duty troops). What contact there remained between Gowon and Ojukwu was carried on by telephone, by letter, or, vicariously, between Enugu's radio station and answering denials and accusations from the other side.

As the weeks went by, Lagos was preoccupied less with the Eastern region's absence from the constitutional talks than with the signs in the West that the old Action Group leadership was restless and moving closer to the East. The West was lukewarm on the question of states, and its constitutional formula was a compromise between federation and confederation. In late November Gowon announced that the constitutional conference was indefinitely postponed. It had run into difficulties which made it impossible for further meetings to take place. A few days later, he came down decisively against confederation, and for the creation of from eight to fourteen new states under an effective central authority.[80] This, charged Ojukwu, was Gowon's attempt to isolate the regional governments and to run the country with a clique of senior civil servants mainly drawn from a certain ethnic group.[81] If a constitution were to be imposed on Eastern Nigeria, the period of negotiation seemed now to be at an end.

It was Mr Malcolm MacDonald, Britain's peripatetic diplomatic fixer in Africa, who set up the Aburi meeting in January 1967 between Nigeria's estranged leaders. Ghana's General Ankrah was prompted to invite both sides, and to act as host; he and police inspector General Harlley sat in on the Aburi sessions and even broke anxiously into the discussion when it got acrimonious. ('I am sure no tempers will rise because I have put a lovely bowl of flowers here with God's grace in it,' said General Ankrah.) The central issue for the Easterners was clearly the legitimacy of the Gowon government. It was Major Mobalaje Johnson, governor of Lagos, who opened the wound. 'If you still have lice in your head, there will be blood on your fingers,' he said; and continued: 'May I ask one question. Gentlemen, is there a central government in Nigeria today?'

To which Lieutenant-Colonel Ojukwu replied, with blistering stress on the 'simple': 'That question is such a *simple* one and anyone who has been listening to what I have been saying all the time would know that I do not see a central government in Nigeria today.'[82] The parting of the ways had come about because the hold on Lagos was 'by force of conquest'. Gowon, said Ojukwu, was Supreme Commander

> by virtue of the fact that you head or that you are acceptable to people who mutinied against their commander, kidnapped him and had taken him away. We are all military officers. If an Officer is dead – Oh! he was a fine soldier – we drape the national flag on him, we give him due honours and that is all. The next person steps in. So the actual fact in itself is a small thing with military men, but hierarchy, order is very important, discipline are *sine qua non* for any organization which prides itself for being called an army. [These remarks of Ojukwu's are taken from the verbatim record.]

Hierarchy, order and discipline were all-important, his army colleagues agreed; but mutiny was another thing. During the July crisis days, Ojukwu had told Brigadier Ogundipe that it was for 'the responsible officers of the army to get together'. He himself had been present when Ojukwu talked on the telephone to Ogundipe, Commodore Wey said. It was all very well for Ojukwu to read the list of army precedence, he implied; but 'I must say one thing, that it is impossible for any man to expect to command any unit which he has not got control over. . . . If an ordinary sergeant can tell a Brigadier – "I do not take orders from you until my Captain comes", I think this is the limit, and this is the truth about it.' In a private off-the-record session, Ojukwu was given an account of Ironsi's death. ('For all the East knows the former Supreme Commander is only missing, and until such a time that they know his whereabouts they do not know any other Supreme Commander,' he had insisted.) By the end of the meeting Ojukwu was insisting that he had nothing personal against Gowon and, to the surprise of the conference, asked for the 'honour' of nominating him as Chairman of the Supreme Military Council, when the agreement reached at Aburi had been implemented. But the Aburi communiqué, vague and ambiguous, papered over very conflicting purposes.

Certainly, the record of proceedings shows that these were far from plain sailing.

At issue was the control of the army; was it to be in the hands of the Supreme Military Council or the Commander?

LIEUTENANT-COLONEL OJUKWU: While I agree that the Supreme Military Council should stay . . . the legislative and executive authority of the Federal Military government should be vested in the . . . Council because previously it was vested in the Supreme Commander. What I envisage is that whoever is at the top is a constitutional chap, constitutional within the context of the military government. . . . He is the titular head, but he would only act when we have met and taken a decision . . . by so doing our people will have the confidence that whatever he says must at least have been referred to us all . . .

COLONEL ADEBAYO: I do not think there is anything wrong provided the Supreme Military Council and the Federal Executive Council do not go into things affecting the regions without consulting the Governors. . . . The only thing I would like to add is because of the state of the army itself, I would like to see an effective Commander of the army.

LIEUTENANT-COLONEL OJUKWU: I will object completely to that last one. We started by agreeing that nobody can effectively command the entire army . . . what I have said is that the army should be commanded on a regional basis.

COLONEL ADEBAYO: If we have those regional commands do you not want somebody on top to co-ordinate?

LIEUTENANT-COLONEL OJUKWU: I said there should be a co-ordinating group to which each region should send somebody, but just for the façade of Nigeria there should be a titular Commander-in-Chief not a Supreme Commander which involves and means somebody who commands over and above the other entities. Perhaps after we have created and generated certain confidence we could again have a Supreme Commander, but it is not feasible today . . .

LIEUTENANT-COLONEL HASSAN: With respect, to summarise the whole thing. The Eastern region will not recognise whoever is the Supreme Commander in the form of association we have now and it means a repetition of the whole history of Nigeria when the politicians were there, to strive to put either a Northerner or an Easterner at the top. It must be an Easterner for Easterners to believe or a Northerner for the Northerners to believe. To summarise, the Eastern people will not recognise anybody in Lagos unless he is an Easterner.

COLONEL ADEBAYO: I do not think we should put it that way.

The session in progress was adjourned at this uneasy juncture.

The Aburi communiqués are vague on many issues. As far as the army went, it was to be governed by a Supreme Military Council under a chairman who would be known as commander-in-chief, and would be head of the Federal military government. All regions were to be equally represented at military headquarters, and promotions were to be dealt with by the Supreme Military Council. Any decision affecting the whole country was to be dealt with by the Supreme Military Council; or, if a meeting were not possible, referred to the military governors for comment and agreement.[83] But no record is available of the two secret sessions which discussed the powers of the head of state; and even the two verbatim reports, one Federal, the other Eastern, differ in several respects. If anything was decided, it was to loosen connexions and weaken the old federal tie between centre and region.[84]

Aburi was no sooner over than the argument started over what had been decided. Three weeks after the meeting, General Gowon issued a statement on Aburi[85] which said that the old Federal constitution would operate; and that, far from being abandoned, the state scheme, under an effective central authority, was 'more urgent than ever'. In between Aburi and this pronouncement, Federal permanent secretaries had met in Lagos, dissected the agreement, and advised Gowon to disown it.[86] In the East the slogan was 'On Aburi We Stand'. In Lagos a draft decree made its appearance, ostensibly to implement the Aburi decisions, but effectively to do the opposite. One final attempt was made to reach agreement round the conference table, this time with legal experts and top civil servants in the seats. Towards the end of March, a 'little Aburi' took place in Ghana, at the Ghanaian government's apparent initiative once again; but this time, in the presence of the Ghanaian attorney-general and other officials. The meeting consisted largely of a dialogue between the attorney-generals of Nigeria and Ghana. By the end of the meeting, the Ghanaian participants took the view that the decree was not an implementation of the Aburi agreement, but, indeed, contrary to the accord reached there. The powers given the Supreme Commander were, for one, totally inconsistent with collective regional control of the army.*

The decree that was finally promulgated on 17 March[87] reflected Aburi up to a point. It gave the regional military governors the right of veto on most important issues, including any decision to carve new states out of their respective regions. The Supreme Commander became Chairman of the Supreme Military Council, and the army was to be controlled by this Council. But the decree incorporated an emergency powers clause (like that held by the civilian Federal government before the coups under sections 70, 71 and 86 of the old constitution) permitting the Supreme Military Council to declare a state of emergency under which, ominously, 'appropriate measures' could be taken against any region that might 'endanger the continuance of Federal government in Nigeria'. The state of emergency could be declared by the head of government with the concurrence of at least three of the military governors. The other three against the East? Under Balewa, the emergency powers of the constitution had been used as a political weapon to oust the Action Group from power in the West; the East feared that the same power would be used to bring down the Ojukwu regional government.

As the conflict sharpened, secession was to be presented as an act of rebellion against Nigeria's legitimate government. In a contest of legalities, which could claim greater legitimacy: Ojukwu's government, or Gowon's? It depended on which side

*The proceedings were tape-recorded but have not been released. The meeting was referred to by C. C. Mojeku, for Biafra, at the Kampala peace talks. Ojukwu, in an interview with Suzanne Cronje, said of it: 'Indeed the last four hours of that meeting was Ghana versus Lagos and the North. . . . It was quite amusing. On arrival at the meeting the Mid-West immediately got up and said "Gentlemen, we are here as observers." And they had travelled all along with Lagos on the same plane! Lagos was so completely confused. No sooner they said that and sat down than the West said they had been asked to observe, not to contribute. So that immediately cleared both the Mid-West and the West. The Ghanaians took over very quickly almost within the first hour and a half. They had done their homework. They had studied critically the Aburi meeting, studied the Decree and everything. They came in and put it quite plainly to Lagos. Finally Lagos had to admit, first of all, that the Decree is not Aburi but Aburi as amended by Lagos . . .'

you were. The Nigeria of the politicians and the constitution of the First Republic had disintegrated with the collapse of that government. Any line of 'legitimate' political authority, however spurious in the hands of politicians who fixed the system and alienated the electorate, was severed then. After January 1966 guns, not constitutions, became the arbiter. But the form of the constitution, for all the elaborate formulations and tortuous discussion, was of little real importance. In the violent state of the country, the real issue was control of the army command. The Eastern region tried at Aburi to negotiate a sufficient share in the management of the armed forces; and when that failed, it no longer felt safe inside the Federation.

By the end of March 1967 the two sides had resorted to economic war. The East had argued at Aburi that the old basis of fiscal relations had been undermined: Easterners could no longer work freely or set up businesses in the North; the population of the East had been swollen by an influx that amounted to an increase of 16 per cent in six months; the Eastern civil service had been swollen by about half, and among the refugees there were 6,000 unemployed railway workers alone. Arrangements were made at Aburi for the Federal government to carry some of these costs; but nothing was done. The sum in dispute, said the East, was over £10 million, including the East's share of Federal revenues; but the Federal budget made no concessions to the needs of the East. So the Eastern regional government issued a Revenue Collection Edict to assert control over its own railways, ports, posts and telegraphs, coal and electricity. Meanwhile the Supreme Military Council had met – without Ojukwu, of course – to devise a three-year programme for return to civilian rule, which included the creation of states, and the introduction of civilians into government.

The Action Group in the West was badly racked at this time. Awolowo fleetingly championed the Eastern cause in a statement suggesting that 'what some people with influence in government circles now want is to help Eastern Nigeria out of Nigeria, and to try to form a new federation on terms which are already cut and dried by them from among the remaining units'.[88] This was the time that the West, through the Western military governor, was demanding the withdrawal of all Northern soldiers from the region and from Lagos. Confederation was tempting to the West, because it would leave the region freer of central control, and its experience of the latter was still raw. But as the tide turned from confederation to a strong federal centre, the Yoruba were swept along with it. They needed Federal jobs in the civil service and the corporations; and where there were top jobs for educators, businessmen and civil servants, the political tendencies followed. Awolowo himself was indecisive – it took the inner circle of the Action Group five full days to make up its mind on the issue of states – but eventually he opted for continued association with the forces closest to him. After his statement on the danger of letting the East secede, he had a police guard over him during the next crucial weeks; and he was, in any event, offered the posts of Commissioner of Finance and Vice-Chairman of the Federal Executive Council. If Western secession in sympathy with the East was ever seriously contemplated, the West, without any support in the army, was demonstrably too feeble even to try it.

In the East, Ojukwu told the Consultative Assembly that they were at the cross-roads: they could accept the terms of Northern Nigeria and of Gowon; continue the stalemate and drift; or ensure survival by asserting their autonomy. Outside the meeting, student demonstrators were demanding secession. On 27 May, Gowon declared a state of emergency, assumed full powers and decreed the existence of twelve states which, among other consequences, landlocked the East Central state of the Ibo people. On 30 May, the state of Biafra was proclaimed. Five weeks later, on 6 July 1967, Nigeria and Biafra were at war.

In Lagos, the permanent secretaries who did the thinking for the centre had seen clearly that declaration on states was a race against time and secession. If Ojukwu seceded first, they calculated, it could be claimed that he had never been part of the states scheme. A leading official told me: 'The psychological need was to beat Ojukwu to it, so that we could defend the creation of states internationally.' This, Lagos achieved. The creation of states and the emergency declaration were devised as a package deal. As Dent has said,[89] the creation of the states represented the concession which the Federal military government had to make to the Middle-Belters for their participation in the war against Biafra.

On the eve of war, the Federal government was far from monolithic; what popularity it achieved was provided by the conflict with the East and Ojukwu. The offer of new states consolidated the support of minorities within a very rickety Federation. The war steadied this structure, by giving it an external enemy.

In the form in which it emerged, the states scheme was in part a creation of young Northerners who had begun to assert themselves after January, when the die-hards of the old administration were palsied by the shock of the Sardauna's death. It was this group that in a memorandum to the Northern military governor urged training for all services – regional, federal, commercial, industrial and small private business – 'so organised as to assume that all Ibos will go *en masse* and immediately'.[90] From this group – some of them academics, but most of them professionally trained civil servants of the same generation as the military men in power – emanated, some time between March and April 1967, not only the first draft map of the twelve states, but also a 'Strategy for Survival' after Aburi.[91] Gowon would be acceptable as head of state, their policy document said; any clash between Northerners would be disastrous. This could be avoided by evolving a more 'dynamic' and 'forward-looking society' (which, with characteristic bureaucratic incomprehension, they thought should be defined by a full-time central planning committee; composed, presumably, of civil servants in the main); by neutralizing some of the ex-politicians known to be corrupt and discredited; and by guiding change in the North into 'constructive channels'. Aburi had been a victory for Ojukwu, because the other members of the Supreme Council had been 'too eager to appease'. The solution, said the young Turks of the North, was the simultaneous creation of states which would 'sustain the efforts of the minorities in their struggle against the tyrannical government of Ojukwu'.

The states scheme was thus an operational decision for

imminent war rather than part of a carefully structured new constitution for a more equitable distribution of power in a new federation. It calculated on turning the minority areas of the East into its soft under-belly, and on depriving the Ibos of Port Harcourt, their outlet to the sea, as well as most of the oil in the region. Inside the Federation, the states scheme struck several bargains in the division of power. The breaking of the North into six states at last met the Middle-Belt demand for autonomy. Carving large states into smaller ones quietened the anxiety of the little Mid-West state, previously squeezed between giants. The declaration of a separate Lagos state kept the seaport under Federal control and denied the Western region – lest it contemplate secession itself – access to the sea; it also gave the Lagotian élitists, ever detractors of the populist politicians in the Action Group, a leverage against Awolowo's influence in the West and at the centre.

In the old Federation, the minority peoples undoubtedly had grievances. And the states scheme may solve some of these. It has, some say, given control of the Federal government to the minorities. They run government at the centre and are able to draw on its resources; they furnish most of the soldiers in the Federal fighting forces; they hold the key permanent secretaryships and they sit on top of the richest oil fields. At last they have found the way to escape from the political dominance and economic deprivation that they suffered at the hands of the three major groups in the old federal structure.[92] But if there is little justice in the domination of minorities by majorities, then there is scarcely more justice in the reverse. Large tribe chauvinism was destructive enough; will small tribe chauvinism be any less so?

The thorniest minority problem is undoubtedly that of those which formerly belonged in the East. The states scheme has been manifestly effective in creating minority groups with a vested interest (especially oil) in the defeat of Biafra. Except in the clamour and cruelty of the war, the minorities have not been asked at all where they wish to belong. Biafra stated its willingness to allow the minorities themselves to decide their future by plebiscite. But plebiscites belong to peace settlements; the issue of the minorities, as of Biafra, will be decided by the way that the war is won or lost. Among the numberless casualties will be those principles of the right to self-determination, or the wrong of secession, which in abstract argument decide all, and in battle settle nothing.

If the new state structure belatedly brought minorities in from the cold, it deliberately pushed the Ibo out. Nigeria claims the states scheme to be the most broadly based federal union yet created in Africa voluntarily by Africans, as distinct from colonial federal establishments; yet, in the process, it went to war with one of the three major constituents of the original Federation. For the trouble with the states scheme is that it did almost as much as the massacres to persuade Biafrans that their enemies were bent on their total destruction.

The threat, and then the act of secession, made first the states scheme and then the war inevitable, it is said. The Ibos were set on secession, and there was no turning them back. Secession is the trump card that North, West and East had each threatened, at one time or another, to pull from the pack. The North fingered the card most frequently, and – until the departure of the East – most recently; as when the mutiny of July 1966 started as a Northern secession coup. Indeed, up to and during the constitutional talks of September 1966, prominent Northern civil servants, including the former head of the service, were saying publicly that the only way out for the North was to go it alone. (At this time, a team of foreign road experts, brought in by the Northern Ministry of Finance, was investigating the possibility of building roads from the region through Dahomey, so as to cut the North's dependence on the South for an outlet to the sea.) But, in the event, it was the Easterners – whose political associations had led the movement for close and effective Nigerian unity, and who, of all Nigerians, moved most energetically across regional boundaries into all parts of the country – who struck out for secession.

Eastern secession thinking had reared strongly during the 1964 Federal crisis; but then it had receded, and the politician-businessmen had buckled down again to their manipulative politics inside the Federation. As the January 1966 coup and its aftermath in the Ironsi government had exposed, not one but two (at least) Ibo political tendencies – the radicalism, however inchoate, of the young majors and their counterparts among the intellectuals, who wanted a purged political system throughout the country; and, side by side, Ibo chauvinism that used Ironsi's government to assert not new policies but élite Ibo interests – so, too, the Eastern crisis produced both secessionists and a unity camp.*

The January coup was hailed in some Ibo quarters, as it was reviled in others, as an Ibo achievement; and those who thought in these terms, many of Ironsi's closest advisers among them, set out to make the most of their opportunity. The backlash of the May attacks produced some initial panic; but the great majority of the refugees who fled to the East filtered back to their homes, employment and business in other parts of the country. The July coup caused a fresh exodus of surviving Ibo soldiers and officers, and, in their wake, of Ibo federal public servants and academics. Now the scares seemed to come too often to be discounted. Support began to grow for an extreme form of regionalism, and many once ardent for unity began to think of secession. Oil revenue would make the East a viable economic unit, and Ibos, spurned in the rest of the Federation, would turn their backs on it and devote themselves to building their own region's prosperity. Displaced civil servants and academics formed the core of a secession lobby.[93] During the three days at the end of July and the beginning of August 1966, when Nigeria had no government at the centre, and the North seemed about to secede, the Eastern Cabinet was united on secession; it was the emergence of Gowon at the centre that brought divided opinions, according to the account of the former attorney-general, who later defected.[94] Then, with the massacres in the

* Some indication of the split within the Eastern camp is revealed in the Federal publication *Nigeria: The Dream Empire of a Rebel* (Ministry of Information, Lagos). Based on documents captured at Enugu, it reproduces a dialogue between Ojukwu and Philip Alale, a major in the Biafran army. Ojukwu argued 'that victory will be through our own singular effort as a people, excluding the Mid-West and the West', and Alale that this 'overlooks the potential revolutionary role of the peoples of the West and Mid-West and even of the North who dread the rule of the Fulani–Hausa oligarchy'.

North, a mood of outrage and defiance spread throughout the region. The pressures of a lobby became a steadily rising popular clamour for making a break or, at least, setting some distance from a Federation that persecuted and massacred Ibos because they were Ibo. Aburi brought a spurt of hope; but then Lagos reneged on the agreement. Many not fervent for secession before Aburi, changed sides after its failure. And side by side with the growing secession movement in these months went Eastern government planning for a reconstituted army and administration that could function independently of Lagos, in case the conflict should, after all, end in a break.

Yet at the same time there were also, within the region, deep pockets of uncertainty about secession; and of opposition, too. The opposition camp, which included trade-union youth activists, and Major Nzeogwu, the hero of January, still placed its hopes for a changed Nigeria in a Southern unity of East and West, against what it characterized as the reactionary feudal North. But Nzeogwu was falling from official grace in the East during the anxious months before the war. He surrendered his position as Director of Military Operations, through which he had played a key part in training the region's reconstituted army.

> Some people [he wrote] still consider me a rival for popularity with the masses and they feel unsafe with me around. Every military training exercise in which I figured prominently was thought to be a plan for another coup! There are many questions on the political problems created by the collaboration of Awo with the Gowon regime. We still want to know the facts. . . . The leadership [in the East] fears my popularity, resents my views on the national issues of the day, and people imagine that I am ambitious. . . . My confidence has never been stronger in the ability of our enlightened and honest folks. There are still a lot of them left even after the calamitous 1966.[95]

Three weeks earlier he had written:

> Our camp is in disarray . . . our contact with the masses is apparent, not real. . . . In our lethargy we shall be witnesses to the rending asunder of the national fabric and the biting away of large chunks of our territory by monarchs of reaction and tribal mob leaders. . . . Even if we become a confederation with component territories

governed in the same manner as the whole republic was previously governed, the same political malaise will remain until progressive men with progressive ideas and executing progressive actions take hold of the helm of state affairs. . . .[96]

Traumatized by their losses in the July coup, and by the massacres that followed, the Ibo people turned in on themselves. Whether élite lobbying incited popular pressure, or the popular clamour itself stiffened élite support for secession, is difficult to say. After the failure of Aburi, and with the start of the economic war at the end of March, attitudes hardened at all levels. Inside Biafra, as inside the Federation, military government had put curbs on popular participation. Consultative assemblies were summoned, but they were totally dependent on the government for information and the scope of their decisions. As the months went by, there seemed so few options in any event. Federal terms seemed calculated to offer the East only humiliation. Doubts and minority points of view were deferred and finally abandoned as the crisis deepened; and patriotism, with a national war effort, became a condition of survival.

Yet hopes of a Southern unity, with the West rising to join the East in radicalizing the Federation, persisted in some quarters even during the first phase of the war. They died in August 1967, when Biafran occupation of the Mid-West failed, and the drive of the Biafran army on Lagos was beaten back at the battle for Ore, in the Western region, 135 miles from the capital. Then the Yorubas, who had been perched on the fence, dramatically switched allegiance to the Federal government.[97] Events seemed once again to justify the secessionists. There seemed nothing for it but to discount all other forces inside the Federation, and to strike out, Biafra for itself.

The Mid-West campaign was the most vital of the war. Facing setbacks on the three military fronts – Nsukka, Ogoja and Bonny – the Biafran army had planned a lightning advance on Lagos and Ibadan. Key to the plan was a coup inside the Federal units stationed in the Mid-West. Inside those units the Ibo were outnumbered two to one in the ranks; but of the eleven officers, eight were Mid-West Ibo. The Biafran army invasion on 9 August was led by a Yoruba officer, Lieutenant-Colonel

Victor Banjo, who had been imprisoned by Ironsi for allegedly plotting against him, and when released had taken a commission in the Biafran army. Benin fell from within as the army coup coincided with the troop infiltration: Banjo proclaimed the Republic of Benin; and the Biafran army set its sights on Ibadan, where, it was thought, Yoruba support would reinforce attempts to change the government in Lagos and thus the face of the Federation. Some say that the fortunes of the war were reversed irrevocably when a misadventure on the road blocked the advance of the Biafran troops long enough for the Federal forces to rally reinforcements and rout the Biafrans. This was a serious military setback, but in addition pronounced political differences emerged on the Biafran side: Colonel Banjo promoted himself brigadier (which enabled him to outrank Ojukwu) and declared the Mid-West under his liberation army to be independent of both sides. It was at this point that a coup d'état against Ojukwu began to unfold. Once again, Ifeajuna was part of it. It was to be a 'One Nigeria' coup to remove both Ojukwu and Gowon; and, if Awolowo played his part, to install him in power at the centre. Suddenly, when the Biafran army was in a more favourable position than it ever achieved at any time of the war, Banjo ordered his troops to evacuate Benin, without firing a shot. (This was on 12 September; and Nigerian troops did not enter the city until 21 September.) There were similar withdrawal orders elsewhere on the front. And the effect on the Biafran army was devastating. As General Modiebo described the impact of the Banjo–Ifeajuna coup: 'Morale was so low that a shot fired in the air would disband a whole battalion.' Not long after, four men were court-martialled and shot in Enugu. They included Banjo and Major Ifeajuna. He had not made the January coup to liquidate Nigeria, said Banjo – whose claim to have played a part in the first coup is as yet unsubstantiated. But if this coup was directed at reuniting Nigeria, its effect was to persuade Biafrans that anything short of total commitment to their own victory would weaken them.

The war, generally expected to be over within a few weeks, dragged on for thirty-one months.* The way of life on either

*Biafra collapsed suddenly in January 1970.

side of the battle-line was as difficult to reconcile as the issues that divided them. Biafra was pronounced doomed from the first days of the war, but was a long time dying. Even as the new state was squeezed into a tiny land-locked enclave that became a children's graveyard – with malnutrition, if not mortars, threatening an entire generation – its people fought back with a determination, a resilience and a panache that spoke of an ardour for their cause that left the other side mystified or infuriated. 'They are all paranoics,' a young poet in Lagos said in desperation. 'How can they not know and tell the difference between victory and defeat? If all must die, who will tenant the earth?' In Biafra, even in the worst days of the war, there were strange and obstinate survivals of the sedate British-patterned life of the better-off: obsessional red-tape bureaucracy and glaring rich-poor inequalities, alongside impressive improvisation for war, suffering and sacrifice. On the Federal side, the war was fought by a conventional army (conscripts, if not of any recruiting law, then of unemployment), while within the élite the most rigorous war effort was a fiercer than usual verbosity for the 'national' cause. In the Federation, the front was far away – except for the few anxious days of the Mid-West invasion. In the capital, if patriotism was most fervent there, so too were the flippancy and frivolity of war, as the wives of the élite hi-lifed round charity balls to raise comforts for the troops, and their husbands – the velvet-cushion commandos, as Wole Soyinka has called them – rode into office and influence on a wave of zeal for all Federal policies and causes. In Biafra there was not only fear, real or imagined, of annihilation by the enemy in war, but the conviction that Ibos would have no future in a Nigeria even at peace.

Within the Federation it was said that Ibos would be re-integrated without difficulty in the Nigeria emerging victorious from the war; or the loaded qualification, 'Yes, they can come back. We know the Ibos will, and they will settle in again – as long as they've learnt their lesson.' Will Ibos find a place – except in small numbers and in menial roles, now that the economy and, above all, the market for jobs and office have adjusted to their absence? It took a pogrom and a war to relieve the pressure on posts for university vice-chancellors, judges, top civil servants, bank and post office clerks, lawyers and corporation men. There is no more gruesome commentary on why Nigeria went to war with itself.

There is also no more inflammable issue in Africa than secession. Nigeria saw it as setting off a chain of fission inside the Federation which might bring down the whole precarious state structure. Africa sees it as showing that there is nothing permanent – and why *should* there be? – about former colonial borders supposedly fixed with independence. The Organization of African Unity (OAU), which identifies its own only hope of survival in a formalistic recognition of the sovereignty and authority of existing states – its constituent members, after all – has refused to dissect the causes or the course of the conflict. To probe the sensitive area of how and why the Nigerian state broke into two pieces, entails a recognition that it is not enough for independence government to have inherited authority from the colonial power: if this is the failing of Nigeria's generation of independence politicians, how many of the OAU member-states are immune? Biafra's case was Africa's nightmare, because Nigeria mirrored the breakdown, actual or incipient, of so many of the continent's independent states and their élite governments.

Biafra's case was also agonizing because it produced the most capricious alignment of powers, both European and African, on the two sides of this African war. Their reasons or rationalizations can have their origin not in the intrinsic issues at stake in the conflict, but in their own particular interests, in Africa or in the world. Disputes between the two antagonists, already difficult enough to resolve, were made much more so by the intervention of big powers. Yet, however outside forces manipulated it, Biafra's secession was not externally instigated; it arose out of the innermost failures of the Nigerian political system. Biafra, it was argued by some seeking to explain their championship of Nigeria, is another Katanga: Ojukwu is a second Tshombe, and the role of Union Minière is being played by international oil companies. The analogy has been shown to be hollow.[98] Oil was not primarily the issue that led to secession in the first place. Oil revenues have, however, grown more central to the conflict, because essentially the war had its origins in intra-élite disputes over power and oil helps to pay for power.

The war was three weeks old when Wole Soyinka issued a poignant appeal for a temporary ceasefire. Ojukwu, he argued, must realize by now that the act of secession was, at the least, a miscalculation. The Federal government, for its own part, needed to recast the entire situation, this time basing its calculation not on guns but on the primary factor of the human will. The 'swift surgical operation' was being conducted with blunt and unsterile scalpels, despite the obvious superiority of Federal arms. The government might well prove its military superiority, but it had also to demonstrate a sense of the future. 'When the East has been overrun, what happens to the Ibo people?' The Federal government was faced with a choice of wiping out all the Ibos or administering a nation which had developed a core of implacable hate and resolution. 'There will be no victory for anyone in the present conflict, only a repetition of human material waste and a superficial control that must one day blow up in our faces and blow the country finally to pieces.... A fight to the finish will finish all, or nothing....'[99] There was one additional compelling reason why some way had to be found to end the strife, wrote Soyinka. Fleetingly, in the Nigeria of 1966, it had seemed that at long last 'the new generation was about to march together, irrespective of religion or origin'. Then there emerged once again 'the by now familiar brigade of professional congratulators, opportunists, patriots and other sordid racketeers, the cheer-leaders of a national disaster whose aim was to exploit Ojukwu's blunders to camouflage their own game of power and position.' Soyinka spent the first two years of the war in prison. The old game of power and position continued to be played, though in this period to the sound of gunfire.

The Army: Thirteenth State

The army 'is battling . . . with the conversion of hooligans and thugs . . . but in any case it is better to keep them in the army and get them disciplined rather than let them loose in the society'.

Brigadier Ejoor, December 1968

On both sides of the war, power lay with the army men and the administrators controlling the state apparatus. The politicians had been called in; but essentially they discharged their functions by will of the military, as both Awolowo and Azikiwe in their different ways discovered.

In Nigeria's Second Republic, control passed decisively from the politicians into the hands of the power bureaucrats. When, on the eve of war, the civil servants and the army were in the midst of their own crisis, they summoned some of the politicians to give the regime a base of popular support. But though these were to run the ministries with virtually the same powers that the former feudal ministers had exercised, they were to operate under the army, in the context of decisions already taken, formally by the soldiers and by the administrators in fact. The military regime had decreed no political parties; and this meant, ostensibly, no politics. Dislodged from parties and government, where they had formerly manipulated communal support, political forces continued their manipulations, but without the old outlets afforded by regional and federal government. Disputes that were once settled by a process of bargaining among the parties or by deals of political expediency now flared into street action (the May and September killings) or came for arbitration before civil servants and soldiers. If expediency was the way of the politicians, the combination of civil servants and army was infinitely more lethal. It is hard to say whether Nigeria might not have gone to war with itself under a civilian government; but surely it would not have done so with such deadly swiftness. The parties and the politicians used tribalism for their own ends; but the very existence of parties insulated the country to some extent from its most explosive forms. Communal conflicts were in part processed through the party, to emerge amended somewhat and more subdued; communal tensions might be dissipated or absorbed in prolonged political manoeuvring. Perhaps this is where Nigerians got their reputation for riding to the brink, and then reining back. The power-bureaucrats have ridden at a gallop; and, in their bravado, did without the reins.

Army men pride themselves on their speed of resolution (it must undoubtedly be easier to reach decisions when you exclude so many 'political' factors). And civil servants like nothing better than principals who are brief and to the point, make up their minds and rarely change them and, above all, defer to them, the trained experts. To bureaucrats of the military and civilian order, all problems have a starkly administrative cast, and any particular problem has a single and direct solution. To the Ironsi government, unification meant a decree that unified the civil service. To the Gowon government, the creation of states meant a decree; and, if the Ibos had stayed, or been frightened, away from the crucial decree-shaping consultation, it was a decree binding on them none the less. An agreement reached at Aburi, after delicate consultation, was countermanded by another decree, written by civil service hands. The army-bureaucrats rejected the methods and motives of the politicians; but substituted nothing at all, except for the terms of reference that their own specialist training – and own group interests – had instilled.

This does not mean that, even under the First Republic, the bureaucracy did not exercise a large corporate slice of influence in the state, though government was manipulated by the more flamboyant politicians. With the displacement and overshadowing of the political class by the January coup, however, control was centralized in the corporate groups of civil servants and army, which used the politicians selectively and had the power, through the gun, to circumscribe their freedom of action. Roles had been reversed; the bureaucrats were on top. Successive crises were diagnosed and treated according to the needs of these two corporate groups, the civil service and the army. In one crisis after another, under both the Ironsi and the Gowon governments, civil servants and soldiers, or aspirant bureaucrats – like students at the universities, or at the training institute for administrators, or at the air force college – sounded national alarums and used the powers of the state when their own interests seemed to be under attack. The interests of civil servants were at the centre of the successive crises in 1966, 1967 and 1968. Decree 34, which threatened the security of a relatively small group of Nigerians, the top Northern civil servants, as well as those who hoped to graduate into these posts, resulted in the May killings and the destruction of the Ironsi government. The weight of Ibo officer-corps promotions in the army was one of the major grievances that stirred the July coup-makers. The drive for new states came from new élites whose members saw in each a job apparatus that would absorb them, giving new men the big jobs and the rapid promotions that independence and Africanization had given to the earlier élites of the African states. At every stage of the constitutional debate – Decree 34; Aburi; the arguments over federal, confederal or unitary government – there has been one prime calculation, in addition to any others that might have been entertained: unification meant that federal posts would be allocated to regional functionaries of high calibre, and men at the centre might be displaced; a federal system tightly controlled from the centre would mean enhanced status and power for the top men of the federal civil service. The interests of the Federal bureaucrats were best served by the preservation of the Federation. But as the crisis developed, the 'unity' forces closed their ranks against the candidates from a large part of the country, the Eastern region. An important group of competitors has been excluded. But, at the same time, new competitors, from the new states, are forming a queue. The shortage of resources and, in a few years, the hardening of promotion opportunities inside the twelve states, could bring a new round of acrimonious and ugly conflict within the élite.

In the Second Republic, the states scheme and the war have thrown up new candidates for the ranks of the privileged and the manipulators of politics and business. The fall of the Balewa regime saw some members of the old 'political class' effaced; temporarily only, they themselves hoped. (Some were forcefully displaced by the corruption probes; others, like Inuwa Wada in Kano, took a back seat in politics while they devoted themselves to business.) The demands of the war made it a lean time for some kinds of entrepreneurship. The most lucrative tenders were for the army, where regular army contractors, or the new ones who had been quick to cultivate army contacts for this and other reasons, got the pickings. It is too soon to tell to what extent the Nigerian officer corps has followed in the best Nigerian traditions of using office to acquire economic interests; but there were murmurs from the other ranks that some officers did not want the war to end, because that would bring an end to the loot as well.

The states scheme produced a large crop of fresh candidates for political and economic power. A new state offers unprecedented openings in politics, business and the bureaucracy; and if the Mid-West state is anything to go by, new élites* devour resources even faster than did the old. For the time being, while the ban on parties lasts, the first in the queue are the civil servants and the representatives of communal or local interests who, in the absence of political parties, gravitate around the administrators or the army men in power. Inside the West, the pressure on the fastest-growing and largest élite is nearer bursting point than ever; but in the North the expulsion of the Ibos left a welcome vacuum for Northerners at levels both humble and elevated, and the creation of new states is bringing new echelons to office in each of them. Emirs, the young men feel, should reign not rule. Though three of the six Northern states remain powerful emirates, Native Authorities have lost their control over police, courts and prisons, and young men are coming to the fore in local government and other manifestations of reform.

How different, though, will the new guard be from the old? Or from those in the Southern élite, who were so much more

*The Begho Tribunal in Benin was told by Dr I. C. Doppler, described as an industrial promoter, and managing director of Technochemi (Nigeria) Ltd, that the Mid-West government lost £5 million on the state's three largest industries, a cement factory, a glass factory and a textile factory, because of the inflation of prices to enable the Lagos-based firm to pay the 10-per-cent contract bribe to the ruling party in the state, the NCNC. (*Daily Times*, 12 January 1968.)

'modern' than the rulers in the hierarchical structure of the old North, but corrupt and, once in power, equally immune to pressures from below? Out of power, the young men, and the radicals and the minorities (NEPU and the United Middle Belt Congress) led rebellion against the hierarchical authoritarian order that enclosed them; out of power, they advocated an ideology of radical reforms. But radicals risen to office do not necessarily make radical governments; nor do they necessarily remain radical. Young men are taking the place of older men; but will they also not take over their policies? And where, as in some states in the North, there has been a reconciliation of new, formerly opposition men and the older conservatives, could this not be based more on the sharing of power than on any agreement over policy, in which the radicals have served to change ideas? Much is talked of the social change coming over the North. But Nigeria will not be the first country where new groups attaining political power do not implement significant reforms, but try rather to integrate themselves in an existing structure of power. When élitist politicians are 'in' and not 'out' of power, the preservation of the *status quo* becomes their goal. The new states, even in the midst of war, were preoccupied with very mundane considerations. Local sons, kept out of the civil service when it was the preserve of the Northern select, now expect to make up for lost time. The scramble for office, government houses and cars, promotion and service privileges, suffuses the swelling civil service, and the aspirants coming up behind from secondary school.

When the six new states were being set up in the North, a prime consideration was not policy-making, but the division of the old North's assets. To many civil servants, the most knotty problem was how to divide Kaduna's two Mercedes cars between six states. I asked an attorney-general from one of the new states what he considered to be his main challenge. 'Oh,' he said, pointing to the shelves behind him. 'There's the question of how we allocate the books in this law library.' Administrative costs are soaring beyond the capacity of treasuries, and budgets are being drafted with eyes on the expenditure but not on the revenue column. Oil, of course, is the great hope; and of all the new interest groups that will use office to entrench themselves economically, the most tenacious will probably come from the 'oil rich Rivers State', as it proclaims itself in its publications. RSG1 (Rivers State Government 1) reads the number-plate of the shiny black Mercedes Benz in the choked early morning traffic rush from Lagos's civil-service-élite suburb of Ikoyi to the complex of offices in the capital. On the back seat, beside a shiny new briefcase, and a smooth new hat, sits the new incumbent. The older political generation came to office the hard way, compared to this acquisition of power by civil service, army or navy* promotion; but, however effortlessly acquired, the office, the prestige, the salary and the openings to economic power are no more readily surrendered.

Will a Nigeria of more, and smaller, states permit a stronger centre; or will the competition of local demands set up more centrifugal forces than the Federal centre can stand? Admittedly, small states will have less leverage on a centre than one previously subject to three powerful partners. But in place of the old monoliths from East, West and North, there could be small state parochialism in twelve different varieties and, given Nigeria's penchant for arrangements of expediency, a bewildering series of alliances at the centre. The constitutional experts are searching for forms of government to induce not inter-state conflict but cooperation. It is not so much the constitution that will determine this, however, as the system of revenue allocation for the states. And oil here is crucial, because conservative estimates put oil revenues at £600 million over the next four years, while the present Federal budget is under £190 million a year.[100] A 1969 commission on revenue allocation proposed that all but 10 per cent of in-shore oil royalties should be retained by the Federal government either for itself or for division among all states. But the oil-rich states would have nothing of this. The old derivation principle remains, under which 50 per cent of oil royalties go to the state of origin. State budgets already reflect

*The military governor of the Rivers State, Lieutenant-Commander Diete-Spiff, is a twenty-six-year-old sailor who rose from meteorological officer to merchant seaman to naval cadet and then Lieutenant-Commander in the Nigerian navy.

imbalances between the states which could produce profound conflicts in the near future. The constitution of the new Federation posits the existence of a strong centre for Nigeria's unity and development; the disposition of oil – and other revenues – could set up centrifugal pressures that will make nonsense of the talk, and the war, for unity. Have not all Nigeria's previous crises been, essentially, over the distribution of the spoils?

Inside Biafra, mobilization for the war and paucity of information obscured the shape of internal politics. To some of its supporters, Biafra's cause was a revival of the possibility for African revolution: because Ibos are the basic revolutionary group in West Africa; and Biafra could have become the area's first viable state, pulling itself up by its own bootstraps, and the rest of the continent by its example.[101] The politicians of the Eastern region, however, were as much responsible for the failures of the First Republic as were any of the others; radical critics emerged, but they made no more of a mark in their own region than did their counterparts in the West. The test of Biafra's revolutionary potential had to lie not in its skill at entrepreneurship, nor even sufferings in war, terrible as these have been, but in the emergence there of some real alternative to the old system. The search for a social policy was begun even in the midst of war; but it is not known how representative was the group, Chinua Achebe included, that was 'putting down what it is we want and what we want to avoid, as a basis for discussion when the war is over'.[102] Nor is it known what concept of social change the group developed. Ojukwu's Ahiara Declaration, which came to be known as Biafra's little green book, stressed self-reliance in the main.

In Biafra, as in Nigeria, power lay with the military, and day-to-day government and policy-making was in the hands of the top civil servants. Like their politician colleagues, who did duty as diplomats for the most part, they were élitist in origin and in outlook. Ojukwu presided over a great pyramid of army and administration. But bricks in that pyramid did include some committees and institutions that hinted at changed concepts of mobilization and policy-making. There was, for instance, a

Political Orientation Committee, which ran an institution training cadres for the army; for the fronts of women, farmers, youth and trade-unionists, mobilized for the war effort; and for BOFF, the Biafran Organization of Freedom Fighters, which was intended not only to operate behind enemy lines rather than fight conventional warfare, but also as a counter to the power of the regular army and its coup-making propensity. A body known as the Socialist Group was the principal initiator, and its members were also represented on a National Guidance Council of young intellectuals planning, or talking about, the shape of the future. In Biafra, now dead, or in Nigeria, now administered and re-formed as one, any re-shaping of the future had to depend on the ability of Africans to carry through those structural transformations in their society without which no African country can really develop. Nigeria has been the classic example in Africa of the havoc caused by self-indulgent élites. And though these may have been somewhat obscured by the war, they will return to prominence, in new formations and new alliances, until groups emerge with a sustained critique of them, and a way out for the society itself.

Furthermore, Nigeria's problem now that the war has ended will be not only how to hold the country together, and govern it, but also how to get the army back into barracks and its maverick commanders under control. Eighteen months after the outbreak of war, the Nigerian army alone (not counting the Biafran forces, which it is virtually impossible to estimate) was ten times the size of what it was when Nzeogwu staged the first coup; in the third year of the war, it was said to have grown by at least half again. Large sections of the original officer corps were wiped out in coups and warfare; but prodigious intake and promotion have raised men from the rank of lieutenant to major in charge of a battalion within a year. Alongside a rise in rank goes a rise in pay, and status. Nigeria's lowest army rate (£17 5*s*. a month for a private) is about eight times the *per capita* income of the average Nigerian. Recruits have been drawn more heavily than ever from the traditional areas of army enlistment; but, above all, the unemployed and the formerly unemployable have found job outlets at last, and steady pay. When the army must be cut back,* these men are unlikely to go willingly back to the street corner. Demobilization will bring problems enough. In 1967 the army was already taking soundings on how it might be phased back into barracks or civilian life. But during the war itself, the army was knee-deep in periodic breakdowns of discipline: some of which have been in the ranks and dealt with punitively, while others in the command have been too delicate to touch. When the instances of soldiers using their uniforms and their weapons to flout the law grew too numerous to ignore, Armed Forces Disciplinary Courts were established, which had nearly all the powers of a general court martial and could be convened at any time by the commanding officer of any unit.[103] Soldiers turned bank robber or hold-up man on the street or in the dance hall were dealt with by these courts. At the front, there were cases of major indiscipline and of large-scale desertions; as in 2 Division, where morale was weakened by its failure to take Onitsha in October 1967, despite repeated assaults across the river and very heavy losses. The unity of the Nigerian army and of Nigeria at war has been symbolized in the figure of General Gowon. His conciliatory style of leadership is an indication of how many pressures in army and administration – and, much less important for the time being, in politics – he has to reconcile. His tenure in office has not been without challenge. Throughout the first months of his government, he was a shaky occupant of the seat that Colonel Mohammed Murtala saw as his own, especially when the colonel lost out on the issue of immediately invading the East. Anti-Gowon moves were smothered several times after that. Throughout the civil war indeed, Gowon paid no visit to the front; and the commanders in the field held sway over their particular war kingdoms. There were three divisions, and each was virtually a law and an organization unto itself. Each drew its own budget; conducted its own arms purchases; handled its own recruiting in its own areas; and vied for allocations of men, arms and supplies from the centre. (Only in its final offensive did the three divisions

* This was written before the war ended. When it had, both Gowon and Hassan Katsina made public statements to the effect that they intend keeping the army at very nearly its present level.

achieve enough coordination to win victory.) Colonel Benjamin Adekunle, conqueror of Port Harcourt and Calabar – megalomaniac, riotous, at times ebullient, at others berserk – was the hero of the war until he sustained a major defeat. If he was at last removed, it was not only because he had ceased to supply sufficient success, but because he had become too pushful at the game of requisitioning the best and largest share, and because he was taking too little trouble to conceal his political ambitions.

If there is a challenge to Gowon's leadership, it must come from within the army, or from politicians who have links with officers who, in turn, have support from the ranks. The army has been called Nigeria's thirteenth state. It is the country's most important constituency, and no serious contender for office can afford to forget this.

As daunting as were the problems produced by the war, the peace could produce issues almost equally intimidating. What is to stop soldiers, in the army, or recently demobilized, from taking steps inside the states to preserve and further their corporate interests? Heroes back from the front deserve a just peace. Can a post-war Nigeria give it to them? And if it does not, will soldiers not act to help themselves? The division of state assets will go on inside the states; at the centre, the battle for the distribution of resources has yet to be fought. The statisticians, the economists, the planners, the permanent secretaries of the ministries, the technical advisers – and, in the background, the international creditors, the bankers, the trading companies, and the condition of the world market – will circumscribe what is possible, perhaps desirable. The outcome will be decided in the contest between the echelons of power in post-war Nigeria; old interest groups and new; and, most belligerent of all, the army.

Conventionally, soldiers in peace-time should once again subordinate themselves to the civil authority. The army should retreat from state office; the soldiers should return to the barracks – though some commanders might leave the army to opt for politics – and the politicians should take over again. Nigeria's army has already shattered the fondest conventions about the military. The army was supposed to be a corporate body with a corporate sense; able, through discipline and training, to avoid the ethnic or other group antagonisms that divided other élite groups. But Nigeria's army was no better able to escape these divisions and antagonisms; officers and other ranks alike broke discipline indiscriminately to identify with communal interests. Once the infection set in, it coursed through the army – a body so compact, so organized for the rapid communication of orders and action. A disciplined army is supposed to obey its officers. Nigeria, during the Congo operation, was said to have one of Africa's most disciplined armed forces. It did not take long for Nigeria to be talked about, however inaccurately in Congo terms.

Young officers are likely, it is said, to intervene in politics not through 'tribal feeling but through the impatience of the young and capable at incompetence and corruption'.[104] What was true for Nzeogwu and the young majors was not true of subsequent young officer actions. New military regimes have in general, it is said, put an end to disorders that have been tearing their countries apart. In Nigeria they tore the country apart even faster, and with sharper weapons. In Africa's new states, it has been said, the national goals of civilian policy-makers (the politicians), the bureaucracy and the army are substantially the same: stability and order, national unity and rapid modernization.[105] Politicians in Nigeria failed to reach these goals; bureaucracy and army failed even more abysmally.

The Nigerian army reflected within itself all the divisions, tensions, contradictions and crises of Nigerian society. The army was distinct only in possessing the instruments of violence. This made it possible for army men to topple an unproductive government, but not to govern productively in its place; to go to war but not to negotiate a peace. If the armed men of Africa's military governments have an ultimate achievement, it was this wretched war. The men under arms, when they were afflicted by crisis, resorted to the only weapons that they had been trained to use, and went into battle. Coup, counter-coup, civilian massacre and war: has there anywhere else been so rapid and gruesome a sequence?

3. GHANA

Competitors in Conspiracy

Those who were directly involved in the overthrowing of Nkrumah have come to believe that God himself must have had a hand in the coup and that the armed forces and the police were merely instruments of God achieving his purposes for Ghana.
Major-General Kotoka, 22 April 1966

In Nigeria, where the coup failed, little was known about the coup-makers, and it was soon not politic to claim to know too much. Ghana's coup, by contrast, sprouted contesting claimants and several official and semi-official versions. Yet much about it remains obscure, and has been made even more so by the emergence, three weeks after the event, of an official version – the work of Police Chief John Harlley. This version was to justify the army–police balance of power in the new regime; to present the action of Ghana's service chiefs for the plaudits of the western world, so as to erase any hint of the rather squalid career considerations that prompted the principal actors; and to cover traces of the sharp in-fighting between army and police for the honours of the post-coup National Liberation Council.

Early on, claimants to the conspiracy had presented themselves with some alacrity. Every conspiratorial thought tended to be translated by the successful coup itself into a daring deed against the all-powerful tyrant; men who had whispered together in corners later seemed to imagine that they had been manning intelligence networks. For instance, the news of the coup had no sooner reached London than one Khow Daniel Amihiya announced, from two furnished rooms in the West Cromwell Road, that he was an ex-intelligence agent of Nkrumah who had been trained by the CIA as the coup's master mind. He had sent out the signal 'Locusts can be operated upon' to start the revolt; and the reply 'Cockerel cooked' announced its success.

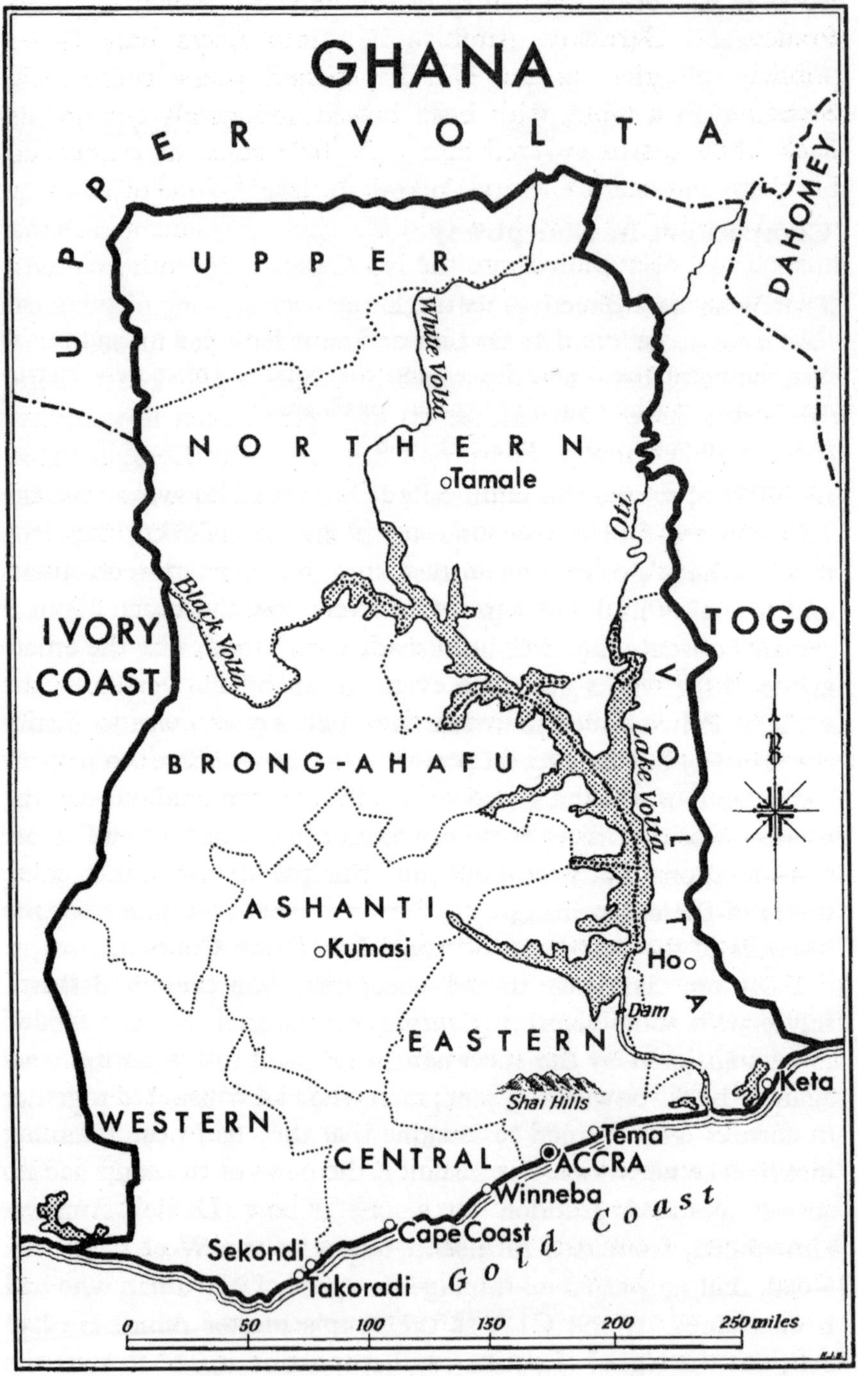

GHANA
UPPER VOLTA
DAHOMEY
UPPER
White Volta
NORTHERN
Tamale
Oti
Black Volta
IVORY COAST
TOGO
BRONG-AHAFU
Lake Volta
VOLTA
ASHANTI
Kumasi
Ho
Dam
EASTERN
Keta
Shai Hills
WESTERN
Tema
CENTRAL
ACCRA
Winneba
Cape Coast
Gold Coast
Sekondi
Takoradi
0
50
100
150
200
250 miles

London had been the centre of his network, which included France and Germany. Amihiya flew into Accra only to be publicly pilloried at an NLC-convened press conference. Standing on a table, with head bowed and hands behind his back while guards covered him with their guns, he renounced his claim and heard General Ankrah declare: 'None of us know him. We will put him in a cold ice chest.'[1] (General Ankrah himself had been pulled into the NLC at the eleventh hour and knew virtually nothing of its origins.)

In Lagos unnamed Ghanaian opposition circles in exile said that the coup had been organized by a group called the Ghana All-Forces Inner Council, set up five years earlier in the army and the police force. There had also been the London-based attempt of former Air Commodore De Graft Hayford, who had been relieved of his command after falling foul of Nkrumah, and who had hoped to draw on army trainees and even ex-servicemen in a plot to topple the president: these plans were still in the blueprint stage, however, timed, it was hoped, for action in September 1966. Then there was the Gbedemah–Busia axis: political opponents in Ghana, they had found common exile cause in scheming for Nkrumah's overthrow. Gbedemah nurtured contacts in the United States and Switzerland. Busia was often in the Ivory Coast, and is known to have had a meeting on at least one occasion with Jacques Foccart, de Gaulle's special intelligence and diplomatic operator in Africa; the French were very interested in getting rid of Nkrumah. But once again the plotting was vague and, without the serious help of foreign intelligence, its outcome was unlikely.

Though General Ankrah found it necessary to warn that the NLC would tolerate no false claimants, and would deal with them appropriately, these intrigues abroad were of marginal interest to an NLC trying to adjudicate a conflict within itself. For the first three weeks in the life of the new NLC were spent arbitrating the contesting claims to coup leadership of army and police. Thus, the first list of NLC membership carried seven names, four army men and three police officers.[2] A second and final list evened the score at four representatives of each force. (The eighth member was Harlley's deputy, A. K. Deku, whom

Harlley subsequently credited as the man who had carried out the intelligence aspect of the planning.[3]) But it was only when Harlley produced a version of events that was to serve as a model for all subsequent accounts[4] that speculation about the police–army argument was quieted.

The NLC had no sooner been constituted than there had been murmurs in the army, especially among the middle-ranking officers, that Kotoka should have been chairman rather than Ankrah; and that while it was the army that made the coup, with the police playing no more than a minor role, the police were now virtually running the Council. What, it was asked, was their claim to their disproportionate share of the power?

The army version, to which Afrifa's account is faithful, was that the coup had been planned by a tiny, closed partnership of two: General Kotoka, then colonel; and his brigade major and staff officer in charge of training and operations, Major, later Colonel, and later still, Brigadier Afrifa. The plot was hatched early in February 1966 when, carrying out a reconnaissance of a training area for the brigade's annual manoeuvres, Kotoka and Afrifa found themselves alone on the road for over five hours, and together fulminated on the evils of the government. A few days after that conversation, confident of one another's complicity, they talked about Nkrumah's forthcoming visit to Hanoi, and agreed that a coup should be staged in his absence. The next morning, without wasting time, the colonel went to Accra to meet Mr Harlley, the commissioner of police. The broad plan for the coup was drafted in Colonel Kotoka's office in Kumasi. 'So far as I knew the only person who knew the details of the plan was Mr Harlley, whom I had not met at that point,' wrote Afrifa.[5]

For a while, a version was current that cast not only the army role as more central than that of the police, but Harlley himself as a last-minute recruit. Members of Kotoka's defence platoon who moved down to the capital as the coup got under way, were detailed to call on senior army, navy, air force and police supporters to inform them of what was happening and to ask for their support.[6] In the capital they drove to police barracks and persuaded the commissioner of police to put the police behind the coup.[7] To a reporter who asked about Harlley's role, Kotoka is reported to have replied, 'Harlley? Who's Harlley?'

The deciding factor in favour of the police claims was provided three weeks after the coup, when the government published *The Decisive Role of the Police*. This was the address delivered by Harlley at Accra central police station to officers and men of the force. As he read the speech, Harlley was flanked by his fellow-members of the NLC; it was an official NLC occasion, for the delivery of the official NLC version of the coup. It reversed the roles of army and police heads in the conspiracy, but justified the army–police balance of power in the new regime. It made the plot one of long-standing and careful coordination in which Harlley himself had pride of place. Was it not, accordingly, natural that so seasoned an operator, who had conspired so long and earnestly but had yet defied discovery, should control the crucial security levers of the new regime? At the same time, the Harlley version gave honoured roles in the planning and execution of the coup – as well as of several attempts that had failed along the way – to those who had to be given office in the NLC. This regime clearly had the political need to allocate roles rather as a Cabinet rewards good party and election campaigners. And so the character list of front-rank conspirators grew, to accommodate not only those who found a place in the NLC hierarchy, but also those whose political support was needed for the new regime, and those on Nkrumah's side (like former Foreign Minister Alex Quaison-Sackey and TUC chief Bentum) who crossed over. What the first Harlley version did not recount, subsequent versions, inspired by it, did.[8] Every time that a coup-maker held forth on the event, or an officially approved chonicler was given access to those in the know, still another instalment was added to the series of mutual compliments and credits that the coup-makers were dishing out to one another. After the first Harlley version, and apart from the limited Afrifa account, there were no independent sources left to tap.

The most fetching aspect of the Harlley version is his improvisation of a sedate if spurious justification for a professedly non-political policeman's resort to coup d'état. How could he reasonably claim that he had the right, indeed the duty, to overturn the regime whose security he was pledged to protect? Harlley retorted that he had acted in his very capacity as policeman, mandated under an act of parliament to prevent crime, and to detect and apprehend offenders; for Nkrumah himself, head of state, was guilty of corrupt practice. This realization had come as a terrible shock to Harlley and to Deku. When Harlley dilated on this period to the Reverend Peter Barker, who interviewed some fifty coup participants for an NLC-approved if semi-official story of the coup, the NLC vice-chairman had an unconvincingly vivid memory for conversations several years old; and if he conveyed little else, it was a compelling portrait of himself, with his tortuous fantasy life of conspiracy. There was the occasion after the assassination attempt at Flagstaff House when he and Deku had chatted together in Ewe:

'... The real trouble is all this corruption in high places – and in Flagstaff House itself.'

'You don't mean that Nkrumah is implicated?'

'That's just what I do mean. I've got proof of it too. This ten per cent on all government contracts is not just private bribery by ministers; it's a systematic plan to finance the party. All the companies know they're expected to pay ten per cent in order to get contracts, so they just add it to their estimates and pay it out cheerfully.... No, I'm afraid we're fighting a losing battle. We're working loyally for the Old Man, trying to stamp out bribery and corruption, but the arch-criminal is the Old Man himself.'

Deku could hardly believe his ears. It was extremely dangerous for anyone to talk in this way: it meant that Harlley trusted him.

'As far as I can see,' went on Harlley, 'we have every constitutional right to apprehend him.'

Harlley lapsed into English to explain that the Ghana police, being in possession of information that the President was involved in criminal transactions, could prepare charges against him. 'A copy of the charges will be handed to the chief justice, the original will be delivered to Nkrumah, and we shall give him an ultimatum – a date and a time at which he must either abdicate or face the consequences.'

'And if he refuses to abdicate?'

'A military task force would be ready in positions surrounding Flagstaff House to effect his arrest. The Commissioner of Police would drive into Flagstaff House in an armoured car, together with the Chief of Defence Staff, to declare Nkrumah destooled and take him away.'[9]

Harlley, it seems, had reflected long and earnestly on section 36 of the act which empowered him to use force to apprehend an offender:

After giving careful thought to these matters I came to the conclusion that in view of the unconstitutional army which Kwame Nkrumah had raised around himself, the Constitutional Armed Forces of the country could be employed to constitute the necessary force as prescribed by the law to enable me to arrest criminals.

Thus was opened the constitutional way to mutiny by a head policeman, in league with the army. Harlley subsequently 'held discussions with certain members of the armed forces. *There was a general agreement to my proposals* [my emphasis]. . . . we held secret meetings, and the plan of action was drawn.' Harlley apologized to senior police officers that they were not put in the picture until the very last minute. It had been necessary to keep strictly to the principle of the fewer the better.

Before the successful operation of February 1966, the plotters had toyed with some extraordinary schemes. There was the plan to chloroform Nkrumah one night when he visited one of his girl friends. Harlley had actually bought the bottle of chloroform it seems; but at the last minute he and Kotoka, then quartermaster-general in the Ministry of Defence, had dropped the plan one afternoon at a tennis party discussion.[10] On another occasion, Otu and Ankrah had been sounded out; each had agreed to act, but only if the other did. This was the plot due to be sprung in mid-1965, during the Commonwealth Prime Ministers' Conference, which Brigadier Hassan, Director of Military Intelligence, sniffed in the air.[11] In the reshuffle following the enforced retirement of Ankrah and Otu, Kotoka was sent to Kumasi as commander of 2 Brigade. He had remarked, when the chloroform plot was dropped, that force had to be met with force; but then, as quartermaster-general, he had had no troops under his command. Now he had troops, although he was 170 miles from Accra.

With the exception of the mid-1965 plot, it is unlikely that there was much serious planning. There was intent, but it did not make for the continuous thread of conspiracy or the intense commitment that Harlley recounted. Of his own extraordinary aptitude for conspiracy, there can be no doubt: when Nkrumah heard the first news of the coup d'état while in Peking, his first reaction was: 'Oh, Harlley will put it down.' The skill with which Harlley gulled Nkrumah all those years could also serve to present an unlikely account of the coup.

It was an intricate and effusive account, certainly. It wove together several conflicting strands in the conspiracy of army, police and civilian elements; it made the coup-makers the country's true custodians of the rule of law. It did, however, omit at least one relevant factor. This was the strong rumour circulating in Accra, and since confirmed by Nkrumah,[12] that his first action on returning from the Hanoi mission would have been the arrest – whether at all justified or not is impossible to say without the evidence – of Harlley and with him Deku, on charges of diamond smuggling or complicity. If even the rumour reached the police chiefs, however, they clearly had no time to lose. Kotoka himself, it is generally agreed, felt insecure and nervous about how long he would last in command. Whatever else Kotoka and Harlley shared – and much has been made of their both being Ewe and quick to rely on one another – they were both uneasy about how long they would endure in their respective police and army command posts.

Wherever the coup plot originated, and whether it was Harlley or Kotoka who was its lynch-pin, it could not have worked without both police and army. What probably happened is that in both army and police force, Harlley and Kotoka – and with Kotoka, Afrifa – were thinking along parallel lines. Harlley was operating, for purposes not yet established, a private little security network. His access to official reports from the regions, which must in some measure have pointed to popular discontent with rising prices, must have been invaluable. But without the army, the police would have found no means of action. When the handful of men in the army decided to move, they realized that the plot would be abortive without the police, the larger force and the one in control of the extensive radio system. The approach was probably from Kotoka to Harlley, and not the other way about;[13] but once a member of the inner circle of three, Harlley became responsible for decisive planning and security on the police and administrative side.

The troops under General Kotoka's command were able to advance on Accra unquestioned and unsuspected because the police signals reporting their progress *en route* were sent ultimately to Harlley himself, or Deku, for further action. The police communications network, which connects 126 administrative centres throughout Ghana, was crucial throughout the night of 23–4 February, and in the days immediately after the coup. Police headquarters in Accra became the operational headquarters of the NLC as soon as it was certain that the battle of Flagstaff House was won. It was the police force that administered the country for the crucial twenty-four hours after the coup began. Above all, a synchronized police swoop on all the leading political supporters of the regime – ministers, MPs and top officials; youth, women and workers' brigade organizers – froze opposition even before it could be alerted. Harlley and Deku planned this exercise together. As Kotoka's troops moved, ostensibly on a training operation, so Harlley devised his own cover for the police swoop. The budget was due to be delivered in the week that Nkrumah left for Hanoi, and it was expected to be unpopular. Under pretext of preparations to counter any anti-government activity, police leave was cancelled and standby ordered. Every police station was alerted for trouble; every area intelligence officer was supplied with a list of top CPP officials and politicians, and was instructed to reconnoitre their addresses, ready for the time when they might have to be offered 'protection'. The security briefing was official and above-board. Harlley and Deku worked on the lists of those who were to be 'protected'.[14] When the order was given, the security round-up worked only too smoothly.

What is significant is how few of the command in either service were drawn into the conspiracy. Harlley, it has been seen already, had to apologize to his police officers for leaving them in the dark. As for the army, though all soldiers were cast as the heroic saviours of their country, only a handful were trusted at coup-making time and drawn into the preparations. Whatever was said once the coup had been successful, the army command was not united for action to overthrow the Nkrumah regime. The 1965 plot, for instance, took Ankrah along with it; but Otu had baulked, and, to Harlley's fury, could not be won over. After the coup, Major-General S. J. A. Otu found himself posted abroad as ambassador to India. The army's former chief of defence staff, Major-General Aferi, found himself his country's ambassador in Mexico; his support for the coup was strongly suspect by the NLC, largely because he had been picked by Nkrumah as successor to Otu. In fact, the coup came within a hairsbreadth of failing, just because it relied on such narrow army support.

Kotoka's consultation with Harlley on 15 February, after he and Afrifa had clinched their coup understanding, fixed the date for action eight days later. Nkrumah would be on his way to Hanoi. Kotoka and Afrifa drew in a very few other army officers. (Lieutenant-Colonel John Addy, garrison commander at Tamale, was told by Kotoka; and though he played no part in the action, he knew that the troop exercises in the north were to be used as a cover.) None of the battalion commanders was drawn in, since Kotoka took care not to move a complete battalion; he had with him his own defence platoon. When he moved it was with some 600 men in thirty-five vehicles, ostensibly testing their readiness for action against Rhodesia.

Only at the very last minute was it realized that, without the Accra-based 1 Brigade and their armoured cars, the coup-makers would certainly fail. Afrifa broached the coup plan to Major Coker-Appiah of the field regiment; and as Colonel A. K. Ocran, the brigade commander, had been a contemporary of his at an Eaton Hall officer training course, Kotoka himself approached Ocran.[15] But this was barely hours before the coup, when troops were already under their orders to move southwards. Ocran had little option, really. It would be hard to explain away the movement of the 600 men under Kotoka, Ocran reasoned to himself. 'We were committed.' At this stage Kotoka produced a sheet of paper of the general plan; it was quite simple: Kotoka's force would capture Flagstaff House, Broadcasting House and the Castle; while Ocran's force would handle the

President's Guard regiments, and seize the cable and wireless station, the news agency and the banks. In addition there were to be arrests of eight key men, among them Major-General Barwah, Colonel Hassan, Director of Military Intelligence, Lieutenant-Colonel M. Kuti, national organizer of the Workers' Brigade, and Colonel D. Zanlerigu, commander of the Guard regiment. The army chief-of-staff was listed among the eight, but Aferi was in Addis Ababa at the time. Kotoka detailed a special team to 'get' army commander Barwah.

The first half of the plan worked well enough. The battalion stationed in Tamale moved south on 23 February to join up with the remainder of the brigade in Kumasi. Striking time was 4 A.M. on 24 February, for the troop exercise was then to be changed into the coup operation. Afrifa was left in command of the column moving on Accra, while Kotoka – under the pretext of seeking medical attention – went on ahead to synchronize actions with Harlley and with Ocran, and to install himself in a house near Flagstaff House. The convoy was already on the road when Colonel Ocran tried to call off the operation. Involved in a routine court-martial proceeding, he had been unable, in the hours since Kotoka had first approached him, to alert all his brigade commanders. He sent a flash to Kotoka, suggesting a postponement; but it was too late. At this point, Ocran set about trying to find his commanding officers. That evening, as they agreed to the coup, Ocran devised a pretext for the operation of the troops: they were to suppress a mutiny by the Guard regiment. 'I knew this would go down very well,' Ocran said.

That night Kotoka and Ocran met briefly to finalize the plan of operations. Their combined forces were to join up at 3.30. But a few hours after Ocran returned to Burma camp, he received a battery of telephone calls, all connected with the impending operation, although the telephone should, according to the plan, have been disconnected by the Signals regiment. One of the calls was from General Barwah, who had received a report that Colonel Hassan of Military Intelligence had been arrested. Ocran promised to investigate; but it was already evident that Major Coker-Appiah's squadron had jumped the gun and carried out some of its arrest assignments prematurely.

Ten minutes later the platoon sent by Kotoka to deal with Barwah arrived, and when the army commander resisted arrest, shot him. He died in the Signals regiment room a few minutes after being taken there. The troops that dynamited their way into the house of Colonel Zanlerigu, the commander of the Presidential Guard, found that he was not there; he reached Flagstaff House in time to alert its defenders. The premature arrests also alerted some of Nkrumah's ministers, among them Kofi Baako, Minister of Civil Defence, who improvised a quick meeting – in the foyer of the Ambassador Hotel – of the Presidential Commission, or those members of it who could be found at that hour. Its sole act seems to have been to alert Commodore Hansen of the navy and Air Commodore Otu, both of whom went to the operations room in the Ministry of Defence to try and rally the army.

Kotoka's final briefing of his troops had taken place punctually, and they had moved off on their assignments. Under Major Afrifa, 'A' Company made for Broadcast House, to seize the radio. 'B' Company, under Captain Sesshie, went into action at Flagstaff House, but considerably below strength: one of its platoons had been held up by a breakdown on the road; and the major part of the attacking force, 2 Brigade and the armoured cars under Ocran's command, did not materialize. The battle for Flagstaff House was still in the balance when at 6 A.M. Kotoka made his broadcast announcing a seizure of power. An hour later he set up combined headquarters with the police at police headquarters. Both Harlley and Kotoka agreed to decline the office of head of state, and to offer it instead to General Ankrah. The general heard of the take-over only when it was in operation. He was used, in Latin American style, as the coup swing man: as highest-ranking army officer, he swung behind the NLC the support of the senior officers not taken into the confidence of the coup-makers.

The countryside police round-up was effectively concluded within hours of the start of the operation. But at Flagstaff House, 2 Brigade and the armoured cars had still not arrived to reinforce Captain Sesshie's troops, who were facing heavy fire, and there was a danger that the battalion of the POGR in the

Shai hills thirty-two miles away would arrive to reinforce Colonel Zanlerigu's men. The Shai hills battalion made no move. This, apparently, was the work of Lieutenant-Colonel Addy, Tamale garrison commander, who was one of the few trusted by Kotoka, and who had fortuitously been called to Accra for the same court martial on which Ocran had been sitting. He had made use of this assignment to call on an old army friend, Major Tetteh, commanding officer of the Shai hills battalion. 'He was very careful about his approach. He said nothing about a coup. He treated it as a casual social call. . . . He sympathized with Tetteh over the delay in his promotion. . . . "Well, old man," he said, as if it were an afterthought, "if ever anything were to happen – you know what I mean – don't move your troops. That's my advice."'[16]

Colonel Ocran's 2 Brigade did not move either until the battle was almost over. The colonel had been summoned to the operations room by the navy and air force chiefs, and he subsequently explained the half-heartedness with which he conducted himself by the military proprieties imposed by the army chain of command. Air Marshal Otu and Commodore Hansen were his seniors, and he was obliged to place himself under their direct command. Indeed, he took orders to counter the coup, but then played for time to negate them. The burlesque in the operations room lasted some hours.[17] Even after the Kotoka broadcast, Ocran remained cautiously mute about his knowledge of the coup; at one point there was a serious risk that contradictory sets of orders would set his own men in combat against each other. One of his orders given under pressure resulted in the engineers being blockaded in their own barracks for a while. Then a chance summons to two battalion commanders, who had been party to the coup planning of the night before, brought an end to the farce. Ocran gave them one set of instructions in the operations room and then accompanied them to whisper instructions for the arrest of the air force and navy commanders. When these two were carried off at gun point, Ocran went along with them, to give the impression that he, too, was under arrest. Only then, three hours late for his coup assignment, did he confide his knowledge of the coup and, leaving the two commanders in the guard-room, hurry away to try and catch up. He had taken no chances on the coup going the wrong way; and his self-confessed irresolution was apparently shared by other officers in his brigade.

By mid-morning, the reinforcements of 2 Brigade had been rushed up, and the Guard regiment at Flagstaff House had surrendered; by the end of the day, the main wall of Flagstaff House had been breached by an armoured car, and the compound occupied. Broadcasts called on civil servants to remain at their posts. The membership of the National Liberation Committee, with the setting up of the Economic Committee of the NLC, was announced. The army promotions were rapid. By noon of coup day, Major-General Ankrah had become lieutenant-general. That week, Afrifa rose from major to colonel; Ocran, from colonel to brigadier; Kotoka, from colonel to major-general.

Swing to the West

In the eyes of western diplomacy the change that has come over the political aspect of West Africa in the past six months looks encouraging. . . . Now a solid block of states under the control of moderate leaders stretches from the Congo to the frontier of Guinea.

A special correspondent, writing in *The Times*, 30 April 1966

Were the Western powers accomplices in the Ghana coup; and, if so, how? For the time being, the dossier of calculated external intervention, or collusion, must remain open. More evidence is needed before one can say with any degree of the certainty expressed by Nkrumah,[18] how direct a part Western powers, intelligence agencies, financial and trading interests played. At the least, they created a climate in which prospective coup-makers were never in any doubt that a move against Nkrumah would be greeted with fervent approbation in the West. As it was, the day after the coup d'état, *The Times* of London recognized that 'Ghana would be worth salvaging again'.[19] Ghana had 'swung back to reliance on the West'.

For two reasons, no particularly deep international conspiracy was needed. In the first place, if the conspiracy was not orchestrated, it found a natural harmony between those inside Ghana and those outside who called a tune different from the one that the Nkrumah government was trying, however fitfully, to play. In the second place, like all Third World countries caught between falling prices for primary exports and the climbing costs of industrial imports, Ghana was inescapably susceptible to external pressures.

When the cocoa price fell, by coincidence or contrivance, Ghana's economy slumped with it. When reserves grew short and Ghana resorted to stiff short-term suppliers' credits, it was held ruthlessly to ransom by foreign firms and foreign governments. If Ghana's own vision of the consequences was blurred, the same could not possibly be said of the hard-sell countries eager to boost their own export earnings at the expense of their poorer customers. Even when it was apparent that Ghana could not finance all the debts that it was accumulating, Western countries – like Britain, with its Export Credits Guarantee Department – eager to improve their sales abroad, continued to guarantee private firms that advanced credits for project costs. The Drevici Group of West Germany, probably Ghana's largest single creditor, alone advanced £60 million in credits.[20] Ghana, noted one observer, 'has been sold a massive shipyard (how Ghana can provide credits to finance the sale of ships is a mystery) by a contractor from one of the several countries where the shipbuilding industry is notably "depressed". Perhaps this is one explanation for the contract?'[21]* (The country was Britain.) The lasting availability of supplier credits, the same observer commented, was 'primarily a function of domestic export promotion efforts in the creditor countries'. Some reputable Western firms are alleged to have used 'the high pressure techniques of an encyclopaedia salesman on a suburban doorstep',

* By 1965 the external debt for suppliers' credits was about £437·4 million, 82·5 per cent of the total debt (Ann Seidman). Of Ghana's debts, 77 per cent were due to be paid between 1963–8, because the typical loans negotiated were medium-term export guarantee credits, especially the borrowings from Britain and West Germany: *West Africa*, 9 April 1966.

in the way capital projects were hawked round to under-developed countries.[22]

Then there was the role of agencies like the International Monetary Fund and the World Bank, supposed to be disinterested mechanisms of international aid and cooperation. Intrinsically, and because of their dependence on United States finance, however, such bodies are preoccupied with the needs and the policies – political where not economic – of the creditor. The Fund and the Bank were concerned with 'stability', not development; orthodoxy, not change. Deserving societies were those that conformed, not those that tried to innovate. Aid policies have been shown[23] to have a bias against radical policies in developing countries. How much greater the sanctions – even if they were not so called – against developing countries whose foreign policy pronouncements were in jagged conflict with those of the principal creditors? A country that could or would not produce a 'climate of confidence' – foreign and pan-African policy included – for foreign investment and aid could scarcely expect the subvention of capital from those whose interests it hurt.* If Ghana was a miscreant society subscribing, by proclamation at least and by deeds where it could, to a different order of development priorities, it could not hope for understanding, let alone generosity. And the profligacy of the Nkrumah regime did provide a pretext for a combination of economic, diplomatic and strategic pressures against his government.

For Ghana, 1965 was the year of the squeeze. There had been mounting pressure in Washington for less indulgent attitudes to Ghana, especially after Brezhnev's visit to Nkrumah and their

*Recall, for instance, the 18 June 1964 Hearing before the Committee on Foreign Relations of the United States Senate:

SECRETARY RUSK: . . . we have made it very clear to Mr Nkrumah that we can't proceed with any confidence in this matter [of the aluminium project] if he is going to steer Ghana down a road that is hostile to the United States or American interests there.

SENATOR LAUSCHE: Has Russia sent in any aid?

RUSK: Russia is sending in some aid to Ghana.

LAUSCHE: If you would supply a statement, a recitation of the facts on Ghana, I think it would be very helpful in the record.

RUSK: If I could speak just off the record for a moment.

(*Discussion off the record*)

joint communiqué. President John Kennedy had been an active supporter of the Volta Dam project, financed by Kaiser; but with the Johnson administration came a hardening of United States economic and political policies towards Nkrumah. 'In its relationship to Africa as a whole,' the United States War Book said,[24] 'Ghana has limited strategic importance. It is doubtful that West Africa, in whole or in part, could become the scene of major operations in the event of a Third World War. There is little of strategic value in the area that would make it a target for conquest.' But by 1965, American attitudes had changed.[25] The first arrival of Soviet arms in Ghana during the Congo's post-independence crisis had caused alarm: were the weapons destined for Gizenga in the Congo? The alarm subsided, but it flared again in 1965. On 8 June 1965, the United Nations man in Accra noted in his report[26] to the UN secretary-general that, in the presence of Major-General Barwah and Major-General Gorshenin, the Russian military attaché, 142 cases of machine-guns had been loaded into the Russian freighter *Gulbeni* at Tema, for dispatch to Pointe Noire and suspected re-routing to Stanleyville in the Congo. Moreover, Nkrumah was building a £6·5 million air base in North Ghana with a three-mile long landing strip, thought by the Americans to offer excellent facilities for Soviet planes *en route* to Havana. In Guinea it had been the identical threat of staging facilities for Soviet planes bound for Cuba that had precipitated feverish activity by United States ambassador Attwood.[27] 'Ghana despite its own economic crisis was a more valuable prize for the East than Guinea had appeared to be five years earlier,' it was thought.[28] Furthermore, Nkrumah was developing intelligence facilities with Soviet and East German help. Nkrumah, it came to be considered in Washington, 'could now threaten the *status quo* in Africa: he could undermine regimes friendly to America, and to the Congolese he could transmit substantial aid. . . . The intelligence facilities which Russians and East Germans were developing with the Bureau of African Affairs were bound to complicate American efforts throughout Africa. . . . By mid 1965 concrete American interests began to be affected.' Thus, Willard Scott Thompson discloses, 'it is not a surprise to learn that during

1965, according to one report, Nkrumah's intentions were the subject of discussion at the highest NATO level'.[29]

It was in 1965 that Nkrumah made a major request for assistance to the Western powers. He was said to be seeking a loan of £1,000 million. He was referred in turn to each capital of the IMF. He also applied for surplus PL 480 food from the United States to help meet Ghana's shortages, and made the 'dual mandate' speech at the opening of the Volta River project*. The United States, however, had embarked on a consistently antagonistic line: investment and credit guarantees were withheld from potential investors; pressure was brought to bear on existing major furnishers of credit to the Ghana economy; and applications made by Ghana to US-dominated financial institutions, like the IMF, the World Bank, and direct to the US (US AID), were turned down.[30]

> As could have been guessed, the Americans were calculating carefully what might be the odds for a coup. The shrewd American deputy chief of mission in Ghana and his equally able successor played their hands very skilfully. Influential Ghanaians were in fact pleading with them that no new assistance be extended to Nkrumah lest (depending on the speaker's viewpoint) it delay the inevitable confrontation with economic reality and extend the life of the regime itself.[31]

In September 1965 a World Bank evaluation mission visited Ghana as part of the government's attempt to get financial assistance. The IMF had sent a mission to Ghana in May of the same year. The conditions laid down were predictable. Ghana's economic programme under the Seven Year Plan should be fundamentally repatterned. State-owned and run corporations should be closed down (not reorganized), and transferred to private enterprise. There would be a liberalizing of policy towards foreign private investment. There should be a scaling down of social amenities and 'unproductive' expenditure under the development plan, and heavier personal taxation. When Ghana tried to renegotiate its loans from West Germany, it was informed that the latter was waiting for the results of the World Bank mission, and in particular was considering Ghana's bi-

*Nkrumah's *Neo-Colonialism: The Highest Stage of Imperialism* was pubished just at that time.

lateral and barter agreements with 'centrally planned' or socialist economies. (The one IMF condition to which Ghana did accede was the cut in the cocoa price paid to producers; this was announced two days before the coup.)

Ghana next had resort to the socialist states. The Amoako-Atta mission of late 1965, described earlier, was crucial. The CPP Cabinet, though, was said to be divided between this solution of extended links with the socialist states, and the IMF demands. In the West, especially Britain, the prospect that socialist states would invade traditional trading preserves like cocoa, minerals and timber, was alarming. (On 12 January 1966, a report of the Cocoa Marketing Board revealed that the United States was the leading purchaser of Ghana's cocoa, accounting for 124,050 of the 567,769 tons exported. Other major purchasers were West Germany, the Soviet Union, Netherlands, Britain and Yugoslavia. However, agreements signed with the Soviet Union in December 1965, contracting for the sale of 150,000 tons of cocoa there, indicated a basic shift in the direction of Ghana's commercial relations.)[32]

Britain had begun to feel that neither its investments (about £150 million strong) nor its trade were safe. The turning point in British attitudes, it has been said,[33] was the departure of Sir Geoffrey de Freitas, who had served as High Commissioner for two years. 'By the time he left there was general agreement that Britain could only mark time till a new regime appeared.' Britain had been hopeful that the new Investment Act introduced in 1963 would provide a partnership of British capital with Ghanaian enterprise under the Seven Year Plan. But Nkrumah assigned the attractive slots in the plan to the state sector, and bought out private investors whose success was threatening . . . by the end of the year, this, and the corrupt system of import licensing, led British commercial interests to consider the Investment Act a dead letter. In the diplomatic field, Ghana was taking Britain to task in the Security Council for its Rhodesia policy, and meanwhile Ghanaian activity at the OAU summit had helped 'narrow Wilson's alternatives'. After the breakdown of diplomatic relations between Britain and Ghana over Rhodesia, 'most of the British officials, regardless of what happened in Rhodesia, thought they would not be back while Nkrumah was still in power'.[34]

Both the United States and Britain – and West Germany, which had been alarmed by a series of articles attacking it in *Spark* at the end of 1965 and the beginning of 1966[35] – were preoccupied with the matter of how to get rid of Nkrumah. But they faced real problems in finding someone to displace him.

Ghana's army, cheered on by the middle classes, proved capable coup-makers; but even if the political and economic interests of the West had not been indispensable in the making of the coup, they were crucial in helping to sustain it. Coups, Edward Luttwak has written,[36] are in the nature of things illegal; how justify and legitimize them? Recognition by foreign powers is essential.

> For many countries of the Third World whose *pays réel* lies outside their own borders, it will be a crucial problem. When much of the available disposable funds come from foreign loans, investments or grants, and when foreign cadres carry out a vital administrative, technical and sometimes even military function, the maintenance of good relations with the particular 'donor' country or countries concerned may well be a determining factor in political survival after the coup.

Recognition, he points out, is generally granted to illegitimate governments after a polite interval, if there are convincing assurances that they will continue with the traditional pattern of foreign relations. Ghana, of course, was expected to *reverse* Nkrumah's pattern of international relations; and this was promptly done. Technicians and experts from socialist states were sent packing, though there was later a public admission that the expulsion of Russian technicians had affected the fishing industry,[37] the Cuban embassy was shut down; a clutch of policy statements made all the agreeable noises. 'Far more important than these declarations is the considerable diplomatic activity which will take place after the coup (and sometimes even before it),' Luttwak adds. 'After the necessary exchange of information and assurances the new government will usually be recognized. . . . Diplomatic recognition is one of the elements in the general process of establishing the authority of the new government;

until this is achieved, we will have to rely on the brittle instruments of physical coercion, and our position will be vulnerable to many threats – including that of coup d'état.'

When it came to diplomatic activity immediately after the coup, the schedule of the French ambassador to Ghana was especially revealing, as he went into quick conclave with representatives of the former French colonies on Ghana's borders. Relations between France and Ghana were sour, as were Ghanaian relations with the Ivory Coast, Togo, Upper Volta and Niger. One of the first rounds in the NLC's intensive diplomatic activity was to clinch new relationships with these immediate neighbours.

The British were disconcerted by the coup. Its political direction suited them perfectly, but they were not expecting it to happen when it did. 'It seems clear from the British reaction to the military take-overs in Nigeria and Ghana – Wilson's instruction to George Wigg to "shake up" the intelligence services – that the appropriate sections in the British embassies in Lagos and Accra were tailing badly behind events or failing to evaluate correctly the information at their disposal,' wrote Roger Murray.[38] When it came to diplomatic recognition, Britain had a problem. Nothing, it was felt in Whitehall, would be clumsier than if a number of 'white states in the group categorized neo-colonial by Nkrumah' were seen to be giving Ghana 'a possessive bear hug or a paternal pat on the head'.[39] It was deemed wiser to wait until a number of African states had taken a decision, so that governments in Europe and other continents should not appear to be trying to influence the course of events in Africa by pressure from outside. Kenya and Tanzania had, after all, walked out of the OAU conference in Addis Ababa in protest against the seating of the Ankrah government delegation; and the United Arab Republic, Mali and Tanzania announced their support for Nkrumah. Britain announced its recognition of the new Ghana government on 5 March. By then a number of African countries had done so: Liberia, Nigeria, Tunisia, the Ivory Coast, Malagasy, Togo, Gambia, Niger and Senegal. After the recognition by Britain, the NLC restored the diplomatic relations which had been severed over Rhodesia.

The first European power to recognize the NLC government was West Germany. Among the Western powers, West Germany's relief was said[40] to be the greatest when the coup succeeded. West Germany had grown convinced that its position was being weakened by the growth in trade between East Germany and Ghana.

Diplomatic recognition was followed by the phase of gift-giving. The NLC begging bowls were held out, and all charity was received with obsequious gratitude. West Germany sent a batch of sixteen pairs of spectacles (additional pairs followed at various times) for some of the released detainees. Britain shipped out a £7,000 consignment of pharmaceutical drugs. Powdered milk was flown in from the United States for distribution to released detainees, and NLC members went personally to receive it at the airport. US food consignments under the PL 480 agreement, which had been refused Nkrumah, were authorized in March, less than a month after the coup, and bags of yellow corn arrived at Tema harbour. An astute US gift – after appeals to Britain had gone unheard, and had provoked NLC expressions of disappointment that Ghana's old ally was lagging in generosity – was equipment and supplies for the army; the heroes were seen in the green gabardine and baseball-type caps of the US forces, until more traditional supplies were located. The American presence was very visible at Accra in generously staffed embassy and US AID offices; in an expanded military mission which paid close attention to developments inside the Ghanaian army; in 'academic' and business probes.[41] US AID offered to supply a US army 'crash programme designer' among other things.[42]

Economic sluices, previously closed, suddenly opened again. Commercial credit that had dried up gushed anew. British businessmen with Ghanaian interests were fluent in their praise of the change. Major-General Sir Edward Spears – who happened to be chairman of the Ashanti Goldfield Corporation – headed a British mission to Ghana and pleaded with the West, especially Britain and the United States, to help the NLC: 'They are carrying too heavy a weight. They are very devoted people who need help.'[43] By the sixth week after the coup, West

Germany had negotiated a new twenty-year loan, half of which would be used to finance the purchase of essential commodities from West Germany.* Seven weeks after the army–police take-over, the price of cocoa began to rise on the world market. By the end of 1968 it was four times higher than it had been in mid-1965.† (The price paid to Ghana's farmers went up, too.) The British government loan to the Volta project had been a tied loan, with interest, and Nkrumah had been unable to have its terms amended; after the coup, the loan was converted into an interest-free, untied loan.

Ghana had done all the right things. General Ankrah announced that the Seven Year Plan was abandoned, and that 'no private enterprise would be forced to accept government participation'.[44] NLC vice-chairman Harlley went on several tours of West Germany; and during one of these, he invited the Krupp group to take part in development projects, discussed the training of Ghana policemen in Germany, and the building of ships for the Volta lake. International Confederation of Trade Union advisers were rapidly on the spot to help Ghana's trade-union movement, and West Germany's Friedrich-Ebert Foundation seconded one of their staff to the Ghana TUC.

The World Bank and the International Monetary Fund were in close and solicitous attendance. No sooner was Nkrumah toppled than the IMF gave immediate aid totalling almost

*In December 1966 a technical and economic cooperation agreement was concluded between Ghana and Germany, and in the summer of 1967 Germany made available a credit of 25 million marks for the purchase of urgent commodities, plus infrastructure projects.

†The movements of the cocoa price in the months immediately before and after the Ghana coup d'état are interesting, though not as significant as some might suspect. For most of 1964 the price per cwt dropped dramatically, reaching 100*s.* by July, and then beginning to slowly rise in the second half of 1965 and the first months of 1966, as follows:

December	1965	170*s.*
January	1966	180*s.*
February	1966	177*s.*
March	1966	184*s.*
April	1966	201*s.*

The price continued to rise and fall somewhat during the rest of 1966 and 1967, but by the end of 1968 had risen astronomically to 480*s.* by the end of that year, then declining somewhat in 1969 to 420*s.* or thereabouts.

£20 million in standby facilities and other drawings. By the end of 1968 Ghana had received over $100 million from the IMF, of which nearly $85 million were obtained after April 1966, in support of the 'stabilization' programme pursued by the NLC. From July 1966 the Fund stationed a resident representative in the country to advise the government on monetary, fiscal and balance of payments policies. An IMF fiscal team was also in attendance to advise an overall review of tax structure and policy. In the three years after the coup, the IMF's views were crucial in influencing creditor countries to accept a postponement of Ghana's debt repayment obligations. The Fund convened and chaired the meetings at which the representatives of the major aid-giving countries and international bodies were present; it was the first time in the Fund's history that it had convened such meetings. The austere conditions imposed by the IMF – like the drastic reduction of government spending in the July 1966 budget – were accepted by the NLC without demur; in return the IMF and the creditor nations staggered debt repayment terms.

Ghana was back in the fold. 'The soldier-policeman government has greatly impressed the International Monetary Fund,' wrote Russell Warren Howe.[45] 'The probability is that Ghana in the next year or so will be a shining example of democracy. It must avoid the danger of presenting an image of chaos and irresolution which would make investors hesitate. . . .' Mr Julian Amery of Britain's Conservative Party pointed out that Ghana was the only country apart from Indonesia where 'a pro-Soviet regime had been overthrown and replaced by one friendly to the West. . . . Ghana is surely one of the countries where, within her limited means, Britain should reinforce success.'[46]

The effects of the coup d'état were threefold. First, it took Ghana back to the political position of several decades earlier and installed in power – or used for political ballast – those whom Nkrumah and the CPP had beaten at the polls; thus the social groups which had expected to inherit office after the colonial withdrawal finally did so, with the help of the police and the army. Secondly, the coup put the running of Ghana into the hands of technocrats: army men, but above all civil servants who saw Ghana's economic problems and all crises of underdevelopment in terms of technical 'efficiency'. This in practice constituted an unquestioning deference to the patterns laid down by outside creditors, economic interests and their 'experts'. Finally, between them these forces of conservative politics, technocracy and foreign capital inaugurated a rapid process of dismantling all attempts, whether failing or successful, to introduce state-owned or socialist aspects into the economy. Private enterprise was embraced like a long-lost lover. No penance was too extreme for a Ghana that had forsaken it. Everything that Nkrumah had tried was denounced and damned: anything that outside powers or foreign capital proposed was gospel. It followed automatically that in the rearrangement of the economy and the political order, the generation and the social forces that had put the CPP into office were to be penalized.

Post-Nkrumah Ghana, wrote Irving G. Markowitz[47] 'was an outstanding example of "technocracy-capitalism", a political prototype that is of newly increasing significance, particularly in the aftermath of the various recent world-wide military coups d'état'. In their search for a social base in Ghana the technocrats aligned with the members of the liberal professions and commercial élites. Ghana's new policy-makers were mostly products either of Sandhurst and Camberley, Hendon Police College, or of Harvard, the London School of Economics, Cambridge and other British or American universities. All but one of the members of the NLC were army or police force careerists who had risen through the ranks, beginning as privates or police constables; none of the officers had received a university education, but they immediately called on those, especially in the civil service, who had. Straight after the coup, at the army's request, the principal secretaries took sole charge of the ministries and the provincial administrations. On their own volition, eight of the most prominent members of the civil service had early issued a statement in support of the new regime.[48] Headed by Emmanuel Omaboe, who had been Nkrumah's chief economic tactician of the NLC, the Ghanaian civil service showed its rubbery, malleable shape. The bureaucrats exhibited a resilience and endurance under two antagonistic regimes which the politicians could never hope to equal, for the civil service on which the NLC fell back was left virtually unscathed by the post-coup probes and shuffles of office. Chiefs and judges were an exception; many elevated by Nkrumah were in large measure deposed or replaced by the NLC. For them and for the leading CPP politicians, the see-saw tipped the other way up.

From the day that the NLC took power, Omaboe with advisers took the country's major economic decisions. He was appointed chairman of the National Economic Committee, composed of seven civil servants and bank officials, ranging in age from thirty-five to forty-one,* who brought all their pragmatic skill into prompt, even precipitate, action to reassure Ghana's creditors. The nine regions of Ghana were headed by military or police officers in conjunction with regional administrative officers. Administrative patterns reverted to bygone colonial days, as in Accra old colonial precedents were thumbed through when instructions for local officials had to be formulated. Once again the chieftaincy system came to be talked about with especial reverence. Chieftaincy, said Harlley, is an essential element in Ghana's national life.[49] It began to look as though the 'natural' rulers, whom even the colonial system had begun to dispense with in self-government formulae, would be called on to fill the political vacuum.

Only in June, in their fourth month of office, did the eight members of the NLC divide ministerial responsibility among themselves.[50] The following month the NLC appointed a Political Committee of twenty-theee members. The body was virtually a *Who's Who* of the old NLM and United Party, the opposition to Nkrumah which had been trounced at the polls a decade earlier. These men, said General Ankrah in answer to

*Other members of Omaboe's economic team included Mr Albert Adamako, the governor of the Bank of Ghana, a barrister and graduate of Cambridge; Mr Kwaku Gyasi-Twum, a product of King's College, Durham, principal secretary in the Ministry of Finance at one time; Mr Kew Arkaah, a graduate of Harvard, a senior Mobil executive before he joined the civil service; and another Harvard product, Mr B. K. Mensah, who studied at the Economic Development Institute of the World Bank. (Biographical details from *West Africa*, 12 March 1967, pp. 287–8, 'Ghana's Rescue Team'.)

criticism, had been chosen 'because they are men who have the right sort of experience to sound out the people'.[51] Chairman of the Political Committee was Mr Justice Akufo-Addo, a former Supreme Court judge. Its members included Dr Kofi Busia, formerly leader-in-exile of the opposition, and all the well-known names from the yester-year of United Party politics: R. R. Amponsah, Joseph Appiah, William Ofori Atta, S. D. Dombo of the former Northern Peoples' Party, which had gone into opposition to the CPP in the North, and Modesto K. Apaloo. No member of the Political Committee had formerly been associated with the CPP except for TUC secretary-general B. A. Bentum, who crossed the floor theatrically, and J. A. Braimah, who had been an early member of the CPP Cabinet but who had been involved in a matter of corruption, had resigned from the CPP and become a significant figure in the opposition. When the political Committee was enlarged towards the end of the year, its additional members included the managing director of Lever Bros in Ghana. (Two of the young technocrats of the Economic Committee were former executives of Mobil and the United Africa Company. Prominent businessmen were also appointed to the board of directors of the Ghana National Trading Corporation, and of the State Hotels Corporation.)

While the Economic and Political Committees worked supposedly side by side, the Political Committee was being rapidly disillusioned to discover that the decisions taken by the Economic Committee prejudged, or rendered unworkable, some of their own guidelines. Policy was in fact steered by one man, Emmanuel Omaboe, who was the country's principal representative in talks with Ghana's creditors, and whose decisions on the rescheduling of debt payments – before Ghana had the opportunity to consider whether these were wise in the long term – conditioned most other significant issues of policy.

The old UP leadership was not well pleased at the retention in office of prominent civil servants. Government by civil servants, complained aspirant politicians, was government by an anonymous body, by the faceless; and under this form of government there was no opportunity for the redress of grievance.[52] The civil servants, no less than judges and academics, had been corrupt or CPP flunkies, they complained, and their record under the Nkrumah regime should be investigated. It was this pressure, with the counter-coup led by Lieutenant Arthur in April 1967 (which was abortive, but which resulted in the death of General Kotoka), and the advice of Mr Adu, the Commonwealth Secretary, that led to a change in July 1967. The principal secretaries in charge of the ministries were displaced by civilian commissioners; and an Executive Council was created from the seven remaining members of the NLC (the vacancy left by Kotoka's death was not filled), together with the civilian commissioners. In Nigeria it had been the conflict in Biafra that had led to the inclusion of civilians in government; in Ghana it was mainly the crisis caused by the abortive coup. Most of the commissioners were relatively young technocrats, from the generation of the élite that came after the United Party.[53] In his speech of appointment, General Ankrah referred to them as 'private gentlemen'.[54] The NLC also created the National Advisory Committee of thirty-one members, which replaced the Political Committee and which included the fourteen newly appointed commissioners and the members of the Political Committee.[55] The politicians were steadily getting further through the door. When finally it was opened to them, it was for a view of politics that, once again as in the old colonial days, were the 'virtually exclusive preoccupation of various personalities and internal factions among the new governing elites',[56] who were committed to the orthodox economic policies prompted by foreign advisers.

Hotfoot to Ghana in the year of the coup, to advise on the restructuring of the economy, came a team of economists from Harvard University. Known as the Development Advisory Service of the Center for International Affairs, it was under the direction of Dr Gustave F. Papanek, who had done similar duty in post-coup Indonesia. (Harvard had been involved in similar advisory capacities in Iran and several Latin American countries.) The United States was delighted with the turn of events in Ghana, wrote Papanek. 'I was anxious to provide strong support for the new government.'[57] Several of the Papanek confidential reports were 'liberated' in 1969, during a student raid on Harvard University Hall; and xeroxed copies were 'deposited by an unknown person' at the office of *The Old Mole* in Boston, Massachusetts, to be published subsequently in a special supplement.[58] These revealed that some people inside and outside the Harvard advisory group had regarded as unfortunate the group's heavy engagement in the preparation of Ghana's post-coup two-year plan; but Papanek reminded them that this 'provided an excellent device to get the advisers into the major problems of the economy, and to give them access to people, documents and ideas that will be invaluable to them later on'. Since the IMF Resident Representative, 'who has gained a unique position in Ghana', was moving on (this during 1965), the Harvard Group would be in an excellent position to move actively into work on crucial, immediate problems of the Ghanaian economy. 'The government,' he observed in his first report, written on 13 December 1966, 'is remarkably receptive to foreign advisers.' It was, after all, such an interesting set of problems: 'an economy that had gone far towards collectivation and centralization and which is now reversing the process to some extent'.[59]

The Papanek reports should be allowed their full say on several issues. On Ghana's debts, which 'increased her vulnerability to foreign pressure', and their rescheduling:

> At the time of Nkrumah's overthrow it might have been possible to repudiate, or at least to scale down, many of the more doubtful debts. The Government decided against this course, partly out of a sense of responsibility and obligation ('a gentleman does not welsh on debt') and partly under strong pressure from the creditors. *Some countries threatened to cut off all aid and all export credit guarantees if the debt were not fully honoured.* Since Ghana had no foreign exchange reserves and imported on short term credit, the failure to guarantee this credit might have meant interruption in imports, perhaps for six months [my emphasis].[60]

Negotations with the creditors proved exceedingly tough, Papanek showed:

> The US, delighted with the turn of events in Ghana, was anxious to provide strong support to the new government, but since it is an

insignificant creditor, it played a relatively modest role in these discussions. Of the major creditors the Dutch have proved flexible, but both the Germans and the British were tough and intransigent, arguing that they did not want to create a *dangerous precedent for negotiations with the Indonesians, the Indians, the Turks and others* [my emphasis].[61]

By 1968 Ghana faced the need for another round of debt renegotiation, hardly a year after the previous round.

Ghana's negotiation position was a difficult one, given the foreign exchange problems of its principal creditor, the UK; the predatory instincts of the second largest creditor, a private contractor named Drevici; and the tough position taken by such leading creditors as Germany and Japan, usually represented by their banking and not their foreign policy or foreign aid fraternity. The outcome will depend in part on the credibility of the implied Ghanaian threat to hand the deadlocked negotiations to a politically elected civilian government or to declare its inability to meet all of its debts on schedule. The Ghanaians are in a better position than in the past to use the latter threat, since Ghana has established its good faith servicing its debts since Nkrumah's overthrow and since its foreign exchange position is somewhat better than at the time of the coup . . . Ghana's position would be further strengthened if it could count on some support from the US, the IMF and the IBRD, but the position of all three has been equivocal. The US has a strong interest in favorable debt renegotiations, especially since US aid on a net basis goes essentially to pay off Ghana's old debts to its US and European creditors and it has urged the creditors to be cooperative and sensible. Its position, however, has been voiced very softly. *Directly and indirectly, through its influence in the IMF and IBRD, the US has concentrated not on pressing the creditors, but Ghana, urging it not to use the implied threat of default.* The US has therefore weakened the creditability of the major bargaining threat which Ghana holds. . . . The IMF has played a similar role, urging the creditors to be cooperative and sensible, but has been unwilling to set the example by stretching out its own debt. The IBRD has been of minor importance in these discussions. *All three (international bodies) point to their statutory requirements not to provide support to countries that default on loans* [my emphasis].[62]

By the second half of 1968, the Papanek reports were warning:

Ghana will become a net exporter of capital to the developed countries. This incongruous situation would exist despite substantial net aid from the United States.... *In other words, Ghana would be a supplier of capital to the UK and some European countries* [my emphasis].[63]

Omaboe was himself having second thoughts by 1967, when the second round of IMF-convened meetings of creditors took place. 'It should be recognized that our economy cannot perpetually be run at the mercy of external balance of payments support,' he said.[64]

When in the middle of 1966 the NLC's first budget was placed before the country, it was the recipe that the IMF had long sought to prescribe for Ghana, full of a strong dose of orthodox classical economics. Government expenditure was to be financed only from revenue available, and the private sector was to be the mainspring of the country's progress.* General Ankrah told the country that the NLC rejected 'any purely theoretical division between the public and private sectors'[65] and was concerned only with the 'best' use of resources. Four major sectors of the economy would be recognized: private; joint private and government; government; and the cooperative. Open to both Ghanaians and non-Ghanaians to assume an increasingly larger share, the private sector would remain the largest both by numbers of persons engaged and by gross output. Active state participation was to be limited to certain basic and key projects. No private enterprise would be forced to accept government participation. To attract foreign capital, tax exemptions were offered for three years, and tax relief for up to ten years, while the repatriation of profits and capital was guaranteed. As for the state-owned and run projects, they were to be turned over to private ownership as rapidly as possible.

The Papanek reports reveal that the NLC had received conflicting advice on the state enterprises and the state farms.[66] (By 1966 there were fifty state-owned and twelve joint state–private enterprises in Ghana.) The initial inclination was simply to sell

* See Kportufe Agama's review of the budget, *Legon Observer*, 30 August 1966: 'The Budget leaves much, far too much, to the private sector.... Thus we have the prospect of the economy's growth, and the welfare of Ghanaians ... placed largely in the hands of those who appear unlikely to act with the enthusiasm which the needs of the country require ...' It was a budget which 'left too much to chance'.

off the state enterprises to foreign companies. But there were second thoughts; although 'the American Ambassador still seems to be pushing for that solution, which I consider completely unrealistic'.[67] Professor Arthur Lewis had pointed out that selling most of the enterprises to foreign companies could be politically disastrous. A UN advisory team, headed by an Egyptian, recommended that the government retain most of the enterprises and place them under highly centralized management. The government wavered. Decisions on a set of policies towards the public sector constituted 'clearly one of the major challenges that still face the government'. Papanek's own view was that the sale of a number of state enterprises 'should provide an excellent opportunity to develop a group of Ghanaian industrial entrepreneurs'.[68] This is the road that Ghana took.

Many of the state enterprises had been poorly conceived, badly sited and hit by shortages of raw materials in the import control chaos. Some had operated at heavy losses because they had been overburdened with unskilled and unqualified personnel. But while some had been steady liabilities to the state, others had shown promising profits, and some looked[69] as though the worst years were over, and they would soon begin to make profits. None of this was of any account to the NLC. The more profitable the enterprise, the keener the NLC appeared to sell it to private enterprise. The state bakery corporation had made a profit, and was one of the first enterprises to be sold to private buyers. The state laundry corporation had made a profit over five years and was 'much in demand'; it was sold to private capital. The paints corporation at Tema was doing well and was reported to be a highly profitable venture; the NLC decided that private investors should be invited to participate. The tyre-making factory was sold out to private enterprise, as was the Sekondi boat-building industry. Among the bidders were Firestone, Associated Portland Cement, Norway Cement Export and Cine of France. Several virtual hand-overs to foreign companies – the Abbott–Ghana agreement over the pharmaceutical factory, which was cancelled when the scandalous terms became known; the handing over of Accra's two largest hotels to Intercontinental Hotels Corporation, USA; the deals with Anglo-

American finance over 200,000 acres on the Accra plains; and, finally, the take-over of the Ashanti Gold Mines by Lonrho – caused storms of protest that the NLC was disposing of Ghanaian national assets with total disregard for the consequences to the economy.[70]

Initially, in shifting over to great reliance on the major private sector, the Papanek reports disclosed, 'it appeared that foreign businessmen would be the major beneficiaries. To correct this dangerous political consequence, the government opted for Ghanaization.'[71] This had several aspects. A back-dated decree was promulgated for the promotion of Ghanaian business enterprises at the expense of 'foreigners', mainly Lebanese and Syrians, in small-scale undertakings. Small businesses, taxi services or workshops with staffs of fewer than thirty had a period of five years in which to train Ghanaians, and three years within which to ensure that half their capital was sold to Ghanaians. Certain reserve industries with annual retail sales of a prescribed sum had to have Ghanaian staffs by 1970.[72] To assist Ghanaians to enter into joint ventures with foreign investors, it was decided that the benefits of the Capital Investment Act would only be given to enterprises where a certain amount of the capital was owned by Ghanaians.[73] The Bank of Ghana launched schemes to help indigenous businessmen with domestic credit insurance, and a special fund was launched, with the assistance of the US PL 480, to boost these entrepreneurs.[74] The budget provided tax relief for enterprises wholly owned by Ghanaians. West Germany loaned an expert to the National Investment Bank of Ghana, which was primarily concerned with promoting small and medium-sized industries.[75] The policy was to kick into being an indigenous ownership class and commercial bourgeoisie to take their place alongside the technocrats and professionals as the mainstay of a conservative political system and a dependent economy. With the commanding heights of the Ghanaian economy in the hands of either foreign companies or a propertied, respectable middle class, the country could be considered 'safe' for the West.

Nowhere perhaps as much as in the post-coup schemes for the handling of Ghana's cocoa crop did the rapture for private enterprise so blatantly turn the clock of the economy back. One of the NLC's numerous commissions of inquiry[76] was instructed to investigate the local purchasing of cocoa. Under the CPP government, the United Ghana Farmers' Cooperative Council (UGFCC) had been the sole licensed buying agent for the Cocoa Marketing Board. The Commission heard farmers' objections to the UGFCC: some on the grounds that politics was mixed with business (the UGFCC was said to favour CPP-supporting farmers); others on the irregularities committed by UGFCC employees in the weighing, handling and purchasing of the crop at buying stations. Yet the Commission was emphatic that the UGFCC had achieved its main objective of moving the nation's increasing cocoa crop from the rural areas to the ports for shipment to overseas markets; that the quality of the cocoa had improved from 1961–6; and that 90 per cent of the cocoa bought up-country was grade one quality, 'an excellent performance by any standard'.[77] However, the farmers who appeared before the Commission were insistent that this system of cocoa handling be demolished; and to this the Commission and the NLC acceded. There followed the astonishing spectacle of the Ghana government inviting back into the field expatriate firms like Cadburys, SCOA, CFAO, the UAC and others which had handled the trade in the 1950s, and encountering refusal. Cadbury Brothers declared: 'We think it would be a retrograde step if expatriate organizations were to become licensed buying agents of the Cocoa Marketing Board on the same basis and relationship as existed formerly.'[78] CFAO replied that it believed 'more efficiency could be achieved at a lesser cost, through monopoly buying by a properly organized and controlled national organization'.[79] Since the expatriate firms were clearly not interested in entering a field that they had left a decade earlier, the Cocoa Marketing Board decided to license as agent any Ghanaian who could finance and handle the purchase of a minimum tonnage of cocoa annually. The field was thrown wide open for the cocoa farmers themselves to become cocoa-brokers and – like the commercial bourgeoisie that was being so assiduously nurtured – to amass capital for entrepreneurship. It was, after all, a government very solicitous towards the cocoa producers, who received two increases in the price paid for cocoa during the NLC's first two years of office.[80] The cocoa farmers and emergent businessmen were to be an important political basis of the new Ghana.

The entry of the army into government not only rearranged the political constituents of power, but also spread the distribution of benefits very differently. The better-off were generally the favoured. The exemption limit of taxable income was raised. The CPP tax on property was abolished, as was the tax paid by cocoa farmers on income from the sale of cocoa. On the other hand, the NLC instituted a charge for school textbooks, while government hospitals and clinics levied charges for drugs and dressings. (To all except civil servants, which prompted an irate letter to the press: 'Did the armed forces fight to liberate civil servants alone?')[81] Devaluation, ordered by the IMF, had lowered salaries; but a commission into the public service subsequently recommended increased scales of remuneration for all government employees.[82] At the other end of the scale, the shutting down of several state enterprises and the retrenchment of the Workers' Brigade created a large force of unemployed. The NLC retrenched 63,000 workers in under two years, the great majority of them (all except 9,000) from the public sector, and most of them construction workers and labourers.[83] The CPP era had set afoot, though it had failed to consolidate, a social and economic revolution in the creation of jobs and opportunity beyond the exclusive ranks of the educated and the propertied. The NLC set out to build a social and economic base of the 'respectable', the propertied and the 'stable' elements of élite society. The early constitutional proposals framed by the committee under the chairmanship of the Chief Justice, Mr Edward Akufo-Addo, produced an electoral system heavily weighted against the age and social generation that had been Nkrumah's strongest supporters. It set the age limit for the vote at twenty-five, in a country where the age group fifteen to twenty-five is larger than any other; it gave extraordinary powers to a president who had to be at least fifty years old; it severely limited the powers of Parliament, and made the judiciary ubiquitous in sensitive executive areas. It was to be government by gerontocracy, the critics taunted. Power was to be allocated to the so-called natural estates of the realm, an ageing and conservative president, the judges and the chiefs; but there was 'an acute contradiction between this distribution of power in political society'[84] and a Ghana numerically dominated by school-leavers and the unemployed, junior civil servants, school teachers and young clerks, and the poor of the rural areas. During the protracted debate on the constitution, there were signs that the NLC itself was divided on the issue of the promised return to civilian rule. General Ankrah seemed in no hurry to relinquish office; seemed, indeed, to be developing political ambitions. On the other hand, Colonel Afrifa, close to Ashanti political aspirations and Dr Busia in particular, was known to have stormed out of NLC proceedings more than once in protest against the slow staging of the return to politics. When the NLC suddenly brought forward the date for the lifting of the ban on political parties, this was said to be not unconnected with signs that Colonel Afrifa had been renewing contacts with the company commanders of his old battalion, the 5th at Tamale. Prolonged tenure of government was not cementing, but chipping away NLC and army solidarity. There had been a nasty scare only fourteen months after the NLC installed itself, when two junior officers, commanding no more than 120 men, had almost seized power. This was the abortive coup d'état led by Lieutenant Arthur in April 1967.

THE COUNTER-COUP THAT FAILED

During the first months of 1967 prominent Ghanaians were receiving cyclostyled sheets from the League of Young Army Officers, alleging corruption in the NLC, denouncing the record of the new rulers, and demanding a change. The League's members, and any direct connexion with CPP forces within or outside Ghana, were never identified. But certainly inside the army there was a simmering resentment at the police share of NLC power; and, inside the junior officer corps, indignation at the uneven rewards doled out to army men after the 1966 coup. The Nigeria army officers who staged a coup had not promoted themselves, it was said; those in Ghana responsible for 24

February should have been given medals for meritorious service, but not promotion.

In the officers' mess of B squadron of the Reconnaissance regiment based at Ho in Eastern Ghana, feeling rose high one evening, when an officer sent from headquarters to umpire exercises described how army promotion examinations were made especially tough so that those on the top would remain there. There was some talk about the number of colonels in the Ghanaian army. 'I said six,' said young Lieutenant Arthur, 'but Colonel Odonkor, the officer from headquarters, said, "There are twelve full colonels in the army." They counted, and got exactly twelve names.' Odonkor added, 'You can see that the top is very very heavy. These people are selfish, all of them.' Second Lieutenant Collison added: 'I think they just add the pip if they feel like it.' From that day on, twenty-six-year-old Lieutenant Sam Arthur told subsequent court hearings, 'I began to develop a hatred for all senior officers, especially the colonels and above.' NLC members, mess talk said, were feathering their nests and had renounced the aims for which 24 February had been staged.

On 4 April Lieutenant Arthur learned that he had failed his promotion examination. Six days later, he found himself in temporary command of the garrison. The idea of staging a coup came to him as he occupied the commanding officer's chair. 'As soon as I breathed the air of importance . . . the first thing which came into my mind was to see if it would be possible to stage a coup with the resources I had.' He had read about the attempt in the Sudan by a second lieutenant; he would be the first lieutenant in Africa to lead a coup. He laid his plans in less than a week. As alternative to government by the NLC, he considered a chief justice, the chancellor of the university and some senior civil servants; then he decided that there were not enough honest civilians in the country. The alternative was a new military junta. 'I counted out all colonels and above, because I knew in the coup I would eliminate them.' One officer was excluded because he was too womanish; another, because his mode of speaking did not befit a head of state. Three candidates were chosen although they were not, apparently, told; and they strenuously – and two of the three, successfully – denied complicity when arrested. They were Lieutenant-Colonel Assassie of the Ghana Parachute battalion, Major S. M. Asante of the Infantry and Major R. A. Achaab, commander of the Recce squadron in Accra. (The latter was court-martialled and jailed.) Lieutenant Arthur had to strike before 21 April because on that day the permanent garrison commander was due to arrive from Reconnaissance headquarters to take his place. On the night of 6 April 1967, he took advantage of an operation in search of armed smugglers near the Togo border to re-route his squadron to Accra. He detailed Lieutenant Moses Yeboah to capture Flagstaff House, and arrest General Kotoka; he sent a sergeant to seize the radio station, and another to the airport; and he detailed Second Lieutenant Oseo Poku to take the Castle and General Ankrah. He claimed an instruction from the commander of the Armoured Reconnaissance squadron, Major Achaab, to enlist the detachment in a coup being organized by the Ghana army. When the unit reached the capital in light armoured cars, it split into four contingents and proceeded to stage a take-over according to the Afrifa–Kotoka pattern of the previous year. Two hours after the start of the operation, Lieutenant Arthur broadcast the displacement of the NLC by the three-officer junta he had chosen. General Ankrah narrowly escaped from the Castle which, after two hours, was virtually abandoned to the coup-makers. General Kotoka was fatally shot in the attack on Flagstaff House. No member of the NLC or the army command emerged to rally forces for a counter-attack; loyal forces seemed to have faded into nothing. Though the firing at the Castle started some time before the attack on Flagstaff House, no warning was sounded and no general alert ordered. When the coup finally petered out in mid-morning, it was not from any counter-attack by government forces, but from the deficiencies of the coup-makers themselves. The Ho units began to run out of ammunition, and Lieutenant Arthur, trying to win over senior officers in Burma camp, found himself tricked or talked out of his bid for control at a strange conference of the coup-makers and the Accra commander. Only then did troops arrive to arrest the mutineers.[85]

A military tribunal, assembled with the utmost dispatch, heard Lieutenant Arthur insist that he was the sole architect of the coup. He had divulged its aim to his two young collaborators, Yeboah and Poku, only when they were already on the road to Accra, he insisted. He was convinced that the NLC members had organized the February 1966 coup for their own selfish ends, and were amassing wealth and betraying the aims they had declared.

He singled out the promotion of Brigadier Afrifa. 'Who knows we shall soon have field marshals in Ghana?' he asked. He criticized the NLC for the promotion of semi-literates as chairmen of regional administrative committees. He regarded the NLC as an illegal government, which was not constitutionally elected by the people. The only difference between his own coup attempt and the 24 February revolution was that his had failed, while the February one had succeeded, Arthur told the court. If his coup had been successful, the same people who had hailed the 24 February coup would have hailed him, too. 'A coup becomes legal when it succeeds, but when it fails it becomes unlawful.' Arthur and Yeboah, who had shot General Kotoka, were sentenced to death, and Poku to thirty years' imprisonment. The NLC ordered a public execution, and a crowd of some 20,000 – with children among them – surged round the Teshie firing range to watch this edifying spectacle of revenge.

How had so small a force almost taken Accra? And what explained the inadequacy of the NLC security apparatus, or the army paralysis during the attack itself? Reports of restlessness brewing at Ho – and at Tamale in the north where Afrifa, who happened to be on the spot, took prompt control during the scare of the counter-coup – seemed to have been lodged with military intelligence, but there discounted. Some said it was sheer bungling; others murmured dark hints of favouritism. Whatever the cause, the Recce squadron managed to travel from Ho to Accra without being detected by military intelligence. (After the Arthur attempt, gates were erected on the roads leading to Accra.) More serious still, when the alert was sounded – Ankrah had apparently managed to telephone from the Castle at an early stage of the firing there – there was no reaction from the army.

(One leading member of the command was said to have spent the dangerous hours in a wardrobe, another in a latrine.) Perhaps the NLC considered itself so popular that it had not bothered about security. But whatever the reason, it was a signal failure. Some heads had to roll. Those responsible for negligence and inefficiency would be removed, Harlley announced. Shortly afterwards, the army commander, Major-General C. C. Bruce, and the navy commander, Rear-Admiral D. A. Hansen, were appointed defence advisers to Ghana's missions in Washington and London respectively. They were transferred without detailed inquiry into their actions, or those of others, during the counter-coup, apparently in a fury on the part of General Ankrah that his fellow-Ga officers had shown such an absence of zeal in quelling a mutiny of which he would have been the principal victim. In the following months, disciplinary action was meted out to young officers and NCOs. Seven officers and close to 200 men were placed in custody. Some court martials ensued, but the procedures left a bitter taste in the military mouth. The privates were discharged from the army and the NCOs jailed, some with heavy sentences. Several officers were individually disciplined, some were sentenced to imprisonment and discharged with disgrace from the armed forces. Others were not given hearings but were simply reduced in rank. The punitive action was haphazard, and rumour was rife that those who got off lightly must have enjoyed protection in high places. If some sort of rough army justice was being done, it was not seen to be justice; and if the abortive coup was prompted by a sense of injury felt by young officers at the hands of the high and mighty command, its aftermath inflamed the injury even more.

The counter-coup and the slap-happy punitive actions in its train illuminated the essential dilemma of an army that has come to power through a coup d'état. When would reward flow from the usurpation of power by army officers; and when punishment? Arthur put his finger on the issue during his court martial: a coup becomes legal when it succeeds; but when it fails it is unlawful. Yet how was the soldier to know whether to obey the order of an officer? This was the dilemma before Corporal Joseph Roland Donkor, who spent the hours of the counter-coup hiding from his company engaged in taking Broadcast House. On the one hand, it was a dereliction of duty for any soldier not to obey his commanding officer; on the other hand, 'I never know if the order is right or wrong,' he pleaded at the court martial of nine NCOs from the disbanded Ho Recce squadron.[86] The prosecution insisted that any order to capture or kill the head of government and commander-in-chief of the army had to be illegal. But the memory of the NLC's rise to power was far too fresh for that to be conclusive. The solution was for a soldier to query the order of the officer with the counter 'Who says so, and why?' But the beginnings of army scepticism meant the end of army discipline, not to say morale; and the entire army knew that. What rapport was left between officers and men, or between senior and junior officers, after the 1966 events, and the grumbles about self-promotion, slumped sharply after 1967; and the army was left pondering the very opposite rewards possible for those who seize government.

It remained for Ankrah to cite yet another consequence of the 1967 events. Rumours had reached armed force headquarters, he said, that the insurrection led by Arthur had been planned by Ashantis and Fantis against the Gas and the Ewes. This was a 'wicked rumour which was absolutely untrue'. The armed forces were a cross-section of all tribes in Ghana. It so happened that the three officers killed in the counter-coup were all Ewe. That was true enough; yet only one year after the NLC had installed itself, there was a growing tendency to put a tribal complexion on most events, and the Arthur coup was no exception.

The feeling in the army that promotion and punishment were not impartial, but precipitate and partisan, also spread to the command. Bruce and Hansen had been removed, but others who could equally have been held responsible for army security lapses were conspicuously left untouched. When Bruce and Hansen were posted to their missions abroad, two of Ghana's three defence chiefs had been displaced. In December 1968 it was the turn of Air Marshal Michael Otu. He was suddenly dismissed from his command, detained and accused of plotting the overthrow of the NLC and the return of Nkrumah. Accused with him was his aide, Naval Lieutenant Kwapong. Otu was charged with having met an executive member of the London branch of the CPP while on a visit to Britain in December 1966; and the seizure of two Russian fishing trawlers in Ghana's territorial waters some months earlier was linked with the Otu plot. Harlley chose to make the allegations against Otu and Kwapong at a press conference; consequently, when the Amissah Commission was appointed to inquire into the charges, Otu and Kwapong refused to answer questions, give evidence or cross-examine witnesses unless they were granted public trial. The commission carried on intermittently; but by October 1969 Otu and Kwapong had been reinstated in the armed forces.

Not long after Otu's removal, General Ankrah himself was ignominiously forced to resign his post as head of government. He left the Castle to the boos of servants and bystanders. He was replaced by Colonel, promoted Brigadier, Afrifa. General Ankrah, it emerged, had accepted sums from foreign businessmen for distribution to politicians, presumably so that they could organize a party around him which would further his presidential chances, largely built on Ga support. And, ironically, by the time that Ankrah came under fire in the NLC, he had himself helped remove his own support in the army, in the shape of Bruce and Hansen. Next came the dismissal from the NLC of yet another Ankrah supporter, the commissioner of police, Mr John Nunoo. It emerged that Nunoo, a Ga like Ankrah, and connected with moves to form a Ga-based political movement, felt that Ankrah's dismissal was intended, and served, to handicap the Ga people in the political stakes then opening. Nunoo charged Victor Owusu, former attorney-general but also a prominent Ashanti politician, with using the Ankrah dismissal to destroy the public image of his political opponents. Politics was barely launched – it was some weeks after the Ankrah and Nunoo dismissals that the ban on parties was lifted, and the elections were still a long time off – but NLC tendencies, despite the oft-repeated army avowals of neutrality, were already finding their place in civilian politics.

Increasingly in 1968 and 1969, both army and politics looked like polarizing along tribal or communal lines: something which even the most fervent critics of Nkrumah agree that he had banished from Ghana. Afrifa in the army and Busia of the old United Party shared Ashanti political aspirations. Harlley and Deku were close to Gbedemah and his fellow-Ewe politicians and business associates; and their political ambitions were strongly represented in the army command by a core of Ewe officers, well positioned at defence headquarters, in 1 Brigade and the navy.

NLC developments and the rising prominence of Ewe officers in the command should not have been significant in themselves. But as politics and parties began to be legalized after 1 May 1969, there was a fumbling paucity of policies and programmes; and with firm purpose absent, regional and local claims and alignments were likely to colour politics. There was a final crisis inside the army. Decree 345, published on 28 April 1969, permitted the revival of parties but disqualified several categories of people – in addition to the 152 disqualified from public office by a decree of February 1969 – from being founding members of a party or holding office in it. These included all who, at any time on or after July 1960, had been members of the CPP central committee or part of its top-level government and party apparatus. The decree disqualified Komla Gbedemah, the leading Ewe politician, and subsequently leader of the opposition in Ghana's new Parliament. Two days later Decree 347 displaced the earlier 345. It stated that only those who had held office on the eve of the coup d'état of 24 February 1966 were disqualified. Gbedemah was free to form a party and to campaign for office. Behind this *volte-face* lay a threat from a portion of the army, led by Ewe officers in Burma camp, to march on the NLC if it did not rapidly reverse the policy that excluded Gbedemah. The first decree had been signed by Afrifa alone; a subsequent decision of the NLC laid down that all decrees had to be the joint decision of all the members, and signed by them all. What army amity had existed was being exhausted by the claims of political competition in the country.

There were thus strong army reasons behind Ghana's return to civilian rule. On 30 September 1969 the NLC repealed the proclamation which had brought it into being; and at a handing-over-of-power ceremony on 1 October, Ghana returned to civilian rule. In the elections contested by five parties, the Progress Party led by Dr Busia, the successor in spirit of the old United Gold Coast Convention, had swept the board. Gbedemah's National Alliance of Liberals had triumphed in the Ewe areas, had been totally eclipsed in the Ashanti and other Akan-speaking areas, and formed the official opposition. The manifestos of the two parties had covered much the same ground in much the same way. There was a constitutional innovation in the shape of the Presidential Commission, which vested three members of the NLC with combined powers: Afrifa, Harlley and Major-General Ocran. Only Ocran retained his service post; Afrifa decided that he would not return to the army, and Harlley resigned his police appointment for the Presidential Commission.

The coup d'état of 1966 and the elections of 1969 had thus reversed the earlier election results of the independence years: but the army in Ghana, uniquely in Africa, had stepped down from the office it had seized, to make way for a constituent assembly, a Cabinet and all the accompanying procedures. There were perhaps two principal reasons. First, the army – and the army command and its advisers knew this well – was neither cohesive nor united: continuance in office between the pulls of regions, and politicians, and generations, seemed likely to tear the army itself apart. Secondly, Ghana's élitist politicians, denied once their heritage of office by Nkrumah and the CPP, were not going to let it happen again. Unlike Nigeria, these were politicians whose reputations had not been soiled in office or compromised by failure in government. They came to power with a fairly clean sheet, though to many it was too clean of programme and policy perspective to augur much in the way of solutions to Ghana's economic and political problems.

It was as though the African pre-independence days were starting all over again in Ghana. It was a plunge back to the political style of old-school politicians, resonant with the rhetoric of democracy and handsome in the trappings of Westminster. The intervening years in Africa had shown that such was only the shadow, not the substance, of what new but still dependent governments needed. One of Nkrumah's failures was that he did not succeed in keeping the tough, corrupt and demanding group intent on property and acquisition out of leading positions in the CPP and government; in Ghana today it is open season for this group, and for overseas private capital, only too interested in making use of this further chance. Nkrumah's government might have been a case of socialism badly manqué; but its successor regime, far from restoring the health of a dependent economy, has delivered it to the system responsible for the poverty and exploitation of all the Third World.

Part VI

Armies in Stalemate

We have today two soldiers at the head of state, that is two national citizens. We are in power as cadres not as military personnel. I do not see why it is necessary to give power back to civilians, there is no problem of military government.

Captain Raoul of Congo-Brazzaville, September 1968

All the African states in which the army has invaded government – and others where the army has not yet left the barracks, but could well do so under provocation – share an incipient state of social crisis. There is a general condition of coup fertility in Africa manifested in four main ways.

1. There is cumulative economic crisis, because political independence alone does not enable Africa to break through the vicious circle of backwardness and dependence which is the condition of colonialism. Some states are visibly and irremediably stagnant; others have some prospects of growth, though not of real development. African states strain to find jobs or opportunity for new entrants to the élite, let alone the vast mass of conspicuously poor. Government is the principal provider of employment, but also, therefore, the principal butt of discontent. Africa's already inflated bureaucracies are confronted by each secondary school and university graduation. There is a constant flow of contestants for the top positions and top salaries in a society growing far too slowly to absorb them.

2. Political crisis is endemic because the temporary and shallow unity of political movements in the pursuit of political independence broke down under the fierce contests for power. Political power is more than office in local council, parliament and cabinet; it is access to the key levers of the economy. Élite leaderships in power use the state to manipulate jobs and contracts for themselves and their followers and, ultimately, to facilitate their emergence as a class. And the conflict of classes in formation can be as intense, if more elusive of analysis, than that of classes long and clearly established. A central conflict, if not the only one, soon developed between the politician–businessmen who dominated the first phase of independence,

and the power bureaucrats, the army men and the civil servants, of the second phase. But the shift from venal politicians to civil servants, however skilled, did not in itself diminish the conflict, or resolve the dilemma of these new states. These are rooted in the manipulation of the state by huge self-serving, fundamentally parasitic élites, while the economy stagnates.

In addition to these ingredients of political turmoil, many of the African states, artificially assembled in the course of conquest, combine disparate peoples; and where there is a faltering supply or an uneven allocation of resources, different sections of the élite fortify their own claims and grievances by identifying them with their particular regional or communal groupings. There are no disputes between the peoples of Africa, only between élites, Amilcar Cabral has said;[1] but in one country after another, if most notably in Nigeria, these élite leaderships have succeeded in polarizing disputes for power and the battle for the spoils along regional and – because region and community often coincide – communal lines.

When the political system is no longer able to contain these conflicts, it has a final resort to a system of reserve authority. This lies in the bureaucracy, the army and the civil service together. Colonialism made Africa essentially a continent of bureaucratic rule and control. After independence, ruling groups, unsupported by the pillars of the economy, were feeble; the bureaucracy, by contrast, was inherited virtually intact and, with direct control over the state's instruments of coercion, proved the more effectual. The last reserve of the bureaucracy has been the army, as cohesive and tightly disciplined as the political parties have been diffuse and slack.

Some African governments tried to assert the political party as against the bureaucracy, but this was done administratively, and not by popular mobilization. These governments succeeded to some extent in changing the forms of administration and even in building a new social base of political power. But as the governments of politicians collapsed, or were challenged, the institutions of power, which had been inherited more or less unaltered from the colonizers, took over control from the forces to which they were expected to be subservient.

3 and 4. Two other sets of factors swing into play in a state vulnerable to crisis, and separately or together they decide whether the army will intervene or not. The one is the role of external forces, the degree of external hostility or encouragement to coup-making. The other is the condition of the army.

Agents or Allies?

The external pressures on Africa can be silent; almost invisible, in the regular rhythm of Africa's dependence. On the other hand, they can be blatant and direct, in the shape of physical intervention; either to incite the collapse of a government and to install a new one, as in the Congo; or to protect a government, even to reinstate one already tumbled by forces within the state, as in Gabon. The elements of crisis – economic and political and military – exist to greater or lesser extent in a number of states where there have been as yet no army coups d'état. It is the external presence that can be decisive in the rising or declining level of incidence; for the absence of coup-making opportunity, or success, is often largely a matter of the protective role exercised by outside forces.

For the West, and especially for the United States, military governments in the Third World have not uncommonly been preferred to civilian ones for their supposedly greater efficiency and resistance to 'communism'. Thus the United States Senate Committee on Foreign Relations heard advice like this in 1959, about Asia:

> The lesson to be derived from recent political developments in South-East Asia is that in most countries of the area the hope for genuinely representative government was premature. It should be the policy of the United States to help wherever possible the officer corps of South-East Asian countries to acquire the administration and the managerial skills necessary in the new tasks they are assuming as the guarantors of their countries' stability.[2]

By 1965, however, the policy-makers of the United States were receiving different advice:

Military coups and military juntas necessarily spur modernization but they cannot produce a stable political order. Instead of relying on the military, American policy should be directed to the creation within modernizing countries of at least one strong non-Communist political party. If such a party already exists, and it is in a dominant position, support of that party should be the keystone of policy.[3]

When it came to the coup d'état in Ghana, Nkrumah himself found the cause transparently clear. In Ghana, he said, the embassies of the United States, Britain and West Germany had all been 'implicated in the plot to overthrow my government. It is alleged' (he does not state by whom) 'that the U S Ambassador Franklin Williams offered the traitors thirteen million dollars to carry out a coup d'état.'[4]

The CIA is the agency whose job it has been to topple governments objectionable to the United States. There has been, among much else, the instance of Iran in 1952; of Guatemala in 1954; of Guyana in 1961; and the abortive Bay of Pigs assault on Cuba. In Ghana, as I have shown, the Western powers had every reason to seek the downfall of the Nkrumah regime. And even though no dollars need pass hands, and no secret codes pass between intelligence operators, the West has its own ways of influencing events before and after a coup d'état, to spur its occurrence and secure its survival. But need the CIA have made the coup d'état in Ghana? It is not good enough to argue that it must have done so because Western purposes ultimately benefitted. The indiscriminate use of the conspiracy explanation is too easily a substitute for analysis of the deeper reasons for political crisis in Africa. The basic structures of African society in new states, Ghana and Mali included, hold the seeds of a coup d'état within themselves. It is precisely because foreign powers and bodies like the CIA understand this well, that their interventions, even very indirect ones, are so effective.

In Africa, except in the pivotal case of the Congo, and of some very small and malleable states, like the former French colonies, the primary initiative for the coup d'état does not seem to have come from outside, but from inside the countries themselves. The principal thrust of the CIA, and of other such external agencies, need not necessarily lie in the instigation or financing of coups. The coup d'état is generally a last resort. More than once, even, a coup d'état in an African state has taken foreign powers by surprise. The intelligence and diplomatic activity of such powers have, rather, been directed to devising mechanisms of control and instigation far more devious and complex than has been credited. They are calculated essentially to influence processes already under way; perhaps to obstruct alternative, and more radical options: but essentially to circumscribe the movement that new states may enjoy. They are designed to avoid rather than to provoke emergency fire-brigade actions.

Who says this? None other than those who conduct these covert intelligence operations. The primary purpose of such operations in the under-developed world, for the CIA and related agencies, 'is to provide Washington with *timely knowledge of the internal power balance*, a form of intelligence that is primarily of tactical significance' (my emphasis). This description comes from no imagined handbook for operators, but from a record of discussions conducted by members of the Group on *Intelligence and Foreign Policy in the Council on Foreign Relations Inc.* The document was 'liberated' from the files of political scientist David Truman, Dean of Columbia College, during a student strike there in 1968. As far as I am aware, the authenticity of this document has not been disputed. It contains none of the startling disclosures usually to be found in forgeries, but rather a more convincing statement of a new and subtle approach to manipulating governments, and one which has been amply substantiated by events. The Group's members included Allen Dulles, academics, journalists, prominent New York lawyers and corporation executives. The Council on Foreign Relations receives financing from the CIA and plays an important part in policy formulation. The 'liberated' document to be published by the Africa Research Group, purports to be the official minute of the meeting held on 8 January 1968, where the discussion leader was Richard M. Bissell Jr; his subject was the nature and means of 'covert intelligence'.

Covert operations, Mr Bissell declared, fall into two classes: intelligence collection, primarily espionage or the obtaining of intelligence by covert means; and covert action, or 'attempting to influence the internal affairs of other nations, sometimes called "intervention" by covert means'. Mr Bissell explained with some precision that:

the underdeveloped world presents greater opportunities for covert intelligence collection, simply because governments are much less highly organised; there is less security consciousness; and there is apt to be more actual or potential diffusion of power among parties, localities, organisations and individuals outside of the central governments. The primary purpose of espionage in these areas is to provide Washington with timely knowledge of the internal power balance, a form of intelligence that is primarily of tactical significance.

Why is this relevant?

Changes in the balance of power are extremely difficult to discern except through frequent contacts with power elements. Time and again we have been surprised at coups within the military; often, we have failed to talk to the junior officers or non-coms who are involved in the coups. The same problem applies to labour leaders and others. Frequently we don't know of power relationships because power balances are murky and sometimes not well known even to the principal actors. Only by knowing the principal players well do you have a chance of careful prediction. There is real scope for action in this area; the technique is essentially that of 'penetration', including 'penetrations' of the sort which horrify classicists of covert operations with a disregard for the 'standards' and 'agent recruitment rules'. Many of the 'penetrations' don't take the form of 'hiring' but of establishing a close or friendly relationship (which may or may not be furthered by the provision of money from time to time). In some countries the CIA representative has served as a close counselor (and in at least one case a drinking companion) of the chief of state . . .

There were situations in which 'the tasks of intelligence collection and political action overlap to the point of being almost indistinguishable'.

In one state, the CIA man might serve as 'private adviser' to a head of state: private, so as to shield this fact from politicians of the local government. In another, the head of state might have 'a special relationship with the senior CIA officers without the knowledge of the US Ambassador because the President of the Republic has so requested it'.

Diplomacy seeks results by bargaining on a government-to-government basis, sometimes openly – sometimes privately. Foreign economic policy and cultural programs seek to modify benignly the economics of other countries [like the Papanek exercise in Ghana described in Part 5] and the climate of opinion within them. Covert intervention is usually designed to operate on the internal power balance, often with fairly short-term objectives in view. An effort to build up the economy of an underdeveloped country must be subtle, long continued, probably quite costly, and must openly enlist the cooperation of major groups within the country if it is to have much influence. On the other hand an effort to weaken the local Communist Party or to win an election, and to achieve results within at most two or three years, must obviously be covert, it must pragmatically use the people and the instrumentalities that are available and the methods that seem likely to work.

And there is more:

The essence of such intervention in the internal power balance is the identification of allies who can be rendered more effective, more powerful, and perhaps wiser through covert assistance. . . . (Typically these local allies know the source of the assistance but neither they nor the United States could afford to admit to its existence.) Agents for fairly minor and low sensitivity interventions, for instance some covert propaganda and certain economic activities, can be recruited simply with money. But for the larger and more sensitive interventions, *the allies must have their own motivation* [my emphasis]. On the whole the Agency has been remarkably successful in finding individuals and instrumentalities with which and through which it would work in this fashion. Implied in the requirement for a pre-existing motivation is the corollary that an attempt to induce *the local ally* to follow a course of action he does not believe in will at least destroy his effectiveness and may destroy the whole operation.

Local allies, not agents, are the key. The very use of the word is a necessary corrective to the obsolete theories of external intervention in the Third World. It is not a matter of a few foreign plotters springing coups d'état or assassinations on unsuspecting states. This does happen, but may be regarded as the exception rather than the rule. To make it the whole picture, or even the main ingredient, is simplistic; it distorts not only the function and purpose of foreign intelligence agencies, but above all the tender and vulnerable condition of Africa. The CIA promotes a strategy to anticipate rather than to initiate – until, as in the Congo, the case is considered urgent. When intervention is ordered, it works because certain groups in the internal power balance want it to work; because the interests of these groups converge with those of external forces.

Not all states in Africa are of equal concern to the big powers. George W. Ball, Under-Secretary of State for Presidents Kennedy and Johnson and a former United States ambassador to the United Nations, argues that the power of the poor countries is limited to creating local situations of violence and instability. They do not by themselves have the ability to precipitate great power conflict, and there are many parts of the world where 'a less anxious policy on our part would pay off'.[5] Patterns of military aid show where the United States places its strongest hopes in Africa. Such aid goes to those states in Africa in which the United States has a 'traditional external responsibility', or special interests, and to those which 'experienced abrupt breaks with the former metropole that threatened to leave voids which Communist powers could fill'.[6] The Congo has been one such state, of course. Ethiopia, strategic not only in relation to Egypt, but also to the Red Sea and the whole Middle East, received 77 per cent of all United States grant aid under the Military Assistance Programme to Sub-Saharan Africa for 1950–66.[7] Kagnew station in Asmara is a United States military communications base involving some 1,300 United States personnel and their dependants. Thus it is understandable that the attempted coup d'état in Ethiopia during 1960 was put down with United States air force, military and diplomatic assistance;[8] and that, in particular, the Emperor was able to fly back into Ethiopia through a United States-run airfield in Asmara. Thus, too, United States has aided Ethiopia in battle against the Eritrean guerrilla movement. The United States is visibly grateful for the Emperor's 'moderating' influence in Pan-African politics. Among the powers training and aiding African armies, Israel has played a phenomenal role, for its military assistance programmes currently operate in at least fifteen African states. Through its own search for allies in the Third World, Israel has apparently become useful for the Third Country technique, elaborated by United States strategists who argue:

Israel's role . . . might be reinforced by imaginative use of the Third Country technique. A free world state wishing to enlarge its assistance flow to Africa might channel some part of it through Israel because of Israel's special qualifications and demonstrated acceptability to many African nations.[9]

(Israel's most important assistance programmes have been in Tunisia and the Ivory Coast, Ethiopia and Congo-Kinshasa: Mobutu had his paratrooper training in Israel, after all, and specialized units like paratroop commandos are the most effective coup-makers.)

Why such emphasis here on the United States and the CIA, in a continent formerly divided among several foreign powers not including the United States? As Conor Cruise O'Brien has shown,[10] the logic of the struggle against 'Communism' has required the United States, in Africa as in south-east Asia, to take over responsibilities abandoned by former colonial powers. In Africa, it was in the wake of the Congo crisis that the United States actively entered the political scene. Up to then, it had been largely a bystander; but after 1960 it came bit by bit to play a role as large as and often far larger than that of the former colonial power,[11] though somewhat different in kind. Since 1945, the Africa Research Group asserts in analysing the role of the United States in Nigeria,[12] it has been a speciality of American foundations and consulting firms to rebuild war-torn economies so that they can more easily be dominated by American companies. For the new shape of Africa's dependence is increasingly the product of huge United States financial and industrial concerns. While, for instance, the State Department was officially neutral in the Nigeria–Biafra war, the corporations were expanding their influence in the spirit of 'reconstruction'. Six months after the war began, Arthur D. Little Incorporated – which has been advising the Federal government on investment promotion and industrial policy for seven years – started work on reconstruction planning. Likewise, an American foundation sponsored Nigeria's Conference on Reconstruction and Development during 1969. The corporations were getting in early; by the time they are finished Nigeria's dependence on them will be deeply embedded.

It was as a result of United States preoccupation with the Congo that we have the single major instance of a coup d'état – two, in fact, in the same country, at an interval of five years – engineered by external forces. Lumumba's offence was to have asked the Soviet Union, once the West had refused, for transport for his troops to defeat the Katanga secession. The issue was not whether the Congo should have a government headed by Lumumba, Kasavubu, Mobutu or Tshombe; but whether an African state should seek an option other than dependence on the West.

In his history of the CIA, Andrew Tully – who records his considerable debt of gratitude to Allen Dulles, and others similarly placed – claims that the CIA came up with the right man at the right time. It seems safe to say that Mobutu was 'discovered' by CIA.[13] Colonel Mobutu was assisted in staging one coup d'état to save the Congo for the West in 1960; and in 1965 he was installed again by a second externally engineered coup. After the first coup d'état, the army played only a caretaker role. The American commitment and presence remained throughout, to buttress the regime in office. It was the CIA that organized WIGMO (Western International Ground Maintenance Organization) to look after the aircraft used by the Congolese army and by the mercenaries whom the Congolese government hired to put down the rebellion in Orientale province. (Later WIGMO was no longer financed by the CIA, but by the Congolese government itself, from money routed to it by the CIA, so that the Congolese should appear more persuasively to be running their own country.)[14] Between them, the United States and Belgium shared the role that Belgium alone had played as colonial power; a Belgian presence, in the shape of teachers, technical assistance, planters and business interests, was augmented by US financial assistance and military support. From Kasavubu to Tshombe there was a succession of governments, all United States-backed, but an increasingly unstable political system in the Congo. Tshombe's governing formula, for instance, depended on an alliance of provincial bosses, and was producing a dissipation of central authority, with much harm to the country's economy, by the plethora of corrupt provincial officials. In 1965, on United States initiative, the army switched from being the power behind the scene, to taking direct control. Mobutu's regime, under United States tutelage, fused the power of the army with that of the new technocratic élite, and by so doing consolidated the centralized power of the state and stabilized the Congo for international capital.

FRANCE THE ARBITER

By contrast with its knowledgeable and active role in other parts of Africa, the United States, far from having instigated the coup d'état in Gabon, as it was accused by France of having done, was taken by surprise. (That is, if the account by former Ambassador Darlington[15] is the complete version: one of the consequences of Bissell-type covert operations is that information about them is sometimes withheld from the ambassador.)[16] In Gabon the American ambassador had kept in constant touch with the senior army officers as well as with the French colonel and his staff who were in overall command, and his reports to Washington 'reflected what they told us, namely that the army was entirely loyal to President Leon Mba. I offer no excuses for our failure to be better informed.' For it was not the command but the junior officers who staged the coup against the president.

While it was French hostility that reversed the Gabon attempt, it was American and British acceptance that sustained two other coups d'état, in Ghana and Nigeria. Britain suffered initially from delayed reaction to the Ghana coup, but the United States rapidly filled the breach. The close attention that U S military attachés and training teams now give to the middle and junior levels of the officer corps suggest that it will not easily repeat the error made in Gabon. In Nigeria British action stabilized two post-coup sheet-anchor governments: first the Ironsi regime, which Britain's High Commissioner prompted into existence to counteract the revolt led by the young majors; and then the Gowon government, which Britain coaxed and consolidated after its own successful intercession to stop a Northern breakaway. Once the break between Nigeria and Biafra was final, and Britain and the oil companies could not play along with both sides, the purposes of Nigeria's ruling élite and the oil companies converged, and Britain committed itself to full-scale support of the Federal army. Where less crucial interests have been at stake, foreign powers have been content merely to watch the conflict and let the contestants themselves decide the issue.

When it comes to the internal power balance so scrupulously observed by foreign powers, African armies are pivotal. The African armies were the creation of the colonial powers; were moulded to the needs of the West; and have been the least decolonized, on the whole, among all African structures and institutions. In the post-colonial period, they remain bonded to the West for training and equipment and aid; their supply lifelines are not inside but outside the country.[17] The African army is also a defence reserve of the Western powers. This is nowhere more strikingly seen than in the case of France and its former possessions in Africa.

France's defence policy in the independence era has been based on two needs: to maintain its own strategic position in Africa 'without an overly conspicuous deployment of forces in Africa itself'; and, as an extension of this, to reserve the right of intervention 'on behalf of' African states and regimes.[18] The policy was devised after the fall of France in 1940, when French strategists reasoned that the bulk of French fighting power could have been withdrawn intact to the strategic North African platform until an African-centred resuscitation could confront Nazi power. From the lesson of its humiliation, it subsequently positioned itself to organize its defences on a Euro-African basis, and thus be able to hold its own in Allied councils as a strong military power.[19] Accordingly, when decolonization came, France not only built national armies for its former possessions with the military hardware coming directly from its own resources, and with the *quid pro quo* that the African states were committed to France for supplies and training,* but it also erected

*The magazine of the French army, *L'Armée*, disclosed during 1968 that about 1,400 senior officers and NCOs of the French army, marines and air

an elaborate system of defence cooperation. Thus, inside Africa, French-trained, French-supervised and French-attuned armies are France's most dependable allies; while outside, France maintains, apart from economic control, a military strike force that in an emergency can make or break an African government. The 11th Division, based in south-west France, stands ready to answer any call for help from any of the eleven African countries bound to France by defence agreements. It consists of five parachute infantry regiments, and three seaborne assault infantry regiments, with adequate provision for men and weapons to be transported by air.[20] The defence agreements generally carry a provision that while the African state alone is responsible for its external and internal defence, it can call on French help under special conditions.

> In several instances, the defense accords included a convention relative *au maintien de l'ordre*. Limited in duration, though with renewal options, these imply a more intimate French commitment to incumbent regimes – a form of personal pact – and they define the channels of appeal and authorisation so that the local French Ambassador has a central role in determining whether French troops shall be brought in and to what use they shall be put.[21]

France's special intervention force is organized to respond within hours to calls for help from African governments; but the help, it has been made clear by France, is to be given only exceptionally. Intervention is not a duty for France. In other words, France has its own criteria. The French Minister for Information, M. Alain Peyrefitte, revealed that at the request of the legitimate African governments, French forces had intervened at least twelve times in Africa between 1960 and 1963; several times in Chad to combat 'insurgency'; in the Cameroun; in Niger in December 1963, to 'discourage' a military uprising against President Diori; twice in Mauretania; in Congo-Brazzaville in September 1962; and, of course, in Gabon.[22] The spate of coups d'état in French Africa in 1966 brought a warning

---

force, the medical corps and the gendarmerie were employed as technical assistants in twelve Francophone countries. These troops are in addition to the 6–7,000 troops of the French army actually stationed in Senegal, Chad, Niger, Ivory Coast, Central African Republic, Gabon and Madagascar.

from General de Gaulle to African military leaders not to spring any more, or he would cut off French aid.[23] A few years later a company of French troops, sent to the Central African Republic ostensibly on a training exercise, was thwarting a counter-coup against the regime of coup-maker General Bokassa;[24] France was protecting the pretender regime. By 1969 it could no longer be concealed that French legions were regularly riding out in Chad to President Tombalbaye's rescue. Sporadic actions against tax collectors and isolated attacks against 'brigands' had become sustained armed resistance under the leadership of the National Liberation Front (FROLINAT). The 'rebellion' (Tombalbaye's term) is in its sixth year. Chad's geographical position largely explains France's anxiety: it is bordered by Nigeria and the Sudan, Niger, the Cameroun and the Central African Republic. Events there could affect the whole core of Africa.[25] And besides, its garrison air base and defence telecommunications system at Fort Lamy are the keystones of the French military organization in Africa.

France thus remains the arbiter of which regimes in Africa are to endure, and which to fall, whether sooner or later. The governments in the smaller, feeble states tend to be expendable; those in the larger and more important ones, which maintain close ties with Paris, could expect France to reinforce them in authority. France's long-standing relationship with President Houphouet-Boigny of the Ivory Coast is the soundest insurance against a successful coup d'état there. The Ivory Coast is not only the richest of the West African states linked with France, but also France's most dependable political ally in Africa. This is not to say that the Ivory Coast is coup-proof. There was an attempt in 1963, when six ministers, including the Minister of Defence, were arrested for plotting, and the loyalty of the army was so suspect that it was sent up-country to be out of the way. But while Houphouet-Boigny lasts, France will play protector; and after he goes, in the event of any dispute over the succession, the outcome will be largely determined by the preference of the French government. Senghor's government in Senegal enjoys similar protection from France, for long-standing sentimental if not such persuasive economic reasons. As for Gabon, it has not only uranium and iron ore, but a very influential French élite of administrators, engineers, managers and businessmen, not to speak of army advisers. Perhaps the request for French intervention during the coup there originated among these expatriates. The formal request under the defence treaty was made by Vice-Premier Paul-Marie Yembit, but twenty-four hours *after* the French had already flown in their troops. The French ambassador was kept in the dark by his own government: while he was busy negotiating a regime to succeed Mba's, the French army was going into action to restore Mba himself. The ambassador and the military attaché tend to run parallel missions in an African state; in Gabon, the military mission seems to have overruled and superseded the diplomatic.

The new state has thus two link systems with the former colonial power. One is between government and government, through the diplomatic mission; the other, between army and army. (Of course, when the army invades government it is much simpler, for the soldier turned president serves both networks at the same time.) The army relationship is in many ways of longer standing and greater intimacy: because the armies were created by the European powers; and, on the whole, African armies continue to receive military aid overwhelmingly from the former colonial power, which also provides most of the military training. Foreign aid and training thus bind an army not to its own government but to an external force; for the army's concern to keep up the flow of military aid will make its interests seem to coincide with those of its supplier power. (Some argue the hypothesis that the speed with which an army jumps to the defence of a regime depends on the degree to which it is maintained by domestic sources.)[26]

The other effect of military aid to Africa is to make African armies stronger, especially in the smaller states, than governments themselves. African armies – with the odd exception here and there, as in the Kenya–Somalia dispute – have no real external defence commitments. Thus the primary impact of military aid is internal. There is no aid as dependable as that pledged to armies, and no aid which produces such rapid and predictable results. At the same time, military aid makes African armies the institutions in the new states which are the most sensitive to foreign pressures, and also the ones most likely to usurp the functions of government. For in the nature of the new African states, building and training armies turns them into instruments for coup-making. The army has disproportionate power by default of the political system, but also by the design of external forces.

The Internal Condition of the Army

Frequently the soldiers strike at government because triggers for action have been cocked inside the army as well as outside. This happened in both Ghana and Nigeria.

To begin with, there is no such thing as a non-political army. Africa's armies are reflections of society and encompass all its interests and conflicts: because the armies do not, like the political parties, have a strong allegiance to an integrated ruling class; nor do they possess a pervasive ideological cast. The armies of Africa are agglomerations of several social groups and interests: they thus play shifting roles, and they adjust to the shifting state of African politics. Political and army triggers for a coup d'état often go off together, since the soldier acts from army grievances, but also because he identifies with his generation, his region or community, his sect (the Sudan) or his political affiliation.

The theory of the non-political army served the purposes of colonial power: an army that questioned policies or politicians might be driven to question colonialism itself, and rule would have been undermined from within by the armies which were used as extensions of the internal security force. The theory was, of course, transplanted to Africa from the domestic needs of the West European states. But even in these states, it often proved on scrutiny to be a fiction, a constitutional concept rather than a constitutional fact.[27] The theory broke down at times of crisis. The Ulster crisis of 1914 showed that the British army was far from neutral in politics. When the Home Rule Bill for Ireland was moving through its last stages in the House of Commons, the Liberal administration was manifestly unsure of the support that it could command in the army. Across the Irish Sea, Ulster volunteers were drilling and secretly importing arms from abroad, supported to the hilt by conservative opinion in England; and through that winter, prominent Conservative politicians were frankly urging the armed forces to mutiny.[28]* If the British army was sharply divided by Home Rule for Ireland, the French army was even more dangerously divided over Algeria. The Fourth Republic would not have fallen without the revolt of significant forces within the French military. De Gaulle reached the Elysée on the momentum of crisis produced by an attempted coup.

If armies have played so small a role in the recent politics of the West, this reflects the composition of advanced industrial societies and in particular the social structure of the armies themselves. Western military men, like Western civil servants, have mostly had to deal with politicians and governments whose outlooks and purposes have not been radically different from their own, so that differences between them have generally been susceptible to compromise and accommodation, and the political loyalties of the military have seldom been put decisively to the test.[29] The fabric of civil organization is such that the military on its own cannot offer an alternative locus of power. Ralph Miliband writes[30] that in the West an overt unconstitutional challenge from the army would have little chance of success unless it were staged in the face of an exceptionally weak or paralysed labour movement, and unless the putschists organized popular support into ancillary mass organizations of the right. It would need, in other words, not only a military putsch, but a Fascist movement. High-ranking officers in Germany and Italy played an important role as allies though not as initiators of such movements, because it is difficult to lead demagogic fascist-type movements from within armies. The regime of the colonels since

* Interestingly, one of the reasons privately expressed by apologists for the failure of the British government to use force against the white rebel regime in Rhodesia is the uncertain response of the British army to such an order. Whether this is a reason or merely an excuse, it does not say much for the supposedly unquestionable neutrality of Britain's armed forces.

their coup in Greece is precarious precisely because it is without the popular base characteristic of European fascist regimes.[31] The infrequency of army intervention as such in the industrialized societies of the West is thus due not to the neutrality of armies but to the nature of the social and political system. Armies in industrialized societies cannot move into politics and government without a substantial degree of support from one class or sector of the population. In Africa, by contrast, where the social structure is still unformed and the political system crumbling, neither the army nor the government that it seeks to displace has a firm social base. The intervention of the army, its physical force alone, will be both swift and decisive.

Politics is present in all armies, though it may be quiescent at times when there are no sharp clashes of interest, and when no specific opportunity for intervention has presented itself. It is, indeed, a variation on the theory of the non-political army which, far from keeping armies out of political action in Africa, precipitates them into it. This is the notion ingrained in Western-influenced and trained armies that they should be independent of government. Armies, after all, had been in existence long before politicians or political parties were allowed; and it came naturally to soldiers to see their authority as not only distinct from that of temporary African governments, but superior to it. The notion had grown that armies and governments should each be master to control their own command structures, their systems of promotion and their training methods. There might be strong political reasons for a state to diversify sources of supplies and training methods, but armies insisted that they were the best judges of these things, and that they reached their decisions solely on 'technical' grounds. To insist otherwise was interference with the autonomy of the army. In Ghana General Alexander and his officers took a firm stand on this. As for reshaping the command by retiring some officers, or promoting others, this might make for security of government, but it was interfering with the autonomy of the army – the state within the state – that insisted on its right to martial freedom, as Geoffrey Bing has picturesquely described it.[32]

Armies were not without politics; the politics they adhered to demanded the right of the army to be master in its own domain. If the other, civil, domain interfered with the military one, was it surprising that the army sought its own remedy? Thus the army, supposed to be the last line of defence for the nation state, was indoctrinated and exercised in precepts alien to those recognizing the sovereignty of government.

The conflict between state and army grew in direct proportion to the attempt of the new state to chart a course from the former metropolitan power; the more strained became the army's life- and supply lines, and the more undermined the rules, conventions and precedents that the African army imbibed from the metropolitan one.

Radically inclined states that have recognized the army as not only a conservative force but a potential for counter-revolution, have tried to neutralize its technical monopoly of violence by building up counter-forces and by diversifying commands. Resort has been made to special military formations like the Presidential Guard in Ghana, or popular militia as in Mali. If the army does not fervently support the goals of the state, however, this move not so much neutralizes as incites it. The Ghanaian army struck largely if not entirely to protect itself from the President's own Guard regiment; the young lieutenants in Mali did so, among other reasons, to clip the wings of the popular militia; Boumedienne struck in Algeria partly because one of Ben Bella's plans was to counter the army with a popular militia. In Congo-Brazzaville in 1968–9 the army saw the Cuban-trained youth movement as a counter to its own armed autonomy.

PALS FOR JOBS

The army strikes at government in defence of its immediate corporate interests, but for other reasons too. The heat of the political crisis in new states is generated largely by the struggle over the spoils between competing layers of the power élite; and the officer corps has a strong stake in the contest, since it is in itself an élite group. When the Cabinet minister, the civil servant and the university academic inherited the salary scales set by departing colonials, so too did the army officer and the police inspector. African armies deliberately preserved European standards of pay; the former British colonies, those of Britain; and the Francophone states, those of the French army. The lieutenant-colonel of a battalion may earn as much as ten or fifteen times the starting salary of the recruit.[33] (In Britain and France the equivalent differential is about five times.)

The military have also been called the best organized trade union in African states.[34] The result of the East African mutinies was a near doubling of Kenyan, and a near trebling of Ugandan and Tanganyikan army pay. In Togo the army was immediately increased after the coup, and in Dahomey Colonel Soglo embarked upon a rapid programme of army expansion.[35] In Upper Volta the military regime decided after the 1966 coup that those soldiers who had served in civilian posts should retain their military salaries, and not be transferred to the civilian wage structure where austerity cuts had been made.[36] The budgets of 1967–8 for Francophone Africa showed that eight out of fifteen states had provided the army with between 15 and 25 per cent of their resources.[37] Already uncontrollable public deficits were subjected to further strain. In Ethiopia the military consumes twice as much of the budget as does education, and twenty-eight times the amount spent on community development.[38] It has been calculated that, in the first fifty-six months after independence, the Congolese army received one-sixth of the state's revenue.[39]

The interests of the officer corps lie in preserving the inflated standards of the African élite; in retaining or increasing the army's share of the budget; and in steadying the state when it shakes under stress, since it has itself such a large group stake in the budget and the economy. Michael Lee[40] considers that the characteristic African coup d'état is a gesture of frustration by the employees of the state. The most pressing competition in the new states is over jobs in the public sector; the most valuable part of the colonial inheritance is the 'senior service', the range of roles formerly occupied by colonial administrators. Soldiers, policemen and civil servants all belong to the state as an organization, and have an interest in preserving their positions; their seizures of power are 'caretaker' actions to preserve a state apparatus from which they benefit so lavishly.

But the men in uniform not only comprise one more contesting layer within the élite; they constitute a distinct corporate group curiously independent, by comparison with industrialized societies, from the social and class forces whose control is generally solidified in the state through institutions such as the army. During the colonial period, the army deployed its coercive power for external forces. This had important consequences in the independence distribution of power in Africa. Ken Post[41] describes how the new state apparatus has come to possess 'a coercive power of its own, inherited from the colonial period, and this power is not the extension . . . of the economic power of some indigenous ruling class'. The politicians derived their position, Post writes, 'from their class and ethnic interests, local ones in the main, but their chief one, which integrates the rest and has a power of its own, was the party'. In political crisis, the balance of power among politicians, bureaucrats and army officers began to change. The political parties, the sources of power peculiar to the politicians, proved unreliable. Popular dissatisfaction with political nepotism and corruption, and generally with the absence of substantial improvements in living standards, eroded the backing which politicians enjoyed from local ethnic interests. 'Moreover they allowed, in many cases, the party structures to wither away, believing that control of state power was sufficient for their purposes. This might indeed have been true, in the short run, had the corporate groups, with their own sources of power undiminished, not existed.' The politicians might try to manipulate and even change the form of state institutions (as in Ghana and Mali); but in the main they were not able to establish firm control over state power and the corporate groups associated with it. The army and the civil service had a degree of autonomy from government and the political parties, and social and class forces, unknown in industrialized states. When the political parties went into crisis, the army could act independently of theirs. Thus, as Post writes, 'the weakness of the bourgeoisie in Africa, and the apparent autonomy of the organs of the state, was manifest dramatically in military coups which placed officer–bureaucrats alliances in power'. When the army struck to defend itself, and its rights to autonomy, it was acting not as an instrument of state power, but as the power in the state. The instrument of power had itself assumed power. Power as coercion became the dominant theme, rather than power as authority.

In colonial days, the legitimacy of government lay with conquest by force and the all-pervading control of the bureaucracy. Once again power now lies in the barrel of the gun and with the control of the bureaucracy. For if army men may seize power, they cannot manipulate it on their own. Within a decade of independence, and in some countries less, Africa has travelled from colonial government to a very close copy of it. Lugard and Lyautey of the last century have given way to Mobutu, Gowon and Bokassa of this one. Once again the pattern of rule is military–bureaucratic in type.

Military Bureaucracies

Once the army seizes government, the corridors of control rarely run from the officers' mess alone. Common to most military regimes installed by coup d'état, is a civil service–military axis in which armies have the physical power to conserve the regime, while the civil service wields effective executive power in the state. The reform coups which serve as levers for change are the exception. In Egypt, the Free Officers Movement took power to itself and rapidly appointed military men to bureaucratic tasks, while the civil service of a disintegrated and demoralized regime played a very self-effacing role. In the Sudan, where the young officer coup of 1969 took power not for the army but for a radical civilian government, one of the first steps to be taken was a purging of the old bureaucracy, lest this, finding the purposes of the new regime inimical, negate its policies through administration. In general, however, the vesting of authority in the bureaucrats is very much a reversion to colonial rule.

Like the colonial predecessor in the early stages of rule by administration, the first act of armies is to ban all politics and all political parties. A new policy must be built, the coup-makers declare, but without politics. The epitaph suggested for Pakistan's Ayub Khan[42] – here was a man who loathed politicians, but whose attempt to create a polity without politics foundered on his ignorance of what the political process really was about – will undoubtedly be as appropriate to Africa's armies in government as it was to Pakistan. For the choices which armies make in the course of outlawing politics are themselves political. 'The politicians ruined the country,' the soldiers declare, 'and we shall do better.' But what sort of policy-making does not entail political choices? What the non-political order does is not to keep out politics, but to keep out radical politics. The decision in the Sudan under the Abboud junta (where administrative methods closely followed those used in Pakistan) to employ indirect rule gave assertion to the most conservative forces in the society: tribal and community heads and local administrators. A reversion to traditional authority is just as much a political move as a progression to revolutionary or reformist authority. In Ghana the army's cry of 'no politics' did not mean, could not mean, a political vacuum; it meant pro-Western, free enterprise, élite-style politics – the very politics, incidentally, which had led to the coup d'état in Nigeria and other states.

The army–bureaucratic coalition which is preoccupied with the decree rather than the debate, and the letter of the law rather than popular support for it, wakes with a jolt to its narrow base of power in time of crisis. The soldiers soon enough discover that they, too, cannot really govern alone, and that they have need of power alliances. Like the political party government previously, the army and the bureaucracy have no firm social or class basis, and find that they are unable to rule for long unsupported. In Nigeria the army drew politicians into government so as to enlarge its power base when the conflict with the East, later Biafra, flared: the authority of the Gowon government was not only denied in the East, but was shaky in the rest of the country; and politicians had to be cast in the role of civilian commissioners, or ministers, to enlist their support and that of their followers. In Ghana the government opened the doors to politicians, after the Arthur attempted coup – when the NLC was so nearly physically defeated in the capital – and its damaging aftermath in the ranks and officer corps of the army itself. Ghana finally went back to civilian rule as much for reasons of potential army disunity as any other.

With rare exceptions, as in the coups which are planned and sustain themselves as levers for or against change (Egypt; possibly the 1969 coup in the Sudan, though it is early to say; and Ghana) the army's take-over of government has not altered substantially the social basis of power in the state. What it has done has been to bring together new amalgams of ruling groups. There have been two principal shifts in the nexus of power: first, from politicians to bureaucrats of the civil service and of the army, as well as to young educated technocrats who were not absorbed into the leaderships of the independence parties; and, secondly, in the redistribution of political power on a regional and ethnic basis.

The army can be the ladder of power for portions of the élite not previously prominent, or dominant, in government. At the crucial formative stages of Africa's new armies, it was not the sons of the traditional, professional or business élites that enlisted, but the sons of the poorer people, generally from more remote, under-developed areas. The coup d'état catapulted into government and authority not only soldiers themselves, as new candidates for political power and economic opportunity, but also – because kinsmen and followers gravitate around men in power – others. Nigeria's new power combination, in which two of the three former majorities balance in office together with minority groups, was arbitrated by the rifle power in the army of one such minority group. Without Tiv ground forces to back it, how far would the demand for a Middle-Belt state have gone? Gowon himself emerged as a nominee of the non-commissioned officers drawn largely from the minority groups. If newer echelons of Northern power today prevail over the old emirates of the North, it is largely because, contrary to legend, it is not the Hausa who form the backbone of the lower ranks in the army, but the minority peoples of the Middle Belt. In Togo four-fifths of the army originated in the North; and though Southerners have continued to run and to dominate the civil service and the professions, the face of Togo's government has been Northern ever since 1963, when a small group of Cabre ex-servicemen shot Olympio and displaced his Southern-dominated regime. When in 1967 Southerners, mostly Ewe, tried an administrative coup against the government, its army protectors came out into the streets with their guns, and the coup evaporated. It was after this abortive attempt to swing power Southwards again, that the army took power directly. Promises to return Togo to civilian government have been made, but broken; the army command resists elections that might immediately shift the balance of power once again to Southerners. In Congo-Brazzaville the removal of Bakongo leaders and influence from government started after the seizure of power by Captain Ngouabi, a member of the Kouyou people from the north of the country. In Congo-Kinshasa, likewise, there has been a steady exit from leading roles by the Bakongo. In Ghana the army command was more equally divided between the various regional groupings, and Northerners have not been so demonstrably advanced through the army; but eyes have been trained on the Ewe soldiers, so well represented in the officer corps and so closely identified with Ewe politicians and aspirations, lest their claims and grievances crystallize in political action through the army. Colonial security entrusted those furthest from political control with the control of force. In the period of coup d'état, possessing the machinery of force leads to command of political power. In enough countries for this to be a significant trend, political power for minority groups has flowed from the barrel of a gun.

New contestants may emerge to compete for power, but the nature of the contest does not change. If anything it grows fiercer, the larger the circle of contestants. The entry of soldiers into government does not significantly change the alignment of social forces; what it does is to put weapons into the hands of particular elements. This is most evident in Nigeria. Here, far from blocking disunity and disintegration, the army has accelerated it. A similar pattern was evident in the Congo, between the first and second interventions of the army.

POWER DIVIDES

As long as the army remains in barracks, or drilling on the parade ground, its command structure and military discipline hold it intact – short of the pay mutiny, that is. Once an army enters government, the possession of power proceeds to divide it: army cohesion disappears as soon as the army stops performing the functions for which it was drilled. There are both political and military reasons for this. Because the armies are agglomerations of interest and social groups, once they have stepped beyond the barracks and must make policy decisions that are not defined in terms of mere military procedure, they soak up social conflicts like a sponge. Armies, indeed, have shown that they can be as prone to divisive loyalties as are politicians and parties. Once the political system divides on communal lines, the division will take the army in power with it. This happened in Nigeria; it is happening in Ghana; and it is certain to happen in Kenya should the army there try to take over government. For as Michael Lee has written: 'Ironically the more a government has striven to make its officer corps representative of the new nation, the more it makes its army vulnerable to complete collapse if the coalition of interests in the civilian sphere also breaks down.' In Uganda and Togo, by contrast, the governments rest their survival principally on the fact that ethnic composition in army and government largely correspond.

Even where communal and regional rifts do not incite division among the soldiers, however, this is no guarantee of military cohesion. African armies are unsettled at the outset, because there is acute resentment between different generations of officers, and fierce rivalry at lower levels. The officers in command positions were the men who rose slowly through the ranks and were promoted with independence and Africanization; younger men, subsequently better educated and better trained at intensive officer courses, consider themselves better qualified to command. Within the middle and younger generations, there is a promotion bottleneck. Instead of careful gradations of age and seniority, there are great clusters of officers similar in age, experience and training; and in each group the career hopes of all but a few seem certain to be blighted. Frustration and conspiracy flourish in such armies.

If armies in power remain united, there is little that will topple them, short of outside intervention. But once armies divide from within, they are far from impregnable, notwithstanding their monopoly of violence. The Sudanese junta fell only after losing support from a significant section within the army. A mutiny of Sierra Leone's other ranks brought down the military government there.

It is essentially the seizure of power that destroys the strongest unifying feature of the army. Once shattered, the sanction against a military seizure of government is broken for ever. A major-general or a brigadier who usurps state power must expect to be emulated by a colonel; and what one colonel can do, another can copy, improve upon, or undo. The military regime will justify its particular coup by the ills, corruption and incompetence of the particular civilian government it has displaced; but the army itself will not be convinced. For once the taboo of the non-political army is shattered, the officers and the soldiers become politicized. They begin to identify not with their seniors, who have defied the rules and have thus broken the obligation of military discipline, but with their equivalents in civilian life, their army generation, their political associates or their kinsmen.

Accordingly, in Africa, every rank has had a turn at coup-making. Colonels and majors – the most competitive and frustrated career grades – are especially well placed, because colonels control the regiments, and majors the companies, and they are in touch with the men and have access to the army hardware. But non-commissioned officers as well, in Togo, in Mali and in Gabon, and in Nigeria during July 1966, have a hand. In Sierra Leone in 1968 the rank and file disproved the old adage that the army worm does not turn and, with the non-commissioned officers, found pay grievances enough initiative to lock up the entire officers corps, and set up their own temporary government.

It is rare for an entry by the soldiers into government not to divide the army, and its command, and to alienate at least a portion of the officer corps; it is even rarer for each successive usurpation of civilian authority not to increase such divisive effects. And the longer an army stays in government, the greater the chances of the counter-coup from below.

On the infrequent occasions, as in Ghana, where the police have joined the army in coup-making, the partnership between the two services has been an additional source of discord and disunity. The police are nowhere as well placed as the army for conspiracy and usurpation of power; since unlike an army, which is accommodated in barracks under a centralized command, the police are dispersed through the country and are more slowly mobilized, if at all, for coup action. But the police are indispensable for security and intelligence work in the hours immediately after the coup; they generally possess the best communications network, not to speak of intelligence service, with the result that police headquarters are often the choice for the headquarters of the coup-makers. Thus, in both Ghana and Nigeria, Generals Kotoka and Ironsi functioned from police headquarters. Uniquely in Ghana the police were partners, though the argument still rages about whether they were senior or junior ones, in the plot for take-over. It was in Ghana that the pre-coup regime had tried to refashion the police force as well as the army, and similar grievances rankled among army and police officers alike. When conspiracy was joined, it thus included police as well as army heads. But a reputation for graft and petty corruption made the police highly unpopular, not least with young army officers.

Back to the Barracks?

Does the possession of power corrupt as well as divide the army? Army men may not seize power with an appetite for it – as in Janowitz's reactive coup, when officers intervene in response to the collapse of civilian institutions[43] – but the appetite is fed by office. The old generals, like Abboud and Ankrah, tend to grow fond of the ceremonial and the perquisites of office; then casual profit is not enough, and business interests stir. The young officers, trim young Galahads in place of the avaricious politicians, enjoy the authority and popular awe. Compared with life at State House, in the ministries and on the diplomatic round, life in the officers' mess is meagre and secluded. And even if the soldier has intervened in government not ostensibly for his own or the army's sake, but for the government's, it is easier to step into than out of power.

Among soldiers in the act of staging a coup, it is a matter of military honour to declare that the army has no political ambitions, no inclination to cling on to power. It was General Soglo of Dahomey who stressed that the place of the army is in the barracks, not in the ministries; that the Dahomean army was not Praetorian. His disavowals of political ambition, personal or corporate, were fluent. But so have they all been: the declarations by Colonel Bokassa of the Central African Republic, Colonel Lamizana of Upper Volta, General Mobutu of Congo-Kinshasa, Colonel Eyadema of Togo. Reassuring words are issued to citizens disinclined to accept the prospect of a more or less permanent military government, and these words may often be sincerely meant; but, as the months go by, they are uttered with diminishing emphasis.

The army has no intention of confiscating power, said Colonel Lamizana the day after the coup d'état in Upper Volta. Five months later the colonel was addressing a fierce and final warning to politicians nostalgic for power, threatening to use the force and power of the army against them. Not long after that, he announced that the army would not surrender power until it could be assured that the parties would find a way to install 'an authentic democracy'. Six months after that, he revealed in a radio broadcast that the army had decided to remain in power for a further four years. Two months later, the army had decided to remain in power for a further four years. Two months later, the army had decided to remain in power indefinitely because there was no other solution.[44] In Congo-Brazzaville, the soldiers argue that army rule is not rule by military government. Said Captain Raoul, whose junta seized power in 1968: 'We have today two soldiers at the head of the state, that is two national citizens. We are in power as cadres not as military personnel. I do not see why it is necessary to give power back to civilians, there is no problem of military government.'[45] According to the captain, military men in government are no longer military men.

After the initial coup d'état the army is likely to move in and out of the barracks to government in successive phases. As crises multiply and political forces prove incompetent, the army steps in partly to mediate, partly to guard its own interests, and partly to reinforce a system that it supports and judges to be in its own interests. The less that is changed by the intervention of the military, the more likely the prospect that it will have to intervene again, even repeatedly. Finer has written that the only way to prevent this *perpetuum mobile* is for the military to produce a successor regime that neither needs the military nor is needed by it. This is the precondition of disengagement.[46] But the very factors which produce the army coup d'état make it impossible for the army to produce a regime free from crisis. The change that is produced by the coup is a change at the top of government and the political system only, and the army – except under the special circumstances of Egypt and likewise of the Sudan since 1969 – is concerned and able to make no more than the most shallow of changes.

In the usual run of coups, there could be several patterns for the future, but perhaps two principal types; that of countries such as Dahomey and Sierra Leone; and that of the Congo. The former states are small and marginal to foreign interests; the latter, the focus of powerful international oligopolies. In Dahomey three interventions by the command and then a young officer coup led, finally, to the return of government by politicians, though a new crop without the corrupt and incompetent record of the predecessors. The army is back in the barracks. The political round is starting up again. Yet nothing has happened to heal the political cleavages or cure the economy. How long will it be before another coup? In Sierra Leone, the former opposition party has been installed in government; but it may come to rule in much the same way as the former government did, for conditions in the country and the patterns of politics have not greatly altered. While in opposition the All Peoples Congress had a radical urban wing; but in power it may well try to prune this. The coup sequence could well start up again. In the Congo the coup d'état steered by external forces has broken the old sequence of politicians tossing government between themselves, and has brought to power new cohorts which, while not altering the social base of power, fuse the army's command of violence with a strong new élite: the university graduates, civil servants, technocrats in commerce and administration and traders, with a few of the old politicians thrown in for good measure. But control lies essentially with those bureaucrats who form the strongest links with the foreign powers really in control of the Congo; behind them hovers the *eminence khaki* of the army.

The coup d'état, which by definition precludes mass participation, is the active symptom of crisis within the power élite. The guns mediate shifts in the balance of internal power and determine who will rule temporarily, but they do not in themselves alter the fundamental character of the society. Though the power of political decision may lie in African hands, the economic resources of the country do not, and nor does political decision in so far as it affects this economic control. The conflict is over very secondary sources of power, while the primary power, not substantially affected by internal changes, is content to let eruptions occur, and for the most part, produce their own results. Where intervention is more prominent or direct, it is where the state is an important enclave of foreign interests; and where the army and the bureaucracy, reinforced in time by some kind of political base, are considered more reliable and more 'stable' than the existing regime.

Armies for Revolution?

For the army coup d'état to open up and not to frustrate radical options, there would have to be not only an army programme for change, but an organized link with radical forces in the country. Between these, they would have not only to seize power, but to safeguard a new regime while it altered the power base.

In this sense, the Free Officers' coup of 1969 in the Sudan has been distinctive. Here were soldiers who staged a coup not to place themselves in power but to produce and secure a civilian government of radical young intellectuals committed to social revolution. Whether they will succeed or not hangs – beyond the immediate danger of counter-revolution from the forces that they seek to dispossess – on whether this radical leadership can galvanize popular support for fundamental social change. For professional armies on their own, by their nature, can create neither a revolutionary mood nor revolutionary possibilities through a coup d'état. Militarism in itself can inspire a nation only if geared to attacking or resisting another nation. Egypt is the sole instance in Africa of a coup d'état that led to major social change; but it is also a seminal case of an army in danger of destroying the very transformations it initiated.

From the first hours of the Egyptian coup d'état in 1952, there was a complete seizure of the state apparatus by the Free Officers; and this was followed by their conquest of the power of decision in all fields: political, economic, social and ideological. After Suez in 1956 and the nationalizations of 1961, Nasser proclaimed that the role of the army was to clear the path of the revolution. Egypt did not want politicians in the army, but the army as a whole would constitute a force within the national political process, and that process was to be devoted to the achievement of socialism. After launching the Charter of National Action, Nasser divided the military into two categories. Officers who continued with their military careers received better training and more privileges than ever previously. Officers who elected to be active in politics had to turn in their uniforms and were stripped of all privileges that came with their rank: in return, they received key positions in the state, soon constituting the great majority of senior diplomatic personnel, and forming a considerable proportion of presidents, directors and board members of public agencies, as well as occupying a large number of ministries and under-secretaryships of state, along with crucial posts in the radio, the press and the information services. Steadily the highest state positions, in the person of the president of the Republic, but also the whole overall direction of the state apparatus and the government, passed into the hands of former military men. In the government of Sidky Soliman installed in September 1966, for instance, the prime minister was an engineering colonel; three of the four vice-presidents of the Council were senior engineering general staff officers; and half the Council of Ministers was composed of former senior and staff officers. This military domination of the political apparatus also extended to the key area of the public sector.[47]

Even the Arab Socialist Union was run in officer-corps style. At three different stages of the Egyptian revolution, political movements were launched for popular mobilization: the National Liberation Rally in 1953; the National Union in 1957; and in 1961 the Arab Socialist Union, with an inner cadre corps known as the Political Organization. Each of these political movements in turn went from torpor to paralysis, intrinsically unable to stir vitality in villages, factories and neighbourhood communities. Instead of a political party running a state, Egypt's state was trying to breathe life into a party. In principle, Egypt had civilian government, since officers in government had taken off their uniforms and severed their connexions with the army; but military control and military methods persisted. There was no political cadre to lead this revolution, because political activity among committed radicals had either been discouraged or suppressed. In the final analysis, the only cadres that the regime could find were in the officer corps, or among the technocrats: and this alliance was increasingly becoming a new privileged élite.

The Egyptian army might have initiated a social revolution, but it was no guerrilla force or popular militia, with deep roots among the people. It was a conventional army, animated by orders from above. In such an army, initiative taken in the ranks is at the least insubordination; and underlings acquire the habit of waiting for commands. No more damaging style of work could be inflicted on a political mass movement. So, in the Arab Socialist Union, leaders were men who had been selected by their superiors for leadership courses: the shock-troops of the Political Organization within the Union were picked 'by the highest possible authority', as an official of the ASU told me in Cairo; and candidates for the youth movement were selected on the recommendation of their teachers or, in the case of students, their university lecturers. It was leadership by appointment from on high; not by popular support and acclaim from below. A critic of this procedure said to me in Cairo during 1967 that a party, to initiate social change,

> is generally built in the course of a struggle, and the struggle is the yardstick by which you judge militancy and leadership and choose your cadres. If Nasser issues a call for militants, 30 million will respond; but how do you select them? We've had fifteen years of discouraging, even suppressing political activity from below; now the problem is how to stimulate it.

In the countryside, there was none of the fury displayed in China's struggle to get its peasants to 'stand up' and break the power of the landed rich. Land reform there was, but initiated by edict and bureaucratic action. Peasant power was passive and subdued, and resistance by the big land-owners was strong if surreptitious. Even the administrative movement was carefully modulated by such processes as giving land-owners transition periods in which to dispose of their land, or paying them compensation. Land reform achieved a certain redistribution of land and rural income, but it did not drastically alter old political patterns in the countryside, for three million agricultural labourers remained practically unorganized, and without them there was no dynamic for change in the countryside. Even when the Kamshish affair burst with dramatic clangour into the sluggish bureaucratic scene of land reform, there was more promise than performance. This affair centred round the murder in a small village of a peasant member of the Arab Socialist Union, and led to the uncovering of an intricate intrigue by a rich and influential family to conceal land holdings considerably in excess of the limits decreed by law. It opened up the countryside to the scrutiny of a special Control Commission to Act against the Remnants of Feudalism: headed, incidentally, by

Field-Marshal Amer, the then army commander-in-chief. Declared policy was to break the grip of the big land-owners on the administration, on the poor peasants and even on the Arab Socialist union, since the political influence of land-owners was still largely intact in the countryside. At Kamshish the poor rose briefly to their feet; but at the top there was still the old reluctance to let any popular movement run its full course. In Egypt the process of national revolution and even industrialization went far, and the professed commitment was to socialism. Yet as Anouar Abdel-Malek has described it, the nature and training of the officer corps; its distrust of popular mobilization; its determination to remain the sole holder of power; its rejection of the role of socialists in the building of socialism; and its view of socialism as evolving not through class conflict, but by the arbitrary direction of the state – all gave control to a powerful apparatus dominated by the military, the technocrats and the administrators, and far from the mass of the people.[48]

It was the Six Day War in 1967 which showed that the state apparatus, led by the military élite, was in danger of undermining the very state and the revolution that it was trying to lead; and which destroyed, in theory at any rate, the pretensions of the army to occupy its hegemonic position in the Egyptian state. For Egypt's military élite showed itself unprepared and incapable in war, and engaged in conspiracy to defend its privilege, by toppling Nasser if need be. After five days of crushing defeat, Nasser's resignation announcement might have left the way open to the generals to stage a coup and grab power. Instead it brought Egyptians pouring into the streets to demand Nasser's return, and refusing to be intimidated back indoors even when their own air force had batteries of anti-aircraft guns light up the Cairo sky to break up the demonstrations. Six weeks later, on the fifteenth anniversary of the coup, Nasser announced that the revolution's greatest victory would be the return to civilian life of the military élite it had brought to power. 'The obstinacy of our generation in keeping the reins of power will prevent the renewal of the people and the appearance of new leaders,' he said. 'Our generation has provided leaders for the transition period. What is necessary now is that other generations step forward to take their place in the government of the country.' Army plotting was charged in a series of trials of top army, defence and security heads; and this forced on Nasser what sounded like a decision to break the political power of the officers and denounce the corporate leading role of the army. The popular risings of early June had given the regime, at last, the beginnings of an alternative base of support. But it is unclear how far the momentum of the June demonstrations has carried, and whether popular outburst is being shaped into popular power. If it is not, an officer corps, grown into an élite with much of the power that the state deploys in its hands, could still undo the social revolution that started as a conspiratorial coup d'état. In that event, Egypt will be a convincing demonstration of the argument that a professional army, however radically attuned, is intrinsically a force unable on its own to create social revolution. This was no armed egalitarian popular movement impelled from below, and enlisting the population in action for change. The army which brought to power a lower middle class helped it use office to entrench its privileges, and to block the farflung social change which alone could build a popular base for Egyptian social revolution.

Algeria's army was founded as an army for liberation war; its base was the poor *fellahin*; and its officer corps was trained in the political aims of the war for liberation. How the course of the war short-circuited the course of the revolution has already been described. The result was to make the army first a competitor for power with the FLN, and then its usurper, but as a bureaucratic state machine, and not as a popularly based revolutionary front.

In 1962 the Tripoli conference of the FLN adopted a programme which echoed the objectives of the Soummam conference during the war. It criticized the ideological poverty of the FLN, and pointed out that 'the amalgamation of the state institutions and the organs of the FLN had reduced the latter to a merely administrative apparatus'. A new bureaucratic class was in danger of developing, it warned. Yet nothing was done to transform the FLN, weakened by successive internal crises from 1962 onwards. Algeria's new bureaucratic élite was born in the years of victory, as the French departed. There was a mass exodus not only of settlers, but of French administrators – though a heavy proportion of top technicians and experts in Algeria remained French throughout* – and into the vacancies stepped Algerians. Furthermore, there was a scramble for the abandoned property of the departing colons: not only for land, which was seized by their agricultural labourers, but also for cars and houses. A small but privileged group grew rapidly out of the triumph of struggle, and at a time when the FLN was exhausting itself in internal wrangles and failing as a mass popular party of the poor and oppressed.

The needle issue for the Algerian revolution was the shape of agrarian reform. The rebellion had its roots in the exploited *fellahin*, and the peasantry was the backbone of the army of liberation. But the shape of agrarian reform was by no means clear. Was there to be nationalization with or without compensation? Was it to be nationalization of land owned by Frenchmen only, or by Algerians too? Was land to be redistributed among the small and dispossessed peasantry; were peasant cooperatives to be formed, in a system of self-management or autogestion; or were state farms to be established in a nationalized sector?

In the army, the debate on independence policy had been more vigorous than in the FLN, though it was not prosecuted in public because of the inhibitions imposed by the Evian agreement. There were two principal tendencies in the army: on the one hand, there was pressure from the ranks for the distribution of the land to the poor peasantry that had been plundered of its proper heritage; and on the other, there was growing support for state farms in the interests of state efficiency and control. Ultimately the latter tendency prevailed, in this intensely corporate, professionally organized army.

*Gérard Chaliand, *L'Algérie – est-elle Socialiste?* (Paris, 1964), p. 89, wrote that in 1963 an astonishing number of administrative officers in the Algerian government were French or had been trained by the French. In the highest levels of the administration, 43 per cent were from the latter two groups, and in the second highest level, 77 per cent. Of administrators in all categories, Chaliand gave the figure of 34,097 who were members of the FLN, and 35,900 who were French or French-trained administrators.

Ben Bella himself, and the political forces that gathered round him, espoused autogestion, not least because workers' control seemed a way of developing a political force in the country independent of, and able to counter, the power of the army. There thus developed, early on, a conflict over this issue between Ben Bella in government and the army. When at the moment of Algeria's independence, French land-owners hurriedly left for France, the system of autogestion seemed to accord with reality. The Algerian state found itself with a large number of abandoned farms for which it was incapable of supplying state administrators and control. Autogestion, the handing over to workers' committees, appeared the only answer, and it happened to be the one supported by Ben Bella's circle of advisers. It was a pragmatic solution almost inadvertently reached during a time of social upheaval; and it was promoted by its advocates as the Algerian road to socialism, despite the fact that it was mostly limited to the agrarian sector. But autogestion never really worked. In the beginning it was asserted with diffidence, partly because Algeria was unsure what the French would tolerate under the Evian agreement (and for years the abandoned farms were known as *bien-vacants*: in-waiting); partly because Ben Bella's government was torn between contesting government pressures; and partly because Ben Bella himself equivocated rather than asserted one policy or another. The army was never reconciled to the idea, however. Though the March 1963 decrees for the confiscation and control of former French lands finally formalized the policy of autogestion, it was evident by then that the agricultural sector was faltering; and the army, still advocating state farms as part of a state sector, could accuse the Ben Bella regime of wasting the patrimony by uneconomic and inefficient policies.

Farmworkers, themselves involved and radical intellectuals, had been won over temporarily to the policy of autogestion, but were disillusioned by its failures and by the restraints put upon it. Ben Bella's promise of mass support in the countryside was not materializing; nor was it in the FLN, which remained in principle the pivot of policy-making, but which existed mostly in name, since both army and government considered real political mobilization far too explosive a prospect. The unions in UGTA (Union Générale des Travailleurs Algériens) had their powers curbed, and were alienated by the regime; and in 1962 the Kabyle, the first region to revolt against the French, and the one which had suffered most from the war but been badly neglected by the Algiers-based government, broke into open revolt under the leadership of Hocine Ait Ahmed. As the FLN frittered away its strength in internal dispute, the army and the administration remained the only organized forces. By 1964 Ben Bella was in search of a firmer base of power, but because the FLN was not rooted in a firm policy or social base, his politics had grown increasingly manipulative. By 1964–5 he needed, Bonapartist-style, to find new allies. He contemplated several courses. One was to win over Kabyle support with a promise to release Ait Ahmed from prison and reconcile himself with the Kabyle leadership. Another was to reforge the FLN so as to give its radical elements their head in political organization. Yet another was a scheme for a popular militia as a counter to the power of the army. When Boumedienne emphatically opposed this last, a compromise resulted whereby the popular militia was to be directed by the FLN, but trained by the army. (A member of Boumedienne's general staff was put in charge of the militia, and he later sided with Boumedienne in the coup against Ben Bella.)

By mid-1965 Ben Bella was preparing to stage a civilian, or political, coup of his own. This was to coincide with the meeting of the Second Afro-Asian Conference, due to open in Algiers on 25 June. Ben Bella was to make a move to the left, in which the FLN would be transformed, after the style of Cuba, into a party with a firm organic commitment to the left, including the Algerian Communist Party; with stronger disciplinary controls; and a marxist training of functionaries and the rank-and-file. It would be a decisive shift to meet worker and trade-union demands; to give autogestion a clear run over the resistance from the Ministry of Agriculture; to free Ait Ahmed, and dispense with certain right-wing ministers in the government. It would also get rid of Boumedienne as head of the army. It was to be a shift by Ben Bella in search of a firmer base of power, but it might have opened possibilities for a new crystallization of forces for social change in Algeria.

The army coup that Boumedienne staged that month was a putsch to pre-empt the Ben Bella move. It was a blow at the top, as Ben Bella's own plan would have been: because between them, the state of apathy into which the FLN had sunk and the manipulative nature of post-independence Algerian politics, had effectively immobilized any initiative other than that taken by the army or government-in-power.

After the coup, the army created a twenty-three-man Council of the Revolution, with Boumedienne as head of state. Like the Ben Bella regime before it, it was an amalgam of individuals and interests; but the core of the new government comprised a business–military élite in which the influence of ministers Bouteflika and Mideghiri, conservative in tendency, was strong. This core came to be known as the Oujda group. The army network already present in the police and security organizations, in the ministries and in the rural administrations, was consolidated by creating a new executive secretariat of the FLN, drawn largely from the army. The role of the FLN was redefined as one of elaboration, orientation, animation and control, but not of supremacy over the state. It was the army that was to be supreme.

Some parts of the army, however, considered that it was not the army itself that governed, but a faction working with the Oujda group, a new army and civil service bureaucracy that ruled in the name, but without the full participation, of the Council of the Revolution, which was rarely summoned. In November 1967, Boumedienne's chief-of-staff, Colonel Tahir Zbiri (who had been appointed to that position by Ben Bella in an apparently abortive effort to counter Boumedienne's influence) moved tanks on Algiers in an unsuccessful attempt to unseat the Boumedienne government. It was a reaction against the new technocrats who were taking over the revolution; a protest against the control of the state by Boumedienne and his intimates without consulting those who had won the seven years' war. They had not calculated, the rebels reasoned, on displacing Ben Bella by Boumedienne, only to have Boumedienne play Ben Bella's role.

The army began to assert its leading role in the execution of policy. Boumedienne made it clear that the emphasis would be on an efficient state. The public sector grew, and with it the civil service. The debate over the autogestion section was resolved in favour of the technocrats, who advocated close state control. It seemed by the end of 1969 that Algeria would develop along the lines of Nasserist Egypt, with the army playing the assertive role above all other forces, but in alliance with technocrats and a lower middle class risen to power, both verbally committed to far-reaching social change but trying to achieve this by state initiative alone. As for nationalizations conducted by the state, they were all very well; but as long as a privileged group was able to use its power in a state-controlled economy to appropriate a huge share of the surplus for its own high standards of consumption, the real crisis of underdevelopment would remain unresolved.[49]

Has there been another way in Africa; can there be another way? Perhaps only where guerrilla warfare is the path to liberation is this likely. Thus paradoxically, the countries last to be free – Portugal's colonies and the powerful white domination regimes of the far South – as well as those already nominally independent, but which realize they have still to wage the real battles of independence – could be those states that will achieve new structures for development by building the revolution as they fight. Guerrilla warfare in its nature cannot be led by élite leaderships, nor can it be fought for élite aims; the problem, as post-war Algeria has seen, will be to conserve the revolutionary impetus generation in battle. In Guiné-Bissau a totally new administration will be built: Cabral has made this clear. Development will be based on the peasantry not on the urban privileged; and the new state will emerge in the revolution as embodied in the PAIGC, the party which leads the battle and the revolution. This is in the conviction that Africa can rescue herself only by radical changes in her own internal structure, and by changes that have a popular base, and popular support.

The Dependence Struggle

In sharp contrast to the swift and incisive blows of the coup d'état stands the popular passivity, even torpor, during and after the action. Here and there strikes, demonstrations and trade-union pressure have precipitated the fall of a government, but nowhere have their initiators proved strong or persistent enough to make a direct bid for power. In Congo-Brazzaville, in Dahomey and in Upper Volta, general strikes toppled unpopular regimes; but, except in Congo-Brazzaville, and there only temporarily, the trade unions simply invited the military to assume power, and their role subsided or was effaced with the advent of army government, or a new government installed by the army. The active unions appear to have been those of the better paid state-employed workers, including civil servants; and perhaps their interests have not been so distinct from the military–bureaucratic formations risen to power through the coup for them to assert contrary pressure. Where the soldiers themselves have staged coups d'état for reform purposes, however vaguely elaborated, the coups were aborted early on, as in Nigeria, or over the course of some years, as in Congo-Brazzaville, because the army reformers could find or create no social forces able to alter the patterns of élite politics. Coups d'état occur because governments are too weak to rule, but radical forces too weak to take power.[50]

If armies either block radical options or are unwilling on their own to open them, where lie the sources for change in Africa? Is a strategy of social revolution possible in areas other than those like Guiné-Bissau, and the embattled south of Angola, Mozambique, Rhodesia and South Africa, where armies not of professional soldiers but of armed radicals are making the revolution in the struggle? It may be asked: is a social revolution necessary? And the answer must be: to break dependence, yes. For dependence is embedded not only in external controls and direction, but also in the absence within new countries of Africa of popular initiative, participation and production. This is not to say that independence has brought no change at all to Africa.

But what development there has been, has been unbalanced. The progress in education has only intensified the crisis: for the products of the new schools have grown more demanding; but the economy, no more self-supporting. Appetites have grown, but not the means of sustenance.

We need a last, brief but close look at the decolonized state.

The conflict in which the coup d'état is the short-cut answer is over very secondary sources of power. Old forms of dependence have altered; new ones have emerged. National colonialisms have made way in the last decade for the giant multi-national corporations. And the principal purpose of these corporations is not the export of capital to exploit cheap labour in the colonies; it is to concentrate investment at home, so as to expand production in the metropolitan country, and to 'organise the market as a colony'.[51] Africa, like Latin America and Asia, has been incorporated into the economic structures of the new imperialism.

> Imperialism [writes Gunder Frank of Latin America] is not only this or that foreign country exploiting Latin American economies; it is the structure of the entire economic, political, social, yes, and cultural, system in which Latin America and all its parts, however 'isolated', find themselves participating as exploited partners. . . . Development cannot radiate from the centre (the capitalist world) to the periphery (the underdeveloped world). The periphery instead can develop only if it breaks out of the relations which have made and kept it underdeveloped, or if it can break up the system as a whole.[52]

By 1965, halfway through the development decade, aid had reached the point where the poor borrowing countries were transferring to their rich donors more for the service of existing loans than they were receiving in new ones. Within only five years of independence, the outward drain from Africa has begun, and Africa can do little about it. When it increases exports of primary products, prices tend to fall on the world market. When it tries to industrialize, the rich industrialized countries place restrictions on the importation of African-made goods. Aid is no answer; it deepens dependence. As for industrialization, the multi-national corporations are directly involved in such economic development as does take place in the new states, and their presence has deepened the structural dependence of the separate African economies on the advanced capitalist centres of production. Heavy industries remain absent; those industries that are developed are for import-substitution goods. The structural weakness of African economies makes them dependent for their foreign exchange earnings on the export of primary products.

With the exception of the oil-producing countries and certain metal producers, underdeveloped economies relying on sales of primary products have, since the end of the Korean-war boom, experienced a slowing down in the rate of growth in total earnings. In the case of Tropical Africa, while the value of exports rose about 55 per cent between 1949 and 1955 it rose only 15 per cent between 1955 and 1960, and lately the position has probably worsened. . . . As Tropical Africa is principally an agricultural producer, though her world position is strongest in minerals, it is safe to assume that a steady and rapid expansion of exports in future is highly unlikely. A few individual countries with important mineral deposits will, of course, represent the exception to the general rule. Imports, on the other hand, have been growing faster than exports, with the result that, in recent years, there seems to be no surplus in the trade account for Africa as a whole. When investment income paid abroad and 'services' are taken into account, Tropical Africa has a considerable deficit on current account.[53]

These dilemmas of development have been common to African states whether they have professed some form of scientific socialism or have been content to offer no prescription at all. Even in the Ivory Coast, deep in the embrace of French capital and French foreign policy, and claiming an economic miracle of West German proportions, the strategy of economic growth based on close links with international capital illuminates the African dilemma. Year by year there has been a favourable trade balance; but the picture is one of French prosperity in the Ivory Coast, not of African prosperity, for the economic boom has left the great majority of Ivorians untouched. In 1965 private funds transferred abroad amounted to twice the total of foreign aid and private capital which came into the country. Ivorian aid to France is gathering momentum![54] African economies may grow under the prompting of the corporations, but dependence will deepen, because their policies are not directed to African self-sustaining growth.

The new phase of dependence has set the economic dilemmas of the newly independent state, but it has also moulded political shapes within. Bourgeoisie and peasantry, worker and white-collar clerk, red-tape administrator and unemployed: what roles do they play while the army leaves the barracks for government?

With the underdevelopment of its economies, has gone the cramping of Africa's bourgeoisie, its indigenous capitalist class. Africa's economies have joined modern capitalism too late, in its old age of monopoly, to get good shares or good seats. The bourgeoisie in Africa is not the dominant class that it is in Europe and America. What industrial development has taken place is the result of foreign capital, foreign technology, foreign initiative. In the shadow of the corporations, the African bourgeoisie's growth has been stunted and faltering. A local commercial bourgeoisie has grown, on import–export businesses, and real estate speculation, but the African entrepreneur is dependent on the patronage of the corporation, whose middle-man he becomes, or on the African state, for capital is accumulated slowly and painfully unless it accrues from state sources. The long-talked-about fundamental contradictions between the roles of the 'national' and the 'comprador' bourgeoisie have proved largely a myth; neither branch of the family has grown to decisive influence or size, let alone dominance.

If the new shapes of dependence have cramped the growth of Africa's bourgeoisie, they have done the same to its working class. Arrighi[55] has produced compelling descriptions of the tiny, stunted working class, but even more significant, a cogent analysis of the trend which will continue to block its growth. In all Tropical Africa, only eleven out of every 100 members of the labour force are in wage employment; and this includes migrant labour, so that the proletariat proper is even smaller. Everywhere government is the largest employer of labour. In Nigeria, for example, four in every ten wage-earners are typical white-collar workers, such as teachers, sales personnel and office staff. In the last ten to fifteen years, wage employment has been relatively static in Tropical Africa.[56] In some countries, indeed, the working class has shrunk in manufacturing and service-industry jobs.[57] Majhemout Diop has written of Senegal: 'It can be said that as long as a new economic and industrial policy is not introduced, the Senegalese working class will develop very slowly.' He suggested that this working class be called pre-proletarian; it lacks the noteworthy characteristics of a proletariat proper.[58] Samir Amin has said[59] that because urbanization has not been accompanied by industrialization, the popular urban masses of Africa's rapidly grown cities have not become a proletariat. The smallness, the slow growth and the heavy white-collar composition of the working class in Africa is no accident; it flows from the capital-intensive investment policies of the international corporations.[60] These require relatively less labour, which is correspondingly higher paid, and also a different composition of the labour force. Accordingly, Arrighi argues, Africa's working class falls into two main strata. The first consists of the workers who inherited colonial salary rates and live a middle-class style of life. The second is made up of those in the lower strata, close to the peasantry from whose ranks they sprang when they were forced off the land in the massive rural exodus that colonialism prompted; they have never been fully incorporated into the urban economy, but are the under-employed and under-paid, or the altogether unemployed, of the urban slums. In the opinion of Arrighi and Saul, these lower strata really belong to the peasantry (and exist in part outside the wage economy). The small minority of the upper stratum, on the other hand, earning three to five times as much, is closer to the élites and sub-élites in bureaucratic employment; this combined category they term the 'labour aristocracy'. The term, they suggest, could be improved upon; and the documentation on which a thorough class analysis must be based is clearly incomplete. But it is crucial to scrutinize African society for those groups whose interests converge with the politics of the corporations; and for those whose interests are deeply antagonistic, and would provide the forces for a second revolution, to break dependence. As the argument runs,[61] the power base of the new state and what stability it achieves must be sought in a consistency between the interests of the corporations, and groups other than the feudal, land-owning or bourgeoisie, which themselves either do not exist or are insufficiently solid to constitute the power base. It is the African élite, sub-élite and privileged stratum of the working class which owe their emergence and their consolidation to corporation capital-intensive policies, that promote the rapid income-growth of these labour aristocracies while restraining the absorption into the wage sectors of the migrant or near-peasant worker. What will break dependence and solve poverty; and who would resist such a policy? Africa needs not foreign capital-intensive, but domestic labour-intensive policies; not the squandering or extravagant consumption of savings, but their investment for capital accumulation. (Capital-intensive policies domestically generated might be another thing, but such a choice is unreal: capital-intensive development can come at this point of time for Africa only from abroad. For domestic capital-intensive policies, labour-intensive programmes must prepare the ground.) Such surplus as Africa produces is repatriated abroad as the reward of the corporations, or devoured by the élites. Any attempt to reallocate the surplus and the élite share, in a drive for primary accumulation, would hit directly at the élite groups that have benefited most from the pattern of growth without development. They would strive not to change but to perpetuate the existing order.

SPRINGS OF CHANGE

From where could change come: from worker-led insurrection, or peasant armies marching to power? The argument – which is the more revolutionary: the peasantry or the working class? – has grown stiff and obstinate with a choice posed in absolute terms. Which peasantry is meant; and what are the spurs to peasant action? For, like Africa's workers, the peasantry is not as homogeneous and undiversified as the labels on the pigeon-holes might suggest.

Eight in every ten Africans remain subsistence or near-subsistence farmers on the land. These are Fanon's disinherited, the wretched of the earth; but, he also argued, they are the revolutionary class of the continent. How disinherited are they, how revolutionary? And, as that is an unreal question so bluntly posed, where and when and how is peasant insurgency to come? For it is not one countryside but several. Here the peasantry has risen to its feet and seized guns. There, it has appeared to offer no challenge to authority or policy. And while it is certain that if the countryside does not change, nothing in Africa will, outside the shuffling of power-seeking groups in the capital, it is not certain that the change will be induced solely or largely by peasant action. 'We are a country of peasants,' Amilcar Cabral has written[62] of Guiné-Bissau, fighting to free itself from Portuguese colonialism. 'Does it represent the main revolutionary force? I must confine myself to Guiné: the peasantry is not a revolutionary force. Which may seem strange, particularly as we have based our armed struggle for liberation on the peasantry. A distinction must be drawn between a physical and the revolutionary force. Physically the peasantry is a great force . . . but we have trouble convincing the peasantry to fight.' In Kenya it was the peasant rising of the Kikuyu that ignited the Mau Mau struggle; and the unemployed and wretched of the towns who supplied and sustained it, until these links between urban slums and the forests were severed, and the rising defeated. It is these dispossessed who will demand a settlement with the political élite which rose to office on their sacrifice, and then abandoned them.

In East and Central Africa, when the colonial administration was under fire during the 1950s, it was facing peasant revolt against government schemes for agrarian change. The pressures of the peasantry at the periphery were at least as important in forcing a shift of colonial strategy as were the demands of the élite at the centre.[63] Rural struggles have been sharpest in the countries penetrated by white settlers. Algeria's war for independence was fought by the peasant *wilayas*, but it was the middle-class élite that captured their victory. Peasant struggle is important. But so is a crystallized ideology and leadership for independence, too. In the Congo after independence, the rural mass in the Eastern provinces where 'the mood in the villages reflected a stunned sense of betrayal'[64] by the politicians, and peasant agriculture went into a catastrophic decline after 1960, peasant rebellion set up an alternative government. The year of the rebellion in Stanleyville saw the assault on city government from the countryside, for the rebel army came from the peasantry; towns did not fall from within but were captured from without by their peasant-based armies. That rebellion might have been 'a social movement which had revolutionary tactics but lacked a revolutionary strategy',[65] yet it took a combination of fighter-bombers from the United States, the enlistment of white mercenaries, and the Belgian–United States paratroop drop on Stanleyville to defeat it.

West Africa's peasantry is different in kind from the peasantries of Kenya, Algeria and the Congo. Across huge regions, there has emerged neither a land-owning aristocracy nor a dependent agricultural force, for there has been little dispossession of the land. The revolution in the countryside will lie principally not in the acquisition of holdings from those who have too much, but in the revolutionizing of production by those who live their lives on the land, and win so little from it, for themselves or the economy. In general, the pattern of land-ownership and cultivation is based on the family and the community. In some regions, land has been brought within the market economy, and marked inequalities of wealth are developing. But in most, especially in West Africa, the peasantry is in the main neither spectacularly wealthy nor desperately poor; on the average they are middle peasants.[66] In Nigeria's Western region, where political divisions have been refined along class lines further than in most other areas of West Africa, there are acute inequalities in income, wealth and land-holding. A gentry class has emerged on the land, and an impoverished peasantry. But as yet there has been no sharp confrontation between landlord creditors and tenant debtors, because there is not yet much rural indebtedness, and there is no landless agricultural proletariat.[67] Landlord–tenant relations are still criss-crossed by family and kinship ties and obligations. Peasant resentment expressed in tax riots is directed at government and the politicians, not at the landed bourgeoisie; conflicts, however fierce, have remained parochial, and peasants have not acted as a social force beyond the confines of their own communities.

The countryside has been left by the privileged in power to

wither in its poverty, and the peasantry has found, or used, no way to change the politics that are pursued in the cities. The peasantry is immobilized for struggle by its dispersal in small local communities, by its being subject to parochial authority; by the vagueness of its political purpose and aims; and by the fact that, while the poorest and most abandoned, the peasantry is in many ways the least touched by crisis. The land fulfils basic consumption needs, even if these are pitifully low; and when there is national crisis at the centre, peasant peripheries remain relatively untouched.

The patterns of Africa's dependence will not change until its peasantry 'stands up', as China's peasantry did. But it may need the mobilization of the urban working and unemployed poor, who are the close cousins of the peasantry; for through them, urban unrest could filter as rebellion into the countryside. Poverty becomes poverty by contrast; it is in the towns, where the privileged live their flashy lives, that the poor and the despised grow most easily disaffected. Searching for the springs of revolution in Guiné-Bissau, Amilcar Cabral[68] delineated a group – 'we have not yet found an exact term for' – composed of young people newly arrived in the towns, with contacts both urban and rural, who make a comparison between the living standards of their own families and those of the Portuguese. It was from the ranks of these that the first guerrilla fighters of Guiné-Bissau were trained. They fight a traditional colonial enemy, of course. The ways and means at the disposal of those seeking and needing change in independent Africa are far different. But the spurs to action for change could similarly come for a new power base, linking a mobilized peasantry with the organized ranks of the dispossessed in the towns.

Settling the revolutionary potential of any force in Africa solely by a genetic-type investigation into the social origins of leadership or rank-and-file runs the risk of becoming a futile exercise in theoretical abstraction.[69] Instead, one must seek out those groups which share a dependence on, and an interest in, the perpetuation of the neo-colonial economic system, whether in the long or only the very short term; and they must be seen not only in statistical tables but in action. Whose interests require preserving the internal structure of the new state; whose interests cry out for the dismantling of the structure? Who strikes to fight his way into the ranks of the privileged; and who to link with those forces that can transform the state of dependence?

Could Africa's omnibus political parties be radicalized from within? Is there not a role for army officers, linked with revolutionary intellectuals and a popular front, as in the Sudan, to join and defend the cause of change? These are real, not rhetorical questions; and they have, essentially, to be posed and answered in Africa, where conditions may lead people to think that the continent is ripe for revolution, but where the other ingredients are largely missing: the instruments and perspectives of change.

In Chad the armed forces led by Frolinat represent not only those left to perish in neglect but those who seek in their deprivation an instrument, if not yet a sustained ideology, for change. But discontent alone is not enough. Those hunting jobs and privilege could dissipate themselves in acrimony against their more successful competitors, through conflict within and around the élite; or they could generalize social protest and raise it to significant heights of action for a radical alternative. The jobless could be immobilized by despair; or they could find the energy of protest, even rebellion. In Africa, governments that were yesterday harassed by unemployed school-leavers will in future be besieged. The unemployed are overwhelmingly the young; 'applicantship' for a job has become a way of life. The cooking pot in the shanty town or crowded back street of the capital no longer stretches to feed the unemployed living on the under-employed; and those beaten by the city must retreat to the countryside, which they left not long before because it, too, offered too little. Even among Africa's large and plastic middle class, frustration could grow to ferment; because although the declarations of 'stability' proliferate, the better life grows more and more elusive. For many who see their place among the privileged, the system is closing up. There are plush positions in the burgeoning government bureaucracies, banks and commercial offices; but not for them. Their rebellion could evaporate into accommodation, as those who protest their disability find room at the top. But accommodation at the top is already crowded, let alone unlimited. A compact of the intellectuals and the bitter young men of the cities trailing links with the countryside could be explosive in changing discontent into organized dissent.

The recognition of the need for change is far from the ability to realize it; but disciplined political movements could, in turn, translate disenchantment with the record of Africa's independence into a drive for real change. Such will not happen, however, until new forces seize the initiative from the privileged élite and the climbers towards privilege, who have so disqualified themselves from the right to rule.

As for rule by the soldiers, this by its nature is emergency action that can have no permanence. The soldiers hold the ring while new internal power amalgams are arranged. They achieve no real alternatives, only postponements of solutions; for while the crisis and the conflict of dependence are temporarily frozen, the 'stability' promised by the military meanwhile shores up dependence itself.

If the 1950s and the 1960s were the years of independence excitement and euphoria, the 1970s are likely to be sober, chastening years. There have been failures of direction not only among those who promised an African paradise on earth, if they were entrusted to run it, but also among those seeking a genuine independence, who had a faulty understanding of the African reality, and of the new crucial corporations and powers. The political compromise of the old imperialisms was conceived, and presented, as total victory over them; and attention was diverted during the celebration of independence from those elements within African society that would ensure not the opportunity for but the impossibility of a changed life for the great majority of Africans.

This book has concentrated on the shape of power inside Africa; not on the power over Africa exercised from outside by investment capital, credit, trade and diplomacy. That is another book, and a required companion to this one. It would have to probe how important these coups have been to continuing foreign control over the continent's economic infrastructure. It would have to trace the relations of multi-national corporations with African governments; the activities of the diplomats and crypto-diplomats, and the planners, technicians and advisers. It would have to scrutinize how Western government and business-investment strategies have been planned and pursued, pre-eminently by the United States.

In 1964 United States capital directly invested in Africa amounted to less than four per cent of capital from that country directly invested abroad. But throughout the African continent, as in Latin America and Asia, there is evidence of mounting American involvement by American money. The multi-national corporations, most of them based in the United States, are richer by far than the individual African states. Ranking African states (gross national product) and corporations (gross annual sales) Nigeria comes thirty-ninth on the list after General Motors, Ford, Standard, Royal Dutch, Shell, General Electric, Chrysler, Unilever, Mobil Oil and others. Ghana is seventy-eighth after Union Carbide; and apart from Algeria (sixty-first) and Morocco (sixty-fourth), there are no other countries in the first hundred.

A United States spokesman* has said:

> The large companies are very big and increasingly are becoming global in their pursuit of international business. It is imperative that both the large companies and governments re-evaluate their relationships and adjust them to the inter-dependence that exists. They both have tremendous economic power. But the nation state is dominant in the political sphere and the multi-national company has access to the world market and is dominant in the commercial sphere. *They need one another*.

How they have used one another is the contemporary story of power over Africa.

Recent statements by United States spokesmen, including the Nixon state-of-the-world address, have served notice on African governments that they should count on less aid in the future and look instead to private interests for help in 'developing their countries'. The 1960 United States Foreign Aid Bill gave birth

* Herbert Salzman, Assistant Administrator for Private Resources, Agency for International Development.

to a publicly funded but privately controlled Overseas Private Investment Corporation (OPIC) to insure and further subsidize United States investors. In the 1970s the American foreign-aid programme is to be reorganized so as to transfer control over it even more explicitly to United States corporations. A report released by the presidential panel headed by the former President of the Bank of America recommends that the United States make more use of such international organizations as the United Nations and the World Bank in order to facilitate investment with fewer political problems.* The World Bank particularly has announced plans to expand its activity in Africa.

In November 1969 a Business International round-table meeting took place in Addis Ababa. (Business International is an influential information-gathering arm of United States corporations.) The talks were off the record, said Business International's executive vice-president, 'with the entire leadership of less developed countries in Africa, Asia and Latin America'. *African Development* commented that 'behind the scenes information reveals that this is the beginning of a big new American raid on Africa. . . . Judging by the talks in the corridors, the American raid, when it really comes, will be on an unprecedented scale. . . . The Americans are asking a higher price than the old, flexible colonial traders ever did.'

The World Bank has recently opened an office in Nigeria uniquely to concentrate on that one country. American aid to Nigeria continued throughout the war; Nigeria still benefits from the biggest US-aid programme in Africa; and the postwar reconstruction plans for Nigeria were mapped out in the back rooms of American foundations, corporations and consulting firms. How can United States economic advisers and investors not try to maintain and revive systems in which international business can best function? The coup d'état often presents them with the finest opportunity. It did in Ghana, where Harvard's Development Advisory Service re-vamped the economy. In Brazil after a recent coup d'état a North American university academic admitted that he had, in an official capacity to the

* This new investment strategy is discussed in *International Dependency*, by the Africa Research Group.

Brazilian government, drawn up the plan for the economy. He added that the Americans had been awaiting this opportunity for years. It is striking how the coup d'état in Africa, with rare exceptions like Egypt, the Sudan and Libya, converges towards the stabilization of the situation for overseas capital.

The government of Africa, in the hands of the politician–manipulators, or the less flamboyant but infinitely more parochial soldier–rulers, is not on the whole tyrannical, but bumbling. Time and again it makes false starts, and spreads false hopes. Condemnation there must be; but compassion, too, for those who talked so boldly about freedom but had so little freedom of manoeuvre. The soldiers illuminate the foundations and the failures of the new states of Africa. Those who have usurped government to consolidate the political system have been driven openly to reveal the armature of state power that supports them; the more it is revealed, the more puny it is shown to be, for its essential supports are not inside but outside Africa. As for the soldiers who seize government to reform or radicalize it, their success or failure will depend on the popular forces for change that they release within Africa; not on the force of armies or the power that flows out of the barrel of their guns.

APPENDIX: PRINCIPAL PERSONS

THE SUDAN

The Politicians:

Ismail al-Azhari, leader of the National Unionist Party (NUP)
Abdallah Khalil, leader of the Umma Party, former army Brigadier
Ali Abd al-Rahman, leader of the People's Democratic Party (PDP)

The Religious Leaders:

Sayid Abd al-Rahman, leader of the Ansar
Sayid Ali al-Mirghani, leader of the Khatmiyya
Sayid al-Siddiq al-Mahdi, who succeeded his father as leader of the Ansar
Sayid Sadiq al-Mahdi, who succeeded his father as leader of the Ansar

The Army Brass:

General Ibrahim Abboud, Commander-in-Chief
Major General Ahmed Abd al-Wahab
Brigadier Hassan Beshir Nasr
Brigadier Mohammed Nasr Osman

The Political Partners of the Army Junta:

Ahmed Kheir
Abu Rannat

Coup-makers among the Brigadiers:

Brigadier Mohieddin Abdallah
Brigadier Abd al-Rahim Shannan

Coup-makers among the Junior Officers:

Major Abdel Kibaida Rahman and others
Colonel Ali Hamid and others, mainly majors and captains of the Infantry Training College

Appendix: Principal Persons

Popular Leaders among the Communist Party, the trade unions, the Gezira Tenants, the students, intellectuals, the Moslem Brotherhood:

NIGERIA

The Politicians of the First Republic:

Dr Nnamdi Azikiwe, First President
*Sir Abubakar Tafawa Balewa, Premier
*Sir Ahmadu Bello, Sardauna of Sokoto, Premier of the North
*Chief Festus Okotie-Eboh, Minister of Finance
*Chief Samuel Akintola, Premier of the West
Chief R. Fani-Kayode
Dr Michael Okpara, Premier of the East, and others

The Army Brass:

†Major-General J. Aguiyi-Ironsi, first Nigerian GOC who restored order after the first coup, and became Head of State
*Brigadier Z. Maimalare
*Brigadier S. Ademulegun
*Lt-Colonel A. Largema
*Lt-Colonel Yakubu Pam, and others
Brigadier B. Ogundipe, now Nigerian High Commissioner in London

The Young Coup-makers:

‡Major Chukwuma Kaduna Nzeogwu
‡Major Emmanuel Ifeajuna
Major T. C. Onwuatuegwu
†Major D. O. Okafor
Captain Nwobosi
Major I. U. Chukuka
Major Ademoyega

* slain in the January coup
† slain in the July revenge coup
‡ killed in the war

The Military Governors:

Lt-Colonel Hassan Katsina
Lt-Colonel David Ejoor
Lt-Colonel F. Adekunle Fajuyi
Colonel Chukwuemeka Ojukwu
Major Mobalaji Johnson

The Revenge Coup-makers:

Major Murtala Mohammed
His uncle, Alhaji Inuwa Wada
Others, mostly unknown

The Politicians Come to Power in the Second Republic:

Chief Obafemi Awolowo
Alhaji Aminu Kano
Chief Anthony Enahoro
J. S. Tarka

The Civil Servants:

Allison Ayida
Francis Nwokedi
Edwin Ogbu
Hamsad Amadu
M. Asiodu

The War Leaders:

Major-General Yakubu Gowon
Colonel Benjamin Adekunle
Major Sule Apollo
Colonel Muhammed Shuwa

GHANA

The CPP Government headed by and including:

Kwame Nkrumah
Finance Minister Kwesi Amoaka-Atta
Krobo Edusei
Kojo Botsio

Appendix: Principal Persons

Kofi Baako
Colonel Zanlerigu, commander of the President's Own Guard Regiment
Major-General C. M. Barwah

The Opposition, including:

Dr K. Busia
K. Gbedemah (in exile)

The Coup-makers in the Army:

Major-General E. K. Kotoka
A. A. Afrifa
Colonel Albert Ocran, commander of the Accra garrison, and some others

The Coup-makers in the Police:

J. W. K. Harlley, the Commissioner
Anthony Deku, Special Branch

The National Liberation Council:

General J. A. Ankrah
Three other army officers and four police chiefs; civil servants, like E. Omaboe; outside advisers like the Harvard Group; politicians of the former Opposition groups

Unsuccessful Coup-makers:

Lieutenant Arthur and others

REFERENCES

1. SILENT CLAMOUR FOR CHANGE

1. E. J. Hobsbawm, 'Peasants and Rural Migrants in Politics', *The Politics of Conformity in Latin America*, ed. Claudio Veliz (Oxford, 1968).
2. S. E. Finer, *The Man on Horseback* (London, 1962).
3. Review article in *Political Quarterly*, XXXIV, 2, April–June 1963.
4. Morris Janowitz, *The Military in the Political Development of New Nations: An Essay in Comparative Analysis* (Chicago, 1964). See also Janowitz's chapter in *Armed Forces and Society*, ed. Jacques van Doorn (The Hague, 1968).
5. Fred van de Mehden and Charles W. Anderson, 'Political Action by the Military in the Developing Areas', *Social Research*, Winter 1961.
6. Van Doorn (ed.), *op. cit.*, Introduction.
7. Martin C. Needler, 'Political Development and Military Intervention in Latin America', *American Political Sciences Review*, September 1968.
8. See for instance, Lucia W. Pye, 'Armies in the Process of Political Modernisation', and Manfred Halpern, 'Middle Eastern Armies and the New Middle Class', *The Role of the Military in Underdeveloped Countries*, ed. John H. Johnston (Princeton, 1962).
9. Veliz (ed.), *op. cit.*
10. Richard Adams, 'Political Power and Social Structures', in Veliz (ed.), *op. cit.*
11. *New Statesman*, 22 December 1967. Review of Veliz.
12. W. F. Gutteridge, *Military Institutions and Power in the New States* (London, 1964), p. 108.
13. Roger Murray, 'Militarism in Africa', *New Left Review*, 38, July–August 1966, p. 53.
14. See 'The Uganda Army: Nexus of Power', *Africa Report*, December 1966, pp. 37–40.
15. Samuel Huntington, quoted by Victor T. Le Vine, 'The Course

of Politics and Violence', *French-Speaking Africa: The Search for Identity*, ed. E. H. Lewis (New York, 1965).

16. Emmanuel Terray, 'Les Révolutions Congolaise et Dahoméene de 1963', *Revue Français de Science Politique*, October 1964.
17. Aristide R. Zolberg, 'The Structure of Political Conflict in the New States of Tropical Africa', *American Political Science Review*, March 1968, p. 80, citing Philippe Decraene, *Le Monde Sélection Hebdomadaire*, 30 June–6 July 1966.

II. THE COLONIAL SEDIMENT

The Grid of Administration

1. John A. Ballard, 'Four Equatorial States', *National Unity and Regionalism in Eight African States*, ed. Gwendolen M. Carter (Cornell, 1966).
2. J. D. Fage, *Short History of Africa* (Harmondsworth, 1962,) p. 197.
3. The phrase is Margery Perham's in her Introduction to John Wheare, *The Nigerian Legislative Council* (London, 1950), p. x.
4. Richard L. Sklar and C. S. Whitaker Jr, 'The Federal Republic of Nigeria', in Carter (ed.), *op. cit.*
5. *ibid.*
6. Lord Lugard, *Political Memoranda* (Lagos, 1918).
7. 'We blacks want to remain French, France having given us every liberty and mingling us without reservation with her own European children,' said Blaise Diagne, first black Deputy from the Senegalese Communes, in 1922. R. Buell, *Native Problem*, II (New York, 1928), p. 81.
8. Hubert Deschamps in '*L'Éveil Politique Africain*' (Paris, 1952).
9. *ibid.*, p. 81.
10. Sir Harold MacMichael, *The Anglo-Egyptian Sudan* (London, 1934), p. 103.
11. *ibid.*, p. 76.
12. Muddathir Abdel Rahim, *The Constitutional Development of the Sudan 1899–1956*. Thesis submitted for the degree of Ph.D. in Government, University of Manchester, May 1964, p. 106.
13. Sir Ronald Wingate, *Wingate of the Sudan* (London, 1955), p. 259.
14. MacMichael, *op. cit.*
15. *ibid.*, p. 104.
16. Michael Crowder, *West Africa Under Colonial Rule* (London, 1968), p. 188.
17. J. Suret-Canale, *L'Afrique Noire*, II (Paris, 1964), p. 95.
18. Crowder, *op. cit.*, p. 188.

19. Quoted in Crowder from '*Le Problème des Chefferies en Afrique Noire Française*', *La Documentation Française* (*Notes et Études Documentaires*) No. 2508, 10 February 1969, p. 7.
20. I. Nicholson, 'Machinery of the Governments', *Government and Politics in Nigeria*, ed. J. P. Mackintosh (London, 1966), p. 151.
21. Rupert Emerson, *From Empire to Nation* (Boston, 1962), p. 38.
22. Colin Cross, *The Fall of the British Empire* (London, 1968), p. 151.
23. *ibid.*
24. *ibid.*, p. 153.
25. Robert Heussler, *Yesterday's Rulers: The Making of the British Colonial Service* (Oxford, 1963), pp. 22–3.
26. *ibid.*, pp. 74–5.
27. *ibid.*, p. 60.
28. *ibid.*, p. 98. See also Robert Heussler, *The British in Northern Nigeria* (London, 1968).
29. Heussler, *Yesterday's Rulers*, p. 164.
30. *ibid.*
31. Delavignette, *Freedom and Authority in French West Africa* (London, 1950), p. 10.
32. Heussler, *op. cit.*, p. 210.
33. Crawford Young, *Politics in the Congo* (Princeton, 1965), p. 577.

Ways and Means of Decolonization

1. Sir Andrew Cohen, *British Policy in Changing Africa* (London, 1959), p. 61.
2. Judd L. Teller, 'The Newest State and Monarch', *The Reporter*, 4 March 1952.
3. Nasser cited by Mohammed Hassanein Heykal in *Al Ahram*, 23–7 July 1962. See Anouar Abdel-Malek, 'The Crisis in Nasser's Egypt', *New Left Review*, 45, September–October 1967.
4. Iain MacLeod, *Daily Telegraph*, 12 March 1965.
5. Donald L. Barnett and Karari Njama, *Mau Mau from Within* (London, 1966), p. 114.
6. *ibid.*, pp. 69–70.
7. Oginga Odinga, *Not Yet Uhuru* (London, 1967), pp. 123–7.
8. Alexander Werth, *De Gaulle* (Harmondsworth, 1965), p. 18.
9. Quoted in Ken Post, *The New States of West Africa* (Harmondsworth, 1964), p. 18.
10. *The Damned* (Présence Africaine edn 1963), p. 55.
11. Gabriel Kolko, *The Politics of the War* (London, 1969).
12. *ibid.*, p. 607.

13. *The Damned*, p. 53.
14. Roger Murray, 'The Ghanaian Road', *New Left Review*, 32, July–August 1965, p. 64.
15. B. B. Schaffer, 'The Concept of Preparation', *World Politics*, vol. 18, No. 1, October 1965, pp. 42–67.
16. See Perry Anderson, 'The Origins of the Present Crisis', *Towards Socialism.*
17. Schaffer, *op. cit.*, p. 51.
18. *Journal of Royal Society of Africanists*, 8 July 1955.
19. Ballard in Carter (ed.), *op. cit.*, pp. 305–6.
20. *Despatch to the Governors of African Territories*, 25 February 1947. See also R. E. Robinson, 'Why Indirect Rule has been Replaced by Local Government', *Journal of African Administration*, July 1950, pp. 12–15.
21. W. P. Kirkman, *Unscrambling an Empire: A Critique of British Colonial Policy, 1956–1966* (London, 1966), p. 66.
22. 'Bureaucracy and Decolonisation: Democracy from the Top', *The New Sociology*, ed. I. L. Horowitz.
23. M. L. Kilson, *Political Change in a West African State: A Study of the Modernisation Process in Sierra Leone* (Harvard, 1966).
24. Max Gluckman, *Culture and Conflict in Africa* (London, 1955).
25. Kilson, *op. cit.*, pp. 285–6.

III. THE SUCCESSOR STATE

White Power, Black Parody

1. The phrase used by Sir Ivor Jennings in *Approach to Self-Government*, Corona, February 1956, pp. 61–2.
2. J. S. Coleman and G. A. Almond, *The Politics of the Developing Areas* (Princeton, 1960), p. 46.
3. James O'Connell in *ODU*, University of Ife Journal, July 1965, Vol. 21, No. 1.
4. M. L. Kilson, *Political Change in a West African State: A Study of the Modernisation Process in Sierra Leone* (Harvard, 1966), p. 24.
5. Thomas Hodgkin and Ruth Schachter, *French-speaking West Africa in Transition*, (Carnegie Endowment for International Peace, no. 528, May 1960), p. 384.
6. P. C. Lloyd, *Africa in Social Change* (Harmondsworth, 1967), p. 141.
7. *ibid.*, p. 143.
8. Ken Post, *The New States of West Africa* (Harmondsworth, 1964), p. 47.

9. Ruth Schachter Morgenthau, *Political Parties in French-Speaking West Africa* (Oxford, 1964), p. 11.
10. Chief Awolowo, *Path to Nigerian Freedom* (London, 1947), p. 64.
11. Letters written in 1871 to Pope Henessey, quoted in E. Blyden, *The West African University*, 1872.
12. Sir Eric Ashby, *African Universities and Western Tradition*, Godkin Lectures at Harvard (Oxford, 1964).
13. Pierre van den Bergh, 'European Languages and Black Mandarins', *Transition*, 34.
14. Jean-Pierre N'Diaye, *Ênquete sur les Étudiants noirs en France* (Paris, Editions Realitiés Africaines, 1962), pp. 107–15.
15. Mbella Sonne Diphoko, *A Few Days and Nights* (London, 1966).
16. Victor T. Le Vine, *Political Leadership in Africa: Post Independence Generation Conflict in Upper Volta, Senegal, Niger, Dahomey, and Central African Republic* (Stanford, 1967), p. 35.
17. *Awo: The Autobiography of Chief Obafemi Awolowo* (Oxford, 1960).
18. *ibid.*, p. 103.
19. Elliott J. Berg, 'The Economic Basis of Political Choice in French West Africa', *American Political Science Review*, No. 2, June 1960.
20. John A. Ballard, 'Four Equatorial States', *National Unity and Regionalism in Eight African States*, ed. Gwendolen M. Carter (Cornell, 1966), p. 297.
21. *ibid.*, pp. 275–9.
22. Immanuel Wallerstein, 'Élites in French-speaking West Africa', *Journal of Modern African Studies*, May 1965, Vol. 3, No. 1, p. 21.
23. Ballard in Carter (ed.), *op. cit.*, p. 325.

Narcissus in Uniform

1. James S. Coleman and Belmont Brice Jr, 'The Role of the Military in Sub-Saharan Africa', *The Role of the Military in Underdeveloped Countries*, ed. John L. Johnson (Princeton, 1962), p. 365.
2. Virginia Thompson and Richard Adloff, *The Emerging States of French Equatorial Africa* (Stanford, 1960), p. 68. See also Abdoulaye Ly, *Mercenaires Noirs: Notes sur une Forme d'exploitation des Africains* (Paris, 1957).
3. Roger Murray, 'Militarism in Africa', *New Left Review*, 38, July–August 1966.
4. Michael Crowder, *West Africa Under Colonial Rule* (London, 1968), p. 260.
5. *ibid.*, p. 258.

6. Coleman and Brice in Johnson (ed.), *op. cit.*, p. 365.
7. Crowder, *op. cit.*, p. 490.
8. W. F. Gutteridge, *Military Institution and Power in the New States* (London, 1964), p. 24.
9. Thompson and Adloff, *op. cit.*, p. 88.
10. Gutteridge, *op. cit.*, p. 100.
11. *ibid.*
12. Lord Curzon, *Memorandum on Commissions for Indians*, quoted in *International Socialist Journal*, Rome, March–April 1966, p. 158, by Hamza Alavi, *The Army and the Bureaucracy in Pakistan.*
13. S. Upkabi, *The West African Frontier Force, an instrument of colonial policy 1897–1914.* MA Thesis submitted to the University of Birmingham, 1964, p. 172.
14. Mac Munn, *The Martial Races of India* (London, n.d.), p. 318, quoted by Alavi, *op. cit.*
15. A. Haywood and F. Clarke, *The History of the Royal West African Frontier Force* (1964), p. 11.
16. M. J. V. Bell, *Army and Nation in Sub-Saharan Africa*, Adelphi Paper No. 21. Janowitz, *The Military in the Political Development of New Nations: An Essay in Comparative Analysis* (Chicago, 1964), p. 52.
17. Crawford Young, *Politics in the Congo* (Princeton, 1965), p. 441.
18. *ibid.*
19. Interview with Francis Monheim in *La Métropole*, Antwerp, 1 April 1964.
20. C. Hoskyns, *The Congo Since Independence* (London, 1965), p. 86.
21. *Report of the Commission of Enquiry into the Disturbances in the Gold Coast*, 1948, col. 231.
22. Gold Coast Government Printing Department, Accra 1945.
23. *ibid.*
24. G. O. Olusanyana, 'The Role of Ex-Servicemen in Nigerian Politics', 1945–60, *Journal of Modern African Studies*, 6, 2. 1968, pp. 221–32.
25. *ibid.*
26. 1 August 1941.
27. *Storms on the Niger* (Enugu, n.d.), pp. 123–4.
28. Olusanyana, *op. cit.*
29. *West African Forces Conference, Lagos 20–24 April 1953* (London, 1954), col. 304.
30. Coleman and Brice in Johnson (ed.), *op. cit.*, p. 370.
31. Federal Parliamentary Debates 1961–2, col. 1250, 11 April 1961.

32. Gutteridge, *op. cit.*, p. 122.
33. Coleman and Brice in Johnson (ed.), *op. cit.*
34. Manfred Halpern, 'Middle Eastern Armies and the New Middle Class', in Johnson (ed.), *op. cit.*, p. 292.
35. Peter Kilner in 'Sudan' in *Africa, a Handbook*, Colin Legum (ed.) (Harmondsworth, 1969) says 300; Coleman and Brice say 400.
36. 20 August 1958.
37. Johnson (ed.), *op. cit.*, p. 378.
38. Pierre Martin, 'Violence in Africa', *War Resisters' International* (n.d.), p. 14.
39. See articles by Russell Warren Howe and Hugh Hanning, *The Statist*, 21 January 1966.
40. Sékou Touré, *L'action politique du Parti Démocratique de Guinée pour l'Emancipation africaine*, Tome 3 (Conakry, 1959), p. 451.
41. This is the account of Russell Warren Howe, who had been on Olympio's staff as adviser. See 'Togo: Four Years of Military Rule', *Africa Report*, May 1967.

Politicians in Business

1. 'Political Parties of Senegal and Unity of its Patriotic Forces' *World Marxist Review*, May 1966, p. 31.
2. Ken Post, *The New States of West Africa* (Harmondsworth, 1964), p. 43.
3. 'Political Science and National Integration – a Radical Approach', *Journal of Modern African Studies*, Vol. 5, No. 1, May 1967, p. 7.
4. R. H. Green and Ann Seidman, *Unity or Poverty? The Economics of Pan-Africanism* (Harmondsworth, 1968), especially the chapter 'Small Countries, Large Firms'.
5. James S. Coleman, *Nigeria: Background to Nationalism* (Berkeley and Los Angeles, 1958).
6. Peter Garlick, *African Traders in Kumasi* (1959) and *African and Levantine Firms Trading in Ghana*, NISER Conference, December 1960. See also Jack Woddis, 'African Capitalism', *Marxism Today*, May 1966.
7. 'The Nigerian Millionaires', *Time*, 17 September 1965.
8. Quoted by Basil Davidson, 'The Outlook for Africa', *Socialist Register*, 1966, p. 218, footnote 21.
9. 'International Corporations, Labour Aristocracies and Economic Developments in Tropical Africa', to be published in *Ideology and Development: Essays on the Political Economy of Africa*, by G. Arrighi and J. S. Saul (forthcoming).

10. Charles Wilson, *Unilever 1945–65* (London, 1968). See also Guy de Lusignan, *French-Speaking Africa Since Independence* (London, 1969), pp. 36–7.
11. For the use of the state by businessmen, see Samir Amin, *Le Monde des Affaires Sénégalais* (Paris, 1968).
12. See especially Exhibit AO 39, I, 24 of the *Report of the Coker Commission of Inquiry into the Affairs of Certain Statutory Corporations in Western Nigeria, 1962* (4 vols.) (Lagos Ministry of Information, 1962).
13. *West Africa*, 4 May 1968.
14. Christopher Allen, 'Sierra Leone Politics Since Independence', *African Affairs*, October 1968, Vol. 67, No. 269, p. 315.
15. The definition of the political class I use is the one developed by Gavin P. Williams in his thesis, *The Political Sociology of Western Nigeria 1939–65*, submitted for the degree of B.Phil. (Politics), University of Oxford, June 1967.

    See also Gavin Williams, 'The Concepts Class, Status, Elite in the Analysis of a Neo-Colonial Economy', paper read to the Sociology of Development Group at the 1969 Annual Conference of the British Sociological Association.

    See also Richard L. Sklar, *Nigerian Political Parties* (Princeton, 1963); and Richard L. Sklar and C. S. Whitaker Jr, 'The Federal Republic of Nigeria', *National Unity and Regionalism in Eight African States*, ed. Gwendolen M. Carter (Cornell, 1966).
16. Williams, 1967, *ibid.*

The State of Bureaucrats

1. Majhemout Diop, *Classes and Class Ideology in Senegal* (Editions du Comité Central du PAI, 1965).
2. *Statistics of Sanctioned Posts in the Public Services of Nigeria.* Prepared by the Chief Statistician, Lagos. Comparative Tables 1960–61 to 1965–6.
3. P. C. Lloyd, *Africa in Social Change* (Harmondsworth, 1967), p. 144.
4. *ibid.*, p. 147.
5. Samir Amin, *The States of the Maghreb* (forthcoming), especially Chapter 7, 'The Birth of the Maghreb States', for the section on Algeria.
6. *ibid.*
7. Economic Commission for Africa, Statistics and Demography

Division, *Survey of Economic Conditions in Africa, 1963–6* (UN), especially the sections on Public Finance.

8. Gérard Chaliand, 'Indépendence Nationale et Révolution', *Partisans:* Special Issue, *L'Afrique dans l'Épreuve*, May–June 1966.
9. Samir Amin, *Trois Expériences Africaines de Développement: Le Mali, La Guinée et Le Ghana* (Paris, 1963), pp. 10–17 and 230–3.
10. René Dumont, *L'Afrique Noir est Mal Partie* (Paris, 1962), p. 65.
11. *Political Leadership in Africa: Post Independence Generational Conflict in Upper Volta, Senegal, Niger, Dahomey and Central African Republic*, Hoover Institute of War, Revolution and Peace, Stanford University, 1967.
12. *ibid.*
13. *The Distribution of Power in West African Political Systems*, unpublished version of a paper presented to the African Studies Center Colloquium, spring 1968.
14. M. Crawford Young, 'Post-Independence Politics in the Congo', *Transition*, 26.
15. Jules Gérard-Libois, 'The New Class and Rebellion in the Congo', *Socialist Register* 1966, p. 268. See also Benoit Verhagen, 'Social Classes in the Congo', in *Revolution*, 1 (12), April 1964, pp. 115–28.
16. Edouard Bustin, 'The Quest for Political Stability in the Congo: Soldiers, Bureaucrats and Politicians', *The Primacy of Politics*, ed. H. J. Spiro (New York, 1966), p. 41.
17. *ibid.*
18. *Transition*, 26, *op. cit.*
19. René Lemarchand, 'The Congo', *Five African States*, ed. G. M. Carter (1963).
20. Gérard-Libois, *op. cit.*, p. 270.
21. Ken Post, *The Nigerian Federal Election of 1959* (Oxford, 1963), p. 48, describes the 'interpretative function' of the new élite.
22. Thomas Hodgkin, *African Political Parties* (London, 1961).
23. For developments inside the Nigerian trade-union movement see Ioan Davies, *African Trade Unions* (Harmondsworth, 1966), pp. 81–4; also Gavin Williams, 'The Political Role of the Nigerian Working Class', a chapter in his thesis, *The Political Sociology of Western Nigeria 1939–65*, submitted for the degree of B.Phil. (Politics), University of Oxford, June 1967. See also G. O. Olusanyana, 'The Zikist Movement: A Study in Political Radicalism, 1946–50', *Journal of Modern African Studies*, 4, 3, 1966.

24. Ken Post, *The New States of West Africa* (Harmondsworth, 1964), pp. 81–2, describes something of the pressures to which students were subjected, especially in Upper Volta and the Ivory Coast.
25. Hodgkin, *op. cit.*, p. 168.
26. C. H. Moore, 'Mass Party Regimes in Africa', *The Primacy of Politics*, ed. H. J. Spiro (New York, 1966).
27. See A. R. Zolberg, *Creating Political Order: The Party States of West Africa* (Chicago, 1966).
28. *ibid.* On relationships between the state and the party, see Bereket Habte Selassie, *The Executive in African Governments: A Comparative Constitutional Order*. Thesis submitted for degree of Ph.D., University of London, June 1967. See also A. R. Zolberg, *One Party Government in the Ivory Coast* (Princeton, 1964) and Victor D. Du Bois on Guinea in *Political Parties and National Integration in Tropical Africa*, ed. James S. Coleman and Carl G. Rosberg Jr (Berkeley, 1964).
29. Zolberg, *Creating Political Order*, p. 105.
30. *ibid.* p. 98.

IV. THE FAILURE OF POLITICS

The Sudan: Pawn of Two Powers

1. *Fourteen Documents on the Problem of the Southern Sudan*, selected with a foreword by Dr Muddathir Abdel Rahim.
   See also Sir Harold MacMichael, 'The Anglo-Egyptian Sudan' (London, 1934) and Keith Kyle, 'The Sudan Today', *African Affairs*, Vol. 65, No. 260, July 1966.
2. Letter from Wingate, dated 27 December 1918, in the Milner Papers, New College, Oxford, quoted in Muddathir Abdel Rahim, *The Constitutional Development of the Sudan 1899–1956*. Thesis submitted for the degree of Ph.D. in Government, University of Manchester, May 1964, p. 106.
3. Anthony Eden, *Full Circle* (London, 1960), pp. 229–35.
4. Mohammed Nuri Al-Amien, *The Rise of Political Parties in the Sudan and their Subsequent Development to 1957*, a Dissertation submitted for the Degree of B.Sc. Hons. at the University of Khartoum, March 1966.
5. J. S. Trimingham, *Islam in the Sudan* (London, 1949), p. 233.
6. Muddathir Abdel Rahim, Thesis, *op. cit.* See also 'Early Sudanese Nationalism: 1900–1938' in *Sudan Notes and Records*, 1966 by the same author.

7. Mohammed Nuri Al-Amien, *op. cit.*, p. 20.
8. Sir James Currie, 'The Educational Experiment in the Anglo-Egyptian Sudan 1900–03', *Journal of the Africa Society*, London 1953, XXXIV, p. 49.
9. P. M. Holt, *A Modern History of the Sudan* (London, 1961), p. 143.
10. K. D. D. Henderson, *The Making of the Modern Sudan: Life and Letters of Sir Douglas Newbold KBE* (London, 1953), p. 268.
11. See Margery Perham's introduction to Henderson, *op. cit.*
12. For an account of the early trade unions, see Saad ed Din Fawzi, *Origins and Development of the Labour Movement in the Sudan.* Thesis presented for Ph.D. degree, June 1955.
13. *New York Times*, 17 May 1957.
14. Sudan: Second Parliament of the Sudan, Weekly Digest of Proceedings in the House of Representatives. First session, 25 June 1958.
15. Leo Silberman, 'Democracy in the Sudan', Parliamentary Affairs, 1958–9.
16. Interview.

Nigeria: The Juicy Morsel

1. James S. Coleman, *Nigeria: Background to Nationalism* (Los Angeles, 1958), pp. 64–7.
2. B. L. Dudley, *Parties and Politics in Northern Nigeria* (London, 1968), p. 134.
3. *ibid.*, p. 118.
4. *A White Paper on the Military Government Policy for the Reorganisation of the Northern Nigeria Development Corporation*, Kaduna Government Printer, Northern Nigeria, 1966.
5. See Ken Post, *The Nigerian Federal Election* (Oxford, 1963), p. 49, and Richard L. Sklar and C. S. Whitaker Jr, 'The Federal Republic of Nigeria', *National Unity and Regionalism in Eight African States*, ed. Gwendolen M. Carter (Cornell, 1966).
6. The Foster-Sutton Tribunal, whose full title is *Proceedings of the Tribunal Appointed to inquire into Allegations of Improper Conduct by the Premier of the Eastern Region of Nigeria in Connection with the Affairs of the African Continental Bank Limited and other Relevant Matters*, Lagos, Federal Government Printer, 1957.
7. *Report of the Coker Commission of Inquiry into the Affairs of Certain Statutory Corporations in Western Nigeria, 1962* (4 vols.) (Lagos Ministry of Information, 1962).

8. Post, pp. 150–56; also published as *The Use of Power in Independent Black Africa*, ed. W. J. Hanna (Chicago, 1964), p. 446.
9. *Journal of Modern African Studies*, Vol. 3, No. 2, 1965, p. 201.
10. B. J. Dudley, 'Federalism and the Balance of Political Power in Nigeria', *Journal of Commonwealth Political Studies*, Vol. IV, No. 1, March 1966.
11. Ken Post, 'The National Council of Nigeria and the Cameroons: The Decision of December 1959', John P. Mackintosh *et al.*, *Nigerian Government and Politics* (London, 1966).
12. *ibid.*, p. 457.
13. Martin J. Dent, 'A Minority Party – The United Middle Belt Congress', *Nigerian Government and Politics*.
14. Post, *Nigerian Federal Election*, p. 442.
15. Dudley, 'Federalism and the Balance of Political Power in Nigeria'.
16. *ibid.*
17. Dr James O'Connell, *Nigerian Politics: The Complexity of Dissent*. Paper delivered to the International Political Association, Brussels, September 1967.
18. Annual Report of the Federal Ministry of Labour 1961–2, Lagos 1964.
19. Federal Parliamentary Debates 1961–2, 11 April 1961, col. 1250.
20. Martin J. Dent, *The Military and Politics: study of the relations between the Army and the Political Process in Nigeria 1966/7*, Paper presented to a Seminar of the Institute of Commonwealth Studies, London, 1968, p. 3.
21. *loc. cit.*
22. W. F. Gutteridge, *Military Institutions and Power in the New States* (London, 1964), p. 106.
23. A. R. Luckham, *The Nigerian Army*, Paper presented to a Seminar of the Institute of Commonwealth Studies, London, 1968, p. 10.
24. *January 15: Before and After*, p. 29.
25. Gutteridge, *op. cit.*
26. Mackintosh, *op. cit.*, p. 590.
27. Peter Enahoro, based on conversations with Dr Azikiwe in Paris, 1968.
28. *Sunday Times*, Lagos, 2 June 1968, p. 14.
29. Nigerian *Tribune*, 16 December 1965.
30. Walter Schwarz, *Nigeria* (London, 1968), p. 198.
31. Patrick Keatley, *Guardian*, 21 January 1966.

32. The Northern premier reported in the *Daily Times*, 19 November 1965; the Federal prime minister in the same paper on 17 November 1965.
33. Patrick Keatley, *Guardian*, 28 January 1966.
34. *Northern Echo*, Members' Newsletter, 21 November 1966.
35. Mackintosh, *op. cit.*, p. 605.

Ghana: Heirs Jump the Queue

1. R. J. A. Rathbone, *Opposition in Ghana: The National Liberation Movement*. Paper presented to the Institute of Commonwealth Studies Seminar, October 1967.
2. Jitendra Mohan, 'Nkrumah and Nkrumaism', *Socialist Register*, 1967, p. 195.
3. Bob Fitch and Mary Oppenheimer, 'Ghana: End of an Illusion', *Monthly Review*, July–August 1966.
4. Rathbone, *op. cit.*, p. 12.
5. Roger Murray, 'The Ghanaian Road', *New Left Review*, 32, pp. 68–9.
6. Harold S. Jacobs, *The Myth of the Missing Opposition: Ghana, a Case Study*, unpublished manuscript, University of California, 1965, p. 20, quoted by Fitch and Oppenheimer, *op. cit.*, p. 75.
7. Fitch and Oppenheimer, *op. cit.*, pp. 82–4.
8. Robert Szereszewski, 'Performance of the Economy, 1955–1962', *A Study of Contemporary Ghana*, ed. Walter Birmingham, I. Neustadt and E. N. Omaboe (London, 1966), p. 62.
9. Fitch and Oppenheimer, *op. cit.*, p. 91.
10. Kwame Nkrumah, *Dark Days in Ghana* (London, 1969), p. 79.
11. *Report of the Commission of Enquiry into Trade Malpractices in Ghana*, Office of the President. The report was delivered in August 1965. See also 'Ghana's Food Failure', *West Africa*, 19 February 1966.
12. Fitch and Oppenheimer, *op. cit.*, p. 120.
13. 1964 Economic Survey of Ghana.
14. *West Africa*, 26 March 1966, p. 341.
15. Nkrumah, *op. cit.*, pp. 90–91.
16. Douglas Rimmer, 'The Crisis of the Ghana Economy', *Journal of Modern African Studies*, Vol. 4, No. 1, 19.
17. G. Kportufe Agama's articles in the *Legon Observer*, 1967–8.
18. Tony Killick, 'Making Ghana Grow Again', *West Africa*, 20 August 1966, pp. 937–8. See also Killick, 'External Trade', *A Study of Contemporary Ghana* (London, 1966).

19. *Africa Report*, April 1966, p. 22.
20. The Volta project is discussed in Fitch and Oppenheimer, *op. cit.*, pp. 123–6, and in the *Legon Observer*, September 1966.
21. Roger Murray, 'Second Thoughts on Ghana', *New Left Review*, 42.
22. Mohan, *op. cit.*, p. 209.
23. *Ashanti Pioneer*, 6 September 1961.
24. Mohan, *op. cit.*, pp. 212–14.
25. *ibid.*
26. *ibid.*, p. 216.
27. Thomas Hodgkin, 'Counter-Revolution in Ghana', *Labour Monthly*, April 1966.
28. *Report of the Commission of Enquiry into Trade Malpractices in Ghana*, Accra, 1965.
29. Adam Fergusson, 'Ghana Redeemed: Black Mischief-Maker', *The Statist*, 4 March 1966.
30. John Kraus, 'The Men in Charge', *Africa Report*, April 1966, p. 17.
31. Colonel A. A. Afrifa, *The Ghana Coup* (London, 1966), pp. 50, 52.
32. Nkrumah, *op. cit.*, p. 47.
33. *ibid.*, p. 37.
34. Kwame Nkrumah, *Challenge of the Congo* (London, 1967), p. 39.
35. Major-General H. T. Alexander, *African Tightrope* (London, 1965), p. 99.
36. *ibid.*, p. 70.
37. *ibid.*, p. 104.
38. *ibid.*, pp. 104–6.
39. *ibid.*, p. 107.
40. *ibid.*, pp. 147–8, Appendix D: *A Cry from the Heart*: '400 Cadets to Russia'.
41. Kraus, *op. cit.*, p. 18.
42. Peter Barker, *Operation Cold Chop: The Coup that Toppled Nkrumah* (Ghana Publishing Corporation, 1969).
43. Geoffrey Bing, *Reap the Whirlwind* (London, 1968), p. 130.
44. Barker, *op. cit.*, p. 20.
45. Robert E. Dowse, *The Military and Political Development*, paper delivered to Conference on Political Development, Sussex, June–July 1968, p. 37. Barker, *op. cit.*, p. 23, adds: 'Harlley gave his deputy Anthony Deku an assignment to keep in touch with their colleagues at the Special Branch, in case they were both moved to another unit; above all, to anticipate Nkrumah's intentions towards the police and the army.'
46. Kraus, *op. cit.*, p. 20.
47. Broadcast, 28 February 1966.

48. Major-General A. K. Ocran, *A Myth is Broken* (Accra, 1968), Chapter 3, 'The President's Own Guard Regiment', pp. 28–39.
49. *ibid.*, p. 31.
50. *ibid.*, p. 35.
51. Afrifa quoted in Bing, *op. cit.*, p. 422.
52. Afrifa, *op. cit.*, p. 42.
53. Ocran, *op. cit.*, p. 47.
54. *ibid.*, p. 99.

V. THE SOLDIERS INVADE: A COUP INVENTORY

1. C. Hoskyns, *The Congo Since Independence* (London, 1965), p. 213.
2. Edouard Bustin, 'The Quest for Political Stability in the Congo: Soldiers, Bureaucrats and Politicians', *The Primacy of Politics*, ed. H. J. Spiro (New York, 1966), p. 28.
3. *ibid.*, p. 41.
4. Russell Warren Howe, 'Togo: Four Years of Military Rule', *Africa Report*, May 1967, p. 7.
5. Interview by Donald Louchiem, *Washington Post*, with several unidentified officers in Enugu prison.
6. Amilcar Cabral, 'Determined to Resist', *Tricontinental*, 9, 1968, p. 123.
7. Richard Greenfield, *Ethiopia* (London, 1965).
8. Christopher Clapham, 'The Ethiopian Coup', *Journal of Modern African Studies*, 6, 4, 1968.
9. *ibid.* See also Clapham, 'Imperial Leadership in Ethiopia', *African Affairs*, April 1969.
10. Christopher Clapham, *Haile Selassie's Government* (London, 1969), p. 24.
11. Greenfield, *op. cit.*, pp. 413–14.
12. Charles F. and Alice B. Darlington, *African Betrayal* (New York, 1968), p. 156.
13. *Le Figaro*, 28 February 1964.
14. Brian Weinstein, *Gabon: Nation-Building on the Ogooúe* (Cambridge, Mass., 1966), p. 175.
15. *New York Times*, 13 March 1964.

COUP CASEBOOKS

1. *The Sudan*

1. Keesings, Vol. 12, p. 16593.
2. Interview.

3. Interview with the former Speaker of the House.
4. Interviews. See also Peter Kilner, 'The Seven Generals', *Africa South in Exile*, April–June 1961.
5. Abd el-Rahman al-Nur in an interview with the writer.
6. Interview.
7. Statement issued by the Political Bureau of the Sudanese Communist Party, 18 November 1958.
8. Interview with Dawood Abd al-Latif.
9. Kilner, *op. cit.*, says the West encouraged Abdallah Khalil's view that 'strong direct rule' was what the country needed.
10. The Inquiry.
11. Interview.
12. See his evidence to the Inquiry.
13. Interview.
14. Shennan's defence statement at his trial, *Morning News*, Khartoum, 29 June 1959.
15. *Morning News*, 6 March 1959.
16. P. M. Holt, *A Modern History of the Sudan* (London, 1961), p. 187.
17. *Morning News*, 9 March 1959.
18. *Morning News*, reports, June and July 1959.
19. Interviews.
20. Interviews with participants.
21. Terms of Reference to the Commission on Co-ordination between the Central and Local Government (Khartoum Government Printer [1962]).
22. The Province Administration Act 1960; the Central Council Act 1962; the Local Government (Amendment) Act 1962.
23. B. S. Sharma, 'Failure of Local Government Democracy in the Sudan', *Political Studies*, February 1967, Vol. 15, No. 1.
24. *ibid.*, p. 65.
25. Dated 20 November 1960.
26. Statement on Foreign Policy, Central Information Office, Khartoum, 29 November 1958.
27. Interviews with student participants.
28. K. D. D. Henderson, 'The Sudan Today', *African Affairs*, Vol. 62, No. 256, July 1965.
29. Keith Kyle, 'The Sudan Today', *African Affairs*, Vol. 65, No. 260, July 1966.
30. *Sudan News*, 26 May 1969.
31. Eric Rouleau, *Le Monde Séléction Hebdomadaire*, 10 September 1969.

32. Policy statements have appeared in issues of the *Sudan News* of May and June 1969. See also *The 25th May Revolution*, Ministry of National Guidance, The Democratic Republic of the Sudan.
33. Interview to *Al Ahram*, Cairo, quoted in *Africa Research*, p. 1405, 1–31 May 1969.
34. *Sudan News*, 26 May 1969. Statement No. 2, page 4.

2. Nigeria

1. Interview with Major Johnson.
2. This among other details of the coup plans was given by Major Ifeajuna to S. G. Ikoku, former secretary of the Action Group, who met Ifeajuna in Accra when the latter fled to Ghana after the coup.
3. Nzeogwu to Tai Solarin, March 1967.
4. Ifeajuna to Ikoku.
5. *Guardian* report (quoted in *West Africa*, 22 January 1966), of an eye witness account by a waiter at the Ikoyi Hotel.
6. Frederick Forsyth, *The Biafra Story* (London, 1969), p. 57; and a report to government officials by Chief J. U. Ndogi in Lagos based on an account supplied by N. C. Perkins.
7. S. G. Ikoku.
8. Nzeogwu to Tai Solarin.
9. Nzeogwu's statement at a press conference, *New Nigerian*, 18 January 1966.
10. Wilton Dillon, 'Nigeria's Two Revolutions', *Africa Report*, March 1966.
11. Interview with Dr Elias, the attorney-general.
12. *New Nigerian*, 17 January 1966.
13. A journalist's account of the press conference on 17 January.
14. *New Nigerian*, 17 January 1966.
15. In an interview with the writer.
16. Account based on information supplied by a senior civil servant in Kaduna.
17. *New Nigerian*, 18 January 1966.
18. *ibid.*, 20 January 1966.
19. *ibid.*, 21 January 1966.
20. Interview with Dr S. Aluko.
21. *Nigeria 1966*, published by the Federal Republic of Nigeria; and *January 15: Before and After*, Volume 7 of *Nigerian Crisis*, printed by the Government Printer, Enugu.
22. See *Nine Months to Crisis*, Government Statement on the Current Nigerian Situation, 21 October 1966.

23. *The Nigerian Situation*, Facts and background. Gaskiya Corporation, Zaria, December 1966.
24. These statements are all from actual conversations with leading figures in the Federation.
25. Reported by Walter Schwarz, *Observer*, 30 January 1966.
26. 23 January 1966.
27. With a journalist of the *New Nigerian*, copy in my possession.
28. Peter Enahoro, interview.
29. *Drum*, September 1966. Interview in Calabar prison.
30. S. G. Ikoku.
31. Dr Elias, the attorney-general, in an interview with the writer.
32. Conversation with Tai Solarin, March 1967, in Enugu.
33. Charles M. Thomas, *African National Developments*, 1967, Aero-Space Institute, Maxwell Air Force Base, Alabama.
34. *West Africa*, 12 February 1966.
35. Lagos Broadcasting Corporation, 21 January 1966.
36. *New Nigerian*, 29 July 1966.
37. Major Hassan Katsina, interview.
38. Peter Pan (Peter Enahoro), in *Nigerian Outlook*, 31 March 1967.
39. Full text in the issue of the *New Nigerian*, 25 May 1966, under the heading 'Breaking the Egg into One Big Omelette: Federation Abolished'.
40. Lagos Home Service, ME/2183.
41. Samson O. O. Amali, *Ibos and their Fellow Nigerians* (published privately but circulated through the Institute of African Affairs at the University of Ibadan). This is a tirade of accusations, trivial and terrible, against Ibos by a young Idoma, drawing principally on Idoma reaction to the coup.
42. Yoruba officer on this training course; his name withheld at his request.
43. See *New Nigerian*, 22 October 1966, for the Northern interpretation of what happened in July.
44. An account of Fajuyi's last hours in State House, written by his brother, is in the writer's possession.
45. *January 15: Before and After*, pp. 46–7.
46. *January 15: Before and After*, p. 48, admits for instance that on the morning after the kidnap Lieutenant-Colonel Akahan was not present at an 'officers' conference' at Battalion headquarters because he was guarded by soldiers in his office.
47. These accounts are based on interviews, some very central to events, whose informants wished to remain anonymous.

48. Lagos Radio. BBC Monitoring Service, ME/2229, 1 August 1966, 10.12 GMT; also *New Nigerian*, 2 August 1966.
49. 1 August, 20.00 GMT. See also *Daily Times*, 2 August 1966, national edition; and 2 August 1966, national edition; and 2 August 1966, first edition.
50. *Daily Times*, 3 August 1966, national edition.
51. *New Nigerian*, 19 August 1966.
52. Press conference statement, August 1966.
53. *New Nigerian*, 4 August 1966.
54. BBC Monitoring service, ME/2232, 4 August 1966.
55. *January 15: Before and After*, p. 49; see Adebayo's comments at the Aburi conference.
56. Lieutenant-Colonel Ejoor, military governor of the Mid-West, described the incident at the Aburi conference, *Africa Research Documentation Service*, No. 3/67, p. 15.
57. *The Times*, 19 August 1966.
58. Statement by Gowon, 10 August 1966.
59. Kaduna radio, ME/2243, 17 August.
60. M. J. Dent, *The Military and the Politicians*, mimeographed paper.
61. For the memoranda submitted to the Ad Hoc Conference see the Federal publication *Memoranda submitted by the Delegations to the Ad Hoc Conference on Constitutional Proposals for Nigeria*, and the Eastern publication *The Ad Hoc Conference on the Nigerian Constitution, Nigerian Crisis*, Vol. 4, 1966, Government Printer, Enugu. The two documents overlap for the most part, but not entirely. The Eastern position is explained in the introduction to its publication, and there is a more complete record of the delegation's several statements on the creation of states, the one issued before and the other after the switch in the stand of the Northern delegation.
62. In the North the *New Nigerian* had been kite-flying for new states, especially the claims of the Rivers and Calabar people, for some months. During the adjournment of the conference, the *New Nigerian* published an article on 23 September, 'An appeal to All-Nigeria Talks: Create Rivers State'.
63. The Eastern constitutional position is explained in *Nigerian Crisis 1966*, vol. 4, see especially the Introduction.
64. Dr James O'Connell, 'Anatomy of a Pogrom: An Outline Model with Special Reference to the Ibo in Northern Nigeria', *Race*, Vol. 9, No. 1, July 1967.
65. Information volunteered by an influential Northerner, whose name is not revealed at his request.
66. An expatriate civil service informant in the North.

67. Civil service informant.
68. *New Nigerian*, 28 September 1966.
69. *New Nigerian*, 29 September 1966. A front-page story was headlined 'No Eastern was molested in the North, says Government'. In Lagos, though, the *Daily Times* gave prominence to the early reports of attacks on Ibos, as in its issue of 28 September 1966.
70. BBC Monitoring Service, ME/2276, 23 September 1966.
71. *New Nigerian*, 3 October 1966.
72. BBC Monitoring Service, ME/2277, 29 September 1966.
73. N. C. Perkins, Administrator of Enugu in 1966.
74. 30 September 1966, front page.
75. *New Nigerian*, 5 October 1966, statement issued from the Federal Military Government Office in Lagos.
76. *Nigerian Crisis 1966*, p. 10.
77. 'Prominent Nigerians from Western Nigeria seemed oblivious to the continued harassment of Ibos, and some even rejoiced that their tribal rivals were being "put in their place"' wrote Donald H. Louchheim in the *New York Herald Tribune*, 3 October 1966.
78. *New Nigerian*, 6 October 1966.
79. *Daily Times*, 12 October 1966.
80. *Towards a New Nigeria*, broadcast to the Nation by the Head of the Federal Military Government, 20 November 1966, Federal Ministry of Information, Lagos.
81. *West Africa*, 26 November 1966, p. 1373.
82. The Aburi proceedings are recorded verbatim in (1) *Meeting of the Nigerian Military Leaders held at Peduase Lodge, Aburi, Ghana, 4th and 5th January 1967* (Federal Ministry of Information, Lagos); (2) *Nigerian Crisis*, Vol. 6, *The Meeting of the Supreme Military Council held at Aburi, Accra, Ghana 4–5 January 1967* (Government Printer, Enugu); and (3) as part of the Documentation Service of Africa Research Ltd (Exeter, England): Documentation Service No. 3/67.

    See also *The Meeting of the Nigerian Military Leaders*, Official Document No. 5 of 1967 (Government Printer, Enugu) for the Eastern record of the Aburi decisions, as well as draft decrees prepared after the meeting. Indispensable as a record of the atmosphere as well as the discussion at the Aburi meeting is the set of twelve gramophone records recorded by the Ghana government and 'Released by Command of the Military Governor of Eastern Nigeria'.

    See, too, Dr F. A. Baptiste, 'Constitutional Conflict in Nigeria: Aburi and After', *The World Today*, July 1967.

83. Annex C, p. 68, in the Federal record of Aburi.
84. See Baptiste, *op. cit.*
85. Opening Statement by the Head of the Federal Military Government and Supreme Commander of the Armed Forces, Lieutenant-Colonel Gowon, to the press on 26 January 1967.
86. For the contents of this confidential memorandum marked Top Secret, see Appendix IV, pp. 55–64, of *Nigerian Crisis*, Vol. 6: *The Meeting of the Supreme Military Council.*
87. Constitution (Suspension and Modification) Decree No. 8 of 1967. G.N. No. 416, 1967.
88. See *Daily Times*, 25 April 1967; also *Financial Times*, 2 May 1967.
89. Martin J. Dent, *The Military and Politics: study of the relations between the Army and the Political Process in Nigeria 1966/7.*
90. Untitled and undated memorandum. Copy seen by the writer in Kaduna.
91. This was the title of a policy document drafted for the guidance of this group after Aburi. The writer read a copy loaned her by a member of the group in Kaduna.
92. Dr James O'Connell, 'The Scope of the Tragedy', *Africa Report*, February 1968, p. 11.
93. Dr James O'Connell argues this in his paper, *Nigerian Politics: The Complexity of Dissent*, presented to the International Political Science Association, Brussels, September 1967.
94. Nabo B. Graham-Douglas, *Ojukwu's Rebellion and World Opinion* (London, n.d.).
95. Letter dated 19 June 1967 to Tai Solarin.
96. Letter dated 30 May 1967 to Dr Tunji Otegbeye.
97. 'I am irrevocably committed on the side of Nigeria as a united country,' said Chief Awolowo, *Daily Times*, 14 August 1967.
98. Ken Post, 'Is There a Case for Biafra?', *International Affairs*, Vol. 44, No. 15, London, January 1968.
99. 'Let us Think of the Aftermath of this War', *Daily Sketch* August 1967.
100. *Financial Times*, Nigeria Supplement, 4 August 1969, p. 17.
101. See for instance Stanley Diamond, 'The Biafran Possibility', *Africa Report*, February 1968, pp. 16–19.
102. *Transition*, 36, 1968, p. 37. The Ahiara Declaration by Ojukwu of 1 June 1969 was a new policy departure.
103. The Military Courts (Special Powers) Decree 1968, of 31 January 1968.
104. M. J. V. Bell, 'The Military in the New States of Africa', *Armed*

Forces and Society, ed. Jacques van Doorn (The Hague, 1968), p. 263.

105. James S. Coleman and Belmont Brice Jr, 'The Role of the Military in Sub-Saharan Africa', *The Role of the Military in Underdeveloped Countries*, ed. John L. Johnson (Princeton, 1962), p. 402.

3. Ghana

1. *Guardian*, 25 February 1966.
2. A proclamation dated 26 February 1966 named seven NLC members: Lieutenant-General J. A. Ankrah, J. W. K. Harlley, Colonel E. K. Kotoka, B. A. Yakubu, Colonel A. K. Ocran, J. E. Nunoo, Major Afrifa.
3. The National Liberation Council Proclamation (Amendment Decree) 1966 of 3 March 1966.
4. *Ghanaian Times*, 11 March 1966. The speech was published as *The Decisive Role of the Police*, Ministry of Information, Accra.
5. Colonel A. A. Afrifa, *The Ghana Coup* (London, 1966), p. 42.
6. *West Africa*, 22 April 1967, p. 517.
7. *West Africa*, 5 March 1966, p. 273.
8. Peter Barker, *Operation Gold Chop* (Ghana Publishing Corporation, 1969), is extraordinarily accommodating. The contents of this book were passed by NLC members, who read the galley proofs.
9. *ibid.*, pp. 20–23.
10. *ibid.*, pp. 74–8.
11. *ibid.*, pp. 76–8.
12. *Africa and the World*, May 1966, June 1966.
13. Some accept one version, others another. Bing, for instance, in *Reap the Whirlwind* (London, 1968), says he believes the plot began with Deku and Harlley, and involved Kotoka only later. The historian, Adu Boahen, in *Legon Observer*, 8 November 1968, says it was laid by Afrifa and Kotoka and only later included Harlley and Deku.
14. Interview with the writer.
15. This account is based on Major-General A. K. Ocran's version *A Myth is Broken* (Accra, 1968).
16. Barker, *op. cit.*, pp. 137–9.
17. For details used here, see Barker, *op. cit.*, Chapter 11; also Ocran, *op. cit.*, especially Chapter 6, 'Plans are Disrupted', pp. 62–7.
18. Kwame Nkrumah, *Dark Days in Ghana* (London, 1969), p. 49.
19. 25 February 1966.

20. Bob Fitch and Mary Oppenheimer, 'Ghana: End of an Illusion', *Monthly Review*, July–August 1966, p. 121.
21. Douglas A. Scott, 'External Debt-Management in a Developing Country', *Financing African Development*, ed. Tom J. Farer (Cambridge, 1965), p. 55.
22. *The Economist*, 30 April 1966.
23. Teresa Hayter, Study to be published by Penguin Books in 1970.
24. United States Government Special Warfare Handbook for Ghana 1/1962, pp. 524–5.
25. *Ghana's Foreign Policy, 1957–1966*, Ph.D. thesis submitted by Willard Scott Thompson to the Board of Social Studies, Balliol College, August 1967, pp. 111–84.
26. Report of the UN Representative in Ghana, Erwin Baumgarten, to UN Secretary-General 6/1965, quoted in W. Scott Thompson, 'New Directions in Ghana', *African Report*, November 1966.
27. Attwood, *The Reds and the Blacks*, London, 1967.
28. Scott Thompson, *op. cit.*, quoting an interview with the UN Representative Mr Erwin Baumgarten.
29. Scott Thompson, *op. cit.*
30. Roger Murray, 'Militarism in Africa', *New Left Review*, 38, 1, p. 53.
31. Scott Thompson, *op. cit.*
32. J. Markowitz, 'Ghana Ten Years After Independence', *Africa Today*, 1968.
33. Scott Thompson, *op. cit.*
34. *ibid.*
35. *ibid.*
36. Edward Luttwak, *Coup d'État* (London, 1968), pp. 163–5.
37. Interview with Anthony Deku in *Legon Observer* Supplement, 17 February 1967.
38. Murray, *op. cit.*
39. Patrick Keatley writing in the *Guardian*, 5 March 1966.
40. Scott Thompson, *op. cit.*
41. See for instance *Le Monde*, 4 January 1968, 'Les États-Unis renforcent leurs positions au Ghana'.
42. Scott Thompson, *op. cit.*
43. *The Times* (London).
44. 3 March 1966.
45. *Rand Daily Mail* (Johannesburg), 13 January 1969.
46. *Daily Telegraph*, 20 April 1968.
47. 'Ghana Ten Years after Independence: The Development of Technocracy-Capitalism', *Africa Today*, XIV, 1, 1967.
48. 'The Rebirth of Ghana', Accra, 1966, p. 47.

49. 12 July 1966, addressing the Chiefs Standing Conference at Kumasi.
50. *West Africa*, 25 June 1966, p. 726, lists the portfolios.
51. *ibid.*, 30 July 1966, p. 847.
52. 'Should the NLC rule as a military junta and not as a political government in order to realise the aims for which the February 24 coup was staged?' asked Dr B. D. Folson of the University of Accra at a symposium in March 1967.
53. *Two Years after Liberation*, Ministry of Information, Accra, p. 21.
54. Ghana Press Release 379/67 of 3 July 1967.
55. Ghana Press Release 385/67.
56. Markowitz in *Africa Today*, *op. cit.*, p. 11.
57. *Report on the Potential Ghana Project* dated 13 December 1966, delivered to the Development Advisory Service of Harvard University, referred to here as the Papanek Report.
58. *Old Mole* Supplement, 11–24 April 1969, Number 11, 'Sticky Fingers in the Pie'.
59. Papanek Report, 13 December 1966.
60. *ibid.*, 20 September 1968.
61. *ibid.*, 13 December 1966, p. 3.
62. *ibid.*, 20 September 1968, pp. 5–6.
63. *ibid.*, p. 5.
64. *West Africa*, 20 May 1967.
65. *West Africa*, 30 July 1966, p. 855. 'Ankrah appeals to Investors'.
66. Papanek Report, 13 December 1966, p. 3.
67. *ibid.*, 15 December 1966, p. 3.
68. *ibid.* ———
69. *Report of the Administration and Operation of State Enterprise, under the Work of the State Enterprises Secretariat 1964-5*, Accra, 1 December 1968.
70. For the scandal of the Ghana–Abbott deal see *Legon Observer*, 8 December 1967, pp. 9–28. When the Ghana–Abbott deal was cancelled, under pressure, a bid for the factory was made by Pfizer. The agreement with Intercontinental Hotels Corporation USA was signed 13 October 1966.
71. Papanek Report, 20 September 1968, p. 7.
72. Bridget Bloom, *Financial Times*, 2 January 1969, 'Ghana ban on Foreign Traders'.
73. Standard Bank's *Annual Economic Review*, September 1967.
74. *Financial Times*, 16 August 1968.
75. *Daily Graphic*, 30 March 1968.
76. *Report of the Committee of Inquiry on the Local Purchasing of Cocoa*, Ministry of Information, Accra.

77. *ibid.*, p. 9.
78. *ibid.*, p. 151: Cadbury Brothers, Bournville, to the Principal Secretary, Committee on Cocoa Purchases, Ministry of Finance, Accra, 25 May 1966.
79. *ibid.*, p. 153: General Manager, Accra, to the Committee on Cocoa Purchases, Ministry of Finance, Accra, 27 May 1966.
80. *Two Years after Liberation*, Accra, p. 13.
81. Daniel Anyete T. Sowa in *Ghanaian Times*, 6 April 1968.
82. *Public Service Structure and Salaries Commission*, Accra, 1967.
83. *Office of the Special Commissioner for the Redeployment of Labour, Summary of the Employment Market Situation*, January 1968.
84. Yaw Tumasi, 'Ghana's Draft Constitutional Proposals', *Transition*, 37.
85. The account of the Arthur-led coup is taken from press reports of court proceedings and Arthur's statement to the police while under investigation. See, for instance, the *Ghanaian Times* of late April and early May 1967; also *West Africa*, 6 and 13 May 1967, and Ghana News Agency Reports.
86. 1 August 1967.

VI. ARMIES IN STALEMATE

1. Amilcar Cabral quoted in Basil Davidson, *The Liberation of Guiné: Aspects of an African Revolution* (Harmondsworth, 1969).
2. US Senate Committee on Foreign Relations, *US Foreign Policy: Asia* (Studies prepared by Conlon Associates), 1959, pp. 61–2.
3. S. P. Huntington, *World Politics*, 17, 1965, p. 429.
4. Kwame Nkrumah, *Dark Days in Ghana* (London, 1969), p. 49.
5. *The Discipline of Power* (London, 1968), p. 234.
6. Chester A. Crocker, 'External Military Assistance to Sub-Saharan Africa', *Africa Today*, Vol. 15, No. 2, April–May 1968, p. 18.
7. *ibid.*
8. Richard Greenfield, *Ethiopia* (London, 1965), pp. 425–9.
9. Arnold Rivkin, *Africa and the West* (New York, 1961), quoted in *David and Goliath Collaborate in Africa* (Cambridge, Mass.), reprinted from *Leviathan*, September 1968.
10. *New Statesman and Nation*, 8 April 1966, 'Non-Alignment'.
11. I. Wallerstein, *The Politics of Unity* (New York, 1967), p. 45.
12. See the forthcoming publication of the Africa Research Group, *The Other Side of Nigeria's Civil War*.
13. Geoffrey Bing, *Reap the Whirlwind* (London, 1969), p. 430.
14. See for instance the series of articles in the *New York Times* during

April 1966, including 'How the CIA put an Instant Airforce in the Congo and Ran a Battle for Government', 26 April 1966.

15. Charles E. and Alice B. Darlington, *African Betrayal*, especially Chapter 7, 'The Coup d'État' (New York, 1968).
16. See Irving Louis Horowitz, *Rise and Fall of Project Camelot* (Cambridge, Mass., 1968). Covert operations, the writer comments, mean that the ambassador will get steep competition from military missions, roving emissaries, finance advisers, academics, undercover men, intelligence men, and above all from military attachés and military missions.
17. M. J. V. Bell, *Military Assistance to Independent African States*, December 1964 (Institute for Strategic Studies, London): 'States pursuing moderate or accommodationist policies tend to develop their security arrangements with their former metropoles and the USA, while the more radical or militant have tried to multiply their dependency relationships.'
18. Chester A. Crocker, 'France's Changing Military Interests', *Africa Report*, June 1968.
19. *ibid.*
20. *Armed Forces of African States* (Institute of Strategic Studies, London) 1966.
21. Crocker, *Africa Report*, *op. cit.*
22. Statement made 26 February 1964, quoted in *Africa Report*, March 1964, pp. 14–15.
23. *Sunday Times* (London), 9 January 1966.
24. *The Times*, 3 September 1969.
25. *Le Monde*, 3 September 1969.
26. See 'The Political Effects of Military Programs', *Orbis*, VIII (4), Winter 1965, cited in J. M. Lee, *African Armies and Civil Order* (London, 1969).
27. Katherine Chorley, *Armies and the Art of Revolution* (London, 1943).
28. *ibid.*, pp. 92–4.
29. Ralph Miliband, *The State in Capitalist Society: An analysis of the Western system of power* (London, 1969); see Chapter 5, 'Servants of the State', especially pp. 129–38. For *Social Affiliations of the British Army Élite*, see C. B. Otley's article in *Armed Forces and Society*, ed. Jacques van Doorn (The Hague, 1968); also the article by M. Abrams, pp. 154–7.
30. Miliband, *op. cit.*
31. Constantine Tsoucalas, 'The Greek Junta', *New Left Review*, 56, July–August 1969.

32. Bing, *op. cit.*, p. 422.
33. Lee, *op. cit.*, p. 92.
34. Aristide Zolberg, 'The Structure of Political Conflict in the New States of Tropical Africa', *American Political Science Review*, March 1968.
35. M. J. V. Bell, *Army and Nation in Sub-Saharan Africa*, Adelphi Paper 20 (Institute for Strategic Studies, August 1965), pp. 11–12.
36. Lee, *op. cit.*, p. 92.
37. *ibid.*, p. 90.
38. Greenfield, *op. cit.*, p. 470.
39. Lee, *op. cit.*, p. 89.
40. *ibid.*, p. 180.
41. *The Distribution of Power in West African Political Studies*, unpublished paper.
42. Neville Maxwell, 'Why Ayub hears no cheering', *The Times* (London), 22 February 1969, p. 8.
43. M. Janowitz, 'Armed Forces and Society' in van Doorn (ed.), *op. cit.*
44. This progression in military permanence is traced by Mirande Hippolyte, 'Coups d'état et Régimes Militaires d'Afrique', *Le Mois en Afrique*, December 1968, p. 36.
45. Speech made in Paris, 11 September 1968.
46. S. E. Finer, 'Military Disengagement from Politics' (Paper presented to the Institute of Commonwealth Studies, 1966).
47. Anouar Abdel-Malek, 'The Crisis in Nasser's Egypt', *New Left Review*, 45, September–October 1966.
48. *ibid:* see also Anouar Abdel-Malek, *Egypt: Military Society* (New York, 1968).
49. Giovanni Arrighi and John S. Saul, 'Socialism and Economic Development in Tropical Africa', *Journal of Modern African Studies*, 6, 2, 1968, pp. 141–69; see p. 151.
50. Tigani Babiker, 'Military Coups d'État in Africa', *Africa: National Social Revolution*, papers read at the Cairo Seminar (Prague, 1967).
51. See the forthcoming publication of the Africa Research Group, *The Other Side of Nigeria's Civil War*, for the role of US corporations.
52. A. G. Frank, *Capitalism and Underdevelopment in Latin America* (New York, 1969).
53. Giovanni Arrighi, 'International Corporations, Labour Aristocracies and Economic Development in Tropical Africa', *Ideology and Development: Essays in the Political Economy of Africa*, G. Arrighi and J. S. Saul (forthcoming).

54. Samir Amin, *Le Développement du Capitalisme en Côte d'Ivoire* (Paris, 1967).
55. Arrighi, *op. cit.*, pp. 11–20, mimeographed version.
56. *ibid.* See Arrighi's table calculated from various government statistics.
57. *ibid.*
58. Majhemout Diop, 'Structure and Position of the Working Class in Senegal', mimeographed version of the paper presented to the Cairo Seminar, October 1966.
59. 'The Class Struggle in Africa', originally published in *Revolution*, 1964, No. 9, under the anonymous signature XXX, reprinted 1969 by the Africa Research Group, Cambridge, Mass.
60. Arrighi, *op. cit.*
61. Apart from the Arrighi article on international corporations, *op. cit.*, which should be read with two others, 'Socialism and Economic Development in Tropical Africa', *Journal of Modern African Studies*, 6, 2, 1968; and 'Nationalism and Revolution in Sub-Saharan Africa', by Arrighi and John S. Saul, *Socialist Register*, 1969; see also 'The Concepts Class, Status, Élite in the Analysis of a New-Colonial Economy' by Gavin Williams, paper read to the Sociology of Development Group at the 1969 Annual Conference of the British Sociological Association (unpublished).
62. Amilcar Cabral, 'The Struggle in Guiné', *International Socialist Journal*, August 1964.
63. See, for instance, John Lonsdale, 'The Emergence of African Nationalism', *African Affairs*, Vol. 67, No. 266, January 1968, p. 24.
64. Weiss and Markowitz, 'Rebellion in the Congo', *Current History*, April 1965.
65. Crawford Young, 'The Congo Rebellion', *Africa Report*, April 1965, p. 11.
66. See Food and Agriculture Organization figures for 1956:

Social Structure of West Africa

	average per capita	
rich peasantry	more than 10 hectares	10 per cent
middle land-owners	2–10 hectares	60 per cent
poor peasantry	under 2 hectares	30 per cent

67. See Williams, *op. cit.*
68. Cabral, *op. cit.*
69. See Romano Ledda, 'Some Problems of Analysis', *Marxism Today*, September 1969; see also the Samir Amin article, reprinted Africa Research Group, 1969.

Index

INDEX